PRAISE FOR *Ask Not*

"Insightful and fascinating analysis . . . [Kennedy] comes off as a skilled, eloquent and inspired craftsman."
—*San Francisco Chronicle*

"*Ask Not* stirs us again with the eloquence of Kennedy's oratory, and deepens our understanding of its place in history."
—Sally Bedell Smith, author of *Grace and Power*

"Thurston Clarke has taken a brief, beautiful speech and re-created an extraordinary moment in time. He understands the power of words, the way they can animate an age and move the world."
—Evan Thomas, coauthor of *The Wise Men,* author of *John Paul Jones*

"With great—and often fascinating—detail, Clarke recounts how the inaugural address was fashioned. *Ask Not* is an elegant and literate celebration of one of the past century's pinnacles of literacy—and a valuable addition to the Kennedy canon."
—*Richmond Times-Dispatch*

"Insightful and engaging. . . . In the end, Sorenson stands revealed as what he's always claimed to be: not Kennedy's ghostwriter, but his scribe. And Kennedy? He comes off as original and eloquent."
—*The Providence Sunday Journal*

"Intriguing . . . *Ask Not* is the product of much diligence. . . . Clarke has made a valuable start by evoking the vivid spirit of that time and documenting a major moment in American oratory."
—*The Boston Globe*

"Clarke is an apt student of the what-he-had-for-breakfast-that-day school of popular history, and as his vivid narrative unfolds in that tradition, we can hear the words of the speech rise from the page. An artful addition to Kennedyana, complete with detailed literary forensics that will inevitably invite a comparison to the present state of political rhetoric and contemplation of what we have lost."
—*Kirkus Reviews*

"Clarke has made an admirable contribution—and he has strengthened the speech-making credentials of JFK as someone who could not only deliver a speech with panache but originate most of the ideas as well."
—*Deseret Morning News*

"In the end, this is a book about a man, a moment and a speech, and Clarke does a terrific job of explaining all three."
—*Pittsburgh Tribune-Review*

"Clarke offers an excellent reconstruction of the details of that frigid, snow-encrusted day in January 1961. . . . a valuable book worth making room for on the crowded Kennedy shelf."
—*Publishers Weekly*

"A spirited narrative . . . fine social history."
—*Library Journal*

"A terse, often cliffhanging re-enactment of the last few days leading up to [Kennedy's] inauguration."
—*The Post and Courier* (Charleston)

"A thoughtfully, gracefully, elegantly written book."
—Peace Corps Writers

"This fine book is part textual criticism, part archival detective work, but most important, a compelling and fascinating story. . . . Clarke has reminded us once again that there was substance behind the charisma, and much to admire about John Fitzgerald Kennedy."
—*The Herald-Sun* (Durham)

"Part of the fun of this book is that Clarke writes good gossip. . . . This is an entertaining and instructive book."
—*The Press-Republic* (Plattsburgh)

PENGUIN BOOKS

ASK NOT

Thurston Clarke has written eleven widely acclaimed works of fiction and nonfiction, including the *New York Times* bestselling *The Last Campaign*, and three *New York Times* notable books: *The Last Caravan*, *Equator*, and *California Fault*. His *Pearl Harbor Ghosts* was the basis for a CBS documentary, and his bestselling *Lost Hero*, a biography of Raoul Wallenberg, was made into an award-winning NBC miniseries. His articles have appeared in *Vanity Fair*, *Outside*, *Glamour*, *The New York Times*, and many other publications. He is the recipient of a Guggenheim Fellowship and a Lowell Thomas Award for travel literature and lives in the Adirondacks in upstate New York with his wife and three daughters. He is currently writing *JFK: The Last Hundred Days*, which will be published in 2013.

Ask Not

THE INAUGURATION OF JOHN F. KENNEDY AND THE SPEECH THAT CHANGED AMERICA

Thurston Clarke

PENGUIN BOOKS

PENGUIN BOOKS
Published by the Penguin Group
Penguin Group (USA) Inc., 375 Hudson Street, New York, New York 10014, U.S.A.
Penguin Group (Canada), 90 Eglinton Avenue East, Suite 700, Toronto,
Ontario, Canada M4P 2Y3 (a division of Pearson Penguin Canada Inc.)
Penguin Books Ltd, 80 Strand, London WC2R 0RL, England
Penguin Ireland, 25 St Stephen's Green, Dublin 2, Ireland (a division of Penguin Books Ltd)
Penguin Group (Australia), 250 Camberwell Road, Camberwell,
Victoria 3124, Australia (a division of Pearson Australia Group Pty Ltd)
Penguin Books India Pvt Ltd, 11 Community Centre, Panchsheel Park, New Delhi – 110 017, India
Penguin Group (NZ), 67 Apollo Drive, Rosedale, North Shore 0632,
New Zealand (a division of Pearson New Zealand Ltd)
Penguin Books (South Africa) (Pty) Ltd, 24 Sturdee Avenue,
Rosebank, Johannesburg 2196, South Africa

Penguin Books Ltd, Registered Offices:
80 Strand, London WC2R 0RL, England

First published in the United States of America by Henry Holt and Company 2004
First Owl Books edition 2005
This edition with a new afterword published in Penguin Books 2011

3 5 7 9 10 8 6 4 2

THE LIBRARY OF CONGRESS HAS CATALOGED THE HARDCOVER EDITION AS FOLLOWS:
Ask Not : the inauguration of John F. Kennedy and the speech
that changed America / Thurston Clarke—1st ed.
p. cm.
ISBN 978-0-8050-7213-6 (hc.)
ISBN 978-0-14-311897-8 (pbk.)
1. Kennedy, John F. (John Fitzgerald), 1917–1963. Inaugural address.
2. Kennedy, John F. (John Fitzgerald), 1917–1963—Inauguration, 1961. I. Title.
J82D91C53 2004
352.23'86'0973—dc22 2003067720

Printed in the United States of America
Designed by Fritz Metsch

FOR

JOHN PYNE JR.

AND

LILY WEST,

to whom we are passing the torch

⚜

A GOLDEN AGE OF POETRY AND POWER
OF WHICH THIS NOONDAY'S THE BEGINNING HOUR.

❦

final lines of the poem written by Robert Frost
for the inauguration of John F. Kennedy

Contents

The Inaugural Address
xiii

PROLOGUE
ARLINGTON NATIONAL CEMETERY
1

PART ONE : THE WORDS
PALM BEACH, FLORIDA
January 10 to January 17, 1961

1 : ON BOARD THE *CAROLINE*
January 10
17

2 : PALM BEACH
January 11 to January 15
38

3 : PALM BEACH
January 16
57

4 : PALM BEACH
January 17
75

5 : ON BOARD THE *CAROLINE*
January 17
94

PART TWO : THE MUSIC

WASHINGTON, D.C.

January 17 to January 21, 1961

6 : WASHINGTON AND NEW YORK
January 17
113

7 : NEW YORK AND WASHINGTON
January 18
123

8 : WASHINGTON
January 19
143

9 : WASHINGTON
January 20
162

10 : THE CAPITOL
January 20
177

11 : WASHINGTON
January 20, 1961, to the Present
202

AFTERWORD
Poetry and Power
217

Notes
225

Bibliography
253

Acknowlegments
259

Index
261

The Inaugural Address of PRESIDENT JOHN F. KENNEDY: *January 20, 1961*

Vice President Johnson, Mr. Speaker, Mr. Chief Justice, President Eisenhower, Vice President Nixon, President Truman, reverend clergy, fellow citizens:

We observe today not a victory of party but a celebration of freedom—symbolizing an end as well as a beginning—signifying renewal as well as change. For I have sworn before you and Almighty God the same solemn oath our forebears prescribed nearly a century and three quarters ago.

The world is very different now. For man holds in his mortal hands the power to abolish all forms of human poverty and all forms of human life. And yet the same revolutionary beliefs for which our forebears fought are still at issue around the globe—the belief that the rights of man come not from the generosity of the state but from the hand of God.

We dare not forget today that we are the heirs of that first revolution. Let the word go forth from this time and place, to friend and foe alike, that the torch has been passed to a new generation of Americans—born in this century, tempered by war, disciplined by a hard and bitter peace, proud of our ancient heritage—and unwilling to witness or permit the slow undoing of those human rights to which this nation has always been committed, and to which we are committed today at home and around the world.

Let every nation know, whether it wishes us well or ill, that we shall pay any price, bear any burden, meet any hardship, support any friend, oppose any foe to assure the survival and the success of liberty.

This much we pledge—and more.

To those old allies whose cultural and spiritual origins we share, we pledge the loyalty of faithful friends. United, there is little we cannot do in a host of cooperative ventures. Divided, there is little we can do—for we dare not meet a powerful challenge at odds and split asunder.

To those new States whom we welcome to the ranks of the free, we pledge our word that one form of colonial control shall not have passed away merely to be replaced by a far more iron tyranny. We shall not always expect to find them supporting our view. But we shall always hope to find them strongly supporting their own freedom—and to remember that, in the past, those who foolishly sought power by riding the back of the tiger ended up inside.

To those peoples in the huts and villages of half the globe struggling to break the bonds of mass misery, we pledge our best efforts to help them help themselves, for whatever period is required—not because the communists may be doing it, not because we seek their votes, but because it is right. If a free society cannot help the many who are poor, it cannot save the few who are rich.

To our sister republics south of our border, we offer a special pledge—to convert our good words into good deeds—in a new alliance for progress—to assist free men and free governments in casting off the chains of poverty. But this peaceful revolution of hope cannot become the prey of hostile powers. Let all our neighbors know that we shall join with them to oppose aggression or subversion anywhere in the Americas. And let every other power know that this Hemisphere intends to remain the master of its own house.

To that world assembly of sovereign states, the United Nations, our last best hope in an age where the instruments of war have far outpaced the instruments of peace, we renew our pledge of support—to prevent it from becoming merely a forum for invective—to strengthen its shield of the new and the weak—and to enlarge the area in which its writ may run.

Finally, to those nations who would make themselves our adversary, we offer not a pledge but a request: that both sides begin anew the quest for peace, before the dark powers of destruction unleashed by science engulf all humanity in planned or accidental self-destruction.

We dare not tempt them with weakness. For only when our arms are sufficient beyond doubt can we be certain beyond doubt that they will never be employed.

But neither can two great and powerful groups of nations take comfort from our present course—both sides overburdened by the cost of modern weapons, both rightly alarmed by the steady spread of the deadly atom, yet both racing to alter that uncertain balance of terror that stays the hand of mankind's final war.

So let us begin anew—remembering on both sides that civility is not a sign of weakness, and sincerity is always subject to proof. Let us never negotiate out of fear. But let us never fear to negotiate.

Let both sides explore what problems unite us instead of belaboring those problems which divide us.

Let both sides, for the first time, formulate serious and precise proposals for the inspection and control of arms—and bring the absolute power to destroy other nations under the absolute control of all nations.

Let both sides seek to invoke the wonders of science instead of its terrors. Together let us explore the stars, conquer the deserts, eradicate disease, tap the ocean depths and encourage the arts and commerce.

Let both sides unite to heed in all corners of the earth the command of Isaiah—to "undo the heavy burdens . . . [and] let the oppressed go free."

And if a beachhead of cooperation may push back the jungle of suspicion, let both sides join in creating a new endeavor, not a new balance of power, but a new world of law, where the strong are just and the weak secure and the peace preserved.

All this will not be finished in the first one hundred days. Nor will it be finished in the first one thousand days, nor in the life of this Administration, nor even perhaps in our lifetime on this planet. But let us begin.

In your hands, my fellow citizens, more than in mine, will rest the final success or failure of our course. Since this country was founded, each generation of Americans has been summoned to give testimony to its national loyalty. The graves of young Americans who answered the call to service surround the globe.

Now the trumpet summons us again—not as a call to bear arms, though arms we need—not as a call to battle, though embattled we are—but a call to bear the burden of a long twilight struggle, year in and year out, "rejoicing in hope, patient in tribulation"—a struggle against the common enemies of man: tyranny, poverty, disease and war itself.

Can we forge against these enemies a grand and global alliance, North and South, East and West, that can assure a more fruitful life for all mankind? Will you join in that historic effort?

In the long history of the world, only a few generations have been granted the role of defending freedom in its hour of maximum danger. I do not shrink from this responsibility—I welcome it. I do not believe that any of us would exchange places with any other people or any other generation. The energy, the faith, the devotion which we bring to this endeavor will light our country and all who serve it—and the glow from that fire can truly light the world.

And so, my fellow Americans: ask not what your country can do for you—ask what you can do for your country.

My fellow citizens of the world: ask not what America will do for you, but what together we can do for the freedom of man.

Finally, whether you are citizens of America or citizens of the world, ask of us here the same high standards of strength and sacrifice which we ask of you. With a good conscience our only sure reward, with history the final judge of our deeds, let us go forth to lead the land we love, asking His blessing and His help, but knowing that here on earth God's work must truly be our own.

PROLOGUE

ARLINGTON NATIONAL CEMETERY

⚜

The whole earth is the sepulcher of famous men; and their story is graven not only on stone over their native earth, but lives on far away, without visible symbol, woven into the stuff of other men's lives.

PERICLES' FUNERAL ORATION

On a low curving wall in Arlington National Cemetery seven sentences from the inaugural address of John F. Kennedy are chiseled into granite tablets below the slain president's grave. The granite, known as Deer Island after the place in Maine where it was quarried, has a pinkish tinge that becomes brighter when worn or sandblasted. It also covers the pavement in front of the wall where the feet of 150 million visitors have turned it pinker every year. The tablets, too, are changing color, but more slowly, as mourners slide their fingers across the three-inch letters, the closest they can come to touching the man who is buried here.

Words carved into the stones of an imperial city usually survive the civilizations they describe. In two thousand years, Washington may resemble Rome, with the ruins of its once-grand buildings scattered across a different sort of metropolis. The White House, Capitol, and Supreme Court may have been renovated, or replaced with structures more in keeping with new technologies or ideologies, leaving behind only their pillars or a cornerstone or frieze. The great memorials to Washington, Jefferson, Lincoln, and Franklin Roosevelt, however, along with the orations chiseled onto them, will most likely remain intact, as will Kennedy's grave. Even if books are burned, or if the written word becomes obsolete or loses its meaning, Americans will still be able to read Abraham Lincoln's Gettysburg Address and his second inaugural, the Declaration of Independence, "We have nothing to fear but fear itself" from Franklin Roosevelt's first inaugural, and these seven sentences from John F. Kennedy's inaugural address.

The first two sentences are from his opening paragraphs, the other five from his concluding ones. They total 226 words, one-sixth of a speech that is the fourth-shortest inaugural address in history. Carved in stone is Kennedy's pledge to:

Let every nation know, whether it wishes us well or ill, that we shall pay any price, bear any burden, meet any hardship, support any friend, oppose any foe, to assure the survival and the success of liberty.

Then come two sentences that spoke to his World War II generation:

Let the word go forth from this time and place, to friend and foe alike, that the torch has been passed to a new generation of Americans.

In the long history of the world, only a few generations have been granted the role of defending freedom in its hour of maximum danger. I do not shrink from this responsibility—I welcome it.

Next, the lines that electrified the young, kindling a wildfire of idealism that blazed across the 1960s, leaving behind scattered, still-glowing embers.

Now the trumpet summons us again—not as a call to bear arms, though arms we need; not as a call to battle, though embattled we are—but a call to bear the burden of a long twilight struggle, year in and year out, "rejoicing in hope, patient in tribulation"—a struggle against the common enemies of man: tyranny, poverty, disease and war itself.

The energy, the faith, the devotion which we bring to this endeavor will light our country and all who serve it—and the glow from that fire can truly light the world.

Then there is the sentence that has been braided into the American soul.

And so, my fellow Americans: ask not what your country can do for you—ask what you can do for your country.

And lastly, the closing sentence, with its obligatory reference to the Almighty.

With a good conscience our only sure reward, with history the final judge of our deeds, let us go forth to lead to the land we love, asking His blessing and His help, but knowing that here on earth God's work must truly be our own.

Like these seven sentences, the Kennedy grave is spare but majestic, unadorned yet elegant. It may be also the saddest place in America aside from the Vietnam Memorial, with which its words have an uneasy relationship.

The slabs of black Maine slate covering Kennedy's corpse and those of his wife and two infant children are simple and stark yet lie on a hillside that commands a majestic view of Washington's great monuments. By design, they lie on an imaginary axis connecting the Lincoln Memorial with the former home of Robert E. Lee that occupies the crest of this hill. The elements of the gravesite are modest: a rough circular rock resembling a millstone surrounds the eternal flame, and plants native to Cape Cod fill cracks between paving stones quarried in the eighteenth century from a location near the Kennedy home at Hyannisport. Still, Kennedy sits high above the white crosses and headstones marking the graves of 260,000 other Americans, and no other American president—not Lincoln, FDR, Jefferson, or Wilson—has such a magnificent grave in the nation's capital. Kennedy's eternal flame is smaller than the one beneath the Arc de Triomphe, yet he is the only president honored by a blaze promising to last throughout eternity, and this reminder of him is situated so it flickers in the White House windows, an inspiration, or reproach, to the men who have followed him.

When Kennedy delivered his inaugural I was in the infirmary of a Massachusetts boarding school. The only other patient was my Latin teacher, a middle-aged bachelor with an explosive temper who had commanded a black infantry unit during World War II's Pacific campaign. We were joined at the television that winter morning by the school nurse, a dour Nova Scotian who had once tended the wounded at a Halifax military hospital. We saw, in black and white, a cloudless sky, sharp light, and air so cold it turned Kennedy's breath into white clouds. When he said, "Let the word go forth from this time and place," it appeared that each word he spoke really *was* going forth into the exhilarating air that everyone in the nation breathed that day.

We saw a Currier and Ives tableau, wintry and patriotic. Wind ruffled the festive bunting, and the marble facade of the Capitol gleamed. Sunlight bounced off snowbanks, and spectators shielded their eyes. Rows of dignitaries filled the platform. The men wore dark overcoats and top hats, outfits for tycoons and statesmen. Eisenhower, Kennedy, Johnson, and Nixon sat in a semicircle of armchairs. Kennedy was young and deeply tanned, whereas President Eisenhower, whom he was replacing, was bald and blinking. The four men's wives, all former and future first ladies (although two of them did not know it yet) sat behind them in the first row on either side of the podium. A faint smile remained frozen on Jackie Kennedy's face, as if she was party to some delicious secret.

No one suspected that Kennedy had dressed in long underwear so that on this cold day he could shed his overcoat and appear youthful and vigorous. No one knew that he was receiving amphetamine injections from a physician who would one day lose his license for dispensing this medicine. No one realized that behind his ringing and confident delivery lay months of secret tutoring from a speech coach. No one imagined that Rose Kennedy was fuming over her row-end seat, or that Eleanor Roosevelt had refused her place of honor because she could not bear being close to Kennedy's father, or that there was so much bad blood between the dignitaries on this platform that if grudges had weight, the entire contraption would have instantly crashed to the ground.

When President Kennedy finished speaking that day, I saw tears on the cheeks of the Latin teacher and nurse, and realized that words capable of touching such well-guarded, deeply-buried hearts must be powerful ones indeed.

Later, after Dallas and Vietnam—and after it became apparent that this would be the last time the Kennedy family would gather in such numbers to celebrate a happy occasion—the photographs, films, and memories of this day would become more poignant and unsettling. And later still, after Kennedy's wife and his son, John Jr., had died, and the cold war had ended, these seven sentences would remain, carved into stone and woven into lives.

A college student who would join the first class of Peace Corps volunteers remarked, "I'd never done anything political, patriotic, or unselfish because nobody ever asked me to. Kennedy asked." After watching the inaugural on television in her college dormitory, Donna Shalala—who would serve in President Clinton's cabinet—was inspired to pursue a career in public service. When she reread what Kennedy had said four decades later, she was astonished to discover that she could still *hear* his voice.

The cardinal who would become Pope Paul VI in 1963 listened over the radio in Milan and was so moved by the "vigorous, classical, and sacred eloquence" of the speech and its "moral significance" that he reread the text numerous times over the years. His landmark 1967 encyclical calling on wealthy nations to alleviate poverty and promote social justice in the third world echoed its themes and language.

On the evening after Kennedy spoke, James Meredith, a black U.S. Air Force veteran, took a step he had been debating for months, typing a letter to the registrar of the all-white University of Mississippi that began, "Please send me an application for admission to your school." Two years later, Kennedy would send twenty-three thousand American troops onto the campus to quell a riot ignited when Meredith attempted to register for classes.

The historian and former White House aide Arthur Schlesinger may have been thinking of Meredith when he concluded his 1965 memoir of the Kennedy administration, *A Thousand Days,* by saying that "the energies Kennedy released, the purposes he inspired, the goals he established would guide the land he loved for years to come." Those years are ending as the young people who heard Kennedy deliver his address retire from the careers it inspired. Soon, his words will have to stand on their own merits, unsupported by the memories of those who heard them. Now, before that happens, might be a good time to ask why the words of this supposedly cool and unemotional man had such an impact on so many lives and elicited such a passionate response.

Praise for the address was so extravagant that it was difficult to believe almost half of the electorate had preferred Nixon. The *New Yorker* compared it to the best of classical oratory, declaring, "We find it hard to believe that an Athenian or Roman citizen could have listened to it unmoved." The *Times* of London detected "the cadence of Abraham Lincoln's oratory . . . [and] Lincoln's sense of the spiritual mission of the great presidential office." The intellectuals, initially the most resistant to Kennedy's charm, offered the most ecstatic reviews. One reads them and imagines tears on even those timeworn cheeks. Archibald MacLeish declared that the speech had left him "proud and hopeful to be an American—something I have not felt for almost twenty years." E. B. White wrote Kennedy that "one of the excitements of American citizenship is a man's feeling of identity with his elected President. I never had this feeling hit me so hard as on January 20, 1961, when, watching on television from a Maine farmhouse, I first saw the lectern take fire, then so much else—thanks to your brave words."

Kennedy's speech moved even the hearts of his adversaries. *Life* magazine, which had endorsed Nixon, reprinted it under the headline "A Great Speech" and said it "rang with a rhetoric rarely found in a political statement." Senator Barry Goldwater, leader of the conservative wing of the Republican Party, remarked, "God, I'd like to be able to do what that boy did there."

The idea of a speech stirring up such excitement now seems quaint and dated, and it is difficult to imagine lives changed by a presidential address. But in 1961, words existed in a precarious and momentary state of balance with the visual, a situation enabling Kennedy, who was comfortable in both media, to become the first television president and the last literate one.

Words are mighty things, but their power waxes and wanes with the times, and they can move different audiences, and generations, in different ways. This may be why "Ask not" has been criticized as a sinister pitch for voluntary fascism and hailed as an inspirational mantra, why passages from a speech advocating peaceful coexistence with the Soviet Union could later inspire both those protesting the war in Vietnam and those waging it, and why passages inspiring the young in 1961 would make the post-Vietnam and post-Watergate disillusionment more bitter, and the cynicism and greed of following decades more discouraging.

Theodore Sorensen was Kennedy's principal speechwriter and aide for over a decade. In his introduction to an anthology of Kennedy's writings and speeches he offered a comment about his boss that originally described the English statesman William Pitt: "It is not merely the thing that is said but the man who says it that counts, the character that breathes through the sentences." But looking for Kennedy's character in his words can be a tricky proposition as, according to conventional wisdom, the real author of his speeches, and the man whose character therefore also breathes through them, is Ted Sorensen.

Richard Nixon was an early proponent of this theory. The only Republican refusing immediate comment on Kennedy's inaugural address, he later told a reporter: "It's easy for Kennedy to get up and read Sorensen's speeches. But I don't think it's responsible unless he believes it himself."

Others have picked up Nixon's torch. Garry Wills, an acknowledged expert on presidential rhetoric following his book about the Gettysburg Address, argues that JFK can "rightly" be called the author of his inaugural address only in the sense that he delivered it, directed its writing, and had the final right to delete or add anything. He concludes, "But Theodore Sorensen, not the author in any of the senses used above, wrote the inaugural address." Even more sympathetic authors are skeptical of Kennedy's claim to his most famous speech. The late *Washington Post* publisher Katharine Graham claimed to be "a real Kennedy enthusiast" but stated, "Along with so many others, we were thrilled by the inaugural speech, which had mostly been crafted by Ted Sorensen, helped by Ken Galbraith." Assertions that Sorensen wrote Kennedy's inaugural address have also appeared frequently in the popular media. In 1988, for example, *Time* essayist Lance Morrow described Sorensen as "the author of so many of Kennedy's speeches, including the inaugural." Educational material sent to teachers across the United States in 2002 to provoke classroom discussions of Public Television's *Great American Speeches* series stated that "John Kennedy's inaugural address has been praised as one of the best public speeches ever. . . . Kennedy, however, did not write the speech himself. Ted Sorensen did."

None of these writers offers any evidence that Sorensen wrote the Kennedy inaugural. Instead, one detects the assumption that since speechwriters wrote the inaugural addresses of other twentieth-century presidents, one must have written Kennedy's, too, and that because Sorensen was the author of so many other Kennedy speeches, he must have been the author of this one as well.

But the issue of whether Kennedy composed his own inaugural address, or simply delivered Sorensen's beautiful words, is not some arcane historical footnote. The speech is generally acknowledged to have been the greatest oration of any twentieth-century American politician. It was also the centerpiece of an inauguration that would turn out to be one of the great political events of that century, a moment when Americans would step through a membrane in time, entering a brief, still seductive, era of national happiness. More than any of the countless books about JFK, it is his inaugural that explains the Kennedy phenomenon to the heart as well as the mind, reaching across the chasm of years to connect the present with the beginning hour of his presidency, and the passion and optimism it excited. To deny him full credit for it not only diminishes his legacy and weakens his claim on the hearts and minds of future generations, it also distances him, and us, from a speech that is a distillation of his experiences, philosophy, and character.

An investigation of the 1961 inaugural address must consider both means and motive. When we do this, we find that not only did John F. Kennedy have the time and talent to write the speech himself, but that the notion that he would have turned the job of composing the most important speech of his career over to any speechwriter—even one as skilled and trusted as Ted Sorensen—contradicts what is known about his character and ambitions.

An inaugural address is unlike any other presidential speech. It is the only one that every president since George Washington has delivered, and the only one a president has ample time to prepare. The months between an election and inauguration are a fallow period for political rhetoric. A new president-elect assembles a cabinet, appoints a staff, and plans a legislative strategy, yet for the first time in months he does not have to deliver any speeches. During the preceding campaign Kennedy had sometimes delivered more than a dozen speeches a day yet still managed to take a keen interest in their content, editing and rewriting some of them moments before taking the podium. It seems inconceivable that he would not have, then, found time during his transition to truly devote himself to a speech that would be one of the yardsticks by which history would judge his presidency.

He knew this speech represented an extraordinary opportunity to present himself, as he chose to be seen, for the pages of history, and few presidents in the twentieth century cared more about history, or its perspective, than John F. Kennedy. One week after his assassination, his widow, Jacqueline, would tell the journalist Theodore White: "History made him [Kennedy] what he was. . . . This lonely sick boy . . . he sat and read history. . . . All the time he was in bed this little boy was reading history, was reading Marlborough, he devoured the knight[s] of the round table." White could appreciate these sentiments because he had also been impressed by Kennedy's knowledge and love of history. On a cross-country flight during the 1960 campaign, White recalled, "[Kennedy] began reeling off a list of names of American historians which I found simply astonishing. . . . His knowledge of history went far back beyond the roots of today's politics, and his reading had a range far beyond the needs of the gamesman."

Kennedy viewed history as determined by the actions of "Great Men" who combined wisdom and courage with oratorical talents and inspiring leadership. Eleven days before his inauguration, he told Massachusetts legislators, "At some future date, the high court of history sits in judgment on each one of us." He hoped this "High Court" would compare him to Lincoln, Churchill, and Franklin Roosevelt, all great orators, and considered his inaugural address an opportunity to link his reputation with theirs for all time.

For Kennedy, history was also a competitive enterprise that measured statesmen, senators, and presidents against one another. He approached any speech inviting comparison with others with the same competitive spirit he brought to politics and touch football. He understood that oratory was an objective measure of a leader's talents, and that the inaugural address was the rhetorical gold standard of the American presidency. In *Profiles in Courage* he had recounted how a single speech by Senator Lucius Lamar of Mississippi had "overnight raised Lamar . . . to the first rank in the Congress and the country." Kennedy's inaugural address presented him with a similar opportunity: the chance to place himself, at the beginning hour of his presidency, in the first rank of American presidents.

Kennedy also cared more about his inaugural than most presidents because he feared he might not live to deliver a second one. Poor health had plagued him throughout his life, and by the time he was elected president at age forty-three he had received the last rites three times. His maladies included a chronic bad back, severe intestinal complaints, and Addison's disease, which he described to the columnist Joe Alsop in 1947 as "a sort of slow-motion leukemia," adding, "the doctors tell me I'll probably last until I'm forty-five," a timetable taking him only into the third year of his presidency, and revealing another reason why he saw the inauguration as perhaps his most influential moment on the public stage.

Even had Kennedy enjoyed perfect health, he was too proud of his demonstrated literary talents and too sensitive to charges that Ted Sorensen had ghostwritten *Profiles in Courage* to risk relying too heavily on others for a work that would be scrutinized by generations of historians and critics.

Kennedy hired the twenty-five-year-old Sorensen as a researcher, writer, and adviser in 1953, when he entered the U.S. Senate. During the eight years that Kennedy served in the Senate, Sorensen became a repository and synthesizer of his experiences, ideas, prejudices, passions, rhetorical tics, and favorite quotations. (Kennedy once told his navy buddy Paul Fay, "Ted Sorensen is getting to be a mirror image of me, reflecting even what I am thinking.") But Kennedy was eleven years older than Sorensen, and the one who had fought in the war, served three terms in the House of Representatives, and knew the leading statesmen and journalists of the time. Sorensen, on the other hand, had little experience beyond Nebraska and Washington, and despite his considerable intellectual gifts, he was the one who more often fitted himself into Kennedy's contours. His speeches sounded as though Kennedy had written them, because many of the words he put into Kennedy's mouth had originated there.

In *Kennedy,* Sorensen's 1965 memoir of the Kennedy administration, he writes that when he and JFK collaborated on a speech they would first discuss the topic, approach, and conclusions; then he would prepare a draft, and Kennedy would edit it. In his book *The Kennedy Legacy,* published four years later, he states that "the final shape of every text was always the President's decision alone," but acknowledges that if the ideas, arguments, phrases were sound, "there was neither time nor necessity for him to rewrite every page—particularly after working together had merged not only our style of writing but also our thinking about the world."

These statements are good summaries of how Kennedy and Sorensen collaborated, but fail to address the occasions when Kennedy composed his own speeches. This might happen if an event was important enough or if Kennedy was dissatisfied with a Sorensen text. We know, for example, that just hours before appearing in the first televised debate with Nixon, he decided that Sorensen's opening statement was "too rhetorical," and took Sorensen's secretary, Gloria Sitrin, onto a balcony outside his hotel room in Chicago to dictate a new one.

Furthermore, we know that during his campaign for the presidency he would frequently carry a Sorensen speech to the podium only to ignore most of it, delivering instead his own extemporaneous oration. Sorensen was probably the finest presidential speechwriter of the century, but his greatest skill lay in channeling Kennedy's intellect—in drafting the elegant landmark speeches of Kennedy's Senate career and presidency, but not the ones that could electrify a campaign rally. He has himself admitted this, writing that "in the vast majority of cases" Kennedy did not follow the speech he had prepared, "deviating sometimes slightly with his own interjections and interpretations, more often substantially, and sometimes completely." The result, he concedes, was that Kennedy's spontaneous remarks "were consistently more effective than his prepared texts because they were delivered with more conviction and vitality."

Sorensen has always loyally affirmed Kennedy's authorship of the inaugural address. In *Kennedy,* he gives some credit to "assistant artisans" among Kennedy's advisers but insists that "the principal architect of the Inaugural Address was John Fitzgerald Kennedy." When asked during an interview in 2002 about his contribution to the inaugural, he carefully replied: "Now this is very delicate ground. I have never acknowledged being the author of the inaugural address. . . . Kennedy was the author in the sense that he decided on every word and, more importantly, on every idea, on every policy, on every concept."

Sorensen's statements have not quieted the skeptics. This may be because they seem to suggest that although Kennedy decided on the themes and ideas, it was Sorensen who wrote the words expressing them. He calls Kennedy the "principal architect" of the inaugural, a phrase implying that he was the controlling intelligence, but leaves unsaid whether Kennedy also provided the bricks and mortar of words and phrasing. He says Kennedy "decided" on every word, but does not say that he actually wrote any of them.

Sorensen is simply telling the truth as he knows it. He knows, for example, that he submitted a proposed draft of the address to Kennedy, and must know, too, that Kennedy included several long passages from this draft in the final address. But what is hard for Sorensen to evaluate, then or now, is how much of the material in his own draft came from Kennedy's previous speeches, earlier writings, and conversation. This is because, as he writes in *Kennedy*, after traveling with JFK he had come to know "all his hopes, dreams, moods, methods, mind," adding that during his long relationship with Kennedy, "their style and standard had become increasingly one."

Few, if any, politicians and speechwriters have enjoyed an intellectual intimacy approaching that between Kennedy and Sorensen. It is this intimacy that often makes it difficult for either man, or an outside observer, to be certain which man originated which phrases in a particular Kennedy speech. But the inaugural address is an exception, a Kennedy speech in which it *is* possible to determine who contributed what.

Most of the speech can be traced to two sources: passages that Kennedy dictated to his secretary, Evelyn Lincoln, on January 10, 1961, and material from a draft written by Sorensen. On close examination, the Sorensen material that Kennedy incorporated into his speech turns out to be largely a compilation of ideas and themes that Kennedy had been voicing throughout his adult life, expressed in words that Sorensen had drawn from Kennedy's writings and extemporaneous speeches. In short, one finds that Kennedy was more than the "principal architect" of his inaugural address; he was its stonecutter and mason, too, the man whose beautiful language, either dictated by him or channeled through Sorensen, cemented together the grand ideas of his speech.

Important, and heretofore overlooked, documentary evidence supports this thesis and proves Kennedy to have been the author of the most immortal and poetic passages of his inaugural address. The most important of these documents was created at about 9:15 P.M. on January 10, 1961, when during a flight from Washington to Palm Beach aboard his private airplane, the *Caroline,* Kennedy asked Evelyn Lincoln to bring her stenographer's pad into his compartment. There he began dictating, and most of the words chiseled onto that curving wall at Arlington appeared for the first time, not in his handwriting or in Ted Sorensen's, but in the lines, loops, and squiggles of Lincoln's shorthand.

Part One

THE WORDS

PALM BEACH, FLORIDA
JANUARY 10 TO JANUARY 17, 1961

Most of them, despite their differences, held much in common—the breath-taking talents of the orator, the brilliance of the scholar, the breadth of the man above party and section, and, above all, a deep-seated belief in themselves, their integrity and the rightness of their cause.

JOHN F. KENNEDY,
Profiles in Courage

I

On Board the Caroline

JANUARY 10

⚜

When John F. Kennedy dictated his inaugural address to Evelyn Lincoln in his private compartment on the *Caroline* on January 10, he was relying on a method of composition he had employed throughout his adult life. It was ideally suited to a restless man, uncomfortable with solitude, who liked doing everything at top speed. He had dictated the college honors thesis that became his first book, *Why England Slept*, and dictated his contributions to his second one, *Profiles in Courage*. In 1947, when he dictated his first major congressional speech, his secretary Mary Davis had expected "this green young legislator" to stumble over his words. Instead, she recalled, "he sat back in his chair and it just flowed out. He had such a grasp of what he was saying, and was able to put it in such beautiful language without any editorializing. . . . It just came and it came, I mean, for fifteen or twenty minutes. . . . He didn't have to say, 'Now, wait a minute. Go back.' . . . It just flowed, and I thought, 'Wow. This guy has a brain.'"

Davis came to recognize it as a typical Kennedy performance. "He never made any preparations," she said. "He just had it stored in the back of his mind somewhere, and when he needed the facts, when he needed that information, he could bring it right out and it was there in final form as I was taking it down in shorthand. . . . When he wanted to write a speech he did it, most of it. I would say 99% of that was done by JFK himself."

Evelyn Lincoln started working for Kennedy in 1952, a few months before he was elected to the Senate and Ted Sorensen joined his staff. Like Mary Davis, she praised his skill at speaking off the cuff, "writing" orally, you might say. In her book, *My Twelve Years with John F. Kennedy,* she describes him scribbling a few lines on a slip of paper while being driven to the Los Angeles convention center minutes after winning the 1960 Democratic presidential nomination. He stared out the window, wrote, then surrendered to a paroxysm of typical Kennedy fidgeting—thumping his knee, folding the paper, drumming his fingers on the dashboard. Minutes later, he delivered a speech thanking the delegates for their support and, Lincoln reported, "the words were rolling out of his mouth as though he had written them weeks before."

Audiotapes of Kennedy's dictation show him seldom pausing or repeating himself. His sentences are short and simple, shorn at their birth of qualifiers and adjectives, and one sometimes hears ideas and phrases destined for his inaugural address. In a 1954 speech criticizing the Eisenhower administration for cutting the defense budget, he spoke of "the problem of *twilight* wars" (the inaugural: "the burden of a long twilight struggle"), and of "alliances cracking" ("we dare not meet a powerful challenge at odds and split asunder").

If Lincoln was unavailable, or if Kennedy had no time to prepare a speech, he would jot down some notes and deliver an extemporaneous address. Even these hastily composed speeches are distinguished by their eloquence and serious themes. The St. Patrick's Day dinner at the Friendly Sons of St. Patrick in Everett, Massachusetts, on March 16, 1958, was the kind of occasion most politicians would have blown off with a boilerplate hymn to the "auld sod." Kennedy's notes show him laying out his views on the relationship between God and the nation, declaring that "freedom is man's natural state," and that "man's nature is based upon the idea of equality of all men before God—the physical side of his nature is the desire to develop his own talents and abilities. What is true of an individual is true of a nation—and history bears testimony to that." (The inaugural: "the belief that the rights of man come not from the generosity of the state, but from the hand of God.") Two months later, he spoke at Memorial Day ceremonies in Brookline and, again relying on some fragmentary notes, proclaimed that "the memory of these young men will abide as long as men are found who will set honor and country above all else. They have become in truth the shining spires of the city to which we all travel."

On January 2, 1960, he began dictating his announcement of his presidential candidacy two hours before delivering it, and while a barber was cutting his hair. He spent the remainder of the morning attending meetings in his Senate office, then revised Lincoln's typescript of his dictation as he spoke to the Washington press corps. He would continue to rely on dictation throughout his presidency.

* * *

Kennedy's decision to wait until ten days before his inauguration to begin his formal work on his inaugural address was a matter of both choice and necessity. On September 15, 1960, the Columbia University professor Richard Neustadt had presented him with an eighteen-point memorandum titled "ORGANIZING THE TRANSITION—A Tentative Check-List for the Weeks Between Election and Inaugural" that became the blueprint for his transition. Neustadt's suggestion number 15, "Preparing the Inaugural Address," cautioned that "it would be well *not* to begin this too early, but instead to wait until the main lines of a first message—that is to say of an initial program—had emerged. . . . It will also help to wait until one knows what international and economic conditions to expect by January 20."

Kennedy had also delayed composing his address because he had been busy presiding over one of the most hectic presidential transitions in history. While his staff worked out of his Senate offices and a downtown suite, his own home served as his personal headquarters. A narrow three-story brick Federal house on Georgetown's N Street with small rooms and a front door opening directly onto the sidewalk, it had proved too small and cramped, so he had spent much of the transition at his father's villa in Palm Beach, making trips to Washington and New York to consult aides, interview prospective members of his administration, and announce appointments from the front steps of the N Street house.

By the time Kennedy boarded the *Caroline* in Washington on January 10, he had traveled over fifteen thousand miles between Washington, New York, and Florida since the election, and his transition was being hailed as a stunning success and a fulfillment of his pledge "to ask the ablest men in the country to make whatever sacrifice is required to bring to the government a ministry of the best talents available." James Reston declared in the *New York Times* that "the changing of the guard in Washington has been achieved with more civility and common sense this time than ever in living memory," and a *Washington Post* writer predicted that "the way Mr. Kennedy has conducted himself . . . and the appointments he has made have encouraged the belief that not only will he be a good President, a fair-minded President, but perhaps a great President."

Kennedy had added to the burdens of his transition by making many of his appointments to second- and third-tier jobs himself and by fussing over each detail of the inauguration ceremony as obsessively as he would fuss over his speech. He was keenly aware that the success of his inaugural, and the judgment of history, would depend on much more than the text of the speech. His friend Ben Bradlee, a *Newsweek* journalist, recalled him relishing the pomp and circumstance of the upcoming affair and liking to be teased "about the fact that he so obviously did relish it."

Kennedy's interest in how things would look at his inauguration hints at more than a simple delight in costume and ritual. He realized that everything that happened at the ceremony, particularly everything that was visible to a television audience of millions, would contribute to how his address was received and judged. He decided that the New England poet Robert Frost would read a poem, and the African-American contralto Marian Anderson would sing the national anthem. He chose morning dress and top hats for men and sent a Secret Service agent to Boston to collect from an attic the Fitzgerald family Bible for swearing the oath of office. He banished his nieces and nephews from the presidential box at the inaugural parade so it would not resemble "kiddies day at the circus," sending them to watch from a window in the Treasury building.

Because he had inspired and charmed his supporters more than any president-elect since Franklin Roosevelt, Kennedy received an avalanche of letters and telegrams during the transition. Many began, "I'm sure you won't remember me . . ." and begged for favors, government appointments, and invitations to inaugural events. A barber who had cut his hair in Rochester, New York, in September wanted to cut it for the inauguration. The town fathers of Craig, Alaska, wanted him to make their village the site of the summer White House. Joe Black, the pitcher for the Brooklyn Dodgers and the first African-American to win a World Series game, wanted to know how he could assist the new nations of Africa. A former lover wanted him to remember her. She sent a billet-doux written on pink stationery in careful finishing-school handwriting that began, "My dear darling Jack, I want to congratulate you on your election as President." It continued, "I wish you had married me instead of that silly Jackie Bouvier. You once asked me to marry you, remember? . . . You were one of the handsomest and strongest PT boat skippers I knew." After several paragraphs in this vein she closed with, "Darling don't forget me please—please? My darling I give you my love forever." Kennedy apparently took this in stride; otherwise he would have destroyed the letter instead of slipping it into his office files. Still, such passion, so fervently expressed after so many years, must have been a distraction.

The two days preceding Kennedy's January 10 flight to Palm Beach had been the most hectic of all. He had flown to Boston on January 8 and slept for the last time in the small Beacon Hill apartment that had been his official Massachusetts residence since 1946. He emerged the next morning without a hat or topcoat despite a biting wind and a temperature in the low twenties, drove to Cambridge, attended a meeting of the Harvard Board of Overseers, and bantered with students chanting, "Speech! Speech!"

After lunch he conferred with his science adviser Jerome Wisner, and his national security adviser, McGeorge Bundy, then returned to Boston to deliver his first formal speech since the election, a farewell address to the Massachusetts State Legislature. In it, he reminded these famously corrupt legislators of John Winthrop's admonition that "we must always consider that we shall be as a city upon a hill—the eyes of all people are on us," and warned that the High Court of History, one never far from his mind, would judge public servants on whether they had been men of courage, judgment, integrity, and dedication. The speech was compared, as he must have hoped it would be, with Abraham Lincoln's farewell to the citizens of Springfield, Illinois, raising expectations even higher for his inaugural.

Kennedy told aides that his Massachusetts speech might have been *too* good, wasting material better saved for the inaugural. One suspects he had the "four questions" in mind. They had been inspired by a passage in Franklin Roosevelt's 1932 tribute to George Norris, the liberal Republican senator from Nebraska. Roosevelt had said, "History asks, 'Did the man have integrity? Did the man have unselfishness? Did the man have courage? Did the man have consistency?'" Kennedy had featured Norris in *Profiles in Courage*, closing the chapter with this tribute. Had he not used these questions in his January 9 speech, he would have probably posed them in his inaugural. His admonition to the legislators that "for of those to whom much is given, much is required" was a paraphrasing of "For unto whomsoever much is given, of him shall much be required," a verse from Saint Luke's Gospel that Rose Kennedy had drilled into all her children, another passage that might otherwise have been destined for the inaugural.

After the speech, Kennedy drove to Logan Airport and flew to New York. During the flight, the reporter Bill Lawrence stopped him in the aisle and said, "God, but you must be rich, and not only in money. Imagine wasting a speech like that on a bunch of clods when you must give an inaugural address in less than a week." A big grin crossed Kennedy's face, and he said, "Don't you worry, Bill. I've got a good inaugural."

While driving into the city, Kennedy ordered tickets to the Broadway hit *Do Re Mi*. He jumped out of his limousine at Fifth Avenue, ran to the "21" Club to eat a quick dinner, and arrived at the theater to a five-minute standing ovation. He slept at his apartment in the Carlyle Hotel, breakfasted with Eleanor Roosevelt, consulted two physicians, met with former Democratic candidate for president Adlai Stevenson, the historian Richard Neustadt, and four New York politicians, dashed to LaGuardia Airport, and conferred during the flight to Washington with former ambassador to Moscow George Kennan, whom he would later appoint ambassador to Yugoslavia.

Kennan's memorandum of the meeting indicates how their conversation would influence Kennedy's dictation to Evelyn Lincoln eight hours later. It was one of several encounters leading Kennan to praise Kennedy as "the best listener" he had ever met. Instead of pontificating, Kennan said, "he asked questions modestly, sensibly, and listened very patiently to what you had to say and did not try, then, to tell jokes, to be laughed at, or to utter sententious statements to be admired." This was, Kennan added, a rare quality among world leaders.

Kennedy briefed Kennan about approaches being made by Mikhael Menshikov, the Soviet ambassador, who had recently lunched with Kennedy's brother Robert, the future attorney general. Two days after the lunch, Menshikov had told former ambassador to Moscow Averell Harriman that secret talks between Kennedy and Soviet premier Nikita Khrushchev should begin as soon as possible. The next day, he had told the same thing to Harrison Salisbury of the *New York Times*. Kennan believed Menshikov was sincere, and that a growing Sino-Soviet rivalry had made Soviet leaders eager to negotiate a disarmament treaty with the United States.

Kennedy explained that he had asked the American diplomat David Bruce to press Menshikov about Moscow's intentions. He then handed Kennan a memorandum from Bruce attached to an unsigned, unletterheaded document purporting to represent Menshikov's personal thoughts, which were considerably more brusque and hard-line than Menshikov's verbal remarks. Kennedy asked Kennan to comment on these contradictory documents.

Kennan said the unsigned document appeared to have been drafted in Khrushchev's office but cleared with a wider circle of people. He explained that the Kremlin was divided into two camps: one believed the Soviet Union would inevitably win the cold war and opposed negotiations with the United States; a second, more moderate faction "was reluctant to burn its bridges." Menshikov's verbal statements, as summarized by Bruce, spoke for this latter group. His written document reflected the hard-line view. Kennan advised Kennedy not to reply to Menshikov or Khrushchev until he took office, then send Khrushchev a confidential message promising that if he was serious about reducing tensions he could anticipate a positive response.

After landing in Washington, Kennedy met in his Senate offices with his future treasury secretary, Douglas Dillon, and his personal attorney, Clark Clifford, then with Lyndon Johnson, Bobby Kennedy, Ted Sorensen, and other aides, advisers, and future cabinet members. His departure for Palm Beach was delayed for three hours by so many last-minute appointments that Evelyn Lincoln had trouble squeezing them onto one page of her engagement book. Her last entry, scribbled at the very bottom of January 10, read, "Dictated several pages of the Inaugural Address en route to Palm Beach."

We like to imagine great speeches are born when great men are left alone with their thoughts and some blank paper. According to the historical myths, Abraham Lincoln wrote the Gettysburg Address on the back of an envelope while traveling by train to Gettysburg, and FDR wrote his first inaugural address in longhand on a yellow legal pad while sitting alone by the fire at Hyde Park. John F. Kennedy's Hyde Park, the sanctuary where he often retreated during the 1960 campaign to dictate letters and speeches, was his compartment on the *Caroline*. A private airplane was an ideal form of transportation for an impatient man who could not tolerate anything—a meeting, conversation, speech, or sex—lasting too long. Kennedy was the first presidential candidate to own one, and aviation enthusiasts believe the speed and mobility that it afforded him made a crucial difference in the close 1960 election. Outside on the tarmac, flashbulbs would pop, reporters shout questions, bands play, and women scream. Then Kennedy would wave, turn, and sprint up the *Caroline*'s metal staircase. The door slammed behind him, the noise and commotion vanished, and finally, among familiar faces and cocooned in the white noise of the engines, he could read, nap, change his clothes, take a shower, and dictate to Evelyn Lincoln.

There is no tape recording of Kennedy's January 10 dictation on the *Caroline*, but we know from Lincoln's notes that he spoke in the same "beautiful language" Mary Davis remembered. He was probably fatigued by the pandemonium of the last two days, and elated by the praise for his speech to the Massachusetts legislature. He probably fiddled with his hair, drummed the arm of his chair, and tapped his teeth with a pencil, as he usually did while dictating to Lincoln. There is one thing about this scene that we know for certain: that as he dictated, he consulted a proposed draft of his inaugural address written by Ted Sorensen.

* * *

Sorensen writes in *Kennedy* that he and JFK had their first discussion about the inaugural address shortly after the November 8 election. Kennedy stressed then that he wanted to deliver a short speech focusing on foreign policy, avoiding partisanship and pessimism, and dispensing with the usual cold-war rhetoric, but letting the Soviets know he would not be bullied. He asked Sorensen to solicit suggestions "from everyone," meaning his ad hoc brain trust of friends, academics, and politicians. He also instructed him to read every previous inaugural address and study the Gettysburg Address to learn its "secret."

The earliest written antecedents of the Kennedy inaugural are the notes Sorensen took at this meeting. On the top of a sheet of yellow legal paper he wrote, "Gloria—CASH!" a reminder to ask his secretary, Gloria Sitrin, to visit the bank. On the left side, he wrote in a column:

4—E areas of agreement
1—C disarmament
5—D United Nations
3—B negotiate
2—A our objectives

The numbers appear to rank the topics in order of importance. The letters set out their logical sequence and reflect Kennedy's desire to convince Khrushchev that he was sincere about reducing tensions between their nations.

In a column on the right-hand side of the page Sorensen wrote:

Count words in draft
Count words in Ike '57, FDR '41, Wilson '17, Wilson '13 [four of the twentieth century's shortest inaugurals]
Leave no copies around, even RNG—MF [speechwriters Richard N. Goodwin and Meyer ("Mike") Feldman]
Add style and eloquence
Shorten sentences and words
Eliminate I specifics [meaning that he should eliminate the first person]
Make it the shortest since TR (except for FDR's abbreviated wartime ceremony in 1945)

At the bottom Sorensen added, "Count to Compare," listing underneath, "Ike, 1951. FDR, 1941. Wilson, 1917. Wilson 1913. Cleveland 1885. Grant 1873." This was further evidence that Kennedy, who strove to keep his speeches under fifteen minutes in order to, as he said, "leave them wanting more," was determined to deliver a brief address.

Sorensen followed Kennedy's instructions and read all forty-three previous inaugurals. He dismisses them in *Kennedy* as "a largely undistinguished lot, with some of our best eloquence emanating from some of our worst Presidents." But the speechwriter Mike Feldman recalls Sorensen telling him that the inaugurals had provided some useful ideas. A close reading of the three previous cold-war addresses, delivered by Truman in 1949 and Eisenhower in 1953 and 1957, suggests that Sorensen's draft incorporated some of their ideas, but the similarities may be coincidental, since these ideas had been in the air since the early years of the cold war and would probably have surfaced in Kennedy's address even had Sorensen not consulted the Truman and Eisenhower inaugurals.

Truman had declared that "democracy alone can supply the vitalizing force to stir the peoples of the world into triumphant action . . . against their ancient enemies—hunger, misery, and despair." Eisenhower had said, "We must . . . help others rise from misery." Sorensen wrote in his draft, "Today the trumpet sounds . . . a call to a broader, more basic struggle against all the enemies of man—tyranny and poverty and war itself." Truman had called world poverty "a threat . . . to more prosperous areas." Eisenhower had called it a "danger to the well-being of all other peoples." Sorensen drafted, "If freedom's way cannot help the many who are poor, it can never save the few who are rich."

Sorensen describes his first meeting with JFK to discuss the inaugural in considerable detail in *Kennedy* but does not mention writing a draft based on this conversation. Instead, he says vaguely that "actual drafting did not get under way until the week before it was due." This statement is true in the sense that Kennedy did not begin dictating his own draft until January 10, and is perhaps an acknowledgment that the real process of drafting the speech did not begin until Kennedy became actively involved in it.

Sorensen states that between the election and early January, "pages, paragraphs, and complete drafts [of the inaugural address] had poured in, solicited from [Joseph] Kraft, Galbraith, Stevenson, [Chester] Bowles, and others," but does not say that one of these "others" was Sorensen himself. He credits these contributors with supplying "several phrases, sentences, and themes," but credits himself with nothing. He declares that "no Kennedy speech ever underwent so many drafts," but does not add that at least two of these drafts were his.

There is an honorable quality to Sorensen's self-effacement. Not only was he reluctant to take undue credit for the speech, he knew Kennedy was proud of his literary abilities and sensitive to charges that he was not the author of his books and articles. Rumors that Sorensen had written *Profiles in Courage* had plagued Kennedy through the 1960 election, and, as Sorensen himself has stated, nothing in Kennedy's life would make him more angry than the charge that he was not the author of his own book. The columnist Drew Pearson had made this accusation during a 1957 ABC television interview on *The Mike Wallace Show*. Kennedy hired Clark Clifford to represent him and threatened to sue for slander. Sorensen provided a sworn statement that he had neither written, nor boasted about writing, *Profiles in Courage*. When Kennedy supplied pages of his handwritten notes and first draft to substantiate his authorship, ABC and Pearson retracted the story, but it remained a touchy subject.

When Kennedy met with Robert McNamara on December 8, 1960, to discuss the latter's appointment to the cabinet, McNamara's first question was "Did you really write *Profiles in Courage* yourself?" Kennedy insisted that he had, then pointedly wrote out an announcement of McNamara's appointment as secretary of defense on a yellow legal pad, walked outside, and delivered it to the press. But McNamara's query, posed to Kennedy a month before the inauguration, must have reminded him that intelligent people remained skeptical about his authorship of *Profiles in Courage*, and made him more determined to write his own speech and to leave documentary evidence for the High Court of History to prove it.

Sorensen's reluctance to diminish Kennedy's legacy by acknowledging his own contributions to *Profiles in Courage*, and to the inaugural address, has not lessened over time. When the historian Herbert Parmet interviewed him in 1977 about his role in writing *Profiles*, Sorensen said, "That was a very sensitive subject while he was alive, very. . . . And I feel some inhibitions in talking about this matter frankly, even today." He finally admitted having had "a substantial role in all that output," but Kennedy's working methods, particularly his habit of redictating Sorensen's material in his own words, indicate that he was seldom a passive consumer of Sorensen's contributions.

Sorensen's first draft of the inaugural address that Kennedy carried onto the *Caroline* was written after the speechwriter shared Thanksgiving dinner with his colleague Mike Feldman on November 24, 1960. According to Feldman, Sorensen spent about three hours in the Feldmans' den writing it. He did not show it to Feldman then ("leave no copies around, even RNG—MF"), but allowed him to read either this draft or a later one before they flew together to Palm Beach to meet Kennedy on December 21. The Thanksgiving Day draft is not in any of Sorensen's files, although he appears to have included four of its passages in *Kennedy*, under a column labeled "First Draft." None of these passages contains any of the speech's most famous sentences, which would be dictated by Kennedy on January 10. One passage includes a phrase that is mercifully absent from subsequent versions, "And if the fruits of cooperation prove sweeter than the dregs of suspicion . . ."

A slip of U.S. Senate memorandum paper in Sorensen's files also indicates that he had written at least one more draft of an inaugural address before Kennedy boarded the *Caroline* on January 10. A column of five typed lines at the top of this memorandum refers to earlier presidential inaugurals. It reads, "Roosevelt 1941 1281 words," "Wilson 1917 1485 words," "Wilson 1913 1690 words." "Eisenhower 1957 1730 words," and then, after a space, "TCS [Theodore Chaikin Sorensen] draft 1693 words." Beneath the typed "1693 words" Sorensen has written in his unmistakable handwriting, " -413," drawn a line underneath it, and written a revised total of 1280, presumably the number of words in his second draft. (Another notation in Sorensen's handwriting at the bottom of this memorandum indicates that his second draft had satisfied Kennedy's requirement that his be one of the shortest inaugurals of the century: "Shorter than Eisenhower 2, Hoover, Coolidge, Harding, Taft, McKinley, Wilson's 2, FDR's 1st & 2nd." When Sorensen was shown this memorandum in 2002, he agreed that it appeared to indicate that he had written at least two drafts of the inaugural.)

The Sorensen draft that Kennedy consulted as he dictated on January 10 must have been, for reasons that will become apparent, a five-page, unsigned, undated, and incomplete typed manuscript available in box 34 of Kennedy's Presidential Office Files at the Kennedy Library. In 2002, when Sorensen examined a copy of this document (hereafter called "the Sorensen Draft"), he remarked that it appeared to have been typed by his secretary, Gloria Sitrin, on her office typewriter. When Sitrin was shown it, she remarked that although she could not be certain, she "thought" she had typed it.

The original of the Sorensen Draft has apparently been lost. The Kennedy Library possesses a photocopy that is lacking its first page. A curator with two decades of experience at the library points out that a small black staple mark in the upper-left-hand corner of the second page of the photocopy indicates that the first page must have been removed *before* the photocopy was made and thus before the library acquired the document. If a Kennedy Library employee had removed the first page of the photocopy, there would be no staple mark on page two.

Of course it is possible that the first page simply became separated from the document and was mislaid. It is also possible that, after deciding to dictate his own introduction, Kennedy absentmindedly ripped off the page and threw it away. But it is also possible that someone removed the page intentionally, and the prime suspects for this would be Evelyn Lincoln, who presumably filed the draft, or Kennedy himself. If the first page had identified Sorensen as its author, it might have been removed to obscure his contribution to the speech. This theory becomes more plausible when one considers the great lengths to which Kennedy would go, during a flight back to Washington one week later, to establish that he had written his own inaugural address.

On January 10, Kennedy treated Sorensen's draft of the inaugural address as he had many of the speeches Sorensen and other speechwriters had prepared for him during the campaign: he largely ignored its opening and closing paragraphs, replacing them with his own original material. He then used the remainder of Sorensen's text as the framework for his own dictated oration, sometimes inserting passages into his dictation verbatim.

Kennedy was known to his aides as a skilled improviser who would often ignore or alter the prepared text of a speech. But if you compare Kennedy's 1960 campaign speeches with the texts released in advance to the press, it becomes evident that he almost *always* ignored a prepared speech, preferring instead to cobble one together from a repertoire of his favorite lines: "I think we can do better," "It's time to get this country moving again," "This is a great country, but I think it can be a greater country," "I don't run for the Presidency promising that if you elect me life will be easier," "Franklin Roosevelt could be a good neighbor abroad because he was a good neighbor at home," and so on.

At one point in the 1960 campaign, the speechwriter Richard Goodwin had supplied Kennedy with what he termed "a proudly-drafted discourse on civil rights." Kennedy put it in his pocket, delivering instead, Goodwin said, "an eloquent extemporaneous exposition of his candidacy." Near the end, he pulled out Goodwin's speech, read a few lines, then added his own passionate conclusion, saying that when future historians (the High Court of History) looked back on the coming decade, he wanted them to cry, "These were the great years of the American life, the 1960s. Give me those years!" (The inaugural: "I do not believe that any of us would exchange places with any other people or any other generation.")

It is one thing to speak off the cuff to an audience of several thousand, but it requires a higher order of courage and skill to wing a live television address watched by several million viewers, as Kennedy did on September 15, 1960, in Harrisburg, Pennsylvania. He used his two favorite Roosevelt quotations in this speech, declaring, "The challenge that faces this generation of Americans is as great as the challenge that faced that generation of Americans who in 1932 Franklin Roosevelt informed that they had a rendezvous with destiny. I believe that our generation of Americans also has a rendezvous with destiny that we are prepared to meet." (The inaugural: "the torch has been passed to a new generation of Americans.")

Evelyn Lincoln writes in *My Twelve Years with John F. Kennedy* that during the January 10, 1961, flight to Florida her boss "dictated and dictated and dictated," making it sound as if they worked for several hours. Her own shorthand notes, however, tell a different story. They fill just seven pages of a stenographer's pad. Even if Kennedy had stumbled over words or frequently paused to organize his thoughts, which is unlikely, his dictation could not have taken more than twenty minutes. He was probably restless and eager to join the other passengers. The flight manifest is unavailable, but we know that several men whose company he enjoyed were on board, including his press secretary, Pierre Salinger; brother-in-law, Peter Lawford; and Carroll Rosenbloom, the owner of the Baltimore Colts football team. There was also a detachment of Secret Service agents, who were perhaps more concerned than usual over the safety of a president who had already survived a suicide bomber and was receiving death threats that Secret Service chief U. E. Baughman was describing as "more than the usual run of prank mail" and "unusually vicious." (Two typical ones: "We are sick of dirty black Catholics. . . . The next bomb will be for Mr. Kennedy," "With a completely divided America there is speculation about your safety. . . . You must surely know that you are no more fit to be President than my tomcat.")

The absence of extensive alterations and deletions in Lincoln's notes indicates that Kennedy's dictation was polished and fluid. The only major exception comes on page two, where she crossed out symbols for "the principles for which our ancestors fought, we now fight for around the globe," then wrote "stet" above them. Kennedy had apparently changed his mind about deleting the sentence. In his speech it would become, "And yet the same revolutionary beliefs for which our forebears fought are still at issue around the world."

A secretary trained in Gregg shorthand who examined and transcribed Lincoln's notes found that Lincoln often abandoned Gregg and fell back on her own idiosyncratic stenographic language. Her shorthand was also rife with misspellings, unorthodox shortcuts, and instances where she spelled out words like *succession, legitimized,* and *tyranny,* a common failing of secretaries with limited shorthand skills, and evidence Kennedy was speaking quickly, and she was struggling to keep pace.

Walt Rostow, a foreign policy adviser in the Kennedy administration, believed JFK sometimes experienced "moments of grace" that enabled him to "go into overdrive" and produce work of extraordinary quality. "Sometimes you could see it in his speeches," Rostow said. "Ideas, rhetoric, movement and personality would all come briefly together. Not for long. But it was special." Rostow pointed to the first televised debate as an example. The inauguration itself was another such moment. And these twenty minutes on board the *Caroline*, when he captured in poetic and immortal language the ideas he had woven into his extemporaneous speeches throughout his campaign, was another.

We do not know whether Kennedy stuffed Sorensen's draft in his pocket, placed it facedown on his desk, or scanned it as he dictated his own opening paragraphs. What is certain is that he was doing what he had done throughout his campaign—putting aside the prepared text of a speech and delivering his own spontaneous oration.

Because the first page of the Sorensen Draft is missing, it is impossible to be certain if Kennedy ignored it entirely or redictated some of its material into his own words. Later in his dictation, when he wanted to incorporate portions of the Sorensen Draft, he did not redictate them but simply instructed Lincoln to insert the material into the text. Because he did not do that at the beginning, and because in his campaign speeches he customarily used his own original material in the opening and concluding paragraphs, it is likely that he ignored all or most of the material on Sorensen's missing page. He also ignored most of Sorensen's second page, which had proposed that he say, for example:

> So let the word go forth to all the world—and suit the action to the word—that this generation of Americans has no intention of becoming soft instead of resolute, smug instead of resourceful. . . .
>
> And the worst is fast upon us, with the threat of hostile power growing in every corner of our planet. . . .

Yet our allies in the West are unfulfilled and insecure. Our neighbors to the South are torn by pressures from within and without. [Here, Kennedy had added in his handwriting, "To our north, Canada, limited by nature and"—the remainder of this line is illegible.] Our friends in less-developed states are diverting resources we are loath to replace into useless power struggles.

The dread secret of the atom we first unlocked spreads slowly, but all too swiftly, around a globe hell-bent for planned or accidental suicide. . . .

The fact that Kennedy had made this editorial change about Canada on the second page, the only place on the Sorensen Draft where his handwriting appears, suggests that he had read it before boarding the *Caroline*. We do not know, however, whether Kennedy had earlier decided to replace these paragraphs with his own material or did so during the flight.

The Sorensen paragraphs that Kennedy replaced were not clumsy or ill-suited to the occasion; they were just not right for a speech meant to equal the best of Lincoln and Churchill. Their tone was also somewhat negative and confrontational, at odds with the instructions he had given Sorensen in November "not to sound pessimistic" and to avoid "the customary cold war rhetoric."

The first page of Lincoln's shorthand shows Kennedy starting his dictation by saying, "An inaugural is an end as well as a beginning." In the final draft of the speech this would become, "we observe today not a victory of party, but a celebration of freedom—symbolizing an end as well as a beginning." Woodrow Wilson had declared in his 1913 inaugural address that an inauguration "means much more than the mere success of a party." Kennedy may not have had this line in mind on January 10, but he had certainly read Wilson's inaugural.

Kennedy dictated, "We must not forget that we are the descendants of revolutionaries." (The inaugural: "We dare not forget today that we are the heirs of that first revolution.") He went on: "The principles for which our ancestors fought we now fight for around the globe," and, "The rights of man [come] not because of the state but because of the hand of God." In the final text these sentences would become, "And yet the same revolutionary beliefs for which our forebears fought are still at issue around the globe—the belief that the rights of man come not from the generosity of the state, but from the hand of God."

This ambitious, some would say reckless, offer to extend the promises of the Declaration of Independence to the world was one Kennedy had often made during his campaign. He had declared at Bangor, Maine, for example, that "the President of the United States represents not only the Democrats of this country, he represents all of the people around the world who want to live in freedom, who look to us for hope and leadership." He sometimes supported this idea with quotations he had been saving in his notebooks since his student days at Harvard, such as Jefferson's comment to John Adams that "the flames that kindled on the 4th of July have spread over too much of the globe to be extinguished by the feeble fires of despotism," and Thomas Paine's declaration that "the cause of America is the cause of all mankind."

He dictated, "Let the word go forth from this place . . . to those who wish us well and those who wish us ill . . . that a new generation of Americans—born in this century, tempered by war . . . do not plan to participate in the defeat of the revolutionary concepts to which this country has always been committed."

These sentences would become, "Let the word go forth from this time and place, to friend and foe alike, that the torch has been passed to a new generation of Americans—born in this century, tempered by war, disciplined by a hard and bitter peace, proud of our ancient heritage—and unwilling to witness the slow undoing of those human rights to which this nation has always been committed, and to which we are committed today at home and around the world."

In 1946, Kennedy had chosen "The New Generation Offers a Leader" as a slogan for his congressional campaign. Throughout the 1960 presidential race he had urged his generation to shoulder the burden of defending their nation at a time of great peril. In an address televised on July 4, 1960, he said, "It is time for a new generation of leadership, to cope with new problems and new responsibilities." At a September fund-raising dinner in Washington he said, "I think this nation will rise to the test, and when we do, Mr. Khrushchev will know that a new generation of Americans is taking over this country."

The second page of Sorensen's draft had opened with "So let the word go forth to all the world," the only phrase from that page that Kennedy included, virtually unchanged, in his dictation. It was one he had previously used in his speech nominating Adlai Stevenson for president at the 1956 Democratic convention. The files for this speech do not indicate whether it was his contribution or Sorensen's, but the hortatory "Let" or "Let us" was one of his rhetorical tics.

* * *

The Sorensen Draft read, "But let every nation know, be it friend or foe, that we shall not yield to threat or force in our vow to keep the peace—that we intend to stand by our commitments—and that we are prepared to do whatever must be done to assure freedom's success and survival."

Kennedy dictated instead, "those who wish us well and those who wish us ill," and ". . . we shall pay any price, bear any burden, meet any hardship, oppose any foe in order to maintain this rich heritage. This much we believe and more." In the final text these phrases became, "Let every nation know, whether it wishes us well or ill, that we shall pay any price, bear any burden, meet any hardship, support any friend, oppose any foe, in order to assure the survival and success of liberty. This much we pledge—and more."

No other passage in the inaugural has been so frequently criticized or misunderstood. The journalist Robert MacNeil condemned it as "soaring hubris." The *New York Times* correspondent Tom Wicker probably had it in mind when he called the entire inaugural "bellicose." George McGovern later said, "That business of bearing any burden and taking on any foe was great at the time but looking back on it, I think it was really quite arrogant and extravagant." Even Kennedy loyalists have taken a swipe at it. Sorensen wrote in 1988 that it "reflected the Cold War atmosphere of the time" and had been a rhetorical mistake. Arthur Schlesinger criticized it as "extravagant rhetoric."

Seen through the lens of Vietnam, it seems reckless and open-ended, but no one singled it out for criticism in 1961 because then it appeared to be simply an eloquent restatement of the obvious—that the United States would not sacrifice its liberties without a struggle. In fact, it was the only stick in a speech offering the Soviets the carrots of negotiation, tolerance, and cooperation.

Schlesinger and other Kennedy aides have explained the bellicosity of "bear any burden" as an understandable, if injudicious, response to "For New Victories of the World Communist Movement," an alarming speech Khrushchev delivered in Moscow on January 6. In it, Khrushchev pledged that the Soviet Union would instigate and support "just wars of liberation" in countries such as Algeria, the Congo, Laos, and Vietnam, and predicted these wars would result in Communist states across the third world. The speech unsettled Kennedy, and he often cited it during the early months of his presidency. But for all the influence it had on thinking in the Kennedy White House, it had none whatever on the Kennedy inaugural address since the Soviets did not release the text until January 17, and Kennedy himself did not read it until January 19, more than a week after dictating his "bear any burden" sentence.

In fact, more than any other line in the address, "bear any burden" shows Kennedy following Richard Neustadt's advice not to write his inaugural address until he knew the state of the world on January 20. Rather than being bellicose, swollen, or extravagant, this sentence was part of a measured response to the schizophrenic Soviet feelers that George Kennan had outlined to him eight hours before. The "bear any burden" sentence was a warning to the Kremlin hard-liners that the youngest man elected president would not be bullied, a message he reinforced later in his speech with "We dare not tempt them [the Soviets] with weakness." Meanwhile, the three pages of the Sorensen Draft that Kennedy was about to instruct Lincoln to insert into his dictation promised cooperation and negotiations.

By the time Kennedy dictated, "This much we believe and more," Lincoln had filled two pages with shorthand and was midway down the first column of the third page. After entering the Gregg symbols for this last sentence she wrote, in regular letters and numbers, "p 3, 4, 5, page (separate) 6."

This can only have been a reference to these pages in the Sorensen Draft. Pages three, four, and five, in fact, correspond precisely to material from that draft that would appear in the inaugural address largely unchanged. These pages consisted of a series of promises addressed to different international audiences, followed by seven paragraphs offering Kennedy's proposals for reducing tensions with the Soviet Union.

After inserting this material into his draft, Kennedy dictated, "Since this country was founded, every generation of Americans has been called at least once to give testimony to its national loyalty. The graves of young Americans who responded now circle the globe." This would become in his inaugural: "Since this country was founded, each generation of Americans has been summoned to give testimony to its national loyalty. The graves of young Americans who answered the call to service surround the globe."

Kennedy had already dictated a version of these sentences to Ted Sorensen when they discussed the speech after the election. As they mulled over several ideas, Kennedy had quickly dictated, "This heritage has been passed on to us by other Americans who in every generation since our nation began have answered the call to service. Many lie buried around the globe." Sorensen had neglected to include this in his draft. On January 10, Kennedy rectified this omission.

* * *

Kennedy dictated sentences containing the phrases "to bear the burdens," "to win this long twilight struggle," and "against the common enemies of man: tyranny, poverty, disease, and war itself." While editing the speech in Palm Beach over the next week, he would merge these phrases with a sentence from page six of the Sorensen Draft to produce: "Today the trumpet sounds its urgent call again—not a call to arms, though arms we need—not a call to battle, although embattled we are—but a call to a broader, more basic struggle." Then he would add a verse from St. Paul's Epistle to the Romans, "rejoicing in hope, patient in tribulation," so the sentence read, "Now the trumpet summons us again, not as a call to bear arms, though arms we need; not as a call to battle, though embattled we are—but a call to bear the burden of a long twilight struggle, year in and year out, 'rejoicing in hope, patient in tribulation'— a struggle against the common enemies of man: tyranny, poverty, disease, and war itself."

Kennedy next dictated four sentences that bear no relationship to anything in the Sorensen Draft.

> In the long history of the world, only a few generations have been granted the role of defending freedom in its hour of maximum danger.
>
> I do not shrink from this responsibility—I welcome it.
>
> I do not believe that any of us would exchange places with any other people or any other generation.
>
> The energy, the faith, the devotion which we bring to this endeavor will light our country and all who serve it—and the glow from that fire can truly light the world.

He had used "defending freedom in its hour of maximum danger" when he announced his candidacy on January 2, 1960, saying, "I have developed an image of America as fulfilling a noble and historical role as the defender of freedom in a time of maximum peril—and of the American people as confident, courageous, and persevering." He liked this phrase so much he used it throughout his campaign. The second and third of these four sentences appear in the inaugural exactly as he dictated them on the *Caroline* that evening. The others appear almost verbatim. The first two are carved into the fourth tablet at Arlington. The fourth sentence is on the fifth tablet.

The word *generation* appears four times in the inaugural address: in "the torch has been passed to a new generation"; "only a few generations have been granted the role of defending freedom in its hour of maximum danger"; "each generation of Americans has been summoned to give testimony to its national loyalty"; and "I do not believe that any of us would exchange places with any other people or any other generation."

None of these passages appear in the Sorensen Draft. Kennedy dictated all four on January 10. They combine his political conviction that each generation has a duty to contribute to the national patrimony with his personal experience in World War II. They also owe something to three quotations he had saved in his notebooks: "This generation of Americans has a rendezvous with destiny," from a speech that FDR gave in Philadelphia in 1936; Daniel Webster's exhortation on the occasion of the dedication of the Bunker Hill Monument: "Let us develop the resources of our land, call forth its power, build up all its great institutions and see whether we, in our time and generation, may not perform something worthy to be remembered"; and Albert Einstein's statement: "A hundred times every day I remind myself that my inner and outer life depend on the labors of other men, living and dead, and that I must exert myself to give in the same measure that I have received."

At the beginning of the 1960 presidential campaign, Sorensen had explained to a political journalist how he and Kennedy collaborated on a speech: "The way Jack worked was to take all the material, mine and his, pencil it, dictate fresh copy in his own words, pencil it again, dictate it again—he never used a typewriter."

Kennedy left no pencil marks on page six, the last page of the Sorensen Draft. Instead, he appears to have been editing it in his mind as he dictated it in the style of his oratorical hero Daniel Webster, about whom he had written in *Profiles:* "He prepared his speeches with the utmost care, but seldom wrote them out in a prepared text. It has been said that he could think out a speech sentence by sentence, correct the sentences in his mind without the use of a pencil, and then deliver it exactly as he thought it out."

The Sorensen Draft contained a version of the inaugural's famous "ask not" sentence. Sorensen had opened his last paragraph, "So ask not what your country is going to do for you. Ask what you can do for your country." Kennedy redictated a version even closer to the final one: "My fellow Americans: ask not what your country will do for you, ask rather what you can do for your country." (The inaugural: "And so, my fellow Americans: ask not what your country can do for you—ask what you can do for your country.") It is tempting to conclude from this that Sorensen was therefore the author of the famous "ask not" line. But the truth, as will soon become clear, is more complicated.

Kennedy added a corollary to "ask not" that was not in the Sorensen Draft: "My fellow citizens of the world, ask not what America or any other country will do for you, but rather what you yourself can do for freedom." This became in the inaugural, "My fellow citizens of the world: ask not what America will do for you, but what together we can do for the freedom of man."

Finally, he dictated a slightly altered version of Sorensen's "Ask of your leaders the same high standards and sacrifice that we will ask of you," then deleted Sorensen's next sentence, "And ask the Lord above to grant us all the strength and wisdom we shall need."

The typed portion of Sorensen's draft concluded with this sentence. But, perhaps sensing this was a weak ending, Sorensen had added in his handwriting, "With a clear conscience our only sure reward, with history the final judge of our motives, let us go forth to lead the land we love, asking His blessing and help, but knowing that here on earth God's work must truly be our own." This was an expanded version of a sentence in Kennedy's January 9 farewell to the Massachusetts legislature that went, "Humbly I ask His help in this undertaking—but aware that on earth His will is worked by men."

Kennedy must have noticed the similarities between it and his Massachusetts speech of the day before. He omitted it from his dictation, replacing it with a trite sentence about "sacrifice," "comradeship," and "lifting the world."

When he had finished dictating, Kennedy asked Lincoln to prepare a typescript before they landed. She typed throughout the remainder of the flight, an indication she was also retyping the three pages he had inserted into the address from the Sorensen Draft. As she typed, she realized that, as she noted in her memoirs, "this was not an ordinary speech." She also noted, "In that dictation, in its original form, was that now famous line: 'Ask not what your country is going to do for you, ask what you can do for your country—my fellow citizens of the world [*sic*],'" and she later attached a memorandum to her shorthand pad showing how Kennedy changed "ask not" between January 10 and the inauguration. She was pulling the last sheet from her typewriter as the *Caroline* taxied to the West Palm Beach terminal. When Kennedy saw it in her hand, he grinned and said, "Oh, I see you have it done."

2

Palm Beach

JANUARY 11 TO JANUARY 15

⚜

Kennedy revised his dictation in the sprawling Spanish revival mansion where he had spent Christmas and Easter holidays since the age of sixteen. It was not a large or ostentatious house by Palm Beach standards, but it had a romantic-sounding name, La Guerida—"den" or "cave" in Spanish—and the cachet of being designed by Addison Mizner, who had become the toast of Palm Beach in the 1920s by building estates with pink stucco walls and roofs of red barrel tiles modeled on the palaces of the grandees of Seville. Mizner offered his clients an architecture of privacy, with high walls, narrow windows, iron bars, and thick doors strengthened by metal studs and braces. The antithesis of front-porch America, it was perfect for a large and public family like the Kennedys who valued their seclusion.

Rose Kennedy once remarked, "It is a long distance in more ways than one from Beals Street, Brookline, to Ocean Boulevard, Palm Beach." But because she and Joe Kennedy lived at both addresses in the same tightwad fashion, it was not really so far at all. One of the most appealing things about Joe and Rose was their indifference to luxury. They spent lavishly on travel, education, and large houses where their family could gather, but were parsimonious about furnishing these houses and heedless about maintaining them. Evelyn Lincoln loyally praised the "quiet beauty and good taste" of La Guerida's furnishings, but the more discerning Oleg Cassini, who designed Jacqueline Kennedy's most famous outfits, recalls cracked linoleum, faded curtains, shabby slipcovers, and a murky swimming pool that he avoided, he says, "at all costs."

During the week he spent at La Guerida before his inauguration, Kennedy sat in the same heavy Spanish colonial furniture he had used since he was sixteen, swam in the same pool, and ate at the same table. Like any adult returning to a house where he grew up, and where his parents still held sway, he must have glimpsed the ghost of his younger self, and the specters of his dead brother and sister, who had also swum in this pool and sat in these chairs. Of the three homes he used during the transition, Palm Beach was the only one he had shared with Kathleen, who had been killed in a plane crash in 1948, and with Joe, killed in action in 1944. Only here could he glance up from the morning newspapers, with their headlines about wars in the Congo, Laos, and Algeria, or up from the draft of his inaugural address, and meet the eyes of his dead brother, whose framed photograph led a procession of family pictures across the baby grand piano, and who had answered his country's call to service "around the globe," not only asking what he could do for his country, but doing it.

La Guerida had the usual gloomy Mizner touches: low-beamed ceilings, filigreed ironwork, lava rock walls, heavy oak furniture, and leaded windows. Its most gracious feature was a layout that encouraged natural ventilation and included patios and courtyards instead of corridors. French doors opened out onto an emerald lawn with curving palms, beyond which was a brilliant beach and the Atlantic. One drawback to the design was that anyone in the surrounding rooms could see anyone sitting on the patios and courtyards, and vice versa. This lack of privacy became even more acute when the house was as crowded as it became during the week of January 10.

There were several dozen people at La Guerida at any given time during those seven days. They included Jack and Jackie, Rose and Joe Kennedy, Rose's niece and companion Ann Gargan, houseguests Peter Lawford and Carroll Rosenbloom, three-year-old Caroline Kennedy and six-week-old John Kennedy Jr., their nurse and nursemaid, Kennedy's valet, George Thomas, and Jackie's maid, Providencia Parades. There was also a staff of cooks, maids, gardeners, pool men, chauffeurs, hairdressers, and barbers commuting or living in the servants' wing, as well as Miss O'Malley, a masseuse who lived at the house and was on permanent call but who was apparently never accorded a first name. Jackie had a personal secretary, Mary Gallagher, and a press secretary, Pamela Turnure, whom she correctly suspected of being one of her husband's mistresses. Kennedy had Evelyn Lincoln, and his parents had Bonnie Williams, who Mary Gallagher thought should have been modeling clothes on Fifth Avenue instead of typing letters. Add to this cast of characters politicians and dignitaries flowing through the house at all hours, Secret Service agents patrolling the grounds, and reporters camped outside the gate, and you have the ingredients of a Preston Sturges or Kaufman and Hart screwball comedy, in which several generations of an eccentric family trip over one another in a creaky mansion where the phones never stop ringing, doors never cease slamming, typewriters clack around the clock, doorbells sound perpetually, and guests never stop arriving and departing.

We can assume that several times this week Rose Kennedy, seventy years old and the mother of nine children, dog-paddled furiously across the murky pool in her usual swimming headgear of two bath caps and a sun visor. Sometimes she scooted through the living room with reminder notes and new quotations she was attempting to memorize pinned to her cardigan, and Scotch tape plastered across her forehead to smooth her wrinkles. Whenever she appeared, her children and their guests—who quickly learned this was a family rule—leaped to their feet as a sign of respect, sometimes even standing up in the swimming pool. Meanwhile, Caroline teetered across the lawn in her mother's high heels, Miss O'Malley "massage-hopped" between rooms, Joe Kennedy, his wrinkled torso glistening with coconut oil, sat in the bullpen, a four-foot-high enclosure by the swimming pool with cushioned benches and wicker chairs where the Kennedy men could sunbathe nude, and Secret Service agents unwrapped and probed the innards of stuffed animals arriving by the hour for Caroline and John Jr., adding them to the menagerie that had swamped a guest room.

We know that JFK's press secretary, Pierre Salinger, held press conferences on the patio, in the living room, and on occasion even in Kennedy's bedroom, and that aides, congressmen, dressmakers, and hairdressers trooped through the ground floor. We know, too, that meetings were convened in the library, living room, courtyards, and even in Kennedy's bathroom, that Jackie and Caroline often retreated to a living-room window seat, pulling a curtain around them to create a snug hideaway where they read and played with dolls as the pandemonium swirled outside. At all hours, people who regretted not contributing to the campaign knocked on the front door, leaving cash-filled envelopes for JFK with the Secret Service agents or pressing them on members of the Kennedy family. One evening Senator Mike Mansfield of Montana stumbled into Miss O'Malley's bedroom, causing her to wake the entire house with her screams. Sometimes the surf wrapped La Guerida in a gauze of salt and white noise, so that like an island or ship at sea, it became lost to its own world and routines. At times, the surf pounded all night, slamming against the sea wall, throwing spray into the palm fronds and sending bedroom walls shuddering, leaving everyone tired and testy the next morning.

* * *

On January 12, the *Washington Post* reported that Kennedy had "settled down" in Palm Beach to write his inaugural. The *New York Times* described him working on "several drafts" and planning to deliver an address equal to the inaugurals of Lincoln, Wilson, Jefferson, and Franklin Roosevelt. Pierre Salinger, most likely the source for these stories, wrote in his memoirs that during this period, "except for a swim and an occasional round of golf, JFK was at his desk in his father's den most of his waking hours," adding that he had made "substantial progress" on his speech. This conforms to the notion that great speeches arise from hours of painstaking work, but bears little resemblance to what was happening at La Guerida that week. Kennedy did spend time revising his dictated draft, but according to Lincoln's appointment book and diary, and newspaper articles, he also played twelve to eighteen holes of golf a day, except on January 12, when he went deep-sea fishing and played only nine. Most days, he spent roughly as much time outside working on his tan as he did inside his study.

Kennedy's schedule that week reflects his aversion to solitude and his horror of boredom. Consider January 11, the day following his arrival. Lincoln recorded in her diary that she arrived at 9:30 A.M. and at 9:33, she took his pills into the dining room. Then, she wrote, "he asked me to call his barber and then he said there must be another airline that would get 'Barbara Lansing' [pseudonym] into New York." A Palm Beach friend telephoned to arrange a golf game, and Kennedy spoke by telephone with the Harvard historian Arthur Schlesinger, who had accepted a position as a special assistant in his White House. When Caroline burst into the room, the future president interrupted his conversation to say, "Hello, Buttons, how are you? How is John-John? How much does he weigh?" After meeting with the Philadelphia political operative Matt McClosky, he walked into the ground-floor library, asked Lincoln to schedule calls with future secretary of state Dean Rusk, the aide Ken O'Donnell, and Ted Sorensen, and had a manicure and haircut while speaking on the telephone with his brother Bobby. At 11:50 A.M., he headed out to the bullpen to darken his tan.

The phrase "healthy tan" has become an oxymoron, but in 1961 a tan was considered evidence of well-being and a way to disprove the rumors about Kennedy's poor health. Hugh Sidey, who covered him for *Time*, remembers the whole family being obsessed with tanning. Jackie used a reflector, Bobby pursued the grail of a full body tan, and Kennedy himself had been traveling with a sun lamp since his 1946 congressional campaign. He worked tirelessly at keeping his tan dark enough to show up on black-and-white television, and at the start of his 1960 campaign had instructed Lincoln to schedule "one full day off per week in a pleasant surrounding, preferably a beach."

The downside of this sun worshipping was that Kennedy's skin was already showing signs of sun damage. On television he looked youthful, but those meeting him in person sometimes had a different impression. Gore Vidal, who shared a stepfather with Jackie, wrote in 1961 that "Kennedy looks older than his photographs. The outline is slender and youthful, but the face is heavily lined for his age. On the upper lip are those tiny vertical lines characteristic of a more advanced age. . . . He is immaculately dressed; although occasional white chest hairs curl over his collar."

On January 11, Kennedy had scheduled Miss O'Malley for a noon massage in the bullpen, but a chilly wind drove them into his bedroom, where she worked on him while he conferred by telephone with Dean Rusk. Then he golfed with the treasurer of the Democratic National Committee and the publisher of the *Miami News,* and attended a reception honoring FBI chief J. Edgar Hoover. According to the columnist Chalmers Roberts, he also found time that day for "pondering drafts of an Inaugural Address designed to tell the Nation the hard and unpleasant facts as he sees them."

Kennedy paid close attention to the text of his inaugural during the next ten days, an indication that he understood that in order for it to be compared to the Gettysburg Address, it would have to read as well as it sounded. Ted Sorensen writes in *Kennedy* of JFK working on his "thoughts" in Palm Beach while he worked on his in Washington, then conferring with him by phone. The speechwriter Feldman recalls Sorensen receiving a call about the inaugural from Kennedy during a weekend brunch Feldman gave for new cabinet members at his home in Washington.

When Feldman had been in Palm Beach in December, he had watched Kennedy reading a newspaper article while speaking with one of his appointees over the telephone. After hanging up, he had summarized the article to Feldman, a performance suggesting that while in Palm Beach he could have been revising his inaugural while having a massage or playing golf. Kennedy often read books, newspapers, or reports while taking a bath, eating a meal, or dressing, by propping a book open on his bureau. He presumably revised his inaugural this way, too, using slivers of time, and working fast.

The accounts of Kennedy editing and revising his inaugural during this week all have him writing his changes in longhand on lined yellow legal pads, and working on the patio, in a first-floor study, or in the secluded ground-floor bedroom he shared with Jackie.

La Guerida's owners have kept the Kennedys' furniture in his bedroom, and seeing it now, one is struck by how modestly they lived. They slept on narrow twin beds with ornate wooden headboards. He worked at a narrow desk and climbed onto a heavy oaken table for his daily massage. It is a small room, twelve feet by fifteen, but its French doors open onto the tennis court, and it appears to be good for sleeping—dark in the morning but cheerful when it catches the afternoon sunlight. It is also relatively quiet, perhaps why Kennedy retreated there to work.

Jackie heard him reciting the speech "in bits and pieces," she said. She remembered piles of yellow legal paper containing his notes and revisions covering their bedroom floor. Whenever he left the room, she climbed out of bed to gather them up. The passages he was revising, like those she heard, must have been the same ones he had dictated to Lincoln, meaning that before he delivered his inaugural, only Lincoln and Jackie could have known how it sounded as well as how it read.

In *A Thousand Days,* Arthur Schlesinger writes about Jackie, "Under neath a veil of lovely inconsequence, she concealed a tremendous awareness, an all-seeing eye and a ruthless judgment." Did she turn this judgment on the inaugural address? Why else would Kennedy read it to her? She had contributed to *Profiles,* suggested literary references and quotations for his speeches, and read him Charles de Gaulle's memoirs, translating them from the French. De Gaulle had begun by declaring, "All my life I have had a certain image of France. This is inspired by sentiment as much as by reason. . . . My emotional side tends to imagine France . . . dedicated to an exalted and exceptional destiny." Kennedy echoed this when, announcing his candidacy, he said, "I have developed an image of America as fulfilling a noble and historical role as the defender of freedom in a time of maximum peril." (The inaugural: "Only a few generations have been granted the role of defending freedom in its hour of maximum danger.")

Schlesinger writes that "morning after morning, puffing a small cigar, a yellow, legal-sized pad of paper on his knees, he [Kennedy] worked away, scribbling a few lines, crossing out others and then putting the sheets of paper in his overflowing desk." In *The Crisis Years: Kennedy and Khrushchev, 1960–1963,* the historian Michael Beschloss also gives him a cigar and has him working during the morning—although given his schedule, one wonders which morning—but places him outside, writing that "in Palm Beach, after rising in his father's house, Kennedy put on sports clothes and sat down on the patio overlooking the gray-blue Atlantic. Puffing on a small cigar, he pressed a yellow legal pad against his knees and scribbled out language for his Inaugural Address."

Schlesinger was not in Palm Beach that week and does not identify his source. When asked about it four decades later, he believed it had been Jackie. Beschloss presumably relied on Schlesinger and on a January 23, 1961, *Newsweek* article containing this account: "He sought to go down in history not only as a great President but as one of inspiring eloquence. He was a professional writer, a Pulitzer Prize winner, and his literary standards were as exacting as his standards of government service. The sprawling house was silent, except for the pulsing of the surf outside, and John F. Kennedy was in a reflective mood as he began to scrawl, barely legibly, on a legal pad of ruled, yellow paper, the words that he hoped would help lead a nation to new heights of greatness, his New Frontier."

There is an eerie, staged quality to this scene, and the more one tries imagining it, the more curious it becomes. The usually bustling Kennedy villa is silent. There is an exchange between Kennedy and an unnamed *Newsweek* reporter (the magazine did not publish bylines in 1961) during which Kennedy gives the impression that he is counting on his inaugural address to establish his reputation as a great orator, and inspire Americans to greatness. But instead of dismissing the reporter so he can concentrate on this important speech, he permits him to remain as a spectator.

So here we have two men sitting alone in Kennedy's ground-floor study, one watching silently as the other writes.

Did Kennedy believe he performed best before an audience? Or have such a horror of solitude he could not stand being alone, even while writing or editing a speech? Did he continue with the interview while he was writing? (He was capable of this.) Or, the most likely scenario, was he proving to a reporter for the nation's second-largest newsweekly that he could write his own speech in his own "barely legible scrawl," without notes or Ted Sorensen? Consider in this regard a letter that Evan Thomas, the editor of *Profiles in Courage*, sent to Emily Danton of Birmingham, Alabama, on December 5, 1960. Danton had asked Thomas to reassure her that Kennedy had written *Profiles*. After making several general points to substantiate his authorship, Thomas wrote, "With my own eyes I saw Senator Kennedy writing parts of the book in his own hand in his hospital room at the Hospital for Special Surgery here in New York." Thomas copied this letter to Sorensen, who probably showed it to Kennedy, impressing upon him the value of eyewitness testimony.

Kennedy may have been performing for the *Newsweek* reporter, but a comparison of his January 10 dictation and the next available draft of the inaugural, the one Evelyn Lincoln typed on January 17, shows how he revised the speech during this week. He removed *conquer* from his "bear any burden" sentence, and he abandoned a clumsy seafaring metaphor. He turned "at a time of maximum danger" into "at an *hour* of maximum danger," and struck out several pessimistic phrases near the end of his dictation, eliminating a warning that Americans were in danger of "sliding and drifting into defeat," and that the price of this might be the "short, quick sacrifice of us all" in a nuclear holocaust.

Alone, or with Sorensen later, he also edited the pages he had inserted into his dictation from the Sorensen Draft, adding "alliance for progress" to "to convert our last good words into good deeds *in a new alliance for progress*," placing "But let us begin" at the end of the paragraph beginning "all this will not be finished in the first one hundred days," and deleting two florid paragraphs at the end of page five. He also reconsidered his deletion of Sorensen's handwritten concluding paragraph, restoring it as, "With a clear conscience our only sure reward, with history the final judge of our motives, let us go forth to lead the land we love, asking His blessing and help, but knowing that here on earth God's work must truly be our own." (He remained so ambivalent about it that when Sorensen came to Palm Beach to help polish the speech, Kennedy told him it sounded an awful lot like the ending of his Massachusetts speech—"but I guess it's OK.")

Kennedy could work so quickly because unlike many politicians he knew who he was and what he wanted to say. He also had an excellent memory. He did not need speechwriters or *Famous Quotations* to supply "defending freedom in its hour of maximum danger" and "the torch has been passed," because they were already part of his personal oratorical archive. The Harvard law professor and future Watergate prosecutor Archibald Cox, who headed a team of Washington-based Kennedy speechwriters during the 1960 campaign, praised Kennedy for having a "sticky mind." A good example of this "stickiness" is his remark following the 1961 Bay of Pigs fiasco: "There's an old saying that victory has a hundred fathers and defeat is an orphan." Kennedy identified it as "an old saying," but Arthur Schlesinger discovered he had borrowed it from a film about Field Marshal Rommel, whose screenwriter had in turn lifted it from the diaries of Italy's fascist foreign minister, Count Ciano.

For years, Kennedy had been saving quotations on scraps of paper, memorizing them, and adding them to notebooks. During the campaign he often stopped at roadside historical markers to record their inscriptions, once telling a friend, "I'm collecting material for my inaugural address." He had inherited the habit of collecting quotations from his mother, who had her secretaries type up lines catching her interest, which she added to her "Expressions Book." She memorized these expressions by pinning them to the front of her bathrobe and repeating them out loud while wandering across her bedroom, "like a schoolgirl cramming for an exam," one secretary recalled. It is not impossible, then, that as Kennedy revised his inaugural address in his downstairs bedroom, recalling some of the quotations he had committed to memory, his mother was upstairs learning new ones.

Jackie Kennedy spent most of this week secluded in the ground-floor bedroom studying floor plans of what she had taken to calling "that dreary *Maison Blanche*," scribbling ideas for improving it on her own yellow legal pads, and exchanging correspondence with Oleg Cassini over an Inauguration Day wardrobe as calculated as her husband's tan.

She was dreading the inauguration but approached her guest list with an attention to detail equal to her husband's. While in Palm Beach she added to her "1-A list" the "Head chef and Wife" of the Georgetown Hospital—"free tickets, but only for the parade." Next to Diana Vreeland, who would suggest she carry a sable muff at the inauguration because of its romantic historical associations, her secretary noted, "Mrs. Kennedy stresses she wants these people to get VIP treatment for the inaugural, parade, and ball, in fact the most VIP treatment of anyone on her list." Other notes requested that Jackie's sister and her husband, Prince and Princess Stanislas Radziwill, receive "very good seats for all events and Mrs. Kennedy wants them with her during the parade." Oleg Cassini's brother and his wife were to have tickets to the "ball, parade—we pay," but "no note to be enclosed from Jackie."

In early December, while Jackie was recovering from the birth of John at Georgetown Hospital, Oleg Cassini had shown her sketches for his proposed inauguration outfit. As she examined his drawing of a fawn-colored wool coat trimmed with sable along the collar and matching pillbox hat, he explained that "all the other ladies will be loaded down with furs like a bunch of bears. Not only will you look even younger, but you'll make the President seem more up-to-date." The ensemble, he promised, would set the tone for her husband's administration. Jackie got it immediately. The minks worn by

Mamie Eisenhower, Pat Nixon, Lady Bird Johnson, Bess Truman, and others seated on the presidential stand would appear dark and dour in black-and-white newsprint and television. A beige coat would make her stand out, and its sable collar would subtly mock their furs.

Her collaboration with Cassini launched a relationship similar to the one between her husband and Sorensen. Just as Sorensen could channel Kennedy, knowing instinctively what he might want to say at a particular occasion, Cassini had an instinct for what Jackie would want to wear. He made this talent sound effortless. "I knew Jack Kennedy wanted to have a youthful and elegant administration," he says, "so I simply matched her clothes to that idea." You could argue, however, that the inaugural outfit he designed for her was a more daring departure from the norm than her husband's address, and that it would make a not insignificant contribution to how that address was received.

Kennedy filled the morning of January 12 with meetings, the afternoon with fishing and golf. On January 13, he met with Dean Rusk, played more golf, and fielded questions from reporters about his ambassadorial appointments. He was meeting with his Harvard classmate Blair Clark on the morning of January 14 to discuss appointments to the U.S. Information Agency when he received a message that Lyndon Johnson, who had been scheduled to spend that night alone in Palm Beach, not only was bringing Lady Bird but had also invited two congressmen and their wives to lunch. Kennedy was stunned. Evelyn Lincoln called it "a very awkward situation."

Rose Kennedy had become increasingly cranky during the transition, and the Johnsons' unexpected lunch party was a last straw. She had already complained in her diary of "a lot of milling around" and a house "full of dressmakers and photographers and assistants," grousing, "If I go into the study, Jack probably is there in conference. If I want to go out the front door to the street, the door is locked behind me almost before I get out." She disapproved when she saw someone swinging Caroline around on the front lawn, and was displeased by a "loose neckline" on a velvet dress Jackie had chosen to wear while being photographed by Richard Avedon.

Jackie and Rose, opposites in most respects, could never bring themselves to acknowledge their only common ground, that both had married serial adulterers and chosen to ignore it. Rose considered Jackie weak and self-indulgent. Jackie saw Rose as cold and slightly ridiculous. Speaking about her mother-in-law in the interview she gave to Theodore White a week after the assassination, she remarked, "His [JFK's] mother didn't really love him. . . . She likes to go around talking about being the daughter of the Mayor of Boston, or how she was an ambassador's wife . . . [but] she didn't love him."

Moments after learning that the Johnsons had invited five others to lunch, Rose asked Mary Gallagher if Jackie planned on leaving her bed to attend, adding, "You might remind her that we're having some important guests. It would be nice if she would join us."

For most of December Jackie had been convalescing from her son's birth by cesarean section. But by the beginning of January she was fit enough to swim and walk on the beach, give an interview to *Time,* have a fitting for her inaugural ball gown, collaborate on an article for the *Ladies Home Journal* ("How to Bring up a Child to Be Happy"), and chauffeur Oleg Cassini around the Seminole Country Club in a golf cart. She nevertheless insisted she was too weak to share meals with her in-laws, and refused to make an exception for Lyndon and Lady Bird Johnson, or "Colonel Cornpone and his Little Porkchop," as she called them. (Later, she and Lady Bird would become close friends and enjoy a lifelong correspondence.) When Gallagher relayed Rose's invitation, Jackie parroted back in her mother-in-law's sing-song voice, "You might remind her we're having important guests for lunch." Gallagher believed her refusal to join the Johnsons inflicted irreparable damage on their already precarious relationship. Afterward, she said, "things between them were never the same."

Lyndon Johnson had a knack for bringing out the worst in Jack and Bobby Kennedy. Evelyn Lincoln noticed that he produced a "smoldering irritability" in her boss, and believed their meetings during the transition had convinced Kennedy that Johnson was crude, devious, and physically repulsive. When Kennedy visited his ranch in November, Johnson had greeted a man widely known to detest headgear of every description with a ten-gallon cowboy hat, then became peevish when he refused to wear it. Kennedy left Texas believing he and Johnson lived in different universes, a conclusion reinforced by the telegram Johnson sent after the birth of his son in which he promised to give Kennedy a heifer calf if he named his son Lyndon Johnson, an indication of how little he understood Kennedy, or how much he enjoyed needling him.

Kennedy was famous for his memory and detachment. When he sat opposite Johnson at lunch on January 14, it is hard to believe he did not recall that at the 1960 Democratic convention this same man had permitted a supporter to refer to him as a "spavined hunchback" and insinuated that Joe Kennedy, the man who owned this house and therefore technically his host, had bought his son the nomination.

Kennedy and Johnson were also a bad fit because Kennedy disliked being touched or crowded and Johnson was famous for his habit of invading the personal space of friends and enemies alike. During a journey across Europe in the summer of 1945, Kennedy had kept a diary notable for its pithy entries. One of the few exceptions was a lengthy story that had clearly engaged his interest. As he told it, "Lady Violet [Violet Bonham-Carter, the daughter of former prime minister Herbert Asquith] had a great habit of bringing her face gradually closer and closer to the subject of her conversation until finally only several inches separated her from the recipient of her remarks. Duff Cooper, Ambassador to France, finally became so infuriated with this habit that, at a dinner party, he suddenly picked up a potato with his fork and dashed it into her mouth saying, 'Excuse me, I thought it mine.'"

Like Lady Violet, Lyndon Johnson would move in close to his quarry, jabbing a finger into his face, and grabbing his shoulder, elbow, or arm, or all three, in quick succession. One wonders if Kennedy was tempted to shove a potato into his hang-dog face when Johnson crowded him during this visit to Palm Beach, frowning and pointing his forefinger to make a point. Lincoln observed that whenever the men were together her boss would begin twitching his right foot and drumming his fingers—classic Kennedy signals of discomfort. When the two men were cooped inside the house during some chilly and showery weather on January 14, Kennedy kept moving from seat to seat to escape a pursuing Johnson. Every time Lincoln came into the living room with a message, they had moved again.

During an earlier visit, Lincoln had arrived at the house one morning to see Johnson, dressed in a silk monogrammed robe, slumped into a dining room chair while waiting for breakfast. He had absentmindedly pulled the *New York Times,* Kennedy's favorite reading, from the carefully arranged pile that was placed by his host's seat every morning. Kennedy, appearing in a simple terry cloth robe, sat down and searched for the *Times* before noticing it at Johnson's elbow, unopened and unread. Johnson made small talk. Kennedy fidgeted with the other papers and sipped at his juice before stalking from the room, angrily ordering Lincoln to bring coffee to his bedroom. She found him staring at the gloomy sky and fuming. "What gall! If he had the paper why didn't he read it?" he asked. "Or at least give someone else a chance to see it?"

This was not the cool and witty man who had charmed the American public. This was the tightly wound, fussy perfectionist familiar to his aides and friends: an impatient man who finished your sentences and had a rich repertoire of nervous tics—brushing his hair off his forehead with the palm of his hand, clicking a pen or forefinger against his head, nose, or teeth, slipping a hand in and out of a pocket, drumming a table with his fingers, and scribbling doodles—to relieve his impatience with people who bored or irritated him as much as Johnson did.

This was the obsessive Kennedy who ate the same breakfast every morning while reading the *New York Times,* insisted that a tureen of fish chowder, made to the same recipe, always be available, changed his wardrobe several times daily, wore as many as five clean shirts a day (yet still smelled faintly of cigars), took several baths a day to satisfy his fetish for cleanliness and soothe his back, changed into pajamas before taking an afternoon nap, had Mrs. French's hair preservative massaged into his scalp at every opportunity, and fussed so much over haircuts that watching him get one was, according to the journalist Hugh Sidey, "a painful experience."

Kennedy may have put the greatest and most dangerous of his obsessions, his clandestine sex life, on hold during this week, although one cannot be entirely sure since one of his lovers, Pamela Turnure, was working in La Guerida. The crowded house and his busy schedule made assignations difficult, but Kennedy could still scheme. His father was a telephone addict who had installed an extension in every room and patio. He had later added a device to ensure that calls could not be overheard from other extensions, a feature enabling him to manage his love affairs without Rose overhearing him. Lincoln noted several telephone conversations that week between her boss and a Washington lobbyist who often facilitated his sexual escapades. "The Senator asked me to close the door of the library as I went out," she reported on one occasion, "so I don't know what they talked about."

On January 11, Kennedy had asked Lincoln to find a way to fly "Barbara Lansing" from Paris to Washington for the inauguration. When Lincoln donated her diary pages to the Kennedy Library, someone decided to restrict access to three containing references to "Lansing." One recorded the price of the tourist-class airfare from Paris to Washington, noting it should be paid by blank check. Another, a typed memorandum, informed Kennedy that "Lansing" had arrived at the Carlyle Hotel on January 15 and was in room 2001. This placed her fourteen floors below the penthouse where Kennedy would be sleeping on January 17.

Kennedy's frenetic adultery has been attributed to his cold and remote mother, his blatantly womanizing father, fear of intimacy, addiction to risk, the steroids he took to control his Addison's disease, and a carpe diem mentality encouraged by his precarious health. All may have been factors, but his own words reveal a lot about his attitudes toward women and sex.

While he was a student at Harvard, he told George Taylor, the young black man who served as his valet, bartender, and driver, "I always make it on the first night. If not the first night, that's the end of the relationship."

In December 1955, he sat by the pool in Palm Beach reading and noting the second volume of David Cecil's biography of Lord Melbourne, the nineteenth-century Whig statesman known for his hedonism, aristocratic style, and intellectual pursuits. The book started Kennedy wondering why he found European history more interesting than American. One answer, he noted, might lie in the fact that American women were "not glamorous." They were instead "either prostitutes or housewives," who "[did] not play much of a role in [the] cultural or intellectual life of [the] country."

At a dinner party in the late 1950s he was seated next to Priscilla McMillan, a Soviet expert who had worked in his Senate office. (She later wrote *Marina and Lee*, a best-selling book about the Oswald marriage.) She gathered up her courage and asked why he had married Jackie. "Because I was thirty-seven years old," he replied, "and people would think I was queer if I wasn't married." But as he spoke, she noticed him staring across the table, unable to take his eyes off Jackie, and realized the truth was more complicated.

She asked another daring question: "Jack, when you're straining every gasket to be elected president, why do you endanger yourself by going out with women?"

There was a long pause. McMillan sensed someone else had posed the same question recently. Finally, he shrugged, and a sad expression crossed his face. He reminded her of a little boy about to cry. "I guess it's because I just can't help it," he said.

Kennedy also considered his infidelities the mark of a great man. When the journalist Marie Ridder asked him at a dinner party during the 1960 campaign how he planned to continue carrying on his affairs in the White House, he breezily replied: "Oh, it'll be much easier because the Secret Service will protect me. Anyway all great men have this failing. Wilson stopped the conference at Versailles to have his 'nooner,' and Alexander the Great had so many sexual appetites he never knew next what gender would appeal to him." He went on, listing other great men who had been unfaithful to their wives, and viewing his sexual morals, as he did so much else in his life, in the context of the sweep of history, and great men.

How a man who spoke and wrote so eloquently about integrity and morality (and who would say in his inaugural address that "a good conscience" was "our only sure reward") could have had so little conscience about his sexual behavior is a question that still mystifies those who thought they knew him. One possible answer is found in a passage he wrote in one of his notebooks shortly before being elected president. He considered it so insightful that he included it alongside quotations from Churchill, Lincoln, and Webster. To be a "positive force for public good," he wrote, a politician needed "a solid moral code governing his public actions." The word *public* was key, implying as it did that a politician's *private* actions and morals were irrelevant to his ability to promote the public good. One finds the same philosophy in his speech to the Massachusetts legislators, in which he defined political integrity as not compromising the sacred trust of the public for "financial gain or political ambition."

Jackie understood better than anyone else the distinction her husband drew between public and private morality. When one of Hubert Humphrey's supporters conceded during a dinner party in Georgetown that her husband was a "fine politician," she shot back, "he may be a fine politician, but do we know if he's a fine person?"

Kennedy was as compulsive about his important speeches as he was about his food, clothes, and sex life. He fussed over every word, dictating, redictating, and editing an address until moments before delivering it, then making further changes as he spoke. Harris Wofford, who collaborated with him on his civil rights speeches during the campaign, felt as if he were participating in policy making because of the way Kennedy sweated over every word.

Kennedy displayed his obsessive attention to detail in his reaction to a ghostwritten speech an aide handed him moments before a 1959 political dinner in Boston. It called for him to introduce Lyndon Johnson as "a Democratic leader without peer or precedent" and proclaim that he would forever "cherish" Johnson's friendship. He took a pencil to the text and reduced Johnson to "the most skillful parliamentarian leader since Henry Clay," said he would "value" instead of "cherish" his friendship, and rather than predicting the audience would "like" Johnson, merely urged everyone to give him "a great welcome."

Arthur Schlesinger remembers handing Kennedy a speech he had written for a gathering of Nobel Prize winners. It contained a labored paragraph about how Thomas Jefferson had been a fiddler, an anthropologist, an architect, and a man of many talents. Kennedy compressed this into: "I think this is the most extraordinary collection of talent, of human knowledge, that has ever been gathered at the White House, with the possible exception of when Thomas Jefferson dined alone."

Kennedy's 1958 address at the Gridiron Club in Washington, D.C., was the kind of high-profile speech that encouraged his competitive spirit. It was to be delivered at a prestigious occasion where the audience of influential journalists and politicians would inevitably compare Kennedy to previous speakers, some of them his rivals for the 1960 nomination. The Gridiron dinner was a "roast" during which a guest speaker became the target of a series of humorous and sometimes nasty attacks, then responded with a witty speech poking fun at himself and his tormentors. Kennedy prepared for it by forming a "Gridiron team" comprising Ted Sorensen, his attorney, Clark Clifford, the journalist Fletcher Knebel, and his father. He gave them the task of collecting and analyzing prospective jokes. After gathering more than a hundred, they met to vote on the funniest. Nothing was left to chance. A printed ballot listed each joke with a space for offering comments. Clifford remembers Kennedy being alternately amused, detached, and intense as he presided over the meeting. Afterward, he sent Clifford, his father, and three journalists a letter asking them to critique his rough draft. "Would you be so good as to indicate what parts, if any, you think should be used, what parts should be deleted, and any other editing, revising, comments or other reactions you have," he wrote. "Please feel free to cut any and all, particularly anything you think unfunny, inappropriate to the occasion or my style, or too broad, too mean, or too petty." He then edited draft after draft, dictating and redictating material to Lincoln while pacing his Senate office, pausing to examine himself in the mirror and fiddle with his hair.

In his critique of the rough draft, Joe Kennedy had praised the content—"I think that the speech is great!"—but, knowing his son's weakness as a public speaker, closed by saying, "A lot of this is so fast that you would have to tell it very slowly and give them all a chance to laugh."

The speech was a smash. As with many of his speeches, its best lines came at the beginning and end. He opened with, "I have just received the following wire from my generous Daddy: 'Dear Jack: Don't buy a single vote more than necessary—I'll be damned if I'll pay for a landslide,'" and concluded, "A recent AP survey asked each senator about his preference for the Presidency—and ninety-six senators each received one vote."

No one at La Guerida that week wanted to read a draft of the inaugural address more than Joe Kennedy. He dropped hints, telling his son his Massachusetts speech had been *too* good, wasting material he should have saved for his inaugural. Time was short, he warned, and it was important that he deliver "a truly excellent speech."

Kennedy just nodded and said, "Yes, Dad."

"Well, I hope you're working on a good one," he persisted, "because it should be good—it should be your best."

"Yes, Dad."

Rose Kennedy reported: "His father took him at his word and didn't ask to see a draft, nor did Jack volunteer to show him; and this, I suppose, was mainly because he kept revising and polishing it, and was still at it the morning of the inauguration. Hence when he stepped to the rostrum neither his father nor I had more than a general idea of what he would be saying."

It would have been easy for Kennedy to hand his father the typescript of his January 10 dictation, or discuss the speech when they played golf. But his inaugural address was far more important than the Gridiron speech, and since then, he had become more wary about taking advice from his controversial father. He may have wanted to keep his father from reading his speech so he could truthfully say that Joe Kennedy had not contributed anything to it, or because he doubted Joe would contribute anything useful. He had kicked off his campaign with a very liberal Labor Day speech in Detroit. The next day, his father called him and said, "If you keep talking that way you'll be buried." After putting down the phone, he told his friend Charlie Bartlett, "I'm not going to listen to the old man anymore. He doesn't understand that for a Democrat to get elected, he has to excite the Democrats."

Kennedy's sensitivity to rumors about his father's influence increased during the campaign. While interviewing Kennedy for a *Time* cover article, Hugh Sidey turned suddenly to the candidate's navy comrade Paul Fay and asked him to assess Joe Kennedy's influence on his son. When Fay replied that he was "the most vital force in the careers of the Kennedy men and women," JFK quickly drew a finger across his throat, signaling Fay to shut up. Afterward, he said, "God, if I hadn't cut you off, Sidey could have headlined his article, 'A vote for Jack is a vote for Father Joe.' This is supposed to be a helpful cover story on a promising candidate, not the kiss of death."

Joe Kennedy had an unflattering public image. He had amassed a fortune through the kind of Wall Street wheeler-dealing contributing to the Great Depression. Franklin Roosevelt had nevertheless rewarded him for his support in the 1932 election by making him the first chairman of the Securities and Exchange Commission, and later, ambassador to Great Britain, where he supported the Chamberlain government's appeasement of Hitler. Returning home in 1940, he destroyed his political prospects by making some ill-chosen public remarks about Franklin and Eleanor Roosevelt. After the war, he channeled his money and energy into his son Jack's political career. Although

JFK was in almost daily communication with his father during the 1960 campaign, he took pains never to be seen or photographed with him, a charade fooling no one. When former president Truman spoke to law students in Richmond in early 1960, he was jokingly asked what would happen when the pope moved into the White House. He replied, "It's not the Pope I'm afraid of, it's the Pop." When he recounted this story to the author Merle Miller, he added, "And that's still true. Old Joe Kennedy is as big a crook as we've got anywhere in the country, and I don't like it that he bought his son the nomination."

JFK had been slowly—too slowly for some—distancing himself from his father. But he still loved him and found it difficult to defy him. After the election he complained to his attorney, Clark Clifford, that his father was insisting that he name his brother Bobby attorney general, even though he had never practiced law and professed not to want the job. When he tried arguing his father out of it, he had shot back, "That doesn't make any difference. I want Bobby to be Attorney General."

Kennedy gave Clifford the bizarre assignment of flying to New York to change his father's mind. Over lunch at Le Pavillon Clifford made a lawyerly presentation of why Bobby Kennedy should not be attorney general. Joe Kennedy listened politely, thanked him for his views, then said, "I do want to leave you with one thought, however, one firm thought . . . *Bobby is going to be Attorney General.* All of us have worked our tails off for Jack, and now that we have succeeded I am going to see to it that Bobby gets the same chance we gave to Jack." Clifford was astonished by the absence of any anger or challenge in his voice. "He was simply telling me the facts," he later recalled. "For a moment I had glimpsed the inner workings of that remarkable family and, despite my admiration and affection for John F. Kennedy, I could not say I liked what I saw."

Perhaps Kennedy feared that his father would meddle with his inaugural speech as he had with his choice of an attorney general, and not trusting himself to resist, decided not to let him read it. During this week in Palm Beach he had to have been acutely sensitive to the issue of his father's influence. An article in the January 8 *New York Times,* headlined "Joseph Kennedy Is Back on Scene After Seclusion in the Campaign," quoted his father as saying that he had intentionally not appeared with his son during the campaign. With the election over, he said, "I can appear with him now any time I want." The article reminded readers that Joseph Kennedy had been an isolationist during the early years of World War II, a friend and supporter of Senator Joseph McCarthy, and that some of his son's advisers considered him "a political embarrassment." It also repeated Joe Kennedy's unfortunate 1957 boast: "I was the one who got Jack into politics. I told him it was his responsibility to run for Congress; he didn't want to do it."

Kennedy also had more at stake, and more to prove, than when he had asked his father to critique his Gridiron speech. Then, he had needed only to convince a small and influential audience that he could tell a joke. On January 20, he would have to convince Americans that the presidency was safe in the hands of the first Catholic and the youngest man ever elected to it, win over leaders of his own party who had opposed his nomination, charm the 49.6 percent of the electorate that had voted for Nixon, capture the imagination of third-world peoples mesmerized by Nikita Khrushchev and Fidel Castro, reduce cold-war tensions without appearing weak, and do it before a live audience of sixty million.

3

Palm Beach

JANUARY 16

⚜

On Monday morning, January 16, Pierre Salinger told reporters gathered for a press conference at the Palm Beach Towers Hotel that Kennedy had made substantial progress on his inaugural speech and that Ted Sorensen had arrived from Washington to help "polish" it. Sorensen writes in *Kennedy* that he and JFK "worked through the morning" of January 16, "drafting and assembling" the inaugural while seated on a patio overlooking the Atlantic. But the January 16 page in the appointment book Evelyn Lincoln kept tells a different story, showing that JFK had a 10:30 A.M. appointment with the *Look* magazine journalist Laura Berquist. Underneath the Berquist meeting Lincoln had noted, "Ted Sorensen Discuss Inauguration Speech," but had not assigned him a time.

Lincoln wrote or typed her diary entries on slips of memorandum paper. Some days she listed Kennedy's phone calls and meetings, but on others, such as January 16, she chronicled his every movement and conversation. Her notes show her arriving at La Guerida at 9:00 A.M. During the next hour she brought Kennedy his pills, took dictation, telephoned the manufacturer of the cigarette boxes he planned to give supporters at the inauguration, then slipped out of the room while he placed a call to "Barbara Lansing," who had arrived the night before at the Carlyle. After hanging up, he disappeared into the bullpen to work on his tan. Lincoln noted next that "at 10:30 Laura Berquist came. Ted Sorensen had come a little ahead of her so he went out to the bullpen and talked to the Senator [Kennedy] about his inauguration speech. Laura went out by the pool and waited until the Senator and Ted had finished their talks."

The only thing we know about these "talks" is what Sorensen recounts in *Kennedy*, where he writes that JFK was "dissatisfied with each attempt to outline domestic goals" in the speech as they made him sound too partisan and divisive. Finally, he told Sorensen, "Let's drop out the domestic stuff altogether. It's too long anyway." According to Sorensen, Kennedy had also suggested that the speech contain a line to the effect that "this won't all be finished in a hundred days or a thousand," adding that he was sick of reading that the first hundred days of his presidency would equal FDR's famous Hundred Days.

There is no doubt that Kennedy and Sorensen met at La Guerida on the morning of January 16, but it seems unlikely they discussed these topics. It would have made no sense for Kennedy to have asked Sorensen to delete any mention of domestic goals because both the Sorensen Draft that Kennedy had consulted on January 10 and his own dictation that evening show this had already been done. Similarly, it would have made no sense to add a line about not promising a hundred days because such a line had already been added.

The best explanation for these errors is that Sorensen was confusing their January 16 meeting with one he and Kennedy had on December 21 at La Guerida, when they had also discussed the inaugural address. In fact, Sorensen's own account of this December meeting describes Kennedy complaining about the press harping on his supposed hundred days.

Whatever discussions Sorensen and Kennedy did have on January 16 were brief. In her 1965 oral history Berquist recalled that she and Kennedy had "sat around and schmoosed for about an hour," leaving little time for Sorensen and Kennedy to have had a long conversation about anything.

Berquist remembers Kennedy shouting, "Hi Laurer!" as she walked toward him. ("That was a big deal—I was 'Laurer.'") Sorensen had just left, and Kennedy was talking on the telephone, his legs dangling over the side of the chair. Before she could sit down, he dragged her over to a baby buggy parked by the pool. As she was admiring his son, he asked, "Are you coming to my inauguration?"

"No one has invited me."

"Well, *I* invite you!"

She was amazed to find him so breezy and unchanged since the election. Charles Spalding, who had known him for thirty years, believed he was happier at his inauguration than at any other time in his life. The journalist Helen Thomas writes that during his transition, Kennedy "was unable to hide his own tremendous sense of exhilaration," adding, "When he would emerge from his home, stand on the front steps and announce the appointment of yet another cabinet official, he exuded the feeling that America was on the march again." Kennedy was also teasing and playful during the final weeks of his transition. One morning he had paused while dictating a letter to Lincoln, examined himself in a dresser mirror, and exclaimed, "My God, look at that fat face! If I don't lose five pounds this week we might have to call off the inauguration." He kidded his best friend, LeMoyne ("Lem") Billings, "Aren't you thrilled to be eating breakfast with the next President of the United States?" When Billings mumbled an unenthusiastic answer, he turned to Lincoln and asked, "Aren't *you* thrilled to be working for the next President?" She deadpanned, "I am overjoyed." He returned to Billings. "See, Lem, it's a privilege for you to be eating with the President!"

Berquist was writing a profile of Jackie for *Look* to accompany photographs Richard Avedon had taken the week before. She knew from experience that Jackie would tell her nothing; she was simply too guarded to be useful. "All these dismal questions!" Jackie had complained during an earlier interview. "I suppose you're going to ask me about Jack's complexes, that he has a complex about his father, and that his father has a complex about Jack, and Jack has one about Joe."

This time Berquist asked Salinger to suggest someone she could interview *about* Jackie. "Talk to the President-elect," he said.

Berquist began by asking Kennedy to describe his wife.

"Well, she has a splendid memory and she speaks many languages," he said. "My sisters are direct, energetic types, and she is more sensitive. You might even call her fey." After finishing Jackie off in three sentences (on another occasion he had told Berquist, "I don't see why you're doing a story on Jackie. You don't even know her. You do know me. Why not do a story on me?"), he began interrogating the reporter about Fidel Castro, whom Berquist had met while covering the Cuban revolution.

Berquist disagreed with Kennedy's hard-line Cuba policy and had sent him a telegram after one of the debates, accusing him of making an ass of himself over Castro. Still, she believed he was educable, and that "if somehow he had gotten enough information, and if he was persuaded, and if he read enough books, and if he talked to people, that he was open-minded enough to change his mind." She sensed he was baffled by Castro's mystique, and envious. When he spoke about him, he could have been a political consultant sizing up a formidable opponent who happened to be, like him, handsome, athletic, and from a wealthy family.

Kennedy was particularly interested in Castro's rhetorical techniques. He gave short speeches; Castro delivered long ones. He was cool and rational;

Castro was grandiloquent and passionate. He had struggled to improve his shrill delivery; Castro was a natural orator. "Why *does* he make those long speeches?" Kennedy asked Berquist, perhaps perplexed that a two-hour harangue could make *anyone* popular.

Three months earlier, at a rally in front of Harlem's Theresa Hotel, where Castro had stayed during the opening of the United Nations General Assembly, Kennedy had proclaimed that the American Revolution, not communism, was the more authentic inspiration for the anticolonial revolution, telling the crowd: "We are the great revolutionary people. We believe in freedom. We believe in independence. The Communists are colonialists, and we are not, and yet for some reason we have lost the imagination of a people [the citizens of third-world nations], and they are beginning to gain it." And before that, he had told a campaign rally in Erie, Pennsylvania, "I would like the people of the world to be reading what the President of the United States is doing, not merely what Castro is doing."

He also wanted Berquist to tell him what Castro was doing in bed. (The men shared a voracious sexual appetite.)

"Who does he sleep with?" Kennedy asked. "I've heard he doesn't even take his boots off."

"I haven't a clue," Berquist replied.

"He runs around making those long speeches, but where are the dames?"

She knew Kennedy loved to gossip about other people's sex lives, but was surprised he would devote time for it so close to his inauguration. "Heavens, he's the President [elect], he's busy," she thought. "He's got all these characters to interview, the cabinet to put together," and, she could have added, a speech to polish.

Billy Graham and Senator George Smathers of Florida arrived at noon to join Kennedy for lunch followed by a round of golf. Salinger had told the press this encounter between the nation's first Catholic president and its second most prominent Protestant clergyman (Norman Vincent Peale came first) would give Graham an opportunity to suggest some biblical verses for the inaugural address.

One wonders what Graham would have thought about the conversation that had just concluded between Berquist and the president-elect. Moving effortlessly from considering whether Fidel Castro screwed with his boots on to discussing biblical verses with Billy Graham was, even for Kennedy, an impressive shift of gears.

In truth, the last thing Kennedy needed was Billy Graham or anyone else suggesting Bible verses. He knew dozens by heart and, for months, had been weaving them into his campaign speeches. He had quoted Deuteronomy in Oakland—"Thou shalt not harden thy heart, nor shut thy hand, from thy needy brother"—and had reminded supporters at Miami's Biscayne Bay Band Shell that "the Bible said it long ago. 'Who will prepare for the battle if the trumpet sounds an uncertain note.'" His inaugural address already contained a passage from Isaiah, "Undo the heavy burdens [and] let the oppressed go free," and an unattributed one from Romans, "rejoicing in hope, patient in tribulation," while its language and cadences—particularly its pledge to help the United Nations enlarge the area "in which its writ may run"—had an Old Testament ring.

The invitation to Graham, however, was in keeping with Kennedy's practice of asking prominent people to offer contributions to his important speeches. Ted Sorensen was lukewarm to the practice, believing it was "sailing close to flattery." Yet Graham had taken the assignment seriously and handed Kennedy a typed list of twenty-five suggestions.

Joe Kennedy had insisted on this meeting, although JFK had resisted, groaning as his father prevailed. Graham was reluctant, too, and had postponed accepting the invitation until his friend Richard Nixon gave his approval. Graham had done everything short of formally endorsing Nixon to ensure his victory. He had delivered an invocation at one of his rallies and written a *Life* article so adulatory that even Henry Luce, *Life*'s powerful publisher and fellow Nixon supporter, had last-minute misgivings and pulled it. Graham substituted a more nonpartisan piece urging Americans not to cast their ballots "on the basis of which candidate is more handsome or more charming," an obvious reference to JFK. "Some say elections can actually be bought," he had written. "I have greater faith in the American people than that."

Kennedy was changing for lunch when Graham arrived, forcing the reverend to spend several awkward minutes on the patio with his father.

Joe Kennedy was blunt. "Do you know why you're here?" he asked.

Graham admitted being perplexed.

Joe Kennedy, now at his most crafty and craven, recounted a flattering story about how he and the president of Notre Dame University had been impressed when they witnessed Graham preaching to sixty thousand people in Stuttgart, Germany. When they visited the pope three days later, they told him about it, and the pope had said he wished he had a dozen evangelists like Graham in *his* church.

While Graham was basking in the Holy Father's praise, Kennedy sprang the trap. "When Jack was elected I told him that one of the first things he should do was get acquainted with you," he said. "I told him you could be a great asset to the country, helping heal the division over the religious problem in the campaign."

Graham insisted that Kennedy was overestimating his influence, but made a vague pledge to help, never imagining that before sundown he would be maneuvered into fulfilling it.

At the Seminole Country Club, Kennedy and Graham rode in one golf cart while Smathers shared another with Billy Reynolds, the president of Reynolds Aluminum. When Graham double-bogeyed the first hole, Kennedy joked, "I thought you were better than that." Toward the end of the round, Graham realized that the other three were making side bets on his putts. Back in the clubhouse, he and Kennedy drank soda pop and talked about Southeast Asia.

Graham and Kennedy left together in the latter's Lincoln convertible. After driving a short distance Kennedy suddenly pulled onto the shoulder, cut the engine, and, in this hedonistic landscape of palm, stucco, and heat, turned to Graham and asked, "Do you believe in the Second Coming of Jesus Christ?"

Graham called the question "unexpected," given that he had made the Second Coming the center of his ministry. But it was in line with Kennedy's practice, inherited from his father, of going right to the foremost expert in any field and asking the crucial question.

After collecting his thoughts, Graham answered, "I most certainly do."

"Well, does *my* church believe in it?"

"They have it in their creeds."

"They don't preach it," Kennedy said. "They don't tell us much about it. I'd like to know what you think."

Graham replied with a bland Sunday school homily summarizing the Bible's description of Christ dying on the cross, rising from the dead, and promising to return. Only when that happened, he said, "are we going to have world peace."

Kennedy was curt. "Very interesting," he said. "We'll have to talk some more about it some day." He pulled back onto the road without another word, treating Graham no better than anyone else who had ever bored him. Then he drove directly to a party where the reverend, still in his golf clothes, found himself uneasy mixing with the Palm Beach socialites.

The consensus of Kennedy's family and friends is that he was theologically unsophisticated but spiritually alive, uninspired by Catholic ritual yet careful to observe it. His sister Eunice believed he was "casual about religious rituals and observances" and "a little less convinced about some things than the rest of us." He attended Mass faithfully and even at the White House knelt by his bed in prayer every night, his hands clasped together like a Norman Rockwell boy. Ted Sorensen, himself a Unitarian, said Kennedy did not "care a whit for theology" and never spoke to him about man's relationship to God, and Arthur Schlesinger thought he was a Catholic as FDR was an Episcopalian, "because he was born into the faith, lived in it, and expected to die in it," but perceived little "organic intellectual connection" between his faith and his politics. Even Cardinal Cushing, who had married him and christened his children, conceded that Kennedy "wore his religion, like his patriotism, lightly."

There is no doubt that when he was younger Kennedy considered Catholic rituals stifling and irrelevant, and observed them to please his family. Yet, oddly, some of the same friends and biographers who have praised his growth in Congress and the White House are unwilling to entertain the possibility that he might have also matured spiritually. They seem unwilling to consider the notion that this famously private man may have also been private about his religious faith. One looks in vain in Kennedy's books, letters, and conversations for clues to his spiritual life. It is in his speeches, however, that one sometimes glimpses, through a glass darkly, his God; and in his inaugural address that one finally meets Him, face to face.

There were clues that Kennedy was developing a livelier spiritual life as he grew older. His aide Mark Dalton claimed to have been "amazed" during the 1946 campaign when Kennedy asked him to wait outside a church where they had just attended Mass so he could return to light a candle for his dead brother. (Dalton called the action "totally unlike him.") Also, while recuperating in Palm Beach in 1955 from the back operation that almost killed him, he spent hours by the pool jotting down thoughts and quotations for *Profiles in Courage*, among them several biblical passages. He selected from Job, "Oh that one would hear me! Behold, my desire is that the Almighty would answer me," and from Ecclesiastes, "For a man's mind is sometimes wont to tell him more than seven watchmen that sit above in a high tower," an expression of his conviction that human reason could solve the most intractable problems.

Five months into his presidency he had been returning to Washington on Air Force One after a tense summit meeting with Khrushchev had made nuclear war seem more imminent. He scribbled on a slip of paper, "I know there is a God—and I see a storm coming; If he has a place for me, I believe I am ready," a quotation he had frequently used in campaign speeches and attributed to Abraham Lincoln, although some scholars have raised doubts about its provenance. But why write out a quotation he knew by heart unless, at this grim moment, putting it down on paper was somewhat like reciting a rosary?

After Kennedy and Graham left the party in Palm Beach, he surprised the minister by proposing another unscheduled stop. "Billy, there are about 300 media people at the Washington Hotel I haven't seen since I've been down here," he said. "I've got to say a word to them. Would you mind going with me?"

The next day the *Washington Evening Star* reported that "newsmen were surprised when the President-elect and the evangelist, both sunburned and in high spirits, strolled into the Press Room." Graham, assuming he was a spectator, took a seat with the press corps. After joking about their golf scores, Kennedy said, "I think some of you expressed an interest in having a few words with Reverend Graham. I am delighted to turn him over to you." Only then did Graham understand that, as he put it in his memoirs, "Mr. Kennedy was using me for his own purposes."

During the ensuing press conference Graham played the role JFK and his father had chosen for him. "I don't think that Mr. Kennedy being a Catholic should be held against him by any Protestant," he said. "They should judge him on his ability and character. We should trust and support our new President." He answered another question with "I suspect that the religious issue will not be raised again in the future, at least to the extent that it was raised in the recent campaign. I think that is a hurdle that has been permanently passed."

Photographs of the two men smiling and relaxed after apparently enjoying each other's company reinforced Graham's statements. The only thing Kennedy had not gotten out of him that afternoon was a satisfactory explanation of the Second Coming of Jesus Christ.

Ted Sorensen had apparently forgotten that Kennedy spent the afternoon playing golf with Graham. In his book he describes his work on the inaugural on January 16 in this single sentence: "That afternoon, as he [JFK] was busy with other meetings at the house, I put his notes, changes and additions into a clean draft, working beside the Palm Beach Towers swimming pool." The "notes, changes and additions" mentioned are not in Sorensen's files or in Kennedy's or Lincoln's. But two copies of the "Clean Draft" that Sorensen assembled that afternoon—and that Lincoln typed sometime later—have survived. One is available in Sorensen's White House files, the other in Kennedy's Presidential Office Files. By comparing the January 16 Clean Draft with Kennedy's January 10 dictation, and with the pages from the Sorensen Draft that Kennedy had then inserted into this dictation, one can see the changes Kennedy and Sorensen made to the speech between January 10 and January 16.

What Sorensen calls the "additions" presumably included the passages Kennedy had dictated to Lincoln on January 10, which replaced the opening and closing of Sorensen's own draft. The "changes" included those Kennedy made to page six of the Sorensen Draft as he redictated some of its passages on January 10.

The "notes" presumably included the sheets of yellow legal paper that Jackie Kennedy had been gathering up from the floor of their bedroom, and that Kennedy had filled with words while being watched by the *Newsweek* reporter. These notes must have contained the phrase "the torch has been passed," since it cannot be found in either the Sorensen Draft or the Kennedy dictation from the plane. It appears in the Clean Draft as, "Let the word go forth from this time and place, to friend and foe alike, that the torch of liberty has been passed to a new generation of Americans." (In the final text the words *of liberty* were deleted.) Kennedy probably borrowed the torch metaphor from the historian Allan Nevins, who used it in his introduction to *The Strategy of Peace*, a compilation of Kennedy's speeches and statements published during the 1960 campaign.

Although the notes, changes, and additions themselves have disappeared, a piece of scratch paper containing Sorensen's cramped handwriting demonstrates how he wove together material from his draft with Kennedy's dictation.

The "trumpet summons us again" sentence, the third one at Arlington, had appeared in the Sorensen Draft as, "Today the trumpet sounds its urgent call again—not a call to arms, though arms we need—not a call to battle though embattled we are—but a call to a broader, more basic struggle against all the enemies of man—tyranny and poverty and war itself." In his January 10 dictation, Kennedy had added the idea of bearing the "burden" of a "twilight struggle," saying, "it may be our fate to bear the burden . . . of a twilight struggle. Today we sound the trumpet again, not as a call to arms, though arms we need, not as a call to battle, though embattled we are, but a call for a broader, deeper struggle against the common enemies of man: tyranny, poverty, disease, and war itself."

We know for certain that these sentences were among those that Sorensen incorporated into the Clean Draft on the afternoon of January 16 because he used as scratch paper the back of a telegram that Kennedy had received on January 11 from Senator Ernest Gruening of Alaska. (Lincoln had written, "Give to Ted S." across its top.) On its back, he inserted Kennedy's dictated references to "twilight struggle" and "burden" into a sentence from his own draft, rewriting it as, "Now the trumpet summons us again—not as a call to bear arms, though arms we need—not as a call to battle, though embattled we are—but a call to bear the burden of a long twilight struggle, year in and year out, 'rejoicing in hope, patient in tribulation'—a struggle against the common enemies of man: tyranny, poverty, disease and war itself."

Writing on scraps of paper is a common habit among busy and impatient people. Kennedy scribbled notes on whatever was handy: the back of letters, airline tickets, envelopes, or telegrams. His handwriting was so poor, and his "doodles" so fragmentary, that for years the Kennedy Library sent them to Evelyn Lincoln for translation. Sorensen copied this Kennedy habit. He had also acquired a faint Boston accent, taken to draping a leg over the arm of a chair and massaging an ankle, gesturing with an upturned palm, and drinking an occasional daiquiri or Heineken, Kennedy's favorite alcoholic beverages.

Sorensen's skillful channeling of Kennedy's ideas and words excited the envy of other aides, and some have used their oral histories to dine on a dish of cold revenge. Ralph Dungan, who also worked in Kennedy's Senate offices, described Sorensen as "an insecure guy" with an "oppressive personality" who "would pitch anybody over," and had "pitched over everything to John Kennedy." And there is a touch of jealousy in Jackie Kennedy's cruel remark to a reporter during the 1960 campaign (when Sorensen spent more time with her husband than she did) that Sorensen was "a little boy in so many ways," who "almost puffs himself up when he talks to Jack."

A profile of Sorensen appearing in the *Wall Street Journal* on January 15, 1961, the same day that he flew to Palm Beach, called him Kennedy's "alter-ego" and said the two men gave "an eerie impression of blending into one person." Laura Berquist, however, had a better take on their relationship. She spoke of Sorensen's "passionate self-effacement" and his "total identification of the self with the hero."

This passionate self-effacement explains some of Sorensen's contributions to the inaugural. The pages from the Sorensen Draft that Kennedy inserted into his dictation account for almost two-thirds of the final version of the speech. Yet, with the exception of "ask not," they contain almost none of the inaugural's most celebrated lines. Some of the material in the Sorensen Draft can be traced to contributions from John Kenneth Galbraith and Adlai Stevenson, some to earlier speeches that were Kennedy-Sorensen collaborations, and some to Sorensen alone. But if you look more closely, you discover that Kennedy was also the original author of much of the material in the Sorensen Draft. The main reason, then, that Kennedy did not tinker much with the passages on pages three, four, and five of that draft was that many of their sentences, phrases, and ideas were already his own.

The Sorensen Draft said, "If freedom's way cannot help the many who are poor, it can never save the few who are rich." Kennedy changed this to, "If a free society cannot help the many who are poor, it cannot save the few who are rich." The same idea was expressed by two quotations Kennedy had collected in his 1945–46 notebook: Thomas Jefferson's "Widespread poverty and concentrated wealth cannot long endure side by side in a democracy," and Daniel Webster's "A general equality of conditions is the true basis, most certainly, of democracy."

Sorensen had written, "Today the trumpet sounds its urgent call again." The trumpet metaphor was one close to Kennedy's heart. He had saved "For the trumpet gives an uncertain sound, who will prepare himself for battle?" from I Corinthians in his notebooks and used this quote in unscripted remarks in Miami on October 18, at a Philadelphia shopping center on October 29, at San Diego on November 2, and at a street rally in New Haven on November 6, sometimes changing the trumpet to a bugle and *sound* to *note*. On January 10, he redictated Sorensen's line, saying, "Today, we sound the trumpet once again."

The Sorensen Draft said, "We dare not tempt you with weakness. For only when our arms are sufficient beyond doubt can we be certain beyond doubt that they will never be employed." This was a restatement of "we arm to parley," a famous phrase from a speech by Winston Churchill that Kennedy had used in extemporaneous speeches or remarks in Seattle on September 6, Fresno on September 9, New York City on September 14, Raleigh on September 17, Salt Lake City on September 23, and Milwaukee on October 23.

Throughout his career Kennedy had woven words, phrases, and constructions from Churchill's speeches into his own rhetorical vocabulary, and as he did so, they became woven into Sorensen's, too. Kennedy had read all of

Churchill's books and had even studied his wartime memoranda, savoring their craftsmanship. The title of his own first book, *Why England Slept*, is a homage to Churchill's *While England Slept,* and, as Kennedy's biographer Richard Reeves pointed out, *Profiles in Courage* is a version of *Great Contemporaries*, Churchill's 1922 study of world leaders at the turn of the century. Churchill opened that book with, "Courage is rightly esteemed the first of human qualities because it is the quality which guarantees all others." Kennedy opened *Profiles* with "This is a book about the most admirable of human virtues—courage."

In 1955, when Kennedy was recuperating from his back operation, he lay in bed reading Churchill for several hours every day, despite the fact that remaining in the same position for any length of time was excruciatingly painful. His friend Paul Fay visited him then, later recalling that "he would take time to memorize some of the passages he had copied down." Kennedy needed only fifteen or twenty minutes to memorize three or four pages of notes, and years later Fay heard him quoting some of the same passages.

Kennedy aide Fred Dutton stopped by his house one evening during the 1960 campaign to find him listening to *I Can Hear It Now,* a Columbia recording of Churchill's wartime speeches. In his introduction to the collection Edward R. Murrow said, "Now the hour had come for him [Churchill] to mobilize the English language and send it into battle, a spearhead of hope for Britain and the world." When Kennedy conferred honorary American citizenship on Churchill in 1963, he used Murrow's line without attribution, praising Churchill for having "mobilized the English language and sent it into battle." And when Kennedy mobilized the English language and sent it into the battles of his 1960 campaign, he also echoed Churchill. He employed Churchill's trademark phrase when he said in a January 14, 1960, speech to the National Press Club, "We will need in the sixties a president who is willing and able to summon his national constituency to its *finest hour.*" Churchill's influence on his inaugural address was no secret. Joe Alsop reported in his January 18, 1961, column that the Kennedy staff was already referring to the speech as "Blood, sweat, and tears."

When Kennedy dictated "pay any price, bear any burden, meet any hardship, oppose any foe" on January 10, he was replicating the cadences of "we shall fight on the beaches, we shall fight on the landing grounds, we shall fight in the fields and in the streets, we shall fight in the hills; we shall never surrender."

Kennedy's summons to "bear the burden of a long twilight struggle" and meet the challenge of "defending freedom in its hour of maximum danger" recalled Churchill's 1940 call to arms—his promise of "blood, toil, tears, and sweat."

At times, Kennedy's urge to send the English language into cold-war battles led him to exaggerate the perils of an already perilous time. Some of this was campaign strategy; but Kennedy had grown up during the 1930s and the pivotal experience of his generation during that decade had been the failure of Western democracies to rearm and confront fascism. The principal heroes of his era were the two men whom Kennedy quoted most: Franklin Roosevelt and Winston Churchill.

Churchill had spoken of a world "made darker by the dark lights of perverted science." The Sorensen Draft contained a sentence urging that "both sides again renew the quest for peace, before the dark powers of destruction unleashed by science engulf us all in ruin." In Palm Beach either Sorensen or Kennedy had changed "engulf us all in ruin" to "engulf all humanity," but otherwise the sentence remained in the final text as written.

The Sorensen Draft had also incorporated sentences and ideas suggested by Adlai Stevenson and the Harvard economist John Kenneth Galbraith. During the December 21 meeting in Palm Beach, Kennedy must have discovered that Sorensen had neglected to solicit suggestions "from everyone" as he had asked in November. Sorensen may have forgotten, or believed their contributions would not merit the time required to read and evaluate them. (The results of a similar effort to solicit ideas for the acceptance speech had demonstrated that even the most brilliant men have tin ears for political rhetoric. One academic had urged Kennedy to proclaim that Americans would not "stand still for long, while some self-appointed political tailor measures them to the size of an Egyptian mummy case"; another had come up with "a patent mattress stuffed with woolly illusions.")

So, on December 23, one day after returning from Palm Beach, Sorensen sent identical telegrams to the historian Allan Nevins (the only member of the acceptance speech team asked back to contribute to the inaugural), John Kenneth Galbraith, the speechwriter Joseph Kraft, future cabinet members Adlai Stevenson, Douglas Dillon, Dean Rusk, and Arthur Goldberg, and three others. The text read: "The President-elect has asked me to collect any suggestions you may have for the Inaugural Address. In view of the short period of time available before Inauguration Day, it would be appreciated if we could have your recommendations by December 31. We are particularly interested in specific themes and in language to articulate these themes whether it takes one page or ten pages. Many many thanks."

One doubts these men welcomed receiving this communication two days before Christmas.

Nevins immediately submitted an entire speech. In his plaintive covering letter he wrote, "I have given it so much work that I hope you will read it carefully." None of his sentences made the Sorensen Draft or the inaugural.

Dillon responded with a brief letter recommending that Kennedy mention the gold crisis and domestic slump, and "reassure friends and enemies that our commitments and determination to expand freedom will be maintained," a suggestion too obvious and vague to be of any use.

Only Stevenson, still testy he had not been appointed secretary of state, was brave enough to complain about Sorensen's peremptory telegram. He fired back his own: "Your wire arrives at most difficult time for me. . . . I will do what I can." He followed with a huffy letter that began, "Due to a myriad of other pressing 'priorities' just now, I have had little time for this." He enclosed a draft he modestly titled "Some Miscellaneous Paragraphs." But it turned out to be Stevenson, who probably cared less than anyone else on Sorensen's list if Kennedy's speech was a succès d'estime, who offered the best suggestions. Sorensen wove three Stevensonian sentences into pages three, four, and five of his draft, and all made the final text, although one wonders if Sorensen informed Kennedy that their provenance was the infuriating Stevenson.

Stevenson had proposed, "We will support the growth of democracy everywhere . . . not because of anything the Russians may say or do, but because it is right." In his draft Sorensen promised the people of the third world, "Americans will help you help yourselves—not because our enemies are doing it, not because we seek your votes, but because it is right." On January 20 Kennedy would deliver these words almost as written.

Stevenson had proposed, "We have not seen one form of colonial control superseded simply to see another far more iron and implacable system take its place." The Sorensen Draft read, "To those new states we now welcome into the ranks of the free, we pledge our word that one form of colonial control shall not have passed merely to be replaced by a far more iron tyranny." This sentence would also appear in the final text virtually unchanged.

Stevenson had proposed, "We cannot expect them [the third-world nations] to be actively on our side. Why should they be? We do want them to be vigilantly and intelligently on the side of their own freedom and integrity." Sorensen changed this to "We shall not always expect to find you on our side. But we shall always expect to find you vigorously on the side of your own freedom." On January 20, Kennedy would say, "We shall not always expect to find them supporting our view. But we shall always hope to find them strongly supporting their own freedom."

The inaugural also expressed many of the ideas Stevenson had championed in his draft and covering letter. He had recommended "all-out support for the U.N." Kennedy would say, "To that world assembly of sovereign states, the United Nations, our last best hope in an age where the instruments of war have far outpaced the instruments of peace, we renew our pledge of support . . . to enlarge the area where its writ may run."

His recommendation that Kennedy speak to "the ultimate goal of worldwide cooperation on the part of the industrialized nations toward lifting the living standards of the under-privileged peoples" may have contributed to "To those peoples in the huts and villages across the globe struggling to break the bonds of mass misery, we pledge our best efforts to help them help themselves."

He had also recommended that Kennedy "create the impression of new, bold, imaginative, purposeful leadership, de-emphasize the bi-polar power struggle, and emphasize the affirmative approaches to peace." Nine short paragraphs from pages four and five in the Sorensen Draft that went into the final text largely unchanged contained sentences such as, "let both sides explore what problems unite us instead of belaboring those problems which divide us," and "Let both sides, for the first time, formulate serious and precise proposals for the inspection and control of arms."

Kennedy had voiced many of these ideas during his campaign; others had been floating around for years. Still, the similarities between Stevenson's proposals and the inaugural are too numerous to be coincidental. Stevenson did not inspire its idealism, concern with poverty, and invitation to cold-war tensions, but at the very least he reinforced Sorensen's and Kennedy's instincts and nudged the address further in these directions.

The Harvard economist John Kenneth Galbraith wrote a letter to Kennedy on July 16 criticizing his acceptance speech for its imagery, transitions, and pacing. He added, "When it comes to oratorical flights and Stevenson-type rhetoric, you give a reasonable imitation of a bird with a broken wing." Kennedy may have had this letter in mind when he asked Galbraith to submit a proposed draft for his inaugural speech. Galbraith knew Kennedy took big-event speeches seriously and was flattered.

On December 23, the same day that Sorensen had sent Galbraith his telegram, Galbraith was enjoying an alfresco lunch in Palm Beach with Kennedy, discussing what Evelyn Lincoln called in her diary "the tone and tenor of the inaugural address." Kennedy had already asked Galbraith to try his hand at writing a draft of the inaugural; now Galbraith watched intently as Kennedy read it. After stumbling across lines such as "Its work will continue without surcease," Kennedy said, "It looks pretty heavy," and asked him to try again. On December 30, Galbraith wrote Kennedy, promising, "Over the weekend I will work on a further version of the Inaugural speech." He submitted his second draft to Kennedy and Sorensen on January 9, 1961.

In his introduction to *Letters to Kennedy* Galbraith writes that Kennedy "did not suffer fools gladly nor did he suffer bad prose," and he therefore lavished more attention on his letters to him than on any other piece of writing. This may explain why the covering letter Galbraith attached to his second draft was a more elegant and polished piece of work than the speech itself, containing lines such as "The conclusions I suppose must evoke God on some rising note. My secular talents do not extend so far. And no man can write another's prayers."

Galbraith also acknowledged in this letter that his second draft included suggestions Kennedy had made on December 23 and ideas contributed by Walt Rostow and Arthur Schlesinger. He called it "preeminently a speech for those who will read it rather than those who will hear it," which may be why Kennedy used so little of it. He also volunteered "to take a hand in smoothing and unifying the tone of the final draft," adding that what made a speech brilliant, rather than just good, was what happened to it in the last half hour. This advice Kennedy took very much to heart.

Galbraith's "John Fitzgerald Kennedy First Inaugural (Second Version)" filled fifteen doubled-spaced pages and began, inauspiciously, with Kennedy warning that he was about to deliver a very dull speech: "I shall speak to you today, plainly and without pretense of rhetoric, about the tasks that are before us. If there is any exultation in what I say, it must come not from words but from the clarity of intention and the depth of determination which lies behind them."

Next came: "It has been said that our task is to insure our survival. But surely we have a higher goal than that. The hedgehog and the three-toed sloth seek survival." "We seek to improve and strengthen our society because it is *our* society." "We must conduct our foreign affairs, as we must conduct our domestic affairs, with all proper economy and prudence. But penuriousness is not the path to greatness."

One struggles to imagine these lines carved into granite, anywhere.

Three of Galbraith's sentences made it into the Sorensen Draft and then into the final text of the speech. "I would add a special word to the Latin

American nations" became "To our sister republics south of the border, we offer a special pledge." His proposal that Kennedy promise economic aid to poor nations, "not as a part of an ideological struggle, not because they are pawns in a cold war, not to buy friendship. We will help them because to do so is right," became "not because the Communists may be doing it, not because we seek their votes, but because it is right." (Stevenson had suggested a similar line, leading to the suspicion that both had borrowed it from someone else. Harris Wofford believes it came from Chester Bowles.)

Galbraith's great contribution was a stirring, Kennedyesque, antithetical statement: "We shall never negotiate out of fear. But we shall never fear to negotiate." Sorensen incorporated this into his draft as, "Let us never negotiate out of fear. But let us never fear to negotiate," and it appeared this way in the final text of the speech.

Kennedy and Sorensen also received dozens of unsolicited suggestions for the inaugural. An acquaintance of Richard Goodwin's urged that Kennedy "modernize our thinking about foreign aid." The chairman of the Committee for Effective Use of the International Court recommended he proclaim, "To forge ahead in all fields in the manner to which we aspire, we must have knowledge." The pollster Lou Harris waited until January 14 to send "Some Ideas on the Inauguration Speech." Even had Kennedy received them earlier, one cannot imagine him saying, "Either we summon up the finest that is in us, or luxuriate ourselves into oblivion."

The best advice came from Gore Vidal, who had lost his bid for a New York congressional seat in the election. He wrote that Kennedy had probably already considered all the suggestions he was about to make, but he would make them anyway: "One: Any challenge to the young people is worth making. . . . You have a remarkable power over their imaginations. For the first time in their short lives they are able to identify with a chief of state. Two: Outer Space. I know this sounds lunatic but we are a nation of actual or putative science fiction addicts. Three: The individual against the mass."

He added that during his own campaign he had noticed "a sense of futility: what can I do I'm just one person against millions." If Kennedy spoke to this fear of the Organization Man, Vidal believed he would encourage "a remarkable emotional response." He closed by reminding Kennedy that he was "free as air" and would be happy to accept a position in the administration. "Remember me," he pleaded, "or I shall be branded forever as the candidate who wrote a movie for Elizabeth Taylor."

Vidal copied his letter to Sorensen, and coincidentally or not, the inaugural echoed its suggestions. Kennedy invited the Soviets to join the United States in space: "Together let us explore the stars." His "ask not" line affirmed that every citizen could make a difference, invoked the theme of individual against the mass, challenged the young, and, just as Vidal predicted, evoked a remarkable emotional response.

4

Palm Beach

JANUARY 17

⚜

On Tuesday morning January 17, three days before the inaugural address was to be delivered, Kennedy and Sorensen sat outside on the patio at La Guerida, editing and polishing the draft that Sorensen had "assembled" the afternoon before. According to the speechwriter, Kennedy "worked and reworked" the "ask not" sentence while consulting three campaign speeches containing a similar line. He had spread all three versions on a low glass coffee table beside him. By this point, Kennedy had apparently decided that "ask not" would be its great and immortal "master sentence," its equivalent of Roosevelt's "the only thing we have to fear is fear itself" and Lincoln's "With malice toward none; with charity for all."

Lord Moran introduced the idea of a master sentence in his memoir of his service as Winston Churchill's wartime physician. He compared it to a master ball in cricket, offering this analysis of the bowling technique of the noted cricketer Wilfred Rhodes by the British author Neville Cardus.

> Flight was his secret, flight and the curving line, now higher, now lower, tempting, inimical; every ball like every other ball, yet somehow unlike; each over in collusion with the others, part of a plot. Every ball a decoy, a spy sent out to get the lie of the land; some balls simple, some complex, some easy, some difficult; and one of them—ah, which?—the master ball.

As an illustration, Moran described a speech Churchill delivered at Harvard University on September 6, 1943. Each sentence, he wrote, was "a spy sent out to get the lie of the land," but one was "the master sentence." In this instance, it was Churchill's final line: "And here let me say how proud we ought to be, young and old, to live in this tremendous, thrilling, formative epoch in the human story." Kennedy was in the South Pacific at the time, but considering his lionization of Churchill, he surely would have read a speech delivered at Harvard. He, in fact, echoed its master sentence when he told a 1960 Shriners convention that he hoped that future historians would look back on the 1960s and cry, "Those were the years of the American life, the 1960s. Give us those years!"

As with a master ball in cricket, there is nothing serendipitous about a master sentence. It is a calculated stroke of genius, usually coming near the end of a speech. The conjunction Kennedy chose to introduce his master sentence, "And so," was a tip-off that everything had been leading up to it.

Kennedy had first articulated his master "ask not" sentence during the campaign in his July 15 acceptance speech in Los Angeles, when he had compared the New Frontier to Woodrow Wilson's New Freedom and Franklin Roosevelt's New Deal, saying, "the New Frontier of which I speak is not a set of promises—it is a set of challenges. *It sums up not what I intend to offer the American people, but what I intend to ask of them.* It appeals to their pride, not to their pocketbook—it holds out the promise of more sacrifice instead of more security."

The campaign speeches containing earlier versions of "ask not" that Kennedy had spread out on the coffee table were ones he had delivered on September 3 in Anchorage, on September 5 in Detroit, and on September 20 in Washington, D.C.

On September 3 he had said in an extemporaneous speech, "Either we move with new leadership, new programs, and a new spirit of education, or we stand still and fall back. This is the call of the new frontier. *It is not what I promise I will do; it is what I ask you to join me in doing.*"

Two days later, before sixty thousand supporters at a Labor Day rally in Detroit's Cadillac Square, he added "our country" to the line and moved it closer to the version in his inaugural address.

There are three texts of his Detroit speech. The first, written in Washington by the speechwriter Archibald Cox, was flat-footed, dense with facts and statistics, and lacked the cadences and language of a typical Kennedy oration. It was supplied to the press in an advance release text, and a reporter for the *Detroit News*, working on a deadline and believing it was the one Kennedy would deliver, criticized it as "diffuse" and "booby-trapped with clumsy figures of speech." A reporter for the *New York Times* pointed out that it bore little resemblance to the speech Kennedy actually used, writing, "Once again, he [Kennedy] indicated that his speech writers were not producing material that satisfied him. In Detroit, he discarded nearly all of his prepared text."

Kennedy and Sorensen had decided against using the Cox speech the night before. In its place, Sorensen wrote a concise address that drew on some of Cox's ideas but was more in tune with Kennedy's style. After a secretary typed up Sorensen's speech on a large-print typewriter, Kennedy brought it to the podium. But then he ignored most of it, delivering instead his own extemporaneous remarks.

The Sorensen version went, "For the New Frontier of which I speak does not sum up the services your country will offer you under my administration. It sums up the services that you must offer your country." Kennedy combined this with the "ask not" sentence from his acceptance speech and said, "The New Frontier is not what I promise I am going to do for you. The New Frontier is what I ask you to do for our country."

In the weeks that followed, Kennedy continued tinkering with "ask not." The advance release text of a speech he delivered at Seattle's Civic Auditorium contained the line "I do not run for the Presidency to emphasize what services this country will offer the American people under a new administration—I run emphasizing the service which the American people must offer their country." As he spoke, Kennedy compressed this to "I do not run for the Presidency emphasizing the services that I am going to bring to you. I run emphasizing the services which the American people must offer their country."

In a nationally televised speech from Washington on September 20, he moved closer to the Detroit version of "ask not," declaring, "We do not campaign stressing what our country is going to do for us as a people. We stress what we can do for the country, all of us."

Sorensen's "ask not" sentence that Kennedy had consulted while dictating on January 10 closely resembled this Detroit version. Sorensen had cut the reference to the New Frontier and substituted "your country" for "I" in accordance with Kennedy's instructions to eliminate the first person from the inaugural. Kennedy's extemporaneous "The New Frontier is not what I promise I am going to do for you. The New Frontier is what I ask you to do for our country" became in Sorensen's draft "So ask not what your country is going to do for you. Ask what you can do for your country." On January 10, Kennedy, with the Sorensen Draft in front of him, merged its two sentences into one, added "fellow Americans," and dictated, "My fellow Americans, ask not what your country will do for you, ask rather what you can do for your country."

Finally, on January 17, with his dictated version of "ask not" and his earlier speeches spread out on the coffee table, he and Sorensen decided that a sentence they had already cut, ground, and polished until it sparkled—a sentence Kennedy was undoubtedly imagining carved in granite—should read, "And so, my fellow Americans: ask not what your country will [he later changed this to "can"] do for you—ask what you can do for your country." Lincoln typed this version into a new draft, and on January 18 a secretary in his Senate office, probably Gloria Sitrin, typed it into the reading copy that Kennedy would take to the podium at his inauguration.

While it is unclear if Kennedy or Sorensen originated the rough version of "ask not" that appeared in Kennedy's acceptance speech, it was Kennedy who connected "ask" and "country" in his Labor Day address in Detroit, and refined the sentence in subsequent extemporaneous speeches. As Sorensen himself wrote, "When a line proved successful at one stop, whether planned or improvised, he used it at the next and many times thereafter." Although the phrasing of "ask not" may have been a joint effort, it was one to which Kennedy made the most significant contributions.

The concept of "ask not"—that the citizens of a democracy have a responsibility to contribute their talents and labors to their nation—was one that Kennedy had articulated long before meeting Sorensen. In a footnote to his prologue to *A Thousand Days*, Arthur Schlesinger writes that "this thought ["ask not"] had lain in Kennedy's mind for a long time. As far back as 1945 he had noted down in a loose-leaf notebook a quotation from Rousseau: 'As soon as any man says of the affairs of state, What does it matter to me? The state may be given up as lost.'"

Bartlett's *Familiar Quotations* and numerous editors and authors have pointed out that "ask not" has numerous analogues. Warren Harding, for example, had told the 1916 Republican National Convention that "we must have a citizenship less concerned about what the government can do for it, and more anxious about what it can do for the nation." In an 1884 Memorial Day address, the Supreme Court justice Oliver Wendell Holmes had said, "It is now the moment when by common consent we pause to become conscious of our national life and to rejoice in it, to recall what our country has done for each of us, and to ask ourselves what we can do for our country in return."

We can assume that someone as widely read and historically savvy as Kennedy would have come across these quotations. He must also have been familiar with the exhortation of his prep school headmaster that what mattered most was "not what Choate does for you, but what you can do for Choate," familiar with Cicero's "you should do something for your country once in a while instead of always thinking about what your country can do for you," and with the verse from Luke that his mother had drilled into him, "For unto whomsoever much is given, of him shall much be required." This was a bare-bones summary of the concept behind "ask not": that because much has been given to the citizens of a prosperous and democratic nation, they are required to make sacrifices for the good of that nation.

"Ask not" was not only the master sentence of Kennedy's inaugural but the master sentence of his life—what his thoughts, books, and speeches had been leading toward for a quarter century. In *Why England Slept* he had written, "But we shall have to be prepared to make long-sustained sacrifices if we are to preserve this way of life [democracy] in the future. . . . All groups must be prepared to sacrifice many of the particular group interests for the national interest." Sixteen years later, in the introductory chapter to *Profiles in Courage*, he reiterated this by saying, "But in public life we expect individuals to sacrifice their private interests to permit the national good to progress."

He had saved in a notebook the following line from Pericles' Funeral Oration: "If a man takes no interest in public affairs, we alone do not condemn him as quiet but condemn him as useless."

He had warned in a 1959 Senate speech that an "economic gap" between wealthy and undeveloped nations was providing an opening for communist ideology, declaring, "In short, it is our job to prove that we can devote as much energy, intelligence, idealism, and sacrifice to the survival and triumph of the open society as the Russian despots can extort by compulsion in defense of the closed system of tyranny."

He had said in a speech to the National Press Club in January 1960 that a president needed "to alert the people to our dangers and opportunities—to demand of them the sacrifices that will be necessary."

Almost forty years to the day after Robert McNamara had met Kennedy to discuss his appointment as secretary of defense and had demanded to know if he was the author of *Profiles in Courage*, he told a reporter for the *Denver Rocky Mountain News* of a recent exchange with Ted Sorensen during a trip they had taken together to Nigeria. McNamara had said, "Look Ted, I'm not going to ask you, but the phrase in President Kennedy's inaugural, 'Ask not what your country can do for you. Ask what you can do for your country'—that phrase had more impact on our country than any other. Now, I don't know whether you wrote it or he wrote it—and I don't want to learn now. But I want to tell you that I know he believed it, and if he didn't write it, he could have." To this, Sorensen replied, "You're absolutely right."

But not only *could* Kennedy have written "ask not," he did write it, contributing not just words but the life culminating in them.

* * *

Kennedy's inaugural address was his philosophical autobiography, informed by his knowledge of the worst modern warfare can do, his fear of nuclear war, his understanding of the dynamics of third-world nationalism, and his encounters with abject poverty. Sorensen, by comparison, had been too young to serve in the war, had traveled little, and spent most of his early adult life in Washington, D.C.

There are five periods in Kennedy's life that, like his character, breathe through its words: his experiences in Europe in 1939, in the Pacific in 1943, in Berlin in 1945, in Vietnam in 1951, and in West Virginia in 1960. The fact that all but one occurred overseas is a reminder that he was both the most traveled man ever to assume the U.S. presidency and an American who had experienced most of the defining moments of his life outside the boundaries of his own country.

His experiences in Europe and Britain during the spring and summer of 1939 taught him two complementary principles: that it is more difficult for a democracy than a totalitarian state to mobilize its citizens for war, and that the best strategy for overcoming this inherent vulnerability is for democratic leaders to inspire their citizens to voluntary acts of sacrifice. These maxims became the thesis for *Why England Slept*, guided his political career, and were expressed in many of his campaign speeches ("In the next ten years we are going to try to develop in this country a sense of public interest comparable to what the Soviet Union is able to develop . . . by the power of the police state"). They also provided the philosophical underpinnings for "ask not" and his call to "pay any price, bear any burden, meet any hardship . . . in order to assure the survival and the success of liberty."

In the spring of 1939 Kennedy took a leave of absence from Harvard in order to live with his parents in London, where his father was serving as U.S. ambassador. He planned to travel extensively through Europe and the Middle East. In May and June he stayed at the homes of Polish aristocrats, crossed eastern Europe by train to Moscow, woke to terrorist bombs exploding on the grounds of Jerusalem's King David Hotel, and encountered pro-Nazi German mobs in the Polish city of Danzig. In August, he visited Prague, Vienna, and Munich, where Nazi storm-troopers stoned his car because of its British license plates. He arrived in Berlin on August 20, 1939, eleven days before the invasion of Poland, and left two days later with a secret message for his father from the American chargé d'affaires warning that war could be expected to break out within a week.

The climax of his prewar experiences came on September 3, 1939, when he took a seat in the visitor's gallery of the House of Commons and listened to

Prime Minister Neville Chamberlain—a democratic leader who had failed to prepare Britain to meet a totalitarian threat—declare that Britain was at war with Nazi Germany. Chamberlain's speech, in which he admitted, "Everything that I had worked for . . . everything that I have believed in during my public life has crashed into ruins," interested Kennedy less than the one that followed from Winston Churchill, newly arrived in the war cabinet. This six-minute speech is not considered first-rate Churchill ("over-prepared and otiose," says his biographer Roy Jenkins), but its call to a generation of Britons "to prove itself not unworthy of the days of yore and not unworthy of those great men, the fathers of our land," stirred the soul of the twenty-two-year-old Kennedy, who was already infatuated with England, Churchill, and history.

Churchill's call to a generation of young Britons to equal the accomplishments of their forebears is echoed in four passages in the Kennedy inaugural address: "Since this country was founded, each generation of Americans has been summoned to give testimony to its national loyalty"; "the torch has been passed to a new generation"; "only a few generations have been granted the role of defending freedom in its hour of maximum danger"; and "I do not believe that any of us would exchange places with any other people or any other generation."

Throughout his political career Kennedy would sometimes choke up when called upon to speak of the young men who had lost their lives in World War II. He had broken down, for example, after telling an audience at an American Legion post in Massachusetts a year after the end of the war, "Greater love hath no man than this, that a man lay down his life for his friends." Films of Kennedy delivering his inaugural address reveal that its emotional turning point, the moment when he began speaking from his heart, came as he proclaimed: "Since this country was founded, each generation of Americans has been summoned to give testimony to its national loyalty. The graves of young Americans who answered the call to service surround the globe." When he dictated these sentences on January 10, and when he delivered them at the inauguration, he was almost certainly remembering his brother Joseph Kennedy Jr. and his brother-in-law Billy Hartington, as well as PT 109 crewmen Andrew Kirksey and Harold Marney, whose graves and memorials were all among those surrounding the globe.

The U.S. Navy patrol torpedo (PT) boats that fought in the Pacific war were flimsy plywood vessels armed with defective torpedoes and commanded by poorly trained skippers, and the PT 109 incident was merely one more fiasco within the larger disaster of the whole program. On August 2,

1943, Lieutenant John F. Kennedy and the twelve-man crew of PT 109 were patrolling the Blackett Strait in the Solomon Islands when a Japanese destroyer suddenly appeared out of the moonless night and rammed them. Crewmen Andrew Kirksey and Harold Marney were killed, and the others were left clinging to the wreckage.

PT 109 was the only torpedo boat to be rammed and sunk by the Japanese, and even sympathetic biographers have questioned Kennedy's failure to see the destroyer and take evasive action. Unquestioned has been the courage he demonstrated afterward. Lashing the badly burned machinist's mate, Patrick McMahon, to a piece of wood, Kennedy clasped the straps of his kapok life jacket in his teeth and spent five hours towing him to tiny Plum Pudding Island. After the other nine survivors arrived safely, he swam back into the Fergusson Passage with a lantern, hoping to signal a passing American warship. He spent the night treading water and passed out on his return. The next day, he towed McMahon for three hours to a larger island promising food and water then carved a distress message onto a coconut that two natives delivered to an Australian coast watcher. During the six days he was marooned, he displayed the kind of physical stamina, leadership, and bravery most men can only wonder if they could summon.

The effect of PT 109 on Kennedy's career was as unquestionable as his heroism. The story made newspaper front pages and newsreels. John Hersey recreated it in an article published in the *New Yorker* that Joe Kennedy arranged to have condensed in the *Reader's Digest*, where it reached a mass audience and became a factor in his son's election to Congress in 1946 and in his future campaigns. What was never specifically pointed out, however, was that Kennedy's courage had been as much moral as physical. He had not killed a single enemy soldier, and his heroism owed everything to his determination and stamina, rather than bravery under fire and an enemy body count.

Kennedy usually responded to questions about PT 109 with comments like the self-deprecatory answer he gave a little boy during a West Coast campaign trip: "It was absolutely involuntary. They sank my boat." But he was too smart and self-aware to believe this. He could have asked the others to take turns pulling McMahon to safety and did not have to risk his life by swimming back into the channel to summon help. The fact that he gave PT 109 tie clips to supporters, displayed the famous coconut on his Senate and White House desks, and wrote a book on the subject of courage is a good indication of what the incident meant to him.

Joe Kennedy had paid to have the *Reader's Digest* article reprinted and distributed to every household in the Massachusetts district from which his son was running for Congress. JFK used PT 109 to further his career in more subtle ways, such as opening *Profiles in Courage* with "This is a book about the most admirable of human virtues—courage," a fairly flagrant act of self-congratulation. His second sentence in that book was "'Grace under pressure,' Ernest Hemingway defined it." Hemingway's definition, of course, is macho nonsense; many courageous acts lack grace, and many heroes are clumsy and terrified. It tells us less about the quality than about how Hemingway and Kennedy wanted to be seen: cool, unruffled, and graceful. The courage that the latter demonstrated in the Pacific, however, owed more to his sense of duty and moral principles. This was the brand of courage he would demand in his inaugural address: not grace under pressure but "high standards of strength and sacrifice," the heroism of citizens meeting their responsibilities.

The dark side of PT 109 was that two crewmen, one-sixth of the men under Kennedy's command, had died in a collision for which he was not entirely blameless. He was too self-aware to ignore his responsibility and too sensitive not to be affected by their deaths. The loss of his brother and brother-in-law were greater personal tragedies, but at least he bore no responsibility for those. He remained bitter that none of the PT boats patrolling nearby had mounted a long or effective search for survivors, despite seeing gasoline burning on the water. His commanding officer, Alvin Cluster, recalled that when Kennedy complained afterward about being abandoned, "the tears were streaming down his face." In Cluster's opinion, Kennedy "felt *very strongly* about losing those two men and his ship."

Behind Kennedy's warning in his inaugural address that "man holds in his mortal hands the power to abolish . . . all forms of human life," and behind his reference to "the steady spread of the deadly atom," and his pleas for Soviets and Americans to "seek to invoke the wonders of science instead of its terrors" and "begin anew the quest for peace, before the dark powers of destruction . . . engulf all humanity," lie the pulverized and gutted buildings of postwar Berlin, and the colorless faces and pale tan lips of its citizens as they scavenged through their devastated metropolis during the summer of 1945.

In the Pacific, Kennedy had experienced war in miniature. On July 28, 1945, two and a half months after the end of the European war and nineteen days before the end of the Asian one, a plane carrying him and Secretary of the Navy James Forrestal circled Berlin before landing, and he saw the results of war on a grand scale, war without limits. On August 22, 1939, he had left behind the bustling, prosperous capital of the most powerful nation in Europe. Now, he noted in his diary, Berlin was "ash gray . . . churned up and powdered stone and brick."

He was traveling as a reporter for the Hearst newspapers and had hitched a ride to Germany with Forrestal, his father's former Wall Street partner. After landing, they drove through the city to Potsdam, where Joseph Stalin, Harry Truman, and Clement Attlee, who had become Britain's prime minister after defeating Churchill three days before, were determining the shape of a cold-war landscape that would also shape Kennedy's inaugural address.

His July 28 diary entry began, "The devastation is complete . . . there is not a single building which is not gutted. On some streets, the stench—sweet and sickish from dead bodies—is overwhelming." Total war had cut Berlin's prewar population of four million in half, and the survivors, he wrote, "have completely colorless faces—a yellow tinge within pale tan lips. They are all carrying bundles. . . . They sleep in cellars. The women will do anything for food."

He had seen photographs and newsreels of the devastation. So had Forrestal, Truman, Admiral William Leahy, and the other Americans gathering at Potsdam. But it was a different experience to confront the three-story mountains of rubble, blackened apartment blocks, and boulevards reduced to footpaths winding between heaps of broken brick, and to drive through the silent, slow-motion city where everyone else walked. Several months later he would tell an audience at a Massachusetts American Legion post that Berlin was "a gutted ruin," its magnificent buildings "merely shells," and, echoing his diary, the faces of survivors "colorless," their expressions "lifeless and dead," their lips "a pale tan." The ruins and horror, he said, "far surpassed anything that I had ever imagined."

Admiral Leahy condemned the ruination of Berlin as contrary to the civilized laws of warfare. Truman wrote he had never seen such destruction and compared it to the sack of Carthage and Rome. "I hope for some sort of peace," he wrote, "but I fear that machines are ahead of morals by some centuries." Yet Truman's horror at what the Allied air forces and Soviet army had done to Berlin did not stay his hand from ordering a similar destruction visited on Hiroshima, and it was while he was surrounded by the bombed ruins of one large city that he decided to drop the atomic bomb on another.

Kennedy never visited Hiroshima, but photographs and newsreels showed a devastation bearing an uncanny resemblance to that of Berlin. In later years, if he wanted to imagine what a nuclear bomb might do to Washington, D.C., he had only to remember Berlin.

* * *

Kennedy was a third-term U.S. congressman when he disembarked in Saigon on October 19, 1951, near the end of a seven-nation fact-finding tour of Asia that had taken him to Israel, India, Pakistan, Iran, and Thailand. Had he not stopped in Vietnam, he might not have pledged in his inaugural to the new nations of the third world that "one form of colonial control shall not have passed away merely to be replaced by a far more iron tyranny," or promised to help "those people in the huts and villages across the globe," or spoken of a "grand and global alliance . . . [to] assure a more fruitful life for all mankind."

Bobby Kennedy said the trip had made "a very, very major impression" on his brother. Foreign policy adviser Walt Rostow called it a "formative experience." JFK and Bobby arrived in Vietnam at a tipping point in the increasingly violent Communist-led guerrilla war against the French colonial administration. The chief of the French Sûreté had been assassinated, a suicide bomber had killed a French general, antigrenade nets covered government ministries and hotels, and French administrators traveled through the Mekong Delta in armed convoys. The two brothers visited Hanoi and the delta, inspected French fortifications, and interviewed French military officers and civilian officials, American diplomats, Vietnamese politicians, priests, and ordinary citizens. After dinner one night, General de Lattre, the commander of French forces in Indochina, rolled out his maps and argued that if France lost the delta, all of Asia would fall to the Communists.

Bobby kept a diary, in which three of the fifteen pages concerning Vietnam are in his brother Jack's handwriting. Bobby noted the people seemed "sullen and resentful," and posited that if an election were held throughout Indochina, Ho Chi Minh would win about 70 percent of the vote, "mainly because he fights the French." He condemned the French for not giving people "sufficient freedom" and complained of too many French flags and streets with French names, and too many French officials. A Vietnamese priest told Jack Kennedy that students from the Catholic universities were leading the revolt. A French army colonel at a frontier post believed France would win, but added, Bobby noted, "that this might not occur during our lifetime!!"

Jack was impressed by a lengthy conversation with Edmund Gullion, a young foreign service officer he would later appoint ambassador to the former Belgian Congo. Afterward, he wrote in his brother's diary: "We are more and more getting identified in the mind of the people with the French. We must do what we can as our contribution becomes bigger to force the French to liberalize political conditions. We are not here to help French maintain colonies."

The visit convinced him that the European colonial empires were doomed, and the new nations arising from their ashes would become cold-war battlegrounds. To win them, the United States would have to offer a better doctrine of political and social revolution than the Communists. At the conclusion of the Asian trip he noted in Bobby's diary, "[The] Reason for spread of Communism is failure of those who believe in democracy to explain this theory in terms intelligible to the ordinary man and to make its ameliorating effect on his life apparent."

When he appeared on the television program *Meet the Press* a few weeks after returning home, he said, "We've allied ourselves in the case of Indo-China with the French very closely which has cost us heavily in the eyes of the natives." He predicted that unless the French pulled out, "this guerilla war is just going to spread and grow and we're going to finally get driven out of Southeast Asia." He repeated the same criticism on the same program the following year, adding that the British position in Iran was "hopeless," and the United States "should have thrown its weight completely with the Iranians." Fifteen months after that, he told *Meet the Press* that "without the support of the native population there is not hope of success in any of the countries of Southeast Asia."

During the 1950s no U.S. senator spoke out more forcefully in support of third-world nationalist movements than Kennedy, or argued more forcefully that the United States should offer the new nations of Africa and Asia economic assistance and an ideology more attractive than communism. He declared in Senate speeches that "every country is entitled to its independence," and that "we should not commit our ground troops to fight in French Indo-China." He wrote in *Foreign Affairs* that one of the weaknesses of Eisenhower's foreign policy was "a failure to appreciate how the forces of nationalism are rewriting the geopolitical map of the world," and urged Americans to face the challenge of helping "the new and underdeveloped nations bear their economic burdens."

On July 2, 1957, he delivered the most controversial and courageous speech of his Senate career, on the subject of Algeria, where France was fighting another brutal colonial war. He proclaimed in his first sentence that "the most powerful single force in the world today is neither communism nor capitalism, nor the guided missile—it is man's eternal desire to be free and independent. The great enemy of that tremendous force of freedom is called, for want of a more precise term, imperialism." He continued, "Thus, the single most important test of American foreign policy today is how we meet the challenge of imperialism, what we do to further man's desire to be free. On this test more than any other, this nation shall be critically judged by the uncommitted millions in Asia and Africa."

Some of the fiercest criticism of the speech came from members of the Democratic foreign policy establishment, who argued that a French defeat would bring chaos to Algeria, humiliate an important ally, and embolden Egyptian president Gamal Abdel Nasser and menace Israel. Adlai Stevenson called Kennedy's attack on France "terrible," "an invitation for chaos," and a threat to NATO. There would be, however, a marked similarity between ideas and phrases in Kennedy's Algeria speech and the suggestions Stevenson would later offer for his inaugural address, making it possible to argue that Stevenson was simply handing Kennedy back some of his own rhetoric.

Anyone reading Kennedy's inaugural for the first time might be struck by his concern for the wretched of the earth, and his insistence that his fellow countrymen had a duty to alleviate their suffering. Americans had become familiar with these themes during his campaign, but because Kennedy considered his inaugural address an opportunity to introduce himself to the world, he was determined to repeat them. During the campaign he had said that the next American president would have to "capture the imagination of the world," and that, "I want Africans and Latin Americans not to quote Roosevelt or Lincoln or Jefferson: I want them to be quoting the next President of the United States." Among the words from the inaugural that he wanted them quoting were his statements that "man holds in his mortal hands the power to abolish all forms of human poverty and all forms of human life" and his pledge to "assist free men and free governments in casting off the chains of poverty."

Kennedy had dictated "man holds in his mortal hands" to Lincoln on January 10. Other passages involving poverty originated in the drafts written by Sorensen and Adlai Stevenson, or reflected Stevenson's recommendation that Kennedy declare "a systematic attack upon the poverty of the world." This was the kind of grandiose liberalism that was supposedly anathema to the more pragmatic Kennedy, and he could have removed or toned down references to world poverty. Instead, he left them in the speech virtually unchanged, and you could argue that his offer to help the impoverished of the earth help themselves, "for whatever period is required," was as extreme, reckless, and open-ended a promise as his one to "pay any price" and "bear any burden."

It is these passages about poverty, more than Kennedy's call for sacrifice and courage, invocation of the Almighty and the spirit of the American Revolution, or celebration of the founding fathers, that distinguishes his inaugural from others. Roosevelt had acknowledged in his first inaugural that "a host of unemployed citizens face the grim problem of existence," but had never uttered the words *poor* or *poverty.* Truman addressed the subject in one paragraph, calling poverty a threat to underdeveloped nations and more prosperous areas of the world. Eisenhower acknowledged that one-third of humankind was struggling to achieve "freedom from grinding poverty," but offered no promise of American assistance. Lyndon Johnson would mention domestic poverty, saying, "In a land of great wealth, families must not live in hopeless poverty." But after him, no president uttered the word *poor,* or dwelled on poverty in an inaugural address.

Kennedy confronted wretched poverty for the first time while campaigning in the West Virginia primary in the spring of 1960. He had seen desperate people in postwar Berlin and in third-world streets, but had never before faced the American poor in their own homes. He arrived in West Virginia tanned and rested after a short Jamaican holiday and, according to Theodore White, who followed him through the state, his shock "communicated itself with the emotion of original discovery." He could scarcely bring himself to believe human beings could survive on the cans of rations he fingered, "like artifacts of another civilization." His friend Charles Spalding, who also accompanied him, said, "If you go into a coal miner's town or into his house and you see the condition his kids are in, and what he's living in, you can't help but be moved." And if these miners are the counterparts of the working-class Boston Irishmen whom you count as your forebears and friends, you are probably moved even more.

After the primary, Kennedy often spoke of the "blight" of West Virginian poverty, of its families receiving "surplus food packages and no hope for the future," and its children taking home their school lunches so their parents could eat. Less than twenty-four hours after delivering an inaugural with more references to poverty, hunger, and suffering than any before or since, he signed his first executive order. It instructed Secretary of Agriculture Orville Freeman to double the surplus food ration given to four million impoverished Americans.

The contrast between Kennedy's fine words about poverty and the luxurious setting where he and Sorensen edited and polished them on the morning of January 17 is an invitation to satire. Aside from telling us that Kennedy wore "sport clothes," and that they sat on the patio, Sorensen is stingy with the kind of detail that might help us better to imagine the scene. One must look elsewhere to discover that the president-elect and his longtime aide sat beside an Olympic-sized swimming pool and alongside a stucco mansion belonging to the richest Irish-American on Earth, or to learn that the man preparing to deliver these idealistic lines about world poverty was dressed by a valet every morning, and had quite possibly, with the exception of the war years, never cooked his own breakfast, washed his own shirts, or even carried them to the laundry.

What saved Kennedy from hypocrisy was an egalitarian spirit that was one of the pillars of his charm. The chief of the Secret Service in the early days of his presidency, U. E. Baughman, believed Kennedy's egalitarian spirit surpassed even that of Truman, and Baughman's wife noticed that whomever Kennedy was with, "he was with them completely," whether it was a Girl Scout presenting him with a plaque or a member of his cabinet. One sensed at once, she said, "that he is thoroughly aware of you and really cares about what makes you tick."

Deirdre Henderson, Kennedy's informal ambassador to the New England academic community during the 1960 campaign, believes his friendships with his resident Irishman and court jester, Dave Powers, and his driver, Muggsy O'Leary, a former Boston policeman, were close and real. A photograph of him and O'Leary attending a Red Sox game together shows Kennedy smiling broadly and smoking a cigar, having a tremendous time. Henderson says that "people like Muggsy, the real people, the cops, the staff in the kitchen, the simple people—they instinctively knew Kennedy liked them, and they returned his affection."

The ability to connect with the common man was a quality he also appreciated in others. He recounted in his 1945 diary a popular story about how Eisenhower had remarked after reviewing the crack British Eighth Army, "To think that I, a boy from Abilene, Kansas, am the Commander of troops like those." To this, Kennedy had added approvingly, "[Eisenhower] never lost that humble way and therefore easily won the hearts of those with whom he worked."

Kennedy's preference for the crofter over the laird was instinctive and authentic. During the summer of 1960, while Jackie was traveling in Europe, he had spent a weekend at the Newport estate of her mother and stepfather, Janet and Hugh Auchincloss. In a letter he wrote his wife afterward, he poked fun at a conversation he had overheard about the "in" castles of England, saying that after one tedious Newport party, "I was taken into the kitchen and introduced to all the help, who were just over from Ireland, and found them much more attractive than the guests."

Despite his million-dollar trust fund, Kennedy really *did* identify with the kitchen help in Newport, and with Irishmen like O'Leary and Powers, probably because he believed he was also being dismissed by the WASP grandees in the front rooms. He had inherited this chip on his shoulder from his parents. His father had been blackballed by every Boston club he tried joining, prompting Rose Kennedy to ask one of JFK's Harvard classmates, "When do you think the nice people of Boston are going to accept us Catholics socially?" After playing golf at the Newport Country Club, JFK had remarked to one of his companions, "Now they [the members] know their worst fears are being realized . . . one of the last strongholds of America's socially elite is being invaded by mongrels without pedigrees." During the 1960 campaign he told Paul Fay, "Do you know it is impossible for an Irish Catholic to get into the Somerset Club in Boston? If I moved back to Boston even after being President, it would make no difference." Fay said he was crazy; any club would take an ex-president. Kennedy shot him a skeptical look, and Fay suddenly understood that his friend still saw imaginary signs reading, "Help Wanted—Irish Don't Apply."

During Kennedy's weeks in Palm Beach Evelyn Lincoln kept her diary and appointment book in fits and starts. She typed or wrote in longhand narrative accounts of what happened on January 1, 2, 3, 5, 11, 16, and 20, but her notes describing the other days in January preceding the inauguration were either lost or never written. She recorded his appointments in a book-sized 1961 *National Diary* from the National Blank Book Company of Holyoke, Massachusetts. Engagements fill many of the January 1 to January 20 pages. Some days she was unable to fit all his engagements onto a single page and instead typed a daily itinerary that she clipped into the book. Some of these itineraries have survived in her files, but others, like the one for January 17, have disappeared. Still, from press reports we know that after conferring with Sorensen that morning, Kennedy met and had lunch with Senator Warren Magnuson (D.-Wash.), the chairman of the Senate Interstate and Foreign Commerce Committee, and then at two o'clock he flew to Washington on the *Caroline*.

Lincoln's diary and engagement book show that while in Palm Beach, Kennedy breakfasted between nine and half past nine, and never scheduled a meeting before ten. Given this fact, and given his meeting with Magnuson on January 17, his morning meeting with Ted Sorensen could not have lasted for much more than an hour. Apart from polishing the "ask not" sentence, we know little else about their editorial discussions. But Sorensen is sure of one thing: that they never performed a rhetorical analysis of the address or consciously employed oratorical devices such as triads, parallel constructions, repetition, or antithetical statements.

Forty years later, Sorensen was surprised to learn that an academic had calculated that twenty-two of the inaugural's fifty-two declarative sentences contained antithetical thoughts or statements. The notion that either he or Kennedy composed the speech this way struck him as laughable. "By that time we had been working on speeches together for eight years and our styles had melded, and we each knew what worked and didn't," he said. "Antithesis was not even a word we used."

They may not have used the word—*antithesis* is defined as "such choice or arrangement of words as emphasizes a contrast," or, more simply, as a "balance of word and structure"—but they used the construction liberally in the inaugural, and in many other speeches.

Kennedy admired brevity and clarity, and antithetical statements therefore came naturally to him because they demand short and simple sentences.

He believed reason could solve any problem, and antithesis invites an audience to reason with the speaker and arrive at a conclusion. Antithetical statements such as "United, there is little we cannot do. . . . Divided, there is little we can do"; "Let us never negotiate out of fear. But let us never fear to negotiate"; and "Let both sides explore what problems unite us instead of belaboring the problems which divide us" were an appeal to reason. "For only when our arms are sufficient beyond doubt can we be certain beyond doubt that they will never be employed" invited the audience to reason together with Kennedy and conclude that the United States needed a stronger military.

Kennedy was impatient, and antithesis is the enemy of ambiguity, a rhetorical shorthand that saves time by reducing a complicated problem to its fundamentals.

He liked routine and order, and antithesis is an orderly presentation of two alternatives. When he said, "For man holds in his mortal hands the power to abolish all forms of human poverty and all forms of human life" and "Let both sides . . . bring the absolute power to destroy other nations under the absolute control of all nations," he was not simply employing a rhetorical device that by its very nature offers the audience a stark choice, but employing it to frame the starkest choice imaginable: between the extinction or survival of the human race.

Nowhere is the merging of Sorensen's and Kennedy's literary styles more apparent than in their use of antithesis. Antithetical statements are scattered throughout the Sorensen Draft and Kennedy's dictation, and they are present in the campaign speeches Sorensen prepared for Kennedy and in the extemporaneous speeches Kennedy delivered in their stead.

If one reads rather than listens to Kennedy's inaugural address, one discovers a prologue of five paragraphs, followed by fourteen paragraphs containing the "pledge'" and "let us" litanies, and an eight-paragraph conclusion. When Kennedy biographer Herbert Parmet interviewed Sorensen in 1977 about his contributions to *Profiles in Courage*, Sorensen said, "The opening and closing paragraphs, which are more personal and more a reflection of his philosophy probably were more heavily influenced by his [Kennedy's] literary style than those that were simply historical accounts." This could also describe their collaboration on the inaugural address, in which the most celebrated lines are found in Kennedy's dictated prologue and conclusion.

At their November meeting, Kennedy had asked Sorensen to determine and apply the "secret" of the Gettysburg Address. After studying the speech, Sorensen concluded that "Lincoln never used a two- or three-syllable word where a one-syllable word would do, and never used two or three words where one would do." He presumably used this "secret" while writing his draft. But as Garry Wills argues in *Lincoln at Gettysburg*, short and simple words are not really characteristic of the Gettysburg Address at all. "Some have claimed, simplistically, that Lincoln achieved a 'down-to-earth' style by using short Anglo-Saxon words rather than long Latin ones in the address," Wills writes. "Such people cannot have read the Address with care." Instead he identifies Gettysburg's "internal wiring" as one of its most important stylistic features, pointing out that "Lincoln interlocks his sentences, making of them a constantly self-referential system. This linking by explicit repetition amounts to a kind of hook-and-eye method for joining parts of his address." By repeating words such as *dedicated* and *consecrated*, and by relying "on a few words in different contexts," Lincoln was able to emphasize "the compactness of themes" and bind his speech together.

The prologue and conclusion of the Kennedy inaugural are bound together in a similar fashion, although perhaps less by design than by the fact that Kennedy had dictated both parts of the speech at the same time.

In his prologue, he spoke of man holding "in his mortal hands the power to abolish all forms of human *poverty*"; in his conclusion, of "a struggle against the common enemies of man: tyranny, *poverty*, disease, and war itself."

He said in his prologue that "the torch has been passed to a new *generation* of Americans"; in his conclusion that "each *generation* of Americans has been summoned to give testimony to its national loyalty," adding three paragraphs later that "only a few *generations* have been granted the role of defending freedom . . ." and "I do not believe that any of us would exchange places with . . . any other *generation*."

He proclaimed in his fourth dictated paragraph that "we shall pay any price, bear any *burden*"; in a concluding paragraph he referred to "the *burden* of a long twilight struggle."

The linkage between the opening and concluding paragraphs of the inaugural, and the use of antithetical statements throughout, created a unity of theme and style furthering the impression that it had been the work of a single author, presumably Sorensen. Instead, the speech Kennedy was carrying back to Washington with him on the afternoon of January 17 was, in every important respect, his own. His next task was to persuade the High Court of History of this fact.

5

On Board the Caroline

JANUARY 17

⚜

Ted Sorensen, Senator Warren Magnuson, Pierre Salinger, Evelyn Lincoln, and the *Time* magazine correspondent Hugh Sidey were among the passengers accompanying Kennedy back to Washington on the afternoon of January 17. Rose and Joe Kennedy had decided to take a commercial flight later that day, while Jackie, who wanted to remain in Palm Beach until the last possible moment, would not fly north until the following afternoon, leaving her children behind under the care of their nanny, Maud Shaw.

After the *Caroline* was airborne, Kennedy invited Hugh Sidey to join him in his compartment. Sidey was not a social or personal friend, but he was as close to Kennedy in a professional sense as any reporter. He had covered him for three years as both a senator and presidential candidate, and had even served as an unofficial oratory coach during the campaign, sometimes advising him on his gestures and delivery. Fond as Kennedy was of Sidey, one wonders if he would have invited him into his compartment if he had represented, say, the *Philadelphia Inquirer* or the *Christian Science Monitor* rather than *Life*, the most influential visual medium in America, and *Time*, believed to have more impact on public opinion than any other newsweekly. Sidey entertained no illusions about their friendship. "I knew he was after *Time* magazine," he says, "but he never humiliated me or caused me any trouble. I did sense that he wanted to own you, and if someone in *Time* had written anything bad about him that would have been the end of me." Sidey believed that under the style and glamour, Kennedy was "basically a serious man on a serious mission." When asked to assess him forty years later, he said: "I can't begin to understand how careless he was about his personal life, and how obsessed he was. But if you separated that out, you had a person who loved and understood history, and could self-consciously place his decisions and career in a historical context. He had courage and a fine sense of honor, but only in his public life. He also had a huge amount of talent and ability when it came to speaking and rousing people—but of course in those days, people wanted to be roused."

When Sidey entered the private compartment, he found Kennedy slouched into a huge leather chair, drinking a glass of milk and sawing into a steak, the kind of meal that, along with his eggs-and-bacon breakfast, and perpetual snacking on ice cream and bowls of milky clam chowder, had raised his cholesterol to perilous levels. Kennedy pushed away his plate, squinted out the window, and picked up a pen and legal pad. He put his feet up on the desk, propped the pad on his lap, and began to fill the first of nine sheets of lined yellow paper with what would become known as the only handwritten draft of his inaugural address.

The Kennedy Library owns these nine pages, and a book published in 2000 with its cooperation includes color photographs of the two most legible ones. It identifies them as "an early draft of the inaugural speech." But if you take the trouble to decipher Kennedy's handwriting and arrange the pages in their proper sequence, it becomes evident that instead of a complete draft of the address, they are merely a reprise of the opening and concluding paragraphs found in his January 10 dictation. This leads to the question of why a man known for making every minute count would have wasted time writing out the same sentences he had dictated the week before.

Kennedy was not in the habit of dating the drafts and notes for his speeches, and none of the inaugural's typed drafts carries a date, yet he took the trouble to write "Jan 17, 1961" in the upper-left-hand corner of this draft, preparing it, presumably, for the High Court of History.

He began, "An Inaugural is a beginning and end is—" then stopped, scratched it out, ripped the page from the pad, and discarded it. He began again, again dating the first page. Like the *Newsweek* reporter watching him write his inaugural two days before in Palm Beach, like Evan Thomas sitting at his bedside in New York Hospital in 1955 as he composed *Profiles in Courage*, Sidey was playing the role of spectator.

Sidey was less astonished by the performance than by its timing, and remembers thinking, "My God! It's three days before the inauguration, and he hasn't progressed beyond a first draft? Maybe he's done the rest, and is just fiddling with the opening."

Kennedy stopped after three pages. "It's tough," he said. "The speech to the Massachusetts Legislature went so well. It's going to be hard to meet that standard." He pushed the pad across the desk to Sidey. "What do you think?" he asked.

It is difficult to imagine any recent president-elect inviting a journalist to comment on a draft of his inaugural address, but Sidey and Kennedy enjoyed the sort of professional friendship that was more common in Washington then. After studying Kennedy's handwriting with mounting despair, he finally said, "Gosh, Senator Kennedy, I just can't read it."

Kennedy picked up the pad and, speaking so softly Sidey had trouble hearing him over the engines, read: "An inaugural is an end as well as a beginning. Today I am linked with the 35 other Presidents, three of whom are with us today and stood in this same place, took the same oath, made the same commitment to the preservation of the American constitution as its founders made today. We are a young people—but an old Republic. But though we are old . . . we must not forget that we are descended from revolutionaries."

He told Sidey he was unhappy with this opening. It was too wordy and rambling. Gesturing out the window toward the horizon, he said, "What I want to say is that the spirit of the Revolution is still here, still a part of this country."

From the next two pages he read, "The concept that the rights we enjoy come not from the generosity of the state but the hand of God," then versions of "Let the word go forth" and "bear any burden" that were almost identical to his January 10 dictation.

He wrote some more sentences, crossed them out, and finally threw the pad down onto his desk in frustration. He pushed his chair back, slapped his waist, and complained about gaining weight during the transition. Sidey noticed the hint of a spare tire but thought the additional pounds had improved his face, making him look more mature.

Kennedy straightened himself in his chair and announced he was concerned by the new Eisenhower budget and the situation in Laos. He picked up the sheet of paper with the twenty-five verses Billy Graham had suggested, and read aloud, "When a man's ways please the Lord, he maketh even his enemies to be at peace with him." "If you hear that in the speech," he said, "you'll know where it came from." In truth, there were already enough biblical verses in the inaugural address of America's first Catholic president.

One doubts it was entirely a lucky accident that passages Kennedy chose to read aloud to Sidey that afternoon happened to be precisely the ones most likely to appeal to Henry Luce, the powerful publisher of *Time* and *Life* magazines. Kennedy was certainly no stranger to Luce's political philosophy. Luce had written the introduction to Kennedy's first book, *Why England Slept*—including the comment that "if John Kennedy is characteristic of the younger generation—and I believe he is—many of us would be happy to have the destinies of the Republic handed over to this generation at once"—and since the 1930s he and JFK's father had maintained a friendship that demonstrates, if nothing else, how easily an appetite for power can overcome any political disagreements.

Luce was the son of a Presbyterian missionary in China, Joe Kennedy the son of a Boston-Irish politician. Luce was a Republican and passionate internationalist who had urged America to intervene in the war against Hitler; Joe Kennedy was a Democrat and passionate isolationist. Yet they had courted, flattered, and circled each other for decades, fashioning a rewarding alliance from an abhorrence of communism and the pleasure each took in throwing his weight around. Jack Kennedy understood this and had once told Sidey, "I like Luce. He reminds me of my father. He's entitled to have his magazine say what he wants because he made it."

Luce ran flattering cover stories in *Time,* praising Joe Kennedy as "an ideal policeman for the securities business" and a man "known and loved by millions of English-speaking men." Joe Kennedy reciprocated by entertaining Luce at the American embassy in London—and sleeping with his wife. Sidey was well positioned to observe the friendship and calls it a "good, tough one that both men enjoyed." It reached an epiphany of sorts on July 15, 1960, when Joe Kennedy went to Luce's apartment in the Waldorf-Astoria to watch his son accept the Democratic nomination. Kennedy puffed excitedly on a cigar as his son spoke. Luce watched impassively but told Hedley Donovan, one of his editors, afterward, "It's quite a thing to sit with an old friend and watch his son accept the nomination for President of the United States." That night, when Joe Kennedy argued that *Time-Life* should endorse his son, Luce replied that he could understand JFK assuming a liberal domestic policy, but *Time* would "clobber him" if he went soft on communism. What remains unknown about this extraordinary evening is what Luce thought of the acceptance speech. Had he given it his full attention, he might have recognized some passages he could easily have written himself.

This son of a missionary believed America had a missionary duty to make capitalism and the promises of the Declaration of Independence available to every soul on Earth. He had first expressed this idea in a prize-winning speech he delivered shortly before graduating from Yale. In it, he criticized the United States for lacking any purpose greater than its own survival, and for joining the Great War to preserve American freedoms at home, rather than guaranteeing them abroad. The great American purpose, he said, should be to become "the implacable and immediate foe of whatever nation shall offer to disturb the peace of the world," and "a defender of good faith throughout the world."

Luce distilled his Yale oration into his "American Proposition," or, as his wife, Clare Boothe Luce, liked to call it, the "Amprop"—the concept that "the American mission is to make men free." It led Luce to become a fervent interventionist, warning in a 1940 NBC broadcast that if Britain and France fell, "we and we only among the great powers are left to defend the democratic faith throughout the world." He also applied the Amprop to the cold war, arguing that the National Purpose, always capitalized in Luce publications, should be not simply to contain communism but to defeat it and extend democracy to independent third-world nations and the Communist states of eastern Europe.

The term *National Purpose* had become a household phrase by 1960, and cause for unending debate, studies, and hand-wringing. Eisenhower responded to the furor with the Presidential Commission on National Goals, staffed by such eminent Americans as AFL-CIO president George Meany, Judge Learned Hand, and former Harvard president James Conant. Its final report, issued during the Kennedy transition, declared that "in the 1960s every American is summoned to extraordinary personal responsibility, sustained effort and sacrifice." Several commentators noticed the similarity between the report and Kennedy's campaign speeches, and the CBS reporter Howard K. Smith said that if he had not known better, he would have sworn Kennedy had written it. Also in 1960, the Rockefeller Brothers Fund issued its *Prospect for America*, an even more extensive series of reports on the National Purpose. Its introduction argued that economic growth should be "the means of contributing to the human betterment which is the central purpose of our society," and that a nation failing to shape events through its own sense of purpose would be engulfed in events shaped by others, ideas Kennedy had been expressing, albeit more elegantly, in his campaign speeches.

Henry Luce had encouraged the National Purpose debate by appointing a panel of eight famous Americans, including Billy Graham, Adlai Stevenson, Archibald MacLeish, and John Kennedy, and commissioning them to contribute essays on the topic, which he published in *Life* during the spring and summer of 1960. The series opened with Walter Lippmann's observation, "The critical weakness of our society is that for the time being our people do not have great purposes which they are united in wanting to achieve," and concluded with "We Must Climb to the Hilltop," a Kennedy essay recommending a National Purpose defined by the Declaration of Independence, Constitution, and Bill of Rights, and characterized by "a sense of idealistic aspiration . . . to build the good society as well as the good life here and in the rest of the world."

Kennedy had not written his acceptance speech to please Luce, but neither was he immune to a debate over the National Purpose, whose terms and language had been largely set by Luce. This is why, when he said in his acceptance speech that "too many Americans have lost their way, their will and their sense of historic purpose," urged Americans to spread freedom and prove America could compete "with the single-minded advance of the Communist system," and told a campaign rally in Jackson, Michigan, "I believe we stand for a great national purpose," one hears echoes of Luce's Amprop.

One does not have to believe that Kennedy had Luce in mind when he dictated passages for his inaugural to Evelyn Lincoln on January 10 to accept that he was influenced by the debate over the National Purpose. When he spoke of the need to "assure the survival and the success of liberty," and prevent "the slow undoing of those human rights to which this Nation has always been committed" at home and around the world, he was speaking words Luce could have written, and expressing ideas Luce had been promoting for decades. Perhaps it was coincidental that he read aloud to Hugh Sidey passages from his draft that owed the most to the Luce Amprop, such as "the principles for which we Americans fought here, we fight for around the globe," or that he told Sidey he wanted to say that the spirit of the Revolution was still part of America. Perhaps there was no calculation in any of this, but inviting Sidey into his compartment to watch him write his inaugural *was* calculated.

As Kennedy and Sidey walked back into the main compartment, Kennedy caught Ted Sorensen's eye and said, referring to his speech, "It'll be a smash!"

Back in his compartment, Kennedy wrote another five pages that also resembled his January 10 dictation. He resurrected the seafaring metaphor in which America was "sailing toward the fixed star that has guided us to our present—the desire for peace," and used the first-person singular, even though Sorensen had insisted that by the morning of January 17 they had eliminated *I* from every sentence but the opening one.

Kennedy wrote out his January 10 dictation because these were the passages he could most easily pull from his memory, and he had wanted Sidey to see him composing his address off the top of his head, not copying it from notes, or from a draft that could have been written by someone else. None of the material in the first eight handwritten pages came from the Sorensen Draft because Kennedy could not write its text from memory. Fewer words were crossed out in the last five pages because Sidey was no longer around to witness the performance, and this is inescapably what it was—a performance with two goals: to convince a representative of the most influential media empire in the world that Kennedy was writing his own inaugural address, and to create a document in Kennedy's handwriting that would convince future historians of this fact. After being accused of winning a Pulitzer Prize with a ghostwritten book, Kennedy wanted to establish that he had not delivered a ghostwritten inaugural.

Many of his actions hint at a performance: throwing away his first attempt at an opening line, staring at the horizon for inspiration, sharing his thought processes, handing Sidey the pad so he could see his handwriting. It was a charade, but an honorable one, performed to reinforce the truth: that Kennedy was the author of the passages he had dictated in this same compartment seven days earlier.

Both Ted Sorensen and Haynes Johnson of the Washington *Evening Star* wrote descriptions of his performance that afternoon. Johnson, who was not aboard the *Caroline*, presumably relied on Salinger, Sorensen, or Kennedy himself. His article appeared on the January 21 front page under the headline "Here's How Kennedy Wrote Own Speech."

> Last Tuesday afternoon, after his plane left Palm Beach, Fla., John F. Kennedy walked to his private compartment, closed the door and sat down at a desk. He was alone.
>
> For about the next two hours, as the plane headed for Washington, the President-elect wrote in longhand with a fountain pen on a pad of yellow paper with blue lines.
>
> Then he called in his secretary, Mrs. Evelyn Lincoln, and began to dictate what he had written. As he dictated, he changed the words and structure slightly.
>
> Mr. Kennedy put the yellow sheets in his pocket and remarked that he had better preserve them. He made a reference to the fact that the rough draft of Franklin Roosevelt's inaugural address had been found only recently.

When Ted Sorensen described the episode in his 1965 *Kennedy*, he did not pretend that Kennedy had been writing a first draft.

> Later that day—January 17—as we flew back to Washington from Palm Beach, working in his cabin on the *Caroline*, the final phrasing was emerging. A Biblical quotation that was later used in his American University speech was deleted. The opening paragraphs were re-dictated by the President-elect to Evelyn Lincoln en route, and he smilingly placed in the plane's desk drawer his handwritten notes from which he had dictated, saying, "An early draft of Roosevelt's Inaugural was discovered the other day—and brought $200,000 at an auction."

Neither account mentions Sidey's presence in the compartment. Sidey's account, however, must be considered the most authoritative since, unlike Johnson, he was an eyewitness, and unlike Sorensen, he filed his story with *Time* immediately afterward. Is it possible that when Sorensen came to write his account four years later, he had forgotten about Sidey's presence, or that at the time he had failed to notice him joining Kennedy in the rear cabin? In any case, when Sorensen examined a copy of the nine pages in Kennedy's handwriting in 2002, he was surprised to see Kennedy had written so much. "I don't know what this is," he said, shaking his head. "My recollection is that we had pretty much finished in Palm Beach, and that Mrs. Lincoln had typed a draft before we left. When we sat down next to each other on the plane I think we were looking at that typed copy, and we may have made an occasional slight twitch here and there."

He paused, as if debating whether to continue, then narrated an account slightly at odds with the one in his 1965 book. "Let me tell you a little story," he said. "Be careful what you do with this. It may not reflect all that well on John F. Kennedy, and I've never done anything in my life that didn't reflect well on John F. Kennedy. During that flight, Jack took a piece of stationary from a drawer—maybe it was a little desk—and wrote a couple of lines, copying them from the text. He winked at me, put it back in the drawer, and said something about Franklin Roosevelt's draft being worth so much."

Kennedy had written three pages in front of Hugh Sidey, then written another five after the journalist left the compartment. The document in the possession of the Kennedy Library, however, consists of nine handwritten pages. Sorensen's 2002 account of the flight makes it clear that Kennedy wrote the ninth and final page in his presence. This page contains a version of "ask not" that is different from Kennedy's January 10 dictation but almost identical to that found in the final text of the speech. It was written by Kennedy with a thinner pen, and on a different type of legal paper, than the first eight pages. It also has the number 33 written in its upper-right-hand corner, while the other eight pages are unnumbered. One far-fetched explanation for these discrepancies might be that after writing the first eight pages Kennedy simultaneously ran out of paper and ink, and picked up a different pad and pen. It is also possible that he wrote this ninth page some time earlier, perhaps under the watchful eye of the *Newsweek* reporter. But this ninth page is almost certainly the one Sorensen watched him writing during the flight, and the one that he put in a desk drawer on top of the other eight pages after winking and referring to the value of Roosevelt's handwritten draft. The pen and pad were different because he wrote the ninth page at a different time in the flight and perhaps in a different section of his plane. He chose to copy "ask not" in his handwriting because he expected that sentence to be the most celebrated. Finally, the wording of "ask not" was closer to the final text because he was copying the version he and Sorensen had polished while sitting on the patio that morning, and that Lincoln had retyped before they boarded the *Caroline*.

It is important to remember that although rewriting his own dictation and copying portions of a typed draft of his inaugural was a charade, it was an honorable one, performed not to perpetuate a fraud but to reinforce the truth: that Kennedy was the author of the passages he had dictated in the same compartment seven days earlier. Behind this charade was Kennedy's misunderstanding of what had occurred at Hyde Park, New York, on the evening of February 27, 1933, and his bitter memories of the *Profiles in Courage* controversy.

In 1956, Kennedy had feared that Drew Pearson's allegation that he had not written *Profiles in Courage* might fatally wound his chance to become president four years later. He told Clark Clifford he could not allow such a direct attack on his integrity to stand, and even after Pearson's retraction, it remained a sensitive topic. The Kennedy biographer Herbert Parmet writes that when JFK learned John Oakes of the *New York Times* still believed the rumor, he handed Oakes a formal letter reaffirming his authorship of the book, and insisted Oakes examine the notebooks he used in preparing it. Oakes later said that Kennedy was "very conscious . . . of the political implications of this kind of story as well as the literary and moral obligations." Kennedy also pressed his *Profiles in Courage* notes on Senator Richard Neuberger of Oregon, another published author, so he could confirm the value of his contribution. For the remainder of Kennedy's Senate career he displayed these notes prominently on his desk, next to the famous PT 109 coconut, presenting them to visitors as proof he had written *Profiles in Courage*.

They were not a complete manuscript, but they were enough to convince the historian James MacGregor Burns that Kennedy had done a substantial amount of work on the book, although he added that Kennedy had received "more help than you or I could hope to get." Parmet examined the audiotapes of Kennedy's *Profiles* dictation as well, and arrived at a less charitable conclusion, saying that the *Profiles* manuscript notes were "very rough passages without paragraphing, without any shape, largely ideas jotted down as possible sections . . . [that] in no way resembles the final product." He dismissed the dictation tapes as "a disorganized, somewhat incoherent, mélange from secondary sources."

Parmet concluded that "the burdens of time and literary craftsmanship were clearly Sorensen's, and he gave the book both the drama and flow that made for readability." But, through no fault of his own, Parmet could not examine Kennedy's unrecorded, live dictation to his secretaries, and some of the notes he dismissed as rough may have been the basis for the dictation of a more polished text. Sorensen's secretary, Gloria Sitrin, met Kennedy for the first time when she flew to Palm Beach to take his *Profiles* dictation in 1955, and she states that although Sorensen contributed a lot of research, much of the book is based on Kennedy's dictation to her.

Anyone who has ever participated in a literary collaboration knows the relationship can easily become contentious, with each party imagining his contribution to be more valuable. Kennedy's anger at the ghostwriting rumors surrounding *Profiles* seems, at this juncture, too visceral to be an act. Rightly or wrongly, he *believed* that he had written *Profiles in Courage*. A memorandum from Sorensen to Kennedy shows that Sorensen considered his contribution at least sufficient to warrant an acknowledgment, something Kennedy apparently had failed to do in an earlier draft. The note is typed on a slip of U.S. Senate paper and titled "Possible changes in Preface." It indicates that Sorensen believed Kennedy was being stingy with his acknowledgments. It read: "1. Final paragraph on Jackie? 2. Mention of Krock and Burns? 3. Mention of Prints and Photos Division people (should there not be any illustrations?) 4. TCS?"

Kennedy revised the preface accordingly, composing in his own handwriting an artfully vague sentence: "The greatest debt is owed to my research associate, Theodore C. Sorensen, for his invaluable assistance in the assembly and preparation of the material upon which this book is based." He had initially written, "Theodore C. Sorensen, who provided . . ." then scratched out *provided,* perhaps because it would have required a more specific accounting of Sorensen's contributions.

* * *

The *Evening Star* story of Kennedy writing a "draft" of his inaugural address in longhand on the *Caroline* on January 17 repeats a version of Sorensen's story: that at some point during this flight, Kennedy put the sheets of yellow paper into his pocket while remarking that the first handwritten draft of Roosevelt's 1933 inaugural address had recently brought $200,000 at auction. Kennedy clearly wanted to make this connection between himself and Roosevelt, emphasizing that just as FDR had sat in his study in Hyde Park six days before his inauguration, writing his inaugural address in longhand on a yellow legal pad, so, too, had he sat on the *Caroline,* writing his inaugural address in longhand on a yellow legal pad three days before his inauguration.

Samuel Rosenman, an adviser and speechwriter to Roosevelt, offered the following description of FDR writing his inaugural in his 1952 book, *Working with Roosevelt*.

> The speech was one of those very few of which the President wrote the first draft in his own hand. He wrote it on yellow legal cap paper, sitting by the fire at Hyde Park on the night of February 27. The original manuscript is now in the Roosevelt Library at Hyde Park, and has attached to it this typewritten note by the President: "March 25, 1933. This is the original manuscript of the inaugural address as written at Hyde Park on Monday, February 27, 1933. I started it about 9:00 p.m. and ended at 1:30 a.m. A number of minor changes were made in subsequent drafts but the final draft is substantially the same as the original."

James MacGregor Burns relied on Rosenman for his re-creation of this scene in his 1956 biography, *Roosevelt: The Lion and the Fox.* First he sets the scene, telling us the weather was cloudy and cold while "inside the warm living room a big, thick-shouldered man sat writing by the fire." He then writes:

> Franklin D. Roosevelt's pencil glided across the pages of yellow legal cap paper. "I am certain that my fellow Americans expect that on my induction into the Presidency I will address them with a candor and a decision which the present situation of our Nation impels." The fire hissed and crackled; the large hand with its thick fingers moved rapidly across the paper. "The people of the United States want more direct, vigorous action. They have made me the instrument, the temporary humble instrument"—he scratched out "humble"; it was no time for humility—"of their wishes."

Phrase after phrase followed in the President-elect's bold, pointed, slanting hand. Slowly the yellow sheets piled up. By 1:30 in the morning the inauguration speech was done.

Schlesinger condenses the Rosenman and Burns versions in his *The Crisis of the Old Order*: "Six days before [his inauguration], Roosevelt in his Hyde Park study, writing with pencil on a lined, legal-sized yellow pad, had made a draft of his inaugural address."

It is inconceivable Kennedy had not read one or all of these three passages. Roosevelt's presidency spanned the most formative years of Kennedy's life, from the time he was sixteen until he was twenty-eight. Roosevelt had appointed Kennedy's father to two positions in his administration, his eldest son had helped Kennedy win the West Virginia primary, his widow had worked still harder to deny him the nomination, and Kennedy had quoted or mentioned FDR in almost every campaign speech. Furthermore, James MacGregor Burns had written Kennedy's authorized campaign biography, Arthur Schlesinger was an important adviser, and their books about Roosevelt had been published within the last five years. Kennedy's offhand comments about Roosevelt's handwritten inaugural draft being valuable prove that he was familiar with the story. He obviously believed that Roosevelt had composed the first draft of his inaugural address in longhand at Hyde Park six days before delivering it, working on it alone for four and a half hours, editing as he wrote, scratching out a few words, and producing a text that closely resembled his final speech. What he could not have known, because it was not revealed until the Roosevelt speechwriter Raymond Moley published his memoirs in 1966, was that this story bore little resemblance to the truth.

Moley prefaced his account by explaining that his collaboration with Roosevelt on the first inaugural address had been no different than on other speeches. After a preliminary discussion of the subject matter and emphasis, Moley would prepare a draft that he and Roosevelt would review. Then he would rewrite it, Roosevelt would make some final suggestions, and the result would be "a joint composition."

The two men had first discussed the inaugural during a campaign stop in San Francisco six weeks before the election but did not mention it again until they were traveling by train from Warm Springs, Georgia, to Florida at the beginning of February 1933. Roosevelt was disembarking at Jacksonville. Moley was continuing to Palm Beach to stay with, of all people, Joseph Kennedy. Moley took rough notes of Roosevelt's suggestions, expanded on them at length in his notebook, and wrote a first draft in his office at Barnard College on February 12 and 13. Once his secretary had typed a second draft, he destroyed his original longhand version to prevent anyone reading it in advance. He edited this second draft and on February 27 brought a retyped version to Hyde Park.

After dinner he and Roosevelt retired to the library, where, for the first time, Roosevelt read his own inaugural speech. Then, Moley wrote, Roosevelt "said he had better write out the text himself," because if Louis Howe [a close Roosevelt adviser who was expected the next morning] failed to see a draft in his handwriting he would "have a fit." Moley took a legal-sized tablet out of his briefcase and settled into a couch in front of the fireplace, watching as Roosevelt copied the speech into his own handwriting, stopping sometimes to discuss a sentence or cross out a word or phrase. At 11:00 P.M. Moley took out his notebook and, he said, "aware of the historical importance of the occasion," wrote, "Before the fire at the library at Hyde Park. Alone w. F.D.R. He is writing inaugural on a card table." This is the only reference to the speech in Moley's notebook, and anyone reading it would assume Roosevelt was "writing" his own speech, instead of copying Moley's draft.

Moley wrote in his 1966 memoirs: "Feeling a keen sense that whatever might be the authorship, he [Roosevelt] and he alone would have to carry the responsibility of what was said on the fateful day of the inauguration, I rose after we had finished and, taking my copy from the table, tossed it in the still-glowing embers in the fireplace. I said as I did so, 'This is your speech now.'"

The following morning Moley made a few changes to Roosevelt's handwritten draft. This is the version that the FDR Library identifies as the first draft of Franklin Roosevelt's first inaugural address. Later that morning Louis Howe redictated the entire draft, adding a paragraph containing "the only thing we have to fear is fear itself." It was later leaked to the press that a passage from Thoreau had inspired this famous line. Moley, however, notes drily: "I am sure that neither Howe at that time nor Roosevelt was familiar with Thoreau's passage. I do clearly remember that the phrase appeared in a department store's newspaper advertisement some time earlier in February. I assume that Howe, an inveterate newspaper reader, saw it, too."

Moley omitted this material from an earlier book and included it in 1966 only after becoming upset by what he calls "the many distortions concerning the origins of this address." He blames them on the note Roosevelt attached to the draft on March 25, which Moley did not learn about until 1964. It was "misleading" at best, he says, and he holds it responsible for Rosenman's erroneous claim that Roosevelt's inaugural "was one of those very few of which the President wrote the first draft in his own hand."

The ironies, of course, are multiple.

While Roosevelt had no hand in his immortal "we have nothing to fear but fear, itself," Kennedy's "ask not," his bid to equal "nothing to fear," arose from his own experiences and earlier speeches.

Kennedy tried to reinforce his claim to authorship by imitating Roosevelt, never suspecting that Roosevelt had copied Moley's draft.

Both men wanted to be considered the true authors of words they sensed would become immortal: Roosevelt performed a charade to establish a claim to words that were not his own; Kennedy unwittingly copied this charade to establish a claim to words that were his.

The final irony came thirty-seven years later, when Kennedy's prediction that his handwritten pages might bring a fortune at auction came true, although not as he had imagined. On March 18, 1998, the sheet of paper on which he had written the date and "An inaugural is a beginning and end is ___" before crossing it out and tossing it away, sold at Guernsey's auction house in New York for $39,000, almost six times the preauction estimate. It was the only Kennedy item to exceed its estimate by such an impressive multiple. Accompanying the page was a photocopy of the nine pages Kennedy had written on the *Caroline*, identified as "Kennedy's first attempt to write the inaugural address."

Sometime during the flight back to Washington, Evelyn Lincoln had recovered this page from wherever he had thrown it and added it to her vast collection of Kennedyana. She willed the collection to her friend Robert White, another Kennedy collector, who put some of her treasure trove up for auction three years after her death. After the news broke, the chairman of the Kennedy Library Foundation described Lincoln as a "compulsive collector" whose obsession had deluded her into believing that President's Kennedy's personal effects and writings were hers to keep. John and Caroline Kennedy criticized Lincoln for breaching the public trust and that of their family by pilfering objects and documents belonging to their father and the federal government.

Their bitter words were the final fruit of a relationship that was far more complicated and spooky than most suspected at the time. Evelyn Lincoln's buckteeth, flamingo physique, and long frontier face pegged her as a timid and passionless factotum. In fact, she was the daughter of a Nebraska congressman and had been a year from earning a law degree from George Washington University when her husband took a teaching position in New

Mexico. On their return, she worked for a congressional committee before deciding that if she had to be a secretary instead of an attorney, she might as well be secretary to the president of the United States. She presciently settled on Kennedy, then only a congressman, after reading his speeches. Next she stalked him, volunteering in his congressional office during his 1952 senatorial campaign and persuading her husband to vacation in New England so they could visit Boston and check out his billboards. The day *before* the election she sent him an eerie telegram congratulating him on his victory. She was days from returning to law school when he offered her a job in his Senate office.

He trusted her with his most intimate secrets but called her "Miz Lincoln." A Kennedy appointee who saw them together for the first time the day before the inauguration noticed "a very close, almost wordless understanding." Her loyalty to him was so unquestioning that Kennedy was once heard to say, "If I said just now, 'Mrs. Lincoln, I have cut off Jackie's head, would you please send over a box?' She still would have replied, 'That's wonderful, Mr. President, I'll send it right away. Did you get your nap?'"—a remark that is cruel and unpleasant on several levels.

Is it possible Lincoln believed he had not sufficiently repaid her loyalty and devotion and considered the articles she kept as fair compensation? Their relationship certainly had its rocky moments. When she was hospitalized in 1955 to have a tumor removed from her back, Kennedy tried to persuade her husband to tell her she would have to relinquish the post of personal secretary. Selfishly, he worried that the woman who may have been his greatest loyalist might be too weak to work at the pace he demanded. He ultimately changed his mind and let her keep her job, but asking her husband to fire his own wife was hardly a Profile in Courage moment, and Lincoln learned about it.

Robert White, the inheritor of Lincoln's memorabilia, relented before the auction, turning over some of the documents to the Kennedy Library, and giving Caroline and John their father's handwritten notes from his 1951 trip to Asia and his mahogany wall clock. But he kept the watch Kennedy was wearing when he was assassinated, and defended Lincoln's collection by arguing it was composed of things Kennedy had given her or asked her to throw away, and that by preserving them she had performed a valuable service to history.

In a 1989 letter to White, Lincoln had identified most of the items as gifts or discards. In her book, *My Twelve Years with John F. Kennedy*, she described an occasion during the 1960 campaign when Kennedy lost his voice and scribbled notes on a pad. "After the Senator left that evening," she wrote, "I went through the wastepaper basket and picked out some notes he had written visitors that day." Beating the cleaning staff to Kennedy's wastebasket may explain how she acquired that $39,000 phrase from his inaugural address, his Ace pocket comb ($1,265), signed telephone credit card ($12,650), unsigned membership card to the American Irish Historical Society ($1,035), a telegram from Lyndon Johnson congratulating him on winning the nomination, his wife's 1960 will, and perhaps even his mother's bathing suit. But how on earth had she come by his college sweater, the flags that flew from the bumpers of his limousine in Dallas, the christening ring he wore as an infant, and a 1943 letter he wrote home from the Pacific declaring that "all war is stupid"?

If Lincoln could have saved the sheets of paper containing the changes he made to his inaugural address during that week in Palm Beach, she most certainly would have. Perhaps she found it too awkward to sift through his bedroom wastebasket, or perhaps Kennedy, knowing her mania, and determined to control which of his handwritten notes survived, destroyed these pages on purpose—much like Raymond Moley throwing his draft into the fire—leaving behind only these nine pages, dated and in his handwriting, for the High Court of History.

During the final hours of the flight to Washington, Kennedy and Sorensen sat together making additional changes—"an occasional slight twitch here and there,"—to the text that Lincoln had typed before leaving Palm Beach. Since this draft has survived in Kennedy's Presidential Office Files, we know what these "twitches" were. All were made in Sorensen's handwriting, and the majority are in the first three paragraphs of the speech, the ones Kennedy told Sidey were proving so difficult to get right.

Kennedy, Sorensen, or both together changed the opening sentence from "We celebrate today not a victory of party but a convention of freedom" to "We observe today not a victory of party but a celebration of freedom," presumably because the word *convention* evoked political conventions and struck the kind of partisan note Kennedy wished to avoid.

The second paragraph had opened, "The world is very different now, empowered as it is to banish all forms of human poverty and all forms of human life." The revision was smoother: "The world is very different now. For man holds in his mortal hands the power to abolish all forms of human poverty and to abolish all forms of human life." Kennedy and Sorensen also substituted *beliefs* for *concepts* at the end of this paragraph, so that "And yet the same revolutionary concepts for which those forebears fought," became

"And yet the same revolutionary beliefs for which our forbears fought." *Concepts* sounded too theoretical. *Beliefs* were worth fighting for.

In the third paragraph, they deleted the unnecessary "of liberty" from "the torch of liberty has been passed to a new generation of Americans."

Throughout the draft they removed harsh and confrontational words. They changed "we dare not meet a powerful *foe* at odds and split asunder" at the top of page two to "For we dare not meet a powerful *challenge* at odds and split asunder." In the next paragraph, they changed remarks directed at the independent states of Africa and Asia from "We shall not always expect to find *you on our side*" to "We shall not always expect to find *them supporting our every view.*"

Evelyn Lincoln had made a carbon copy of this draft, and it survives in Ted Sorensen's White House files. "COPY" is printed in red block capitals at the top of every page. Before landing in Washington, Sorensen wrote the changes that he and Kennedy had made to the original onto this COPY. If one lays this original and the COPY side by side, it becomes apparent from the discrepancies in his handwriting that Sorensen had copied the edits from the original onto the COPY.

When the *Caroline* landed, Kennedy took the original with him while Sorensen kept the COPY. Before they met again, twenty-four hours later, each would make more changes to his respective copy of the address. Then they would combine them into a final Reading Copy that would turn out to be anything but final.

Part Two

THE MUSIC

WASHINGTON, D.C.
JANUARY 17 TO JANUARY 21, 1961

What was spoken
was spoken well.
What was unspoken
needed to be unspoken.
It was none of our business if his back hurt.

MOLLY KAZAN
from a poem written after John F. Kennedy's assassination

6

Washington and New York

JANUARY 17

⚜

After JFK's assassination, Jackie Kennedy told Bobby Kennedy, "I've got to talk to somebody. I've got to see somebody. I want to say this one thing." She invited the journalist Theodore White to Hyannisport and, during the emotional interview given a week after Dallas, compared the Kennedy White House to King Arthur's mythical court at Camelot. She began by explaining that sometimes when she and Jack were in bed in the White House, he would ask her to play the Broadway musical *Camelot* on their old Victrola. He liked the last song the best, the one ending, "Don't let it be forgot, that once there was a spot, for one brief shining moment that was known as Camelot." She told White the line had become "almost an obsession" with her, and the one thing she wanted him to write was this: "There'll never be that Camelot again."

White believed that comparing the Kennedy presidency to Camelot was a misreading of history, but included it in his article anyway because, he said later, he had been bewitched by Jackie's ability to frame the tragedy in such human and romantic terms. He was still under her spell fifteen years later when he wrote in his memoirs that her good-bye to Camelot had also been a "farewell to an America never to be recaptured," and that after Dallas, Americans had "passed through an invisible membrane in time which divided one era from another."

We like to think that any tragedy large enough to scar the national memory and peel away a layer of America's onionlike innocence must also be a historical turning point. Pearl Harbor and September 11 were such moments, but Kennedy's assassination, like FDR's sudden death, was more of a trauma than a turning point. In fact, it was the inauguration of John F. Kennedy, and not his death, that closed one era and launched the next; and it was on January 20, 1961, not November 22, 1963, that Americans stepped through an invisible membrane in time.

On the 1950s side of that membrane were filing clerks, passenger trains, propeller planes, Jim Crow laws, post-Sputnik pessimism, *Life, Look,* and the *Saturday Evening Post,* and an unbroken succession of Protestant presidents. After Kennedy's inauguration came computers, jet planes, freedom riders, moon-shot optimism, the television age, and an Irish Catholic president. In 1957, Eisenhower's inauguration committee had held the last traditional "Minorities Dinner," a patronizing event whose menu listed gefilte fish, minestrone soup, and Greek salad. In 1961, an Irish Catholic, one of the minorities, took the oath of office, making it easier for Irish-Americans, African-Americans, Jews, gays, women, Hispanics, and others to assume prominent positions in previously off-limits professions. At Roosevelt's 1933 inauguration, African-Americans had danced at a "Colored People's Ball," and at the Truman and Eisenhower inaugurations blacks were tokens. In 1961, five hundred African-Americans served on inaugural committees, and five thousand attended an inauguration that *Ebony* praised for having "more Negro participation than any other in history." At his inauguration eve gala, Kennedy introduced his African-American aide, Louis Martin, as a member of his "political family," and at his inaugural ball, he danced with African-American women.

The Kennedy inauguration also marked a change in Americans' attitude toward their government. Before 1961, many had considered the federal government remote and menacing. Kennedy, however, suggested it could be benevolent, even altruistic, and people of accomplishment in education, business, and the arts responded by seeking positions in his administration. His friend Charlie Bartlett wrote in his newspaper column about executives eager to leave the private sector to launch "a new era in the national life," and Eisenhower, who had experienced difficulty finding qualified appointees for second-tier government jobs, was heard to remark that he wished he could have persuaded men of the same caliber to work for him.

In the 1950s, many of the intellectuals leaving their universities to join the administration had been "eggheads" or "pinkos," faintly ridiculous or faintly un-American, and in 1952 the State Department refused to issue a passport to the Nobel Prize–winning scientist Linus Pauling because his anticommunist statements were insufficiently fervent. Kennedy appointed McGeorge Bundy, John Kenneth Galbraith, Walt Rostow, Henry Kissinger, and Arthur Schlesinger to influential positions in his administration, and academics suddenly became the wise men of government, mandarins, and eventually the most cold-blooded of cold warriors.

The position of artists in American life changed, too, with Kennedy's inauguration. In 1957, the Eisenhower inaugural committee had forbidden the National Symphony Orchestra to play a composition by the Pulitzer Prize–winning composer Aaron Copland at the Inaugural Concert because the House Un-American Activities Committee had mistakenly listed Copland as a communist sympathizer. On January 14, 1961, Pauling and Copland were among 168 prominent intellectuals who received telegrams from President-elect and Mrs. Kennedy informing them, "During our forthcoming administration we hope to seek a productive relationship with our writers, artists, composers, philosophers, scientists and heads of cultural institutions," and inviting them to attend the inauguration as honored guests.

Kennedy's inauguration would be the first to be seen as well as heard by a large international audience. Until the Coolidge inauguration was broadcast on radio, the only Americans who heard an inaugural address were those standing within earshot of the president. (Even that was no guarantee, and in 1917 a gale-force wind made Woodrow Wilson's inaugural unintelligible to everyone except his wife and Chief Justice Taft.) Herbert Hoover's inaugural was the first to be recorded on a newsreel with sound, and Harry Truman's the first to be televised. Ten million Americans, more than had witnessed all previous inaugurations combined, watched his ceremony. The Kennedy inauguration would be the first one broadcast live internationally by radio. Simultaneous translations would make his inaugural accessible to more foreigners than any other speech in U.S. history, and a trans-Atlantic cable would enable British viewers to watch the ceremony ninety-nine minutes later, the shortest time a European audience had ever waited to see a North American event. Meanwhile, live dawn-to-dusk television coverage would permit sixty million Americans to see their great national pageant in its entirety for the first time.

The 1961 inauguration would also prove to be a landmark in the rapidly shifting fortunes of television and the written word. Kennedy was in competition with Harding for the title of most physically attractive president of the century, and aside from Woodrow Wilson, he was the most literate. He was also the first presidential candidate to mount both a literary *and* a television campaign for the office, the only one comfortable in both media, and the perfect man for a time when Americans were teetering on a balance point between image and word.

In the late 1950s, Kennedy and Sorensen had churned out articles under his byline for periodicals ranging from *Life, Look,* and the *Saturday Evening Post* to *Foreign Affairs* and *Girls Scouts* magazine. His father considered the picture weeklies so important he had persuaded him to delay announcing his engagement to Jackie until the *Saturday Evening Post* could publish an article naming him the Senate's "Gay Young Bachelor." Kennedy took his literary campaign so seriously that in addition to cooperating with the de rigueur campaign biography, he published *The Strategy of Peace,* described on its front cover as "the foreign policy speeches and statements on defense, peace, national security and related domestic issues of a leading Presidential candidate."

During the primaries, Kennedy became increasingly aware of the influence and requirements of television. He noticed that even the poorest West Virginia shacks had aerials, and was impressed by a survey concluding that twice as many Americans relied on television as on printed material for information about the campaign. He bought broadcast time in individual states for speeches targeted to local concerns, taped infomercials on regional issues, and delivered major speeches before large and sympathetic live audiences, rather than in sterile television studios. His Harvard roommate Blair Clark, an executive at CBS, believed he had a "natural instinct" for television and "never forgot that he was an actor in a public drama." A classic instance of his instinct came during his West Virginia primary campaign, when he stared straight into the camera and told viewers that when a man takes the presidential oath, "he puts one hand on the Bible and raises the other hand to God. . . . And if he breaks his oath, he is not only committing a crime against the Constitution . . . he is committing a sin against God." At this point, he raised his hand from an imaginary Bible and repeated in a soft voice, "a sin against God," demonstrating an understanding for the kind of demeanor and gestures that worked on television.

Before the first debate against Nixon, Kennedy's brother-in-law, the actor Peter Lawford, had recommended that he look directly into the camera, as if it were an old friend sitting across the dinner table. At the studio, the media consultant J. Leonard Reinsch had him change from an off-white into a blue pastel shirt. Before the second debate, Reinsch browbeat a janitor into turning up the thermostat so that Nixon, who had perspired heavily during the first encounter, would have to mop his brow again. A poll conducted for CBS reported that four million voters made their choice for president after the four debates, and that Kennedy was the choice of 78 percent. During the transition Kennedy told the newsman Howard K. Smith he had won the election on the night of the first televised debate, and consulted Blair Clark on how he could best use television during his inauguration and presidency.

The inauguration would be the last moment of rough parity between the print media and television—between word and image. Five days later, Kennedy would conduct the first live televised press conference, and Russell Baker reported in the *New York Times*, "It [television] has a new star with tremendous national appeal and the skill of a consummate showman, the President of the United States." Afterward, the balance was tipped forever in favor of the visual. In March 1961, Kennedy gave a press conference while standing before huge maps of Laos that dramatically illustrated the advance of Communist forces. The following summer, Sorensen wrote a memorandum complimenting Kennedy on his televised speech about Berlin. He recommended that in future the cameras shoot more close-ups, "which give a close personal feeling," and not show the president's hands holding the manuscript of a speech. To prevent viewers from seeing Kennedy perspire and wipe his brow, Sorensen recommended limiting the number of people in the room and installing a fan or air conditioner underneath his desk.

The inauguration was also a turning point for Washington, D.C., when it became the imperial capital of an imperial presidency. The playwright Arthur Miller, who attended the Kennedy inauguration, believes "something new and rather imperial had entered our public business" on January 20, 1961. Ted Sorensen later decided that the 1961 inauguration launched an era of imperial presidencies, and came to blame the Watergate scandal on "Camelot-like glorifications of the Presidency." He mused that the Kennedy administration, "with its high ideals and spirited approach, unintentionally raised public expectations of the Presidency to a level that facilitated subsequent attempts to monopolize power in the White House, and no single event did more to promulgate these high ideals than the inauguration."

On January 10, Kennedy had left behind a sleepy little backwater whose principal celebrities were politicians and journalists. The next day, the Presidential Committee on Information Abroad issued a statement conceding that "our National Capital in the eyes of many is regarded, from a cultural standpoint, as a provincial town." On January 17, he returned to all-day traffic jams, chartered trains pulling into Union Station by the hour, oversold hotels, and a dawn-to-midnight schedule of parties jammed with tycoons, movie stars, academic stars, and the most talented writers, artists, and musicians in the country—an elite of poetry and power. Most would depart on January 21, but a few would stay, and many would return.

The Inaugural Committee had mailed out 40,000 engraved invitations in the mistaken belief that most of their recipients would consider them pleasant souvenirs. But a transition that had dazzled even the most cynical journalists had worked its magic on the rest of the nation, and tens of thousands of ward heelers and campaign volunteers descended on Washington, invitations in hand, demanding tickets to the ceremony, parade, and an inaugural ball. On January 17, the committee had to add a fourth ball at the Statler Hilton, then a fifth at the Shoreham. Carpenters built another 3,700 seats along Pennsylvania Avenue, and the committee boasted that whereas 750,000 spectators had seen Eisenhower's second parade, a million would turn out for Kennedy. The committee had allocated 18,000 seats and 3,000 preferred standee locations in the Capitol Plaza, and was advising the additional 20,000 people expected to witness the inauguration ceremony to arrive early for a view of the presidential platform. The only store in Washington renting fur coats warned that its stock of mink stoles had become "dangerously low," and a convoy of trucks arrived from Chicago on January 17 with new supplies of top hats, dinner jackets, morning coats, and ruffled shirts.

Before Tom Wolfe sent up the fads and conceits of the 1960s, he was Thomas Wolfe of the *Washington Post*, whose articles about the 1961 inauguration hint at the prose to come. He described Washington on the eve as "gilt-edged, mink-lined, silk-hatted, 100-proof," a city where you could leap from a hotel window "and hit nothing but minks and bouffant hairdos." Celebrities met at parties "like colliding comets," and for the first time ever, the city was "cornering the glamour market." And all this glamour could only make the already glamorous John F. Kennedy and his inauguration more glamorous still.

By January 17 the people gathering in Washington for the inauguration had come to resemble an audience awaiting the entrance of a leading man, restless and expectant, imagining him standing in the wings, preparing to take the stage and bring the play to life. The star, meanwhile, sensing their anticipation and adulation, hesitated, postponing the moment when he would surrender himself to his admirers.

After the four-hour flight from Palm Beach during which Kennedy and Sorensen had edited the inaugural address, the *Caroline* landed at National Airport at 6:00 P.M. Kennedy was driven to his home in Georgetown, where he met with his future budget director, David Bell. He then changed into black tie for a dinner dance at the home of his sister and brother-in-law Jean and Stephen Smith. They had invited 130 guests, a mixture of close friends, family, and entertainers performing at the Democratic fund-raising gala at the Washington National Guard Armory on January 19. Of all the parties Kennedy had agreed to attend during the next three days, the Smiths' promised to be one of the most enjoyable, yet he dined alone at home first and arrived more than an hour late. The most likely explanation is that he wanted to watch Eisenhower deliver his televised farewell address, a speech some would come to praise for its candor and prescience, and judge to be superior to Kennedy's inaugural.

Eisenhower's speech was both a stinging reply to Kennedy's campaign rhetoric and an advance rebuttal of his inaugural address. Nothing during the campaign had angered Eisenhower more than Kennedy's accusation that his administration had presided over a decline in American prestige and military power. Kennedy had warned of a dangerous and, as it turned out, imaginary missile gap with the Soviet Union, and would declare in his inaugural speech that "we dare not tempt them with weakness. For only when our arms are sufficient beyond doubt can we be certain beyond doubt that they will never be employed." Eisenhower anticipated this by warning in his farewell address of the emergence of "a permanent armaments industry of vast proportions" and "the acquisition of unwarranted influence, whether sought or unsought by the military-industrial complex," adding that this complex might "endanger our liberties or democratic processes."

Kennedy's "ask not" would call for a relationship of sacrifice and commitment between Americans and their government. Eisenhower was suspicious of such a sweeping commitment. In an earlier speech to the National Rural Co-Operative Association he had said, "Government at all levels has certain obligations to you and me." Now, in his farewell address, he advocated "balance between our essential requirements as a nation and the duties imposed by the nation upon the individual." After Eisenhower finished, Edward R. Murrow commented, "The Eisenhower concern, as I read it, was a fear that we may lose our liberties while preparing to defend them," a notion utterly at odds with the speech Kennedy was planning to deliver in three days.

The Washington-Hollywood coupling that distinguished the 1961 inauguration was dismissed by many as a transitory phenomenon, unique to the starstruck Kennedys and the Kennedy-struck stars. Few suspected it would become a permanent feature of America's political and entertainment landscape, or that the January 17 party at Jean and Stephen Smith's home in Georgetown would be a seminal event.

The venerable *Evening Star* society reporter Betty Beale called the Smith party "a combination of the Lincoln Memorial and Grauman's Chinese Theater." The gossip columnist Maxine Cheshire believed it had "the glamour of a Hollywood premiere." Outside the Smiths' home there were certainly all the trappings of a premiere: blinding television lights and exploding flashbulbs, processions of limousines, a police cordon, and delirious fans spilling into the street, slowing traffic, and waving autograph books. They applauded as celebrities climbed from Cadillacs, and screamed "Bobby Kennedy!" as loudly as "Tony Curtis!" These were not the excited bobby-soxers who had turned out for Kennedy's campaign, but his Georgetown neighbors, sophisticates cheering Janet Leigh, Gene Kelly, Frank Sinatra, and Milton Berle. Kennedy's friend Paul Fay was starstruck, dazzled by his first taste of what he termed "the unbelievable excitement that John Kennedy gave to the Presidency."

The de facto guest of honor was Frank Sinatra, who was producing the inauguration eve gala. As he escorted Nat King Cole's wife to the door, a reporter asked if she was his date. "Where do you come from?" Sinatra snapped. "Bulgaria?" Reporters described Sinatra as "unsmiling" and providing "a moment of quick drama." But the Kennedy-Sinatra drama would prove to be anything *but* quick, and this incident, more harbinger than aberration, foreshadowed some of the perils of the Washington-Hollywood alliance, and of a Sinatra-Kennedy melodrama of several acts that would reach one of its several climaxes a year later when Sinatra, enraged, inebriated, and screaming vulgarities, took a sledgehammer to the concrete helipad he had built for the presidential helicopter at his Palm Springs estate, a pleasure dome of booze and broads he had imagined becoming the West Coast White House.

Kennedy arrived at the Smith party with Washington's version of a Hollywood entourage, a wedge of Secret Service agents. A reporter described him as "relaxed, tanned, and healthy," although *tanned* was probably the only accurate adjective. His health was abysmal, and he seldom felt relaxed at large gatherings. The Cleveland department store heiress Kay Halle, a Washington insider who served on his Inaugural Committee and who was an astute observer of accomplished men (having received sixty-four proposals of marriage by her count, including inquiries from Averell Harriman and Randolph Churchill), once noted that during the fourteen years Kennedy lived in Washington before becoming president he almost never attended large parties and was only occasionally seen at intimate ones. (At these, he had the infuriating habit of cornering the most distinguished guest and picking his brains.) She considered him reserved but not shy, and thought he avoided parties because he had a sense of his own destiny, and every moment seemed keenly important to him.

According to Fay, Kennedy walked into the Smiths' living room flashing his handsome smile, "but also displaying that slight uneasiness he felt at a social gathering . . . [one] based on the fear that he might be trapped by people he didn't especially want to talk to." The party was also making other guests anxious and uneasy. Hollywood and Washington were probing each other, unsure of the protocol. Charlie Bartlett, the journalist who had introduced Jack and Jackie, sensed that Jimmy Durante and other entertainers disliked Washington and felt uncomfortable, "slightly out of place."

The Kennedy side also seemed uncertain how to behave. One of Kennedy's sisters startled her table by standing up in the middle of dinner and announcing, "I've got to go peeps." After Jimmy Durante and Nat King Cole sang a polished duet, Kennedy whispered to Fay, "I think the crowd is ready for a little '*Hooray for Hollywood*'." Fay had sung this number in navy amateur shows, shouting out the words in his gravelly voice. Ever since, Kennedy had been demanding that he perform it at unlikely occasions. Recalling the stunned faces greeting his most recent rendition, on New Year's Eve at the Everglades Club in Palm Beach, Fay refused to play the fool again. To please his brother, Ted Kennedy danced a Charleston and sang "Won't You Come Home Bill Bailey," producing looks of amazement on the faces of the Hollywood guests.

Kennedy left the party at 10:15 to fly to New York. On the way to National Airport he stopped at a buffet dinner being given in his honor at the Statler Hilton by the Los Angeles financier Bart Lytton. His appearance turned the six hundred guests into an unruly mob. Women shrieked that they had seen him, spoken to him, touched him. A photograph shows him surrounded by police, flashing a nervous smile as disembodied hands reach from the crowd. "President-Elect Braves Crush of Guests," said a headline. The accompanying article claimed that this private man, who disliked even his close friends touching or crowding him, and who had appeared uneasy at a party one-sixth this size, had greeted this pawing with "good-natured reserve." A truer indication of his state of mind may be that he stayed only twelve minutes.

Pierre Salinger and Evelyn Lincoln accompanied him to New York and stayed on lower floors of the Carlyle Hotel. Their memoirs are silent about how he spent this night. We know he brought his draft speech to New York, and that sometime during the next fifteen hours he made some handwritten notations on it. He could have started editing it when he arrived at the Carlyle, but he probably entertained "Barbara Lansing," the woman he had flown in from Paris and installed on the twenty-first floor.

Kennedy's thirty-fourth-floor penthouse reflected his family's wealth more than any of his other homes. But the crowds gathering around Madison Avenue and Seventy-sixth Street whenever he was in residence saw only another East Side skyscraper, not the seven-room duplex with its solarium, French antiques, twin terraces, winding staircase, and sweeping skyline views, not the Pissarro, Mary Cassatt, and Gilbert Stuart oils on loan from Madison Avenue galleries that hung on its walls, not the enormous painting by the black impressionist Romare Bearden that dominated the living room and that the civil rights leader Roy Wilkins considered "an encouraging sign."

The views from the penthouse were so dramatic it would have been almost impossible not to pause and admire them. So it is likely that sometime that evening, either alone or with "Lansing" at his side, Kennedy stood in his solarium, surrounded by glass and suspended over the lights of the city, or gazed out of his living room picture window, the lamps behind him dim, the traffic noise muffled, the city sparkling. And if he did, then this sweet moment, coming three days before his inauguration, with Manhattan at his feet, must have been one of the most intoxicating of his life.

7

New York and Washington

JANUARY 18

⚜

Pierre Salinger told reporters that Kennedy had come to New York to confer with Governor Luis Muñoz of Puerto Rico and Hugh Gaitskell, the leader of the British Labor Party. But these were relatively minor engagements for a man who would become president of the United States in two days. The real reason for the trip was that after spending a week polishing his address, Kennedy wanted to polish his appearance.

In *Profiles in Courage* he had written that Daniel Webster's "striking appearance" constituted "half the secret" of his oratorical power, convincing "all who looked upon his face that he was one born to rule men." He described Webster as having a "slender frame," a "theatrical but formidable presence," an "extraordinary head," "tanned complexion," and "crag-like face," and noted that one contemporary had called him a living lie, "because no man on earth could be so great as he looked."

Kennedy had emulated Webster's oratorical skills by dictating his inaugural; now he was out to match his appearance. Forty-three years old is not so young that a politician whose appeal owes something to his beauty and youth can afford to ignore his looks. Kennedy had Webster's "tanned complexion," but his slender frame had filled out during the transition, and there was a serious edge to his jokes about his "fat face." The last time Americans had seen him up close was during the debates, when he had weighed twenty pounds less. Not only did the extra weight conceal the sharp cheekbones he considered among his best features, it was at odds with the lean New Frontier image he wanted to project, and an inaugural summoning Americans to struggle and sacrifice.

Kennedy's vanity was no casual vice. Faced with choosing an official portrait for the inaugural program, he had recalled liking an Alfred Eisenstadt photograph in *Life*. But rather than using that particular shot, he examined the contact sheets of the session, searching for an even more flattering one. Several years before, he had spent a day being photographed from every angle by the same fashion photographer who had done the actress Grace Kelly. He had pored over those contact sheets, too, apparently deciding that he looked best staring sideways into the middle distance, a pose that came to be featured in his official campaign photographs.

The conundrum of Kennedy's vanity was that the youthful appearance so appealing to some voters persuaded others that he was too young to be president. In 1960, the average age of the men leading the United States, Britain, France, Germany, the Soviet Union, Nationalist China, and Communist China was seventy-two, older than at any time in history. Being twenty-nine years under the average made Kennedy seem more vigorous, but also more inexperienced. To counter this he pursued a strategy of presenting a youthful appearance but sounding wise, looking young on the screen but sounding old on the page.

Kennedy's first appointment on Wednesday, January 18, was a 9:00 A.M. telephone conference with his New York internist, Dr. Eugene Cohen. After hanging up, he told Lincoln that Cohen believed his added weight was only temporary, resulting from trading the irregular and infrequent meals of the campaign for a more sedentary transition. "I'll have my usual breakfast," he announced, the implication being that had Cohen's diagnosis been any different, he would have demanded a grapefruit. Several minutes later, he was tucking into his usual calorie-rich morning meal, and any thoughts of starving a few pounds off his face during the next forty-eight hours had been abandoned.

His next engagement was a 10:00 conference with Eddie Adams, an Associated Press photographer who had covered his campaign and seven years later would take the shattering photograph of the execution of a Vietcong prisoner by a South Vietnamese general that would galvanize American opposition to that war. Adams cannot remember if he photographed Kennedy that morning, but since their meeting lasted only fifteen minutes and they were not personal friends, they probably discussed how Kennedy would look in photographs of the inauguration.

Kennedy spent 10:15 to 11:00 A.M. with two CBS executives, his Harvard roommate, Blair Clark, and Fred Friendly, who would soon become the president of CBS News. There is no record of that meeting, but it is a safe assumption that, on the eve of delivering a speech to the largest television audience in history, Kennedy might have wanted to discuss how television, and CBS in particular, would cover it. It is possible he showed his copy of the address to Clark and Friendly, drawing their attention to "ask not" and other key passages so that the CBS cameras would be trained on him, rather than on the crowd or other dignitaries at the Capitol, when he delivered them, which is precisely what happened two days later.

Clark and Friendly had also conferred with Kennedy at the Carlyle on December 1, and after that meeting Clark had reported that they had discussed "a whole new concept" of television and the presidency. Kennedy recounted the details to Ben Bradlee and asked him to send a summary to Ted Sorensen. In his letter to Sorensen, Bradlee wrote: "Basically, Clark and Friendly's premise is that there has never been a successful speech delivered on television. . . . Sooner or later, they contend, a television speech comes down to a man reading. This is particularly true of White House television, where attempts to solve the problem have been limited to using two flags instead of one for background, removing glasses twice instead of once, etc. The chief cause of this stereotype, Clark and Friendly believed, was that TV speeches had heretofore been staged by TV executives, or TV production types, rather than creative TV talent."

Bradlee concluded by saying that Kennedy had expressed "great interest" in their "bold ideas" for correcting this problem. Clark and Friendly are dead, and Bradlee cannot recall the specifics of these ideas, but they probably entailed eye-catching backdrops, multiple camera angles, sound bites, and other elements of the modern photo opportunity. Bradlee's letter suggests it was no lucky accident that the Kennedy inaugural would be the first "successful speech" delivered on television by an American president, and that some of the striking visual images of that day, such as Kennedy facing the audience on a bitterly cold day without a topcoat, were not entirely accidental.

Every vain person has his favorite feature. For Kennedy, it was his thick chestnut-brown hair. Before her marriage, Jackie had told her cousin John Davis that her husband was so vain about his hair that he had a hairdresser come in almost daily to keep it looking "bushy and fluffy." Kennedy kept a hairbrush in his desk drawer and was so worried a photographer might catch him grooming himself that while traveling by motorcade he was careful to pull out his comb only while traveling through an underpass or tunnel. When the UPI photographer Stanley Tretick threatened to wire them with flashbulbs, Kennedy had replied, "I hope they're all misfires."

Kennedy hated hats because they hid his hair, but he could not avoid wearing one at his inauguration. Jackie thought he looked terrible in ordinary ones but handsome in his naval officer's cap and in a top hat. So at her suggestion, or to draw a contrast with Eisenhower, who had worn a pedestrian homburg at his swearing-in, Kennedy announced that men at his inauguration would wear silk top hats.

At noon on January 18, John Garside of the Cavanaugh Hat Company brought a selection of top hats to the Carlyle. Kennedy spent fifteen minutes trying them on and chose two. He must have been pleased to read in the *Washington Post* that as Garside left, he praised him for having "an ideal head" for a hat, a nearly perfect oval—but not pleased enough to wear Garside's hat any more than necessary at his inauguration.

The tailor Samuel Harris spent the next fifteen minutes with Kennedy, taking measurements for two new business suits and making final adjustments to the dark gray cutaway coat, pearl gray vest, and striped trousers he would wear for the ceremony. Harris told reporters that a second fitting had been necessary because his client had "put on a little weight." When asked if the new suits would be two-button, already a Kennedy trademark, he replied, "Certainly, two button. We don't follow Ivy League or beatniks. We make gentlemen's clothes."

Before marrying Jackie, Kennedy had been a sloppy dresser who favored baggy suits, clashing shirts and ties, and ratty tennis shoes. She persuaded him to wear the elegant and understated clothes that became his trademark. He soon became conscious of not only his appearance but that of those around him, scolding his friend Bill Walton for wearing brown shoes in the evening, and telling Paul Fay his button-down collar was "Too Ivy League" and offering to order some custom-made ones with straight collars from his New York shirtmaker.

Kennedy lunched on January 18 with Hugh Gaitskell and the former diplomat and New York governor Averell Harriman at Harriman's East Side townhouse. Afterward, he had his teeth cleaned and polished by his New York dentist. His tan would make his teeth appear whiter on television, and his white teeth, in turn, would make his tan appear even darker. He was then driven to LaGuardia Airport to catch a scheduled flight to Washington. A Secret Service agent noticed his overcoat lying on a chair in the Carlyle penthouse and had the police rush it to the airport in a squad car. An airport worker dashed onto the tarmac as the plane was leaving the gate, waving over his head like a pennant the same coat Kennedy would leave draped over his chair when he rose to deliver his inaugural.

The next day, the *New York Daily News* ran a photograph showing him sitting by the window on this flight, reading some papers. The caption said, "JFK reads typed transcript of speech on the plane to DC on 1/18." Kennedy may have marked up his copy of the draft during this flight. But we know that sometime between arriving in Washington, D.C., from Florida at 6:00 P.M. on January 17, and returning to the capital from New York on the afternoon of January 18, he edited the second-to-last paragraph, turning "My fellow citizens of the world: ask not what America will do for you[,] but what you can do for freedom" into "My fellow citizens of the world: ask not what America will do for you, but what together we can do for the freedom of man," making the enterprise seem more a cooperative venture than a challenge. On the line promising "those peoples in the huts and villages of half the globe" that the United States would help them help themselves "not because our enemies are doing it," he wrote *others* above *our enemies,* and *may* above *are doing it.* In the final draft, *the communists* replaced *others.* Still, Kennedy's reluctance to describe the Soviets as "enemies," like his elimination of the word *foe,* is more evidence that he wanted his speech to be conciliatory.

While Kennedy was in New York, Sorensen was showing his COPY (that is, his carbon copy of the January 17 draft) to a carefully chosen circle of men in Washington. On January 18 he lunched with the influential *New York Herald Tribune* columnist Walter Lippmann. Inviting Lippmann to critique the address was courageous and shrewd. He had written the memorandum that led to Woodrow Wilson's "Fourteen Points," and helped with the acceptance speech that Al Smith, the first Catholic presidential nominee, had delivered at the 1928 Democratic convention. He was also known to be a ferocious line editor who demanded lucid and concise prose.

Although Lippmann and Joe Kennedy had been professional friends of long standing, Lippmann had been lukewarm to JFK's presidential candidacy. By the time of the Democratic convention he was beginning to change his mind and writing that Kennedy had outgrown his youthful mistakes. During the campaign Lippmann became a fervent partisan, calling Kennedy "a natural leader, organizer and ruler of men." Kennedy repaid Lippmann's compliment by adding him to his roster of unofficial advisers and seeking his advice on cabinet appointments. On January 18, the same day that Lippmann met with Sorensen, he had declared in his column, "Without pretending that everything is perfect, that every selection is ideal, and that everything is sure to be right, there is, I am convinced, solid ground for confidence in the Administration which Mr. Kennedy has organized."

The draft Sorensen showed Lippmann was so polished he could only suggest replacing *enemy* with *adversary* in the sentence opening, "Finally, to those nations who would make themselves our enemy . . ." As Sorensen made this change to his COPY, he told himself Kennedy would approve of eliminating the more confrontational *enemy.*

After the inauguration, Lippmann praised the address in his column as a "remarkably successful piece of self-expression." He called it "brief," "deliberate," "decisive," "efficient," and "ardent." He concluded that it "exemplified the qualities which the world has come to expect of the President," but omitted mention of his own contribution. According to his biographer, Ronald Steele, "A few years later [during the Vietnam War] he would deplore the speech—with its exhortation to ask, 'what you can do for your country'—as jingoist rhetoric." Lippmann never admitted to passing up an opportunity to soften this rhetoric, perhaps because when he read it on January 18, it struck him not as an exercise in jingoism but as an invitation to arms control and cooperation, a call to "begin anew" and "explore what problems unite us instead of belaboring the problems which divide us."

Sorensen spent the remainder of the afternoon in Kennedy's Senate offices, an eight-room suite where staff members were struggling to unwrap and acknowledge a deluge of letters, packages, and dozens of stuffed donkeys, gifts from the public for John Kennedy Jr. Sorensen showed his COPY to Dean Rusk, John Kenneth Galbraith, and JFK's brother-in-law Sargent Shriver, who in turn showed it to Harris Wofford, a former campaign aide working with Shriver on the transition. None could resist trying to put their stamp on it.

Rusk, who would become secretary of state in two days, toned down Kennedy's brusque challenge to citizens of other nations to "ask what you can do for freedom," to "what together we can do for freedom," crossing out the *you* in Sorensen's draft and writing *together we* underneath. Kennedy had independently reached the same conclusion while in New York, marking up his copy so it read, "what together we can do for the freedom of man."

Galbraith had devoted more time to the inaugural than anyone but Sorensen and Kennedy. He had written a first draft, discussed it with Kennedy in Palm Beach on December 23, and submitted a second one to

Kennedy and Sorensen on January 9. Sorensen now asked him to critique the COPY. In a diary entry made four days later Galbraith could not conceal his disappointment that the speech Sorensen showed him on January 18 bore so little resemblance to either of his drafts. It must have been discouraging for someone who lavished attention on every word he wrote for Kennedy to discover the latter had discarded most of his carefully considered sentences. The problem was that Galbraith had written an essay, whereas Kennedy wanted a speech. Galbraith had written for a nation of readers; Kennedy had dictated for a nation of readers, listeners, and viewers—for the passing literate age, and the emerging visual one.

Galbraith put on a brave face, recording in his diary that the draft he read in Sorensen's office was "short, economical of words and said something." It was "less daring" than his but "probably a lot wiser." He was pleased that some of the language and tone from his draft had survived in passages about aid to poor countries, and that Kennedy had taken one line almost verbatim from his second draft, turning his "We shall never negotiate out of fear. But we shall never fear to negotiate" into "Let us never negotiate out of fear. But let us never fear to negotiate." It was "a low score," he conceded, "but not completely negligible." He added that "a ghost-writer is like an unloved dog in a poor family. He must be content with scraps." His "scrap" was the kind of antithetical statement Kennedy and Sorensen adored, as he must have realized when he wrote it. Arthur Schlesinger praised it as "the distinctive note" of the inaugural and one "close to JFK's heart." It is also one of eight passages from the inaugural to have made it into Bartlett's *Familiar Quotations,* where John F. Kennedy, instead of that "unloved dog," John Kenneth Galbraith, gets the credit.

When Galbraith met Sorensen on January 18 he made what he called "mostly cosmetic" suggestions. He argued that the term *joint ventures* in the sentence beginning "United, there is little we cannot do in a host of new joint ventures" sounded as though Kennedy was proposing a mining partnership. He recommended replacing it with *cooperative ventures.*

He urged Sorensen to eliminate the hectoring tone of "We shall not always expect to find you on our side. But we shall always expect to find you vigorously on the side of your own freedom—and to know that those who foolishly seek power by riding on the tiger's back inevitably end up inside." Sorensen removed *our side,* substituted *hope* for *expect,* and softened it to "We shall not expect to find them supporting our every view. But we shall always hope to find them vigorously supporting their own freedom of choice—and to remember that in the past, those who foolishly sought to find power by riding on the tiger's back inevitably ended up inside."

Galbraith criticized the tiger metaphor as out of tune with the conciliatory nature of the rest of the speech, but Sorensen refused to delete it, and it survives in several quotation anthologies. Metaphors are rare in inaugural addresses, and it seems odd that Sorensen would have resisted striking out a comparison of communism to a wild beast, particularly after eliminating references to the Soviets as the "enemy" and "foe." Perhaps he and Kennedy considered it an important counterweight to the rest of the address, or he sensed Kennedy was fond of it because of its Churchillian provenance. It had appeared on one of the three pages of the Sorensen Draft that Kennedy had inserted into his dictation. But Sorensen had probably picked it up from Kennedy, who had surely read it in the fiery speech Churchill had delivered in the House of Commons after the 1938 Munich agreement, in which he proclaimed, "Dictators ride to and fro upon tigers which they dare not dismount. And the tigers are getting hungry." Churchill's tiger riders were Hitler and Mussolini, dictators who risked being eaten by the evil forces they had unleashed. Kennedy turned the tiger into a communist tyranny ready to devour third-world countries.

None of the changes Kennedy or Sorensen made on January 18 would have as much effect on the reception of the speech as an area of low pressure appearing that afternoon on weather maps as a blob of clouds, rain, and counterclockwise winds stalled over Arkansas.

An inauguration is a pageant designed to unfold outdoors, with a new president taking his oath and delivering his address on the steps of the Capitol, followed by a parade flowing down Pennsylvania Avenue. It is glorious in sunshine, miserable in rain or snow, and a disappointment indoors. William Henry Harrison and Millard Fillmore's wife died of pneumonia after enduring cold and rainy inaugurals. Snow forced William Howard Taft's ceremony indoors, and bitter cold did the same to Ronald Reagan's second. A downpour turned Franklin Roosevelt's second parade into a miserable event. Benjamin Harrison delivered his inaugural from underneath an umbrella, rain muffled his words, and a sea of black umbrellas covering the crowd gave the event a funereal aspect. A stiff wind made Ulysses Grant's second inaugural inaudible, and guests at his ball danced in their overcoats while cooks used hatchets to hack open roast turkeys that had frozen in the unheated building. In 1933, Congress passed the Twentieth Amendment, moving Inauguration Day from March 4 back to January 20—a date promising drier but colder weather, and a greater chance of snow.

On January 1, 1961, the Inaugural Committee had issued a press release announcing that Dr. Irving Krick, the president of a private weather forecasting service in Denver, was calling for fair but cold weather for Inauguration Day. Krick's forecast carried weight because he had been General Eisenhower's weatherman during the war and had accurately predicted conditions for both of his inaugurations. He was a registered Republican but was offering his services because, he said, he admired Kennedy's "forthright and sincere approach."

On January 18 the *Evening Star* predicted that Inauguration Day would be "cold and windy, with some sunshine and a high of not more than 35 degrees," adding that "to add a touch to the city's festive air, the forecaster says there will be some snow tomorrow. But it probably won't be very much." That same day, a *Washington Post* reporter interviewed the meteorologist in charge of the National Weather Bureau's Washington station at National Airport. He described him as surrounded by ringing telephones and nervous subordinates, muttering to himself, and worried that the low pressure over Arkansas might wreak havoc with the inauguration. On January 19, an article in the *Post* forecast "a measurable amount of snow" for that afternoon, totaling "one or more inches," but a story in the same paper headlined "Forecast: Snow into Rain, Rain into Snow" said the Weather Bureau was predicting "no significant accumulation."

Jackie Kennedy left Palm Beach on the *Caroline* at 2:00 P.M. on January 18 accompanied by an entourage including her personal secretary, Mary Gallagher, her press secretary, Pamela Turnure, and the UPI reporter Helen Thomas. Until now, she had treated Thomas no better than other reporters covering the transition, refusing her requests for interviews and ignoring her. Thomas had spent November and early December standing outside 3307 N Street, trying to divine Jackie's moods by studying her facial expressions and body language whenever she appeared at the front door, and concluding she "feared and dreaded" becoming first lady.

Thomas had followed her to Palm Beach in December, filling her days by interviewing her hairdresser and the owner of her diaper service. Her only notable success had been her friendship with Mary Gallagher, who had slipped her aboard the *Caroline* for the January 18 flight. Thomas was hoping for an exclusive interview, but Jackie sat on the opposite side of the plane behind a wall of staffers. Again Thomas was forced to read her expressions and mannerisms. She concluded she was returning to Washington "with some trepidation," probably an understatement of Jackie's unease as she neared the moment when she would have to occupy the Maison Blanche. She had complained to Oleg Cassini in December, "I seem to be mercilessly exposed and don't know how to cope with it." During his visit to Palm Beach in early January she had begged him, in a sentence sounding as if it had been first formulated in French, "You must come and visit us because the solitude of this place [the White House] will be immense for us." Several days before leaving La Guerida she had written a sardonic note to Adlai Stevenson that concluded, "I shall be seeing you very soon, in that tranquil, peaceful period lying ahead, January 20th."

If Jackie was less enthusiastic about occupying the White House than her predecessors, it may have been because no other first lady had given birth by cesarean section seven weeks before her husband's inauguration or had so recently contemplated divorcing him.

Clark Clifford's observation that "strains seriously threatened the Kennedy marriage during the late fifties" is confirmed by the journalist Marie Ridder, who recalls a day in 1958 when Jackie came alone to a luncheon party at her home. Asked about her husband's whereabouts, the future first lady replied, "Oh, he's probably off with some bimbo," adding breezily, "I'm thinking of divorcing him." Ridder was less surprised than others by this remark because five years before at the Kennedy wedding she had overheard Jackie asking Polly Tunney, the wife of boxer Gene Tunney, "How does a married woman cope with an unfaithful husband?" Tunney had answered that she never stopped believing in her heart that she was the only one he loved.

Ridder relayed Jackie's threat to her husband, the journalist Walter Ridder. After lunch, he took Jackie for a walk and said, "Look, he's got a really good chance of being President. You don't want it on your conscience."

"Well, you know I love him," she replied. "But he's impossible," which is about as succinct a summary of the tragedy of their marriage as one can imagine.

Jackie may have dreaded the inauguration, but she approached it with her usual calculation and attention to detail. While working as the Inquiring Camera Girl for the *Washington Times-Herald* in the early 1950s, she had asked politicians, celebrities, and the man on the street lightweight questions such as "Which first lady would you most like to have been?" and "If you had a date with Marilyn Monroe, what would you talk about?" She recorded their answers, snapped their photographs, and learned which colors and clothes looked best in black-and-white newsprint, one reason she appreciated the genius of the beige wool coat Cassini was proposing for the ceremony.

As she flew north on January 18, the Reception for Distinguished Ladies, one of many inaugural events she had declined to attend, was unfolding at the National Gallery. The invitation had asked guests to wear "either a favorite new hat or special new hair-do," enough in itself to persuade her to skip it. (Had she gone, she would have been pleased to see that every lady wore a mink stole, cape, or coat, an indication they would also be wearing mink on January 20.) The invitation promised "women appointees" in the receiving lines, but since Kennedy had appointed only two women to senior positions in his administration, his mother, sisters, sisters-in-law, and the wives of his cabinet members joined Bess Truman and Lady Bird Johnson in shaking six thousand hands. Rose Kennedy worked longer than anyone, setting a "greeting record," and probably fuming that the future first lady was not at her side. Jackie's mother, Janet Auchincloss, told a reporter, "I must not talk when the photographers are taking pictures." She explained her daughter had warned that if she opened her mouth while being photographed, her face might appear distorted—an Inquiring Camera Girl maxim explaining the masklike smile remaining frozen on Jackie's face throughout the next two days.

Martha Washington missed her husband's first inauguration and traveled up the Eastern Seaboard to New York by carriage a month later, according to "The Presidents' Ladies," a series of articles running in the *Washington Post* that week that Jackie must have read. Parades, bonfires, church bells, and dashing military units greeted her along the way, and her husband placed a notice of her arrival in New York newspapers. He sailed across the Hudson on his inaugural barge to welcome her to the city, and as they traveled back across the harbor together cannons fired salutes, and crowds jamming the wharves cheered.

When Jackie landed in Washington at 5:00 P.M. on Wednesday, January 18, the *New York Times* reported that "nobody" was on hand to greet her. This presumably meant nobody of importance, no member of the Kennedy family, delegation of Democratic dignitaries, or husband, who was at this moment flying down from New York. Although Jackie was not "greeted" in the strictest sense of the word, she was met by photographers, Secret Service agents, and other travelers, who waved and beckoned from behind a fence. She started toward them, then stopped in her tracks, seemingly unable to make herself shake their hands.

She wore a bold checkered tweed suit that looked stunning in the black-and-white photograph appearing on the front page of the *New York Times* the next morning. It was dusk when she disembarked, but she wore oversized sunglasses, useful for controlling photographers. She removed them, offered a radiant smile, then put them back on.

She was driven directly to 3307 N Street. Little had changed since she left the house on December 9. Batteries of television and newsreel cameras still filled the street, their power cables snaking like vines into basement windows, their lenses pointed at the front door like the rifles of a firing squad. When the front door opened, newsreel cameras whirred, shutters clicked, the crowd cheered, and reporters bundled into polar explorer coats craned their necks to peer into a house where phones never stopped ringing, packing boxes lay scattered across floors, and the perpetually drawn shades on the street side of the house left the downstairs rooms in a perpetual twilight.

After arriving back at N Street Jackie secluded herself on "the comparatively peaceful second floor," according to Mary ("Molly") Van Rensselaer Thayer. (The Kennedys trusted Thayer so much that she was permitted to portray Rose Kennedy on the Massachusetts inaugural float.) Jackie had collaborated with Thayer on a four-part biography for the *Ladies Home Journal* that would appear on Inauguration Day and become a book. Thayer followed it with her 1967 *Jacqueline Kennedy—The White House Years.* In the foreword she thanked Jackie for replying to written questions, allowing access to files, and encouraging friends to be interviewed. The volume has no footnotes, but much of its material, by its very nature, could only have come from Jackie. Thayer devotes about a fifth of her book to the fifty-four hours between Jackie's arrival in Washington and the inauguration, evidence of how deeply these hours had been carved into Jackie's memory.

The event most closely resembling the notorious open house following Andrew Jackson's 1829 inauguration that had left the White House in tatters was a January 18 reception in honor of Vice President–elect Lyndon Johnson in the Statler Hilton ballroom. It was open to anyone willing to pay five dollars for a roast beef sandwich, a glass of champagne, and a Lyndon Johnson handshake. Kennedy drove directly there from National Airport, arriving at 6:30 to find nurses bending over guests who had fainted in the crush and fire marshals imploring guests to leave so those jammed onto stairwells could shove their way inside. Upon his arrival, everyone stampeded toward Kennedy, leaving Lyndon Johnson alone, like a seal stranded on a rock after the tide has rushed to sea.

Kennedy's first words to his future vice president were "You've lost some weight, haven't you?" It was an odd remark, given he had seen Johnson in a bathing suit four days earlier, and spoke more to Kennedy's obsession with his own weight.

Johnson was flattered. At least he could beat Kennedy in something. He patted his stomach and boasted of losing twenty pounds since the election (the same amount Kennedy had gained) by using a popular diet drink. Kennedy tolerated twelve minutes of this banter—the same amount of time he had stayed at the Lytton party the night before—before leaving Johnson to get on with shaking eight thousand hands.

Back at N Street Kennedy met with Sorensen. This was their opportunity to compare the changes each had made to his respective copy of the address. Sorensen recalls that by then he and Kennedy believed the speech was in good shape. ("He was a man who wanted to be confident of his material," Sorensen says, "and he felt sure about that speech.") Sorensen wrote Kennedy's changes onto his COPY, so that *freedom* became *freedom of man,* and *enemies, others.* It may also have been at this meeting that Sorensen replaced the vague *others* with *communists,* noting in the margin that *communist* should not be capitalized. This was because Kennedy wanted to refer to communists in general, rather than the Communist Party in a specific country.

Sorensen's COPY now contained three sets of editorial changes: those he and Kennedy had made to the original typescript during the January 17 flight to Washington and that he had transferred to the COPY; those he had made to the COPY between 6:00 P.M. on January 17 and 6:00 P.M. on January 18, some as a result of suggestions offered by Rusk, Lippmann, Galbraith, and others; and those Kennedy had made to his copy of the typescript while he was in New York during this same twenty-four-hour period.

That evening Sorensen gave the COPY to a secretary for typing. Gloria Sitrin believes she was the one who used a large-print typewriter to type the fourteen-page Reading Copy on three-hole paper that she then clipped into a black loose-leaf binder. This was the text that Kennedy would carry to the lectern, and Pierre Salinger would release to reporters on the morning of the inauguration.

Sometime after Sitrin finished, Sorensen or someone else attached a memorandum to this Reading Copy titled, "Changes in Inaugural Speech—to Be Read and Approved by Senator."

The authors of this memorandum were Harris Wofford and Louis Martin. Wofford had advised Kennedy on civil rights issues during the campaign and worked in the transition for Kennedy's brother-in-law Sargent Shriver. Louis

Martin was an African-American publishing executive who had also worked in the campaign and transition. When they read Sorensen's COPY on January 18, they had been disturbed it made no mention of the struggle by African-Americans for equal rights. During his campaign, Kennedy had declared that "the challenging, revolutionary sixties . . . demand that the President place himself in the very thick of the [civil rights] fight," and promised to end racial discrimination in public housing "with the stroke of a presidential pen" by signing an executive order. Further, he pledged to members of the NAACP, "To the extent that these tasks [the struggle for equal rights] require the support, the guidance, and the leadership of the American Presidency—I am bold enough to try." After all this, it seemed incredible to Wofford and Martin that Kennedy would not seek to inspire Americans to end racial discrimination in his inaugural address. Their memorandum, proposing two additions to the speech, forced him to decide how much moral passion and political capital he was willing to invest in the battle for civil rights.

Their first suggestion was to add "at home and around the world" to the last sentence of the fourth paragraph, so that it read, ". . . and unwilling to witness or permit the slow undoing of those human rights to which this nation has always been committed, and to which we are committed today *at home and around the world.*" This addition was the shortest, and the least likely to attract attention. By burying "at home" in the middle of a sentence ending "around the world," Kennedy could refer to the civil rights movement yet maintain the international focus of his address. Had the sentence instead ended ". . . around the world and at home," it would have drawn more attention to human rights in the United States.

Their second suggestion was to add a sentence to the paragraph near the conclusion that posed two rhetorical questions: "Can we forge against those enemies a grand and global alliance, North and South, East and West, that can assure a more fruitful life for all mankind? Will you join in that historic effort?" The Wofford-Martin memorandum suggested that Kennedy add a third question: "Are you willing to demonstrate in your own life—in your attitude toward those of other races and those here from other shores—that you hold these eternal truths to be self-evident?"

They had crafted this sentence to appeal to Kennedy's concern that segregation was alienating the newly independent nations of Africa, and handing the Soviets a cold-war propaganda victory. But it added thirty-three words to a speech Kennedy was determined to make one of the shortest in history, and contained the hackneyed phrase "from other shores." Its closing line, "that you hold these eternal truths to be self-evident," was also confusing since there had been no mention earlier in the speech of any "eternal truths," and not everyone might recognize its reference to the Declaration of Independence.

The memorandum presented Kennedy with four choices:

1. He could adopt both additions and alienate the southern Democrats, who had voted for him in overwhelming numbers, and the powerful southern congressmen, who controlled key committees and whose support was essential to passing his legislative program.
2. He could reject both additions and disappoint black civil rights leaders and black voters who had provided his margin of victory in several states.
3. He could adopt only the first addition.
4. He could adopt only the second addition.

When Kennedy was in the Senate, Joe Clark, a Democratic senator from Pennsylvania, had asked him about his position on the Catholic Church's opposition to making birth control information available to the poor. Kennedy had replied that a change in the Church's position was bound to come, but in the meantime, he said, "I intend to be as brave as I dare." Including both of the Wofford-Martin suggestions would have been brave and daring; choosing, as he did, only "at home and around the world" was as brave as Kennedy dared to be.

It was not the most courageous choice, nor the most cowardly, but then Kennedy had never been that courageous about confronting racial discrimination. During his 1946 campaign his black manservant George Taylor had recruited a contingent of black high school and college girls from Cambridge to work for him as volunteers. Although they labored side-by-side with the white girls in the Kennedy headquarters, the Kennedy sisters would sometimes invite the white volunteers to eat at a local restaurant while sending sandwiches up to the black girls. Taylor complained about it to Kennedy, saying, "Jack, I think that's ______. They're all giving their time. They're all human beings. Why segregate in this way?" Kennedy said, "George, you're thin-skinned. That's one of the things of the time." Taylor protested that Cambridge was more liberal and the girls could have eaten together. Soon afterward he left politics and Kennedy's employment.

You could say in Kennedy's defense that his decision about which passage to add to his inaugural reflected the times. In these times, Sammy Davis Jr. had chosen to skip the inauguration because he feared being heckled, as he had been at the 1960 Democratic convention, about his romance with the Swedish actress Mai Britt. In 1961, the freedom riders, James Meredith, the

Birmingham school bombing, and the March on Washington were all in the future, and it would not be until 1963 that Kennedy would tell Americans that civil rights were "a moral issue as old as the scriptures and as clear as the American Constitution."

At the very least, "at home and around the world" provided a bridge between the idealism of a speech focused entirely on foreign affairs and the major domestic issue of the day. It linked "defending freedom in its hour of maximum danger" abroad to defending freedom in Mississippi, and opposing the spread of communism abroad to guaranteeing voting rights in the American South. Kennedy added it because he must have sensed that for a man who had won the presidency with the overwhelming support of black Americans, not to refer to their struggle for civil rights in his inaugural address would have been shameful.

Sometime on the morning of January 19, at Kennedy's instruction, a secretary removed the second page from the Reading Copy of the inaugural, fed it into a typewriter, and added "AT HOME AND AROUND THE WORLD" in capital letters that were less than half the size of the reading copy type. This made the phrase appear to be exactly what it was, a whispered afterthought.

The books by Lincoln, Thayer, and Gallagher do not tell us what happened at N Street on the evening of January 18. The *New York Times* reported the next day that "the future first lady rested, as her physician had decreed," but it is unclear whether she came downstairs to dine with her husband or remained in her second-floor bedroom, perhaps imagining her large and fractious family, gathering at this moment in homes and hotels across the capital. She and her husband had been invited to a small dinner party at the Georgetown home of Florence Mahoney, the wealthy widow of the president of the Cox newspaper chain. She had declined Mahoney's invitation, but he had accepted, then changed his mind and sent his last-minute regrets. But after spending several hours at home, perhaps restless and bored, annoyed by the clutter and turmoil, and exasperated by his perpetually exhausted wife, he strolled over to the party.

He entered without knocking and appeared in the living room unannounced. The twenty-six guests laid down their dessert spoons, shot to their feet, and applauded. It was a typical Georgetown party: round tables in ground-floor rooms, caterers, cigars, black tie, and a guest list mixing old money, no money, new money, politicians, academics, and journalists. Among those in attendance were the socialites Charles and Jayne Wrightsman, Arthur

Schlesinger, the columnist Joe Alsop, former president Truman, Robert Frost, and Frost's close Washington friend, future secretary of the interior, Stewart Udall. Kennedy grabbed a chair and placed himself between America's two silver-haired avatars of plain speaking, Harry Truman and Robert Frost—the Democrat who had worked harder than any to sabotage his candidacy, and the poet he had feared might upstage him at the inauguration.

Kennedy and Frost had been circling each other for years. Kennedy had discovered Frost's poetry while in prep school and had copied lines from his poems touching on sacrifice, heroism, and courage into his notebooks. He had told graduates at the 1956 Harvard commencement, "If more politicians knew poetry and more poets knew politics, I am convinced the world would be a little better place to live," and often ended campaign speeches with Frost's "But I have promises to keep / And miles to go before I sleep. / And miles to go before I sleep."

Frost, in turn, had praised *Profiles in Courage* as "a pretty lofty book," telling a visiting Russian poet, "You can't imagine how gifted that lad [Kennedy] is." During a press conference the year before his eighty-fifth birthday he had replied to a question about the "decay" of New England by saying, "The next President of the United States will be from Boston. . . . He's a Puritan named Kennedy. The only Puritans left these days are the Roman Catholics."

Kennedy thanked Frost with a graceful letter that led to a meeting. "We knew right off we'd sized each other up right," Frost said afterward. Months later, he hailed Kennedy's election and wondered if his support had provided the slim margin of victory.

Frost had also cemented an unlikely friendship with Stewart Udall, an Arizona Mormon who was serving his fourth term in Congress. He attended "poetry and politics" dinners at Udall's home in Washington, visited his Arizona ranch, and agreed with him that Kennedy would do more to promote the arts than any recent president.

Kennedy had summoned Udall to N Street in December and offered him the position of secretary of the interior. After accepting, Udall suggested that Kennedy invite Frost to speak at his inauguration. Kennedy was wary. "You know Robert Frost always steals any show he is part of," he said. "The same thing would happen to me that happened to Lincoln at Gettysburg, with Edward Everett [the noted classical orator who had preceded Lincoln]. I want my inaugural address, and not Frost's speech, to be the main topic of discussion in the country." Still, having Robert Frost consecrate his presidency was irresistible. The man was a cultural icon and national sage, the winner of four Pulitzer Prizes, and the holder of so many honorary degrees that he slept under a quilt made of his academic hoods. Who better to introduce an inaugural address calling for sacrifice, and dispel any lingering doubts that Kennedy was too young and untested to be president, than a man whose life and work was synonymous with frontier values like hard work, thrift, sacrifice, and living close to nature?

"Couldn't he read a poem?" Kennedy asked Udall. "That way he wouldn't be competing with me."

Frost was a registered Democrat who had disliked Roosevelt and felt estranged from the party, but he was thrilled by Udall's appointment and Kennedy's invitation. His reply came in an exultant telegram: "I may not be equal to it but I can accept it for my cause—the arts, poetry, now for the first time taken into the affairs of statesmen."

When Udall and Kennedy met a week later. Udall explained that instead of composing an original poem, Frost would prefer to recite "The Gift Outright," a sixteen-line hymn to the frontier and manifest destiny beginning, "The land was ours before we were the land's." It was perfect: a frontier poem for the New Frontier president. But Kennedy could not resist fine-tuning it. He asked if Frost would provide a more optimistic ending for the occasion. Negotiations ensued, and Frost finally agreed to substitute *will* for *would* in the last line, so it read, "such as she was, such as she will become."

This was their last communication until Kennedy pulled up a chair next to Frost at Florence Mahoney's party. One wonders if Kennedy suspected he had finally met a man whose ego matched his own. Or that Frost was planning to do precisely what he feared most, and that the *Washington Post* on January 21 would lead its main Inauguration Day story with "Robert Frost in his natural way stole the hearts of the Inaugural crowd yesterday."

The conversation between Frost, Kennedy, and Truman ranged over poetry, fiction, Mark Twain, Thomas Carlyle, and the Soviet Union. Truman had bought a set of Twain's complete works when he was a boy, and had displayed on his White House desk a framed Twain quotation: "Always do right. This will gratify some people and astonish the rest." Kennedy considered Carlyle one of his heroes and had saved in a notebook Carlyle's observation that "the courage we desire and prize is not the courage to die decently but to live manfully," a good line for a man in such precarious health.

During the campaign, Truman had been overheard saying, "I just don't want Joe Kennedy's boy in the White House." Margaret Truman later admitted that her father had opposed JFK because he "could not overcome his visceral dislike of Joe Kennedy." He had made a last-minute attempt to sabotage

Kennedy's candidacy by blasting the Democratic convention as a "mockery" controlled by "one candidate." Looking into the television camera, he had directed a question to Kennedy that touched on the sensitive issues of his age and religion, asking, "Are you certain that you are quite ready for the country, or that the country is ready for you in the role of President in January 1961?" He then called him "Senator Joseph F. Kennedy," a slip revealing the real target of his animus.

Truman's attack left Kennedy infuriated and agitated. He had paced up and down the living room of his hotel suite, yanking on the back of a sofa so hard one witness feared he was going to pull it over on himself, all the while delivering a monologue about how Truman and the old men who were out of politics ought to stay out and let a new generation take over. In a caustic public reply he said, "Based on my observation of him in 1952 and in 1956, and last Saturday, Mr. Truman regards an open convention as one which studies all the candidates, reviews their records, and then takes his advice."

After a perfunctory meeting at the Truman Library in August, Kennedy and Truman announced a "peace pact." Asked by a reporter if this meant he had changed his mind about supporting Kennedy, Truman snapped, "The Democratic National Convention settled that—and that's all there is to that," scarcely a ringing endorsement. Truman wrote former secretary of state Dean Acheson, "You and I are stuck with the necessity of taking the best of two evils or none at all. So—I'm taking the immature Democrat as the best of the two."

Not long after the inauguration, Truman told the author Merle Miller that he had not seen Joe Kennedy since threatening to throw him out of a window in the Ritz-Carlton in Boston—a statement only strictly true if Truman had shut his eyes throughout the ceremony at the Capitol, where he occupied seat A4 on the presidential stand, across the aisle from Joe Kennedy, who was in seat A11. The window incident had occurred in 1944, when Truman was running for vice president. He was at the Ritz to meet a local politician, and, as he told it to Miller, "Who should be in that suite but old man Kennedy, the father of that boy that's in the White House now. . . . [He] started throwing rocks at Roosevelt, saying he'd caused the war and so on. And then he said, 'Harry, what the hell are you doing campaigning for that crippled son-of-a-bitch that killed my son Joe?'" To this Truman had replied, "If you say another word about Roosevelt, I'm going to throw you out of that window."

(There are no truly sympathetic biographies of Joseph Kennedy, and some authors have seized on the Ritz incident to blacken his reputation further. But if you consider that the man Truman had threatened to pitch out the window was a father who had recently lost his beloved eldest son in a war he had opposed, who could not talk about this son publicly without breaking down, who mistakenly believed that Roosevelt had personally sent him on a suicide mission, and who knew that Roosevelt's son Elliott had been on the crew of an escorting plane, close enough to be briefly blinded by the explosion, then his rage becomes more understandable.)

Not seeing Joe Kennedy for two decades had not diminished Truman's loathing. He claimed to detest only two men: former Missouri governor Lloyd Stark and Richard Nixon, who would be seated two seats away at the inauguration. He could easily have added to his list Dwight Eisenhower, who would be five seats away: "One of the most . . . difficult people I have ever encountered in my life." Or Joe Kennedy: "as big a crook as we've got anywhere in this country, and I don't like it that he bought his son the nomination for the President." Or Bobby Kennedy, three rows behind him in D9: "I just don't like that boy, and I never will." Or for that matter all the Kennedys, who would be surrounding him on all sides: "All they're interested in is getting the power. They don't care a hoot in hell about using it."

Within a year, Truman would be comparing Kennedy to President McKinley, a "gutless wonder . . . [with] . . . ears so close to the ground they're full of grasshoppers." But tonight he offered him a tepid toast, saying, "I know you will solve the problems that we are facing." He then abruptly left Mahoney's party, driving himself back to the Mayflower Hotel, and leaving his wife and daughter stranded.

Had Adlai Stevenson, Eleanor Roosevelt, Hubert Humphrey, Lyndon Johnson, or other members of the Democratic establishment spoken as candidly as Truman did to Merle Miller, they would have echoed his complaints about John Kennedy's father, family, youth, ambition, and ruthlessness. Johnson would have been cruder, Stevenson and Roosevelt more subtle, but it added up to this: the most skeptical and hostile audience Kennedy would face at the Capitol would not be the crowd in front of him, or those watching on television, or the millions of Americans who had voted for Nixon, but the grandees of the Democratic Party seated around and behind him on the presidential stand.

Neither Evelyn Lincoln's appointment book nor the newspapers tell us how long Kennedy stayed at Mahoney's party. We only know he woke at 6:45 A.M. on January 19 to the roar of a motorcycle, threw open his second-floor bedroom window, and shouted down, "How about a little more quiet on my last day as a private citizen?"

8

Washington

JANUARY 19

⚜

Kennedy was observed brushing his hair with one hand while turning the pages in a black loose-leaf notebook with the other as he was driven from N Street to the White House for a 9:00 A.M. meeting with President Eisenhower. He was using this ten-minute drive, as he would other moments throughout January 19, to reread his speech and memorize some lines.

President Dwight Eisenhower, who awaited him at the White House, had little use for the Kennedy family. In his parlance, Teddy was "The Bonus Baby"; Bobby, "That Little Shit"; and the former junior naval officer succeeding him, "Little Boy Blue" or "The Young Whippersnapper." Yet, for all his talk, after meeting Kennedy in December, Eisenhower had softened his opinion, telling aides he was impressed by the younger man's grasp of the issues, and praising him as "a serious, earnest seeker of information." Kennedy did not experience a similar conversion. He continued viewing Eisenhower as a "non-President," and just as shallow as he had expected.

The differences in age, temperament, and background between these two men were considerable, and the way each approached his inaugural address underscores how little they had in common. Eisenhower had referred to composing the speech as "a job," writing in his diary, "I don't care much about the words if I can convey the ideas accurately." On January 12, 1953, he gathered the members of his future cabinet at a New York hotel and read them a draft written by the speechwriter John Emmett Hughes. He was not pleased when they applauded at its conclusion, saying, "I read it more for your blue pencils than I did for your applause." He then asked them to "tear it to pieces." Kennedy, on the other hand, showed his speech only to a handpicked circle of advisers, and cared so much about its words that he continued editing them until the last minute.

The meeting between Eisenhower and Kennedy on January 19 began with a forty-five minute Oval Office tutorial on the nuts and bolts of nuclear Armageddon. Eisenhower started by warning Kennedy that "Only the tough problems get to you. If they are easy, they will be settled at a lower level." Pointing to a man sitting just outside the door, he asked, "See that officer with the satchel?" He carried the codes for a nuclear strike as well as communications equipment connecting a president with the missile silos and SAC (Strategic Air Command). Summoning the officer over, Eisenhower had him open his satchel so Kennedy could see its contents: a small telephone, a rudimentary computer, and a loose-leaf notebook containing the codes. Eisenhower next called in a naval aide and ordered him to summon a helicopter. The man barked "Opal Drill Three" into the telephone, and six minutes later a Marine Corps helicopter landed on the lawn. This was how a president escaped the White House when the Soviets launched a nuclear strike.

In his memoirs Eisenhower described this meeting as "a sober one," and you sense him striving to make it as sober as possible. Even if you discount the nuclear satchel and evacuation helicopter as a little chief-executive horseplay, some hazing before Kennedy joined the most exclusive club on earth, there was still a strong hint of "Well, young man, you wanted this job so badly; here's what it really involves."

Kennedy and Eisenhower joined senior aides and the incoming and outgoing secretaries of state, defense, and treasury for a joint conference in the White House Cabinet Room. The fact that such a briefing was necessary points to one of the weaknesses of the American system. In a parliamentary democracy, future cabinet secretaries such as Dean Rusk, Robert McNamara, and Douglas Dillon would have been serving as opposition party shadow ministers, becoming familiar with their positions. Instead, six weeks before, Rusk had headed the Ford Foundation while McNamara had been president of the Ford Motor Company. Their lack of preparation meant that advice from their counterparts in the outgoing administration could not fail to make an impression on them, influencing their decisions and policies during the early months of their tenure.

Eisenhower shocked everyone on the Kennedy side, except perhaps Kennedy, by warning that the most serious international problem facing the United States was the struggle between Communist guerrillas and U.S.-supported government forces in the small, land-locked Southeast Asian nation of Laos. A Communist victory there would be a "great tragedy," he said. If it happened, it would be "just a question of time" before Communists seized power in Cambodia and Vietnam. After this statement Kennedy's attorney and adviser, Clark Clifford, sensed the atmosphere in the room turning from businesslike to grim. In a passage in his memoirs based on notes he took during this meeting, he expressed surprise that Eisenhower would link the national security of the United States so directly to the fate of Laos.

Kennedy asked Eisenhower's secretary of state, Christian Herter, if he believed the United States should intervene militarily. Herter said yes. Laos was "the cork in the bottle." If it fell, then Thailand, the Philippines, and Taiwan might be next.

Kennedy posed the same question to Eisenhower.

"If we permit Laos to fall then we will have to write off the entire area," the former general told the men who would become the principal architects of American policy for the next eight years. "We must not permit a Communist takeover. Unilateral intervention would be our last, desperate hope."

"How long would it take for an American combat division to enter Laos?" Kennedy asked.

"Twelve to seventeen days," answered Secretary of Defense Thomas Gates.

No one on the Kennedy side knew enough about the region to challenge Eisenhower's assessment. "The tone of the old soldier—on the last day of public service, half a century after entering the United States Military Academy—had a powerful effect on Kennedy, Rusk, McNamara, and me," Clifford wrote. "None of us had been prepared for the seriousness Eisenhower attached to Southeast Asia."

In a memorandum Kennedy dictated to Evelyn Lincoln later that morning, he claimed he had sought this meeting with Eisenhower in order to reassure the public about the "harmony" of the transition, and because he was eager to solicit his opinion about Laos. "I thought particularly it would be helpful to have some idea as to how prepared they were for military intervention," he said. But one suspects that this memorandum was somewhat disingenuous, and that Kennedy did not want to admit having being blindsided by Eisenhower's emphasis on that small Southeast Asian nation.

Kennedy did not take notes during this meeting, but like Clark Clifford, McNamara did. Four decades later, he would identify it as one of eleven pivotal events and decisions leading to American involvement in Vietnam, complaining in hindsight that the Eisenhower team had offered "no thoughtful analysis," only "the ominous prediction that if Laos were lost all of Southeast Asia would fall." He insisted the conference had made a deep impression on

Kennedy and his cabinet, profoundly influencing administration policy. One must treat such ex post facto remarks cautiously, particularly when they appear in memoirs written after their author has acknowledged that the Vietnam War had been a debacle. But the notes and memoranda written during or shortly after the meeting support McNamara's conclusion that Eisenhower's remarks shook the Kennedy cabinet, resulting in the administration devoting more time to Laos than to any other foreign or domestic problem during the following months.

Kennedy may have been less shocked than Rusk, McNamara, or Clifford, but he was surprised by the breezy manner with which Eisenhower, Gates, and Herter advocated military intervention. The irony of the same man who two days earlier had warned in his farewell address of the dangers of the military-industrial complex now recommending that this complex be used to save Southeast Asia from communism was not lost on Kennedy. "There he sat," he later told his friend and adviser Ken O'Donnell, "telling me to get ready to put ground forces into Asia, the thing he himself had been carefully avoiding for the last eight years." Future treasury secretary Dillon believed that, in his words, "Eisenhower and Herter both got a certain inner satisfaction from laying a potentially intractable problem in Kennedy's lap." Dillon's observation carries weight since he had served under Herter in the State Department and knew him and Eisenhower better than anyone else in the Kennedy cabinet did.

Kennedy's postmeeting memorandum to Lincoln does not mention Cuba. But McNamara reported Eisenhower saying, "In the long run the United States cannot allow the Castro government to continue to exist in Cuba." Clifford noted that Eisenhower had recommended the training of anti-Castro forces in Guatemala be "continued and accelerated." These were the same forces Kennedy would send ashore in three months at the Bay of Pigs.

Eisenhower's alarming presentation of the Laotian crisis also had the flavor of a hazing. He had warned Kennedy during their Oval Office meeting that no decision reaching his desk would be easy. Now, minutes later, he was presenting him with the kind of decision that might result in him summoning that evacuation helicopter for real. And what is one to make of his comments to a journalist two months later when, referring to Kennedy's answers to questions about Laos at a press conference, he said, "That boy doesn't know what the hell he's doing. He doesn't even know where Laos is. You mean Americans have to fight in that goddamned place?" Had Eisenhower forgotten what he had said on January 19, or had he said it to scare Kennedy and his cabinet secretaries?

After the meeting ended, Kennedy told O'Donnell that it had proven, to his amazement, that "things were really just as bad as [he] had said they were during the campaign." The briefing had come too late to affect the words of his inaugural but, like Khrushchev's alarming speech of January 6, not too late to confirm its relevance. The knowledge that the cold war was even more perilous than he had imagined when he dictated his draft to Lincoln nine days earlier could only have convinced him that its emphasis on foreign affairs was merited and timely, and added passion and conviction to his delivery. If Eisenhower was right about Laos, then young Americans might soon be, as Kennedy would say tomorrow, "granted the role of defending freedom in its hour of maximum danger." He might be summoning them to prove their "national loyalty" in Laos, and "the graves of young Americans" killed there might be added to those of others "who answered the call to service." Preventing a Communist takeover in that country might also be the first thing Americans could do for their country.

The meeting concluded at 11:00 A.M. As Kennedy was leaving the White House, a reporter asked if he was "excited." He considered the question for several seconds before replying, "Interested," more grace under pressure.

Kennedy was driven directly to the Georgetown home of his friend Bill Walton, a former war correspondent and magazine editor turned abstract artist. Salinger told reporters Kennedy had gone to Walton's so he could stay out of Jackie's way while she prepared to move into the White House, but Mary Gallagher's description of N Street as "a battlefield of beauty with the troops charging in all directions" is probably a better explanation for his self-imposed exile. Back at N Street, Oleg Cassini's dressmakers were fitting Jackie into her gown for the gala, the beautician Gudney Lindholm was applying a Cyclax of London facial, her New York hairdresser, "Kenneth" [Kenneth Batelle], was styling her hair into a medium-length bouffant, and his assistant, Rosemary Sorrentino, was straightening it, a service she had also been providing to Marilyn Monroe.

Despite being surrounded by packing boxes and beauty industry courtiers, Jackie found time that morning to dictate a handbook for the new owners of 3307 N Street that identified the best neighborhood florist, grocer, and bookstore, and the most reliable gardener, electrician, and caterer. Two years later, she would tell Bill Walton that her time at the White House had been the happiest she had ever known. Organization had been the key, she explained, and her life became "ideal" once she organized it along the lines of a campaign plotted by Field Marshal Rommel.

The two hours Kennedy spent at Walton's house have a wonderfully manic and improvised quality. Evelyn Lincoln answered a front-hall telephone while Walton typed press releases on an old portable, opened the front door, and brought visitors into a high-ceilinged Victorian parlor where Kennedy sat beside a coal fire. As a crowd gathered outside, police diverted traffic and journalists shouted questions at everyone climbing Walton's front steps.

The chairman of the Joint Chiefs of Staff, General Lyman Lemnitzer, came at 11:30 for fifteen minutes. Then Ted Sorensen arrived with seven nieces and nephews who were visiting from Nebraska. While Kennedy shook their hands, Sorensen noticed the Reading Copy of the inaugural lying open on a nearby chair.

Najeeb Halaby, Kennedy's choice to head the Federal Aviation Agency (FAA), arrived at noon. His impression of Kennedy during their brief meeting was that he was "a man very much relaxed, in command of himself and the situation after a rather hectic week." Others had made similar observations that day, with Anthony Lewis writing in the *New York Times* that Kennedy "appeared the calmest man in the increasingly frenzied city."

Kennedy decided to announce Halaby's appointment on the spot. Walton typed out a two-sentence statement, and as Kennedy stood on the front step reading it to the press, snowflakes began swirling from a darkening sky, dancing across the television lights, and frosting his chestnut hair.

The coming storm would prevent Kennedy from joining seven crewmembers from PT 109 who gathered at the Touchdown Club in downtown Washington. But he was there in the stories they retold of how a Japanese destroyer had collided with their ship, and how "the skipper" had saved their lives. Patrick McMahon, who had been so badly burned Kennedy had clasped the straps of his kapok life jacket in his teeth and towed him to safety, was the center of attention. When he and the other men rode down Pennsylvania Avenue the next day on a replica of PT 109, they would provide a powerful visual reminder that the man who in his inaugural address had just demanded courage and sacrifice from Americans, had already demonstrated the same qualities himself.

One reads of people staring out windows on January 19, hypnotized by the accumulating snow, of conversations becoming languid as backyards and sidewalks whitened, parties becoming gayer as snow muffled the city, and well-lit rooms seeming smaller and more welcoming as night fell and the snow increased.

The syndicated newspaper columnist Rowland Evans joined Kennedy and Walton for a lunch of chipped beef and baked potatoes. The atmosphere was "magical," he said. As the coal fire flickered, everyone stared through the dining room windows at snow piling up on the frozen lawn. Kennedy told some off-color stories before delivering a monologue about how he planned to use black American diplomats, and how he had found the best men for the State and Defense Department subcabinet positions. Evans had known Kennedy for years but had never seen him so expansive and relaxed. He remembered this as one of the most fascinating conversations of their friendship. When lunch ended, Walton went outside to ask the reporters if anyone could spare a cigar for the president-elect.

At 3:00 P.M. Kennedy visited the governors' reception at the Park Sheraton Hotel, finding it organized along the lines of a livestock barn at a state fair. Each governor stood in a stall decorated with his state flag and containing samples of local products and a homegrown beauty queen. According to the *Evening Star,* Kennedy's deep Florida tan received oohs and aahs from the women. As at the Statler Hilton, he was the magnet and everyone else the filings. Twenty-five beauty queens had to lock arms and form a cordon to prevent him being crushed by well-wishers.

Wherever Kennedy went in his final hours as president-elect, crowds rushed forward, pressing against sawhorses, tripping over television cables, thrusting out hands, and shouting his name. At the events he did not attend, he was present in thoughts and conversations. On this memorable afternoon, people saw bleachers lining Pennsylvania Avenue, license plates from every state, women wearing Jackie's bouffant hairdo, bookstore windows filled with copies of *Profiles in Courage,* and they thought of him. They saw television crews cruising down Pennsylvania Avenue in open trucks, pointing cameras to where he would stand the following day. They waited thirty seconds for a dial tone because the telephone system was overloaded, heard mounted policemen playing recordings of sirens, whistles, and barking dogs to prepare their horses for the parade, and they thought of John F. Kennedy.

While Kennedy shook hands at the governors' reception, more fame, intelligence, and creativity than had ever been assembled in one place, according to the *Washington Post,* was gathered at Walter Lippmann's for a "tea" at which photographs showed every writer, artist, composer, philosopher, and Nobel Prize–winning scientist clutching a highball glass. Novelist John Steinbeck's wife said, "To hell with the snow, I'm going to *everything,*" and playwright Arthur Miller was said to tower over everyone "benignly." Beyond that, we have to imagine the conversations between painter Mark Rothko, writer John Hersey, poet W. H. Auden, and the other "Invited Intellectuals." But we *can* be sure that the name of the man who had brought them to Washington passed their lips.

While the beauty queens were saving Kennedy from being crushed to death, prominent female Democrats had gathered at the Women's National Democratic Club to plot his 1964 campaign. Katie Louchheim, whom Kennedy had appointed to a minor post at the State Department, urged the women to begin working at the grass roots to ensure he won by a huge majority. The president-elect skipped their gathering, but Lady Bird Johnson stopped by and, in the custom of the times, the newspapers ignored what she said, but reported what she wore.

Kennedy was even the center of attention at the Nixon household. That morning, at his last press conference as vice president, Richard Nixon had said he would not rule out running against Kennedy in 1964. That evening, according to Julie Nixon, her mother was in "a funny mood," imitating Lyndon Johnson's drawl and threatening to wear "an outrageous outfit" to the inauguration. Her sister, Tricia, swore she would not watch the ceremony on television because, as she told her father and as he told audiences for months afterward, "If they had counted the votes right, we would have won."

While twelve-year-old Tricia Nixon sulked, thirteen-year-old Suellen Fulstone was flying from California to attend the ceremonies at Kennedy's invitation. She had caught his attention by using money earned working on her family's cattle ranch to buy time on a Reno, Nevada, television station and deliver a five-minute speech urging his election. A reporter meeting her at National Airport described her as having "a cool head as well as a pretty face." She was also infected with the giddy optimism of the times, telling the press she planned to become a geneticist and win a Nobel Prize, although for the moment she would settle for dancing with President Kennedy at his inaugural ball. As it turned out, she would spend twenty minutes at one of the balls talking with Jackie, more time than Jackie would spend conversing with anyone else on January 20, which can be taken as evidence of Fulstone's charm or of Jackie's boredom with the rest of the company on offer.

One-hundred-five-year-old Nettie Moulden had said "Good Morning" to President Abraham Lincoln at the age of ten, witnessed every inauguration from Lincoln's second to Eisenhower's first, and boasted an autograph book beginning with "A. Lincoln" and including every president since. Like most Washingtonians, she had a hearty appetite for political news. Her septuagenarian daughters read the newspapers to her every morning, and according to the oldest (who was seventy-eight), Moulden followed the 1960 election closely. But whether, as she lay dying at her home on Rhode Island Avenue on John Kennedy's last afternoon as a private citizen, she replayed in her mind the inaugurations of Grant, Hayes, Garfield, Harrison, Arthur, Cleveland, McKinley, Roosevelt, Taft, Wilson, Harding, Coolidge, Hoover, Roosevelt, Truman, and Eisenhower is unknown. On January 23, three days after the inauguration, and eight days before her one hundred and sixth birthday, the only woman on Earth who could have compared from personal experience John F. Kennedy's first inaugural address with Abraham Lincoln's second passed away.

Every city handles heavy snow differently. In New York, subways keep things moving, people head into the parks to sled, and even the heaviest accumulations seem insignificant when measured against the skyscrapers. Buffalo and Minneapolis take blizzards in stride, but in Washington snow is always a surprise and a disaster, proof of Kennedy's quip about it being a city of "Southern efficiency and Northern charm."

The eight inches paralyzing Washington on January 19 fell as a biting, sleety snow that stung cheeks and frosted spectacles. On the ground it became a cementlike morass that threatened heart attacks, panicked Sun Belt Democrats, and sent federal workers home an hour early, which turned out to be an hour too late. It trapped fifteen trolley cars at Dupont Circle, blocked bridges with cars that had been abandoned after breaking down or running out of gas, and supplied journalists with colorful vignettes such as this one from Tom Wolfe: "At 4:00 P.M. a uranium blonde named Lola Totti, who said she was an actress from Nevada, came out of the Statler and put on her sunglasses. Asked why, she said, 'you don't want me to go snow blind, do you, baby?' "

On the spur of the moment, Kennedy asked Truman to come back to N street, and they left the governors' reception together at 4:00 P.M. Like most cars in Washington that day, Kennedy's Lincoln Continental lacked snow tires or chains. It skidded on Rock Creek Parkway and detoured around a ramp blocked by abandoned vehicles. Back at N Street the two men sat by a fire in the library, making small talk and watching snow cover the branches of a magnolia. The real purpose of the invitation became evident as Truman was leaving and a cameraman snapped a photograph of him and Kennedy standing together on the doorstep, smiling broadly under halos of snowflakes. Truman was ghostly pale. Kennedy, with his dark tan and white teeth, resembled a stage minstrel. Truman told reporters, "[Kennedy is] a nice, decent young man . . . [who] knows the history of government as well as anyone I've met and that includes me." Then, softening his earlier attack on his inexperience and youth, he added that he was "young enough to stand the gaff of being President."

The governors' reception was the last well-attended inaugural event of the day, and five hundred of its guests ended up having to sleep on cots in the ballroom. As the snow increased, the crowds at the teas, receptions, and dinners shrank, and Kennedy had to skip a cocktail party for Eleanor Roosevelt and a buffet dinner at the home of Katharine and Philip Graham.

The only sane response to a major snowstorm is to go home and wait for the plows. But in Washington on January 19 people insisted on finishing what they were doing and heading to the next event. When Oleg Cassini realized the coat he had designed for Jackie to wear at the inauguration ceremony had only a thin silk lining, the snow did not prevent him from driving to and from the tailor who was sewing in a heavier one. Adlai Stevenson's flight was diverted to Richmond, but instead of sleeping there, he rented a car, drove through the worst of the storm, then broke down on one of the bridges leading into the city. Joe and Rose Kennedy made it to their engagements thanks to a powerful sedan and a young man with a shovel. Eighty-six-year-old Herbert Hoover circled for an hour in his private air force plane before reluctantly returning to Miami. Seventy-six-year-old Charlotte Morglieth spent four hours driving in from Alexandria to attend the inaugural concert at Constitution Hall, then dropped dead in the lobby. Secretary of State Christian Herter was trapped in his limousine for two hours on his way to a dinner party before giving up and sharing a bottle of Scotch with another motorist.

Leonard Bernstein and Bette Davis flagged down a police car and persuaded its officers to drive them along sidewalks to the armory so they could perform in the gala. Robert Frost remained in his hotel room composing a forty-two-line verse titled "Dedication," which he planned on reciting as a surprise introduction to "The Gift Outright." Truman stayed in his suite at the Mayflower. Pierre Salinger's secretary, Sue Vogelsinger, brought the former president one of the advance copies of the inaugural she had typed for the press. Truman answered the door in his slippers and invited her inside to meet his wife. It struck her as extraordinary that no Secret Service agents were in evidence, and that anyone could have knocked on the former president's door.

Norman Mailer had predicted Kennedy would make Americans adventurous again, and in Washington on the eve of his inauguration, they were already having a grand adventure. Hollywood stars hitched rides in snowplows, men in white tie huddled like hoboes around oil-drum fires, and matrons in evening gowns slid down snowbanks. Adults who were already feeling as youthful and vigorous as Kennedy had promised to make them built snowmen and threw snowballs, and all the usual magic that accompanies a large snowfall happened, and more. Up and down the East Coast, schools, factories, and businesses closed, and the three-foot snowfalls and ten-foot drifts created a vast snowbound community stretching from Virginia to Maine. People gravitated to their television sets, and some must have wondered whether this storm meant the gods were angry, pleased, or simply taking note of Kennedy's inauguration.

One drawback to employing a large staff is that bad weather can suddenly turn them into houseguests. Back at N Street, Evelyn Lincoln and Mary Gallagher took over an upstairs bedroom next to the Kennedys. Jackie's personal maid, Providencia Parades, converted a ground-floor sitting room into a bedroom for herself and her sons and mother. Miss O'Malley bedded down somewhere, and the last thing Mary Gallagher recalls of that night is falling asleep while receiving one of her massages. The transformation of his house into a storm shelter did not dampen Kennedy's spirits. He poked his head into the bedroom where Lincoln and Gallagher were eating dinner off trays and asked, "Aren't you ladies going to the Gala?" They explained they could not get home to dress. "There's always a bright side," he said. "At least you'll be here in the morning."

He appeared in Jackie's bedroom as Rosemarie Sorrentino was applying lacquer to her hair. Jackie had told him earlier that Sorrentino also did Marilyn Monroe, and Kennedy, who had not yet met Monroe, had asked if she was as temperamental as her reputation. Sorrentino's reply to this question is unknown, nor is it known if Kennedy would later consider it portentous that at the very moment he was taking the oath of office, Monroe was in Juarez, Mexico, divorcing her third husband, Arthur Miller, who was himself then sitting in the VIP stand at the Capitol, watching the soon-to-be lover of his soon-to-be ex-wife become president of the United States.

In the days preceding the inauguration Kennedy had become almost as concerned with Jackie's appearance as his own. The week before, Gallagher had forwarded this message to Mary Thayer from Jackie: "Jack is insistent, in one of the *Ladies Home Journal* articles, you use the Jacques Lowe color photograph which Jacques recently sent me to Palm Beach—one where [I] have on [a] yellow check dress." Jackie stressed to Gallagher that this simply *had* to be done.

Minutes before leaving for Constitution Hall, Kennedy summoned Gallagher into Jackie's bedroom and asked if she thought Jackie should wear a diamond necklace threaded with emeralds. Not realizing that she was being called upon to settle a dispute, or that Jackie was opposed to wearing jewelry with Cassini's gown, Gallagher voted for the necklace, saying she thought it added a touch of color against the pearl-white satin. Jackie remained silent, annoyed at her husband for second-guessing her judgment, and at Gallagher for taking his side.

Kennedy telephoned Bill Walton to warn that he could not pick him up as planned because only Constitution Avenue had been cleared of snow. However, if Walton got himself to N Street, he could ride with them to the inaugural concert. Walton took off running across Georgetown, wading through snowdrifts and arriving breathless just as Jackie descended the staircase. She held a necklace in each hand—the emerald one Kennedy preferred, and a diamond necklace that would be less visible against her gown. She asked her husband and Walton which they preferred. Both voted for the emeralds, and her rebellion was over.

The moment Jackie appeared in the doorway of N Street, television lights blazed, and policemen revved motorcycles. Snowflakes fell like confetti, and a Secret Service agent opened a black umbrella over her head. She raised the hem of her gown with both hands and, facing the harsh night without a fur or wrap, hurried to the limousine in satin slippers. Photographs of this moment appeared on front pages the following morning and have become New Frontier icons. Glance at them quickly and you see only Jackie. She is framed in the center of every picture, and everything else—the night, the umbrella, the topcoats worn by her husband and the Secret Service—is black or a shade of gray. Perhaps it is the agent holding an umbrella over her head like a footman, or her Cinderella gown, its sole adornment a satin cockade evoking her French heritage, or that, as in many inauguration photographs, she is the only woman, but one looks at these photographs and sees royalty heading to a ball. Most show her smiling as she descends the steps, but one, taken as she emerged from the house, and before she remembered her Inquiring Camera Girl lessons, reveals the trace of a grimace, and that she had tucked the emerald necklace under the collar of her gown.

* * *

Anyone who has ever traveled in a motorcade knows the rush that comes with weaving through traffic and speeding through stoplights to the wail of sirens while pedestrians try to peer inside to see who is important enough to merit VIP treatment. Kennedy had traveled in hundreds of motorcades, but this time nature had stopped traffic, and his limousine was one of few vehicles heading down Constitution Avenue. He and Jackie and Bill Walton stared out its frosted windows, stunned into silence by the snow-muffled city. They drove at ten miles per hour, but still the policemen in their motorcycle escort skidded and fell, and several times Secret Service agents had to get out and push. Streetlights glowed like pale moons, and whale-shaped hillocks of snow showed where the plows had buried cars. As they drove through Rock Creek Parkway workmen cheered and lit their way though the darkened underpasses with dazzling pink flares.

The Kennedy party arrived at Constitution Hall on time for an 8:15 concert only to find orchestra members still straggling in by foot and only a few hundred people scattered across 3,800 seats. They spent thirty minutes backstage with the conductor Howard Mitchell, who had lavishly praised Kennedy for insisting only classical music be performed on this night. (The high point of Eisenhower's 1957 inaugural concert had been Fred Waring's Pennsylvanians singing "Mamie, We All Love You.") Kennedy preferred Broadway show tunes but feigned an interest in serious music. He had invited celebrities like Jack Dempsey and Helena Rubenstein, who were known to appreciate classical music, to attend the concert, and had asked a hundred famous Americans to contribute short essays explaining what great music meant to them. The results were banal and predictable, but the real purpose of the exercise, like the last-minute invitation to the intellectuals, was to make Maria Callas, Bernard Baruch, Kirk Douglas, William de Kooning, and Mickey Mantle, who all sent essays, feel they were a part of his inauguration, to merge their fame with his, and convey the impression that although he had barely won the popular vote, most prominent Americans applauded his election.

The highlights of the concert were to be *From Sea to Shining Sea,* commissioned from the Pulitzer Prize–winning composer John La Montaine for the occasion, and *The Testament of Freedom—A Setting of Four Passages from the Writings of Thomas Jefferson,* a Randall Thompson composition written in 1943 for the two-hundredth anniversary of Jefferson's birth. The four passages it celebrated, "A Summary of the Rights of British America in 1771," "The Declaration of Causes and Necessity of Taking Up Arms," "The Declaration of Independence," and "Letter to John Adams, Monticello, September 12, 1821," had been printed on an insert to the program. While waiting for the concert to begin, Kennedy slipped the insert into his pocket.

At 8:40 P.M. the Kennedys took their box to a standing ovation and remained in their seats for thirty minutes, long enough to hear the La Montaine and Thompson compositions. The music critic Irving Lowens headlined his review in the *Evening Star* "Inaugural Concert Excellently Done," praising La Montaine's piece as "craftsmanlike and appropriate," and the Thompson composition as "beautifully sung." But Lincoln Kirstein wrote in the *Nation* that *From Sea to Shining Sea* was "a piece of alarming mediocrity," dismissed Mitchell as not in the first rank of American conductors, and accused him of leading the chorus in "a horrendous rendition of Randall Thompson's grisly *Testament of Freedom*." Lowens, however, came closer to understanding the real purpose of the concert, closing his review with a sentence that must have delighted Kennedy: "The presence of this pair [Jack and Jackie] at the concert and their choice of its content is a symbol of civilized delight in the arts and mature reverence for genuine spiritual values." He then unwittingly undermined this observation by writing that Kennedy had drummed his fingers on the rail in front of him throughout the concert, a tic anyone knowing him well would have recognized as evidence not of delight and reverence but of boredom and impatience.

The Kennedys and Walton left at 9:20 and headed down Constitution Avenue to the National Guard Armory, passing a floodlit Washington Monument and Capitol. Outside, soldiers attacked snowdrifts with flamethrowers, Boy Scouts brushed snow from the grandstands with rolled-up newspapers, and work crews warmed themselves at bonfires. As they neared the armory, Kennedy asked the driver to turn on the lights inside the car so the crowd could see Jackie. "We made her sit forward," Walton recalled. "She looked like the Snow Queen . . . very glittering and marvelous."

Kennedy had another motive for wanting the interior illuminated. While the crowd was admiring Jackie, he pulled the inset to the concert program from his pocket and read Jefferson's four passages, comparing them in his mind with his inaugural. Several of their sentences had counterparts in his address.

Jefferson had written to John Adams in 1821 that "in short, the flames kindled on the fourth of July, 1776, have spread over too much of the globe to be extinguished by the feeble engines of despotism." Kennedy would say, "To those new States whom we welcome to the ranks of the free, we pledge our word that one form of colonial control shall not have passed away merely to be replaced by a far more iron tyranny."

Jefferson had declared in 1774 that "the God who gave us life gave us liberty at the same time." Kennedy would say, "And yet the same revolutionary beliefs for which our forebears fought are still at issue around the globe—the belief that the rights of man come not from the generosity of the state, but from the hand of God."

Kennedy shook his head and said, "Better than mine!"

By the rhetorical standards of 1961, his inaugural address was spare and elegant, but compared to Jefferson at his best, it *was* slightly wordy and bombastic. "The rights of man come not from the generosity of the state, but from the hand of God" was good, but "The God who gave us life gave us liberty" was shorter and better.

As Kennedy entered the armory a journalist asked if he had "a good speech" ready for the next day. Kennedy flashed a winning smile and, banishing the doubts of a moment before, and understanding that the more an audience is told a performance will be great the more it is likely to believe it, replied, "It's a smash!"

Frank Sinatra and Peter Lawford greeted the Kennedys at the curb. The Hollywood couturier who had designed Sinatra's eight inauguration ensembles had called them "elegantly tailored and terribly chic," predicting they would make him (and presumably not Kennedy) "the most elegantly dressed man in Washington." His outfit for the gala at the armory—a black jacket outlined in gold braid, trousers in a tiny white-and-black check, black patent leather oxfords, white kid gloves, and black smoke pearl stickpin—would have made him resemble a suave Beelzebub (which was more or less how Jackie Kennedy saw him). But, angered by the crass publicity, Sinatra had ditched this elaborate costume, wearing instead an elegant dinner jacket.

Jackie forced a smile as he escorted her into the cavernous armory, but gripped his hand so tightly he thought she was nervous or angry. He whispered some soothing words. She elbowed him in the ribs and, with a smile still frozen on her face for the cameras, muttered, "Look, Frank. Just smile. That's all you have to do, okay?"

Lyndon and Lady Bird Johnson's limousine arrived right behind the Kennedys', and they climbed out in time to see Sinatra's back as he escorted Jack and Jackie inside. The gossip columnist Maxine Cheshire wrote that Sinatra's failure to wait for the Johnsons had been "a thoughtless act of rudeness" that had alienated many in the crowd. It was just the kind of boorish Rat Pack behavior that appalled Jackie, who proposed thanking Sinatra for staging the gala by giving him a book about etiquette, "not that he would ever read such a thing," she told her husband.

She did not know, yet, that Sinatra had introduced Jack to his mistress Judith Campbell, but suspected he was a major procurer of women she called "bimbos." He had courted Kennedy relentlessly, singing the praises of "That Old Jack Magic," offering "High Hopes" as a campaign theme song, and renaming the Rat Pack the "Jack Pack." She refused to appear at rallies with him or his chick-chasing and hoodlum-friendly cronies, and worked behind the scenes to banish him from the campaign. But with the election over, Kennedy's obsession with Hollywood gossip and Hollywood starlets, and Sinatra's obsession with Kennedy, had led to this inauguration eve fund-raiser, touted as the largest gathering of stars in entertainment history, a "lollapalooza of a show," "a show millions of dollars couldn't buy," and "the biggest one-night gross in the history of show business." It was less charitably described afterward as "the biggest load of corn in farm-surplus history."

Kennedy was popular in Hollywood and on Broadway. Many performers had quickly accepted Sinatra's invitation; others he begged, bribed, and perhaps blackmailed. He had persuaded Leonard Bernstein to conduct the orchestra, and two Broadway producers to darken their shows so Ethel Merman could sing "Everything's Coming Up Roses," and Anthony Quinn and Sir Laurence Olivier could perform a dramatic reading. The distances the stars had traveled impressed reporters, who took it as evidence of their enthusiasm for the New Frontier. Gene Kelly had flown from Switzerland, Sidney Poitier from France, Shirley MacLaine from Japan, and Ella Fitzgerald from Australia. Nat King Cole, Tony Curtis, Janet Leigh, Louis Prima, Jimmy Durante, Keely Smith, Bette Davis, Harry Belafonte, and others whose names were bigger then than now had come from the East and West coasts.

It was assumed that this odd bouillabaisse of hoofers, opera stars, vaudeville comedians, Broadway belters, and classical actors could not fail to give a great show. But Sinatra recognized that the price of filling his gala with so many famous names was a largely middle-aged cast, and joked about having assembled "the finest older talent in the country," and there being hardly anyone "young enough to get into the Kennedy Cabinet."

Americans who preferred the gossip columns to the political pages could not help but be impressed, however, that so many famous entertainers had traveled so far to celebrate Kennedy's inauguration. "Sinatra, Olivier, Merman, Berle, Durante, and Belafonte" was a powerful incantation, voodoo that made Kennedy and Washington appear more glamorous and sensual.

The Washington armory resembles a giant Quonset hut perched on granite blocks and is a ghastly venue, ugly from the outside and depressing inside.

The gala audience sat on twelve thousand collapsible wooden chairs arranged around a central platform. The makeshift sound system faded out or pierced the ears with banshee screams. Most of the audience and cast arrived unwashed, exhausted, wet, hungry, and cold, wearing street clothes rather than costumes or black tie. They kept on their overcoats and wraps and mobbed concession stands, where the only hot food was a hot dog. Backstage, Sinatra drank and hurled obscenities, raging, "Fuck Lawford! I'm not gonna do this show. I'm out!"

The program began ninety minutes late. The cast and local glee clubs marched down the aisles holding red, white, and blue balloons, and singing "Walking Down to Washington," a Kennedy campaign song that had flopped. Then Anthony Quinn, Fredric March, and Sir Laurence Olivier recited a piece so solemn one reviewer predicted it would make the swearing-in "sound like belly laughs." Milton Berle cracked jokes like "I'd rather have this snow storm with Kennedy than a sunny day with the other fellow," and Jimmy Durante trolled for laughs in a toupee resembling Kennedy's thick mop of hair. Nat King Cole poked fun at Nixon's vice presidential running mate, Henry Cabot Lodge, to the tune of "Mona Lisa." Sinatra sang, "That old Jack magic had them in his spell / That old Jack magic that he weaves so well," and a mawkish rendition of "The House I Live In" that had even Jackie dabbing her eyes.

The *Washington Post* described an "erratic show" smacking of the nightclubs. The *Evening Star* said the wisecracks and parodies lacked even the sophistication of a Gridiron Club show. Sinatra sensed it was a flop, carping to the audience, "I don't get big laughs, I just get intellectual laughs."

There were a few high points. Leonard Bernstein conducted a stirring "Stars and Stripes Forever," and Ethel Merman stopped the show by belting out to Kennedy, "You'll be swell! You'll be great! Gonna have the whole world on a plate!"

The best performance came from the de facto leading man, the president-elect. He entered to the loudest applause and closed the show with a tribute linking Frank Sinatra and Thomas Jefferson, a speech he must have composed on the spot when Jefferson was fresh in his mind. He said he was proud to be a Democrat because since the time of Jefferson the Democratic Party had been identified with the pursuit of excellence, and thanks to Sinatra, they had just seen an excellent show. He declared, "The happy relationship between the arts and politics which has characterized our long history I think reached culmination tonight." (The gala was in fact the beginning rather than the culmination of a lengthy relationship between Hollywood and the imperial presidency.) He concluded by saying, "I know we're all indebted to a great friend—Frank Sinatra. After he has ceased to sing, he is going to be standing up and speaking for the Democratic Party. . . . And I want him and my sister Pat's husband, Peter Lawford, to know that we're all indebted to him, and we're proud to have them with us."

Bobby Kennedy was overheard muttering to those surrounding him, "I hope Sinatra will live up to the public image the President has given him by such recognition." Needless to say, he did not. Fourteen months later Bobby would give Lawford the ticklish job of telling Sinatra that instead of staying at his home in Palm Springs as planned, the president would be the guest of his archrival, Bing Crosby. Lawford cited "security concerns" and blamed the Secret Service, but the real reason was an FBI memorandum describing links between Sinatra, the mobster Sam Giancana, Judith Campbell, and Kennedy. Sinatra was so furious that he sledgehammered his unused presidential helipad and expelled Lawford from the Rat Pack. But he continued idolizing Kennedy and playing the recording of his inauguration eve tribute for guests.

Joe Kennedy hosted a supper dance after the gala at Paul Young's Restaurant, a venerable politicians' hangout. It would be his last great moment of reflected glory before, like Sinatra, he faded into the background. The party featured the society bandleader Lester Lanin and a buffet of high-WASP food such as Lobster Newburg and Strawberries Romanoff. It had been scheduled for midnight, but the gala ran so late that the first guests did not arrive until 2:00 A.M.

Joe Kennedy continued hoping his son would show him the inaugural address. He cornered him and repeated his criticism that he had wasted his best material on the Massachusetts legislators. "I just don't think you should have used that speech up in Boston, because that was a real humdinger," he said. "Do you *really* have something that's going to, you know, awaken America tomorrow?"

"I think so, Dad," Kennedy replied, still refusing to take the bait.

He escaped into the pantry with his friend Paul Fay. "Have you ever seen so many attractive people in one room?" he asked. "I'll tell you, Dad really knows how to give a party."

Fay was concerned that Kennedy was staying out so late. "My God!" he exclaimed. "In a few hours you've got to deliver your inaugural address."

Kennedy was nonchalant. "Listen, I've memorized the speech. I know it cold, and I won't sleep anyway."

Fay could reconstruct this conversation decades later because, as was the case with many Kennedy friends, the inauguration was among the most memorable events of his life. It represented the climax of their friendship and the moment it changed forever. Fay remembers recalling that night the first time he had met Kennedy in the South Pacific. Fay had been so impressed after hearing him address a group of new arrivals that he told them, "I'll give anyone here a thousand-to-one odds that he'll be President one day."

Kennedy left the pantry promising to go home. But he was reluctant to end what Ken O'Donnell called "his last carefree night on the town." On the way out he joined O'Donnell and Dave Powers for a glass of champagne. "You two are living like Presidents tonight," he said. "I suppose you'll be laughing it up here for another three hours after I go home and get into bed with my inaugural address."

He arrived home at 3:28 A.M. to find Jackie too excited to sleep. Back at the party, Joe Kennedy told his departing guests, "Just wait until you see the party we throw four years from now."

9

Washington

JANUARY 20

⚜

Kennedy woke on January, 20, 1961, the day of his inauguration, as he did every morning: his valet, George Thomas, knocked gently on his bedroom door and said, "Eight o'clock, Senator." His answer, "I'm awake, George," signaled Thomas to enter the room, draw his bath, and lay out his clothes.

Kennedy had slept only four hours in a house filled with overnight guests, and risen to a city reeling from snow and cold. He was four hours away from becoming president of the United States, yet his only deviation from his usual morning routine was to walk down the hall to the room where Evelyn Lincoln had spent the night, knock on her door, and ask for the Reading Copy of his inaugural address. She had been so worried it might be mislaid that she had slept with it. Pulling it from underneath her covers, she passed it through a crack in the door. Her room adjoined his bathroom, and minutes later she could hear him reciting passages from it as he took a bath.

Had Kennedy wanted only to familiarize himself with his speech and make some mental edits, he would not have needed to read it out loud. By the morning of January 20, he was convinced it would be, as he had told Sorensen and others, "a smash!" but he was less confident about his delivery.

The oratorical Kennedy we remember is the witty and confident winner of the televised debates, and a president who spoke in a slow, resonant voice about civil rights and the Cuban missile crisis. Because one seldom sees films of his earlier speeches, it comes as a shock to discover that during most of his career he was a mediocre public speaker. Even the author of his own campaign biography, James MacGregor Burns, complained that his delivery often "seemed to drain the drama out of situations loaded with possibilities."

Kennedy was aware of his shortcomings. When he appeared on *Meet the Press* in 1951, an aide had computed how fast he was speaking, and noted the results in the margins of the transcript. His pace of 3.6 to 4.4 words per second might have been good for a tobacco auctioneer, but not a politician. Audiotapes and clips of other early television appearances show him rushing his words, speaking in a high-pitched and unmodulated voice, and in a thick Boston-Harvard accent. The journalist Cabell Phillips praised his performance with small groups during the 1960 primaries but reported him reverting to "a flat, hurried monotone" when facing larger audiences. At a news conference following his January 2, 1960, announcement of his candidacy, he snapped out answers to reporters' questions so fast they complained of missing much of what he said. His delivery of his acceptance speech was so clumsy it convinced Nixon he could whip him in a televised debate.

Kennedy's delivery was also hampered by nerves and his innate reserve. An enthusiastic crowd of seven thousand had waited for hours to greet him at the El Paso airport on September 12, 1960, but instead of shouting, gesturing, or flattering them with folksy compliments about their city and state, he had spoken a few lines about getting America moving again. Several days later, the *Look* correspondent William Attwood told him he sensed the crowd had been disappointed, and suggested he try emulating other politicians and wave his arms in the air to encourage a bigger reaction. Kennedy shook his head and, borrowing Attwood's notebook and pencil (he was saving his voice for the day's speeches), wrote, "I always swore one thing I'd never do," then drew a picture of a man thrusting his arms high in the air, Nixon-style.

Progress came slowly to Kennedy because he was not simply trying to eliminate bad public speaking habits, but to overcome some basic character traits such as his impatience, restlessness, and unwillingness to do anything slightly undignified.

An informal committee of Jackie, his brother-in-law Stephen Smith, and the *Boston Globe* reporter Robert Healy critiqued his performance during the primaries. A turning point came when his shrill delivery of his acceptance speech badly damaged his vocal cords. The Boston voice therapist David McClosky traveled to Hyannisport every day for the next three weeks, teaching him to relax, exercise his throat, and speak from his chest. McClosky soon joined the campaign as his personal voice trainer. He coached him in daily vocal exercises and attended rallies, flashing hand signals whenever Kennedy spoke too softly, rapidly, or with insufficient inflection and feeling. Kennedy was a determined pupil and followed McClosky's regimen of spending thirty minutes a day barking loudly in the bathtub.

* * *

Kennedy continued reading his inaugural aloud as he dressed and walked downstairs to breakfast. He was fussy about this meal, and it was always the same: four strips of lean bacon (broiled not fried), two soft-boiled eggs (cooked exactly four and a half minutes), orange juice (freshly squeezed), buttered toast, marmalade, and coffee (heavy on the cream and sugar). This morning he ate from a tray perched on a luggage rack by the living room fireplace. Jackie sat opposite him, eating her usual breakfast of toast and honey, orange juice, and coffee with skimmed milk. He liked to read the newspapers with breakfast, but this morning he barely glanced at the front pages before returning to his speech, sometimes reading it to Jackie between bites of food.

Pierre Salinger arrived during breakfast to find him in a "jubilant mood" and still searching for ways to improve the speech. Kennedy asked him if he had read it.

Salinger, who had prepared the advance release text for the press, said, "It's great!"

At 8:55, Kennedy left his house to attend mass at nearby Holy Trinity Church.

Imagine a brilliant sun in a piercing blue sky, dazzling snowbanks, trees sheathed in ice, and a city of glistening marble. Imagine air so exhilarating it electrifies the senses and an ideal light for black-and-white television, with knife-sharp shadows and an art-film palette of shadings, the kind of day when you can see to the horizon. Imagine all this, and you have Washington, D.C., on the morning of John F. Kennedy's inauguration.

Rose Kennedy relied on her diary, memory, and the recollections of her children to reconstruct the events of this day in her 1974 autobiography. The book is long and uneven, crammed with scraps from letters, diaries, and interviews, polished by a ghostwriter, and vetted and sanitized by the family, but the nine pages she devoted to January 20, 1961, are distinguished by their emotional honesty and vivid imagery. Like her son, she kept to her routine that morning: attending mass and then eating her usual breakfast of French bread, sliced one inch thick and lightly toasted, butter and honey, and a cup of Sanka laced with gelatin to keep her nails strong and her hair glossy. Shortly after eight o'clock, she set off on foot for the Catholic church nearest the house that she and Joe had rented for the week. Snowdrifts covered the sidewalks, so this diminutive, seventy-year-old woman, dressed like a babushka in an oversized overcoat with scarves wrapped around her neck and over her head, trudged half a mile down the middle of empty streets in her thick galoshes, walking, as she usually did, alone.

For Rose Kennedy, the emotional high point of January 20 may not have been the inauguration, but her son's attendance at mass that morning. She claims not to have known he would be at Holy Trinity until she noticed his Secret Service detachment; "I realized he was there of his own volition," she wrote, "[and] that he wanted to start his Presidency by offering his mind and heart, and expressing his hopes and fears to Almighty God, and asking His blessing as he began his great duties." Here, finally, was proof that her efforts to raise him as an observant Catholic had not been wasted.

She took a seat on a side aisle near the rear. Minutes later, he walked down the center aisle and slid into a pew near the altar. She believed her coat and scarves disguised her, and was too embarrassed by her tatty clothes to make herself known to him. But Barbara Gibson, who later became her private secretary, believes she took a seat near the aisle in order to be easily visible, and that Kennedy purposely ignored her, perhaps to underline his independence. The issue is not trivial because one studies unscripted public encounters like this one for evidence their relationship was as close and loving as Rose maintained, or as distant as Jackie believed.

The sun streamed through stained-glass windows and fell on Kennedy's pew, making it difficult for observers to determine whether he was squinting or closing his eyes in prayer. It will never be known if when he knelt in prayer that morning he was performing for the journalists leaning against the hissing radiators at the rear of the church, silently reciting the Lord's Prayer, asking God for guidance and strength, contemplating what Billy Graham had told him about the Second Coming, reviewing his inaugural address, recalling the 1953 marriage of Jackie's sister Lee at this altar, or conjuring up Angie Dickinson, Janet Leigh, and the other starlets he had been ogling six hours earlier.

Hugh Sidey was at Holy Trinity and believes Kennedy's attendance at mass that morning was a political ploy rather than genuine expression of faith, but admits this is only a hunch because Kennedy did not wear his religion on his sleeve and had rebuffed Sidey's attempts to interview him on the subject. What *is* certain is that Kennedy was inscrutable about his faith and pursued a policy best expressed by a statement made by the British statesman Benjamin Disraeli, which he had saved: "My religion is the religion of all wise men. Wise men never tell."

After mass Kennedy stopped at the house across the street from his own to present a bronze plaque thanking its occupants, Charles Montgomery and his daughter, Helen, for providing shelter, coffee, and telephone lines to newsmen covering the transition. It read, "In the cold winter of 1960–61 this house had an important role in history. From it was flashed to the world news of pre-Inauguration announcements by President John F. Kennedy." It was a gracious gesture to make on such a busy morning, but in character for someone who shrewdly courted the press and could not pass a historical marker without reading it. The plaque remains the only reminder of those heady days in Georgetown and is still fastened to the side of the former Montgomery house at eye level. Kennedy's own former home is unmarked, but a sign at Holy Trinity Church states that on November 1, 1963, "this martyred Chief Executive" attended his last mass in Washington here.

Back at N Street Kennedy interrupted Evelyn Lincoln in the middle of a massage. (Miss O'Malley was working on her feet.) He asked to see the Reading Copy of his inaugural, and one senses from Lincoln's account that he was irritated when she explained that Secret Service agents had already taken it to the Capitol and placed it on his seat.

While he dressed, Pierre Salinger stood on the front step, reading journalists a mendacious statement about the health of a man who was currently surviving on a secret regimen of cortisone, Novocain, amphetamines, and more. It declared that he had recently undergone a complete physical examination, and that his New York physicians, Drs. Janet Travell and Eugene Cohen, had judged his health to be "excellent." To this the *New York Times* would add, "Bronzed by the Florida sun during his pre-inauguration holiday, with his brown hair neatly brushed, he looked the picture of health."

Charlie Bartlett and Ben Bradlee were personal friends of long standing, but Kennedy had successfully concealed from them two fundamental truths about himself: that throughout the years they had known him he had been in almost constant physical pain, and that he had been engaging in a multiplicity of extramarital affairs. Their professions of ignorance are heartfelt and credible, but they lead to two conclusions: first, that Kennedy was an intensely private man, stoical about his pain and devious about his personal life; and second, that if they could be so ignorant about his health and sex life, one must treat with skepticism some of their other observations about him, such as that in the days and hours preceding the inauguration he was calm and relaxed. Instead, the more closely one examines Kennedy's final hours as president-elect, the more nervous and irritable he appears, and the more one suspects that his relaxed public demeanor was more "grace under pressure."

Kennedy had planned to wear a cutaway coat, light pearl waistcoat, gray striped trousers, and a white shirt with a detachable collar. As he began dressing, he discovered that his jokes about his "fat face" had been only too true. In fact, he had gained so much weight during the final weeks of the transition that he could not fasten his wing collar. He held his breath and stretched his neck but was still unable to slip a stud through both collar holes.

Secret Service agents raced to his father's house and borrowed an assortment of collars. All proved too large or small. Kennedy became increasingly upset, and soon everyone was rummaging through bureaus and closets. Meanwhile, the chairman of the Joint Congressional Inaugural Committee, Senator John Sparkman of Alabama, and the House Speaker, Sam Rayburn—who had told Johnson in 1960, "Lyndon, you better run, otherwise we're going to have a Catholic in the White House"—arrived at N Street in a limousine, ready to escort the Kennedys to the White House so they could join the Eisenhowers for coffee.

At last, with the two Democratic legislators whose support was crucial to his legislative program sitting outside, someone found a collar that could accommodate the suddenly heavier Kennedy jowls.

It was 10:50 on Kennedy's watch, ten minutes before he was expected at the White House, before he was at last dressed and ready to go. He paced the front hall impatiently, twirling his hat in his hand, unaware that Jackie, who was nervous they would arrive at the White House late, had set his watch twenty minutes ahead.

He put his hat on and took it off several times before asking Mary Gallagher if he should walk out of the door carrying it or wearing it. "You look handsome either way," she said. "Carry it in your hand if you want, but please get started."

Jackie was in the living room, touching up her makeup and examining herself in a compact. He stuck his head into the room and snapped, "Come on, Jackie! For God's sake, let's go." Jackie, knowing they would arrive early if they left now, continued to take her time, further exasperating him.

As they finally walked down the hall shaking hands with the household staff, someone shouted, "It's a great day for the Irish!" Kennedy laughed, waved, perched the top hat on his head at a jaunty angle, then stepped outside to the cheers of several hundred spectators. As they approached the car, Jackie was overheard to say, "I want you to wear it [the top hat] every time you go out." It was either an affectionate dig or her way of taking him down a peg.

He was climbing into the limousine when he realized he had forgotten something and dashed back into the house. Rosemary Sorrentino never learned what he had returned for, but remembers that when he looked up and saw her and Kenneth, Jackie's hairdresser, standing at a window, he waved at them. It was at this moment, she recalled, that Kenneth began liking him—"when he saw that the man who was on his way to be sworn in as President wasn't too big to wave to us—the hired help."

CBS began its live broadcast at 10:45. Viewers tuning in then saw the Kennedys emerge from their limousine at the White House as the correspondent Robert Trout said, "The President-elect is looking quite tan from his Florida stay."

Even on television you could see, and hear, the cold. People had pulled up their collars like spies and picked their way carefully down icy sidewalks, taking baby steps and watching their feet. Snow covered the hoods of the motorcade limousines, and a stiff wind ruffled flags, shook branches, and stirred up little tornadoes of swirling snow. Every breath and spoken word left behind a white cloud, like the balloon in front of a cartoon character.

The twenty-nine minutes that Jack and Jackie spent in the White House that morning are among the least remembered of that day. The only report on the Eisenhower coffee, which the Johnsons and Nixons also attended, comes from Mary Thayer, who writes that Jackie tried to be as unobtrusive as possible and took a seat on a couch next to Pat Nixon, who ignored her.

The event struck most as a banal exchange of pleasantries, but for Jackie it was anything but routine. Her last White House visit had come on December 9, just hours after she left the hospital following her son's birth. She had requested a wheelchair in advance, but Mamie could not bear the thought of pushing the wife of a political opponent through the White House. The chief usher, J. B. West, who adored Jackie and portrayed Mamie Eisenhower as a dragon lady in his memoirs, *Upstairs at the White House,* wrote that when Mamie summoned him to discuss this wheelchair, "her carefully manicured fingernails drummed the night table," and she said, "I'll tell you what, we'll get a wheelchair, but put it behind a door somewhere, out of sight. It will be available *if she asks for it.*"

When Mamie's grueling tour ended, West reports that she stepped "regally" into her limousine and headed off to play canasta with her friends, while Jackie walked alone to her three-year-old station wagon, pain already darkening her face. She began crying as she was driven through the White House gates, not so much from fatigue as from the shock of seeing its drab living quarters. She told one friend that they almost sent her back to the hospital with a crying jag. Later, she compared them to Moscow's Lubyanka prison, and a hotel "decorated by a wholesale furniture store during a January clearance," and complained that Mamie had not offered her "even a cup of tea."

Whenever Mamie mentioned Jackie to West after this visit, it was always, he said, "in the voice she reserved for disapproval." On the morning of January 20 she summoned him to her bedroom to complain of reading in the morning papers that Jackie planned on sleeping in the Queen's Room that evening. She reminded West that *she* had always kept this as a special guest room. West understood this to mean that you had to *be* a queen to sleep there, and Jackie was no queen. Perhaps this is why Thayer, who was relying on Jackie's recollections, described the atmosphere at this coffee as "painfully strained."

Jackie and Mamie rode from the White House to the Capitol in a Cadillac limousine together with Senator Styles Bridges of New Hampshire. It was a moment neither woman could have anticipated with much pleasure, but here they were: Mamie in a gaudy "tomato red" suit, matching hat, and bulky mink, Jackie in Cassini's fawn coat trimmed with a whisper of sable; Mamie, who had shared a bed with her husband during forty-five years of marriage, and Jackie, who did not plan on sharing the same bedroom with her husband on their first night in the White House; Mamie, who had spent most of her White House evenings sitting next to her husband as they ate their supper off trays perched in front of his-and-hers televisions, and Jackie, who would fill her husband's evenings with intimate dinner parties and concerts; Mamie, the daughter of an Iowa meatpacker who had never attended college and loved canasta and mahjong, and Jackie, the daughter of a philandering, alcoholic New York stockbroker, who had attended Vassar and the Sorbonne and been named Debutante of the Year. Here they were, then, two women riding together to the Capitol who, because neither suspected the infidelities the other had endured in her marriage, believed they had nothing in common.

As the limousine pulled away from the White House, Mamie turned to Senator Bridges and said, "Doesn't Ike look like Paddy the Irishman in his top hat?"

Jackie reported this comment to Arthur Schlesinger, who included it without comment in *A Thousand Days*. Thayer gave it a fuller treatment in her book, writing that Bridges looked visibly distressed and Jackie said little, while during the rest of the drive Mamie "chatted on effortlessly."

A casual slur is more devastating than a considered one. "Paddy the Irishman" meant taverns, graft, and the feckless, dim-witted Mick of countless jokes. That the slur has since been defanged owes not a little to the Kennedy presidency. Considering that several generations of the Kennedy family had been at the receiving end of anti-Irish prejudice, and that JFK had acknowledged anti-Catholic and anti-Irish prejudice in his acceptance speech by saying that his party had "taken on what many regard as a new and hazardous risk," Mamie's remark was either careless and insensitive or profoundly wicked.

Jackie herself was seven-eighths Irish, and the remark clearly burned itself into her memory and must have been doubly unsettling because awaiting her at the Capitol was her mother, Janet Auchincloss, who, although Irish herself, viewed the Kennedys as occupying a lower social stratum, and had complained before Jackie's marriage that "the wedding will be just awful—quite dreadful. There will be one hundred Irish politicians!" And preparing to watch the ceremony on television were millions of Americans who had voted against her husband, according to postelection polls, because he was a "Papist," a "Mick," a "Paddy."

When the women's husbands had posed together on the steps of the White House just before leaving, one reporter noted that Eisenhower was the more relaxed of the two. They rode to the Capitol ahead of their wives in a bubble-topped limousine, and both seemed flummoxed by their top hats and kept putting them on and taking them off. Kennedy brought up the subject of D-Day, no doubt imagining it a safe topic for these tricky moments. He asked Eisenhower's opinion of *The Longest Day,* the recent best-selling book about the Normandy invasion by Cornelius Ryan, a Kennedy supporter who had been with him in Hyannisport on election night. The supreme commander of Allied forces in Europe told Kennedy he had not read Ryan's book. Kennedy remarked to Bobby afterward that Eisenhower appeared not to have read much of anything.

Americans watching the CBS broadcast of the inauguration saw a motorcade of limousines, Secret Service cars, and open trucks filled with reporters and cameramen. They heard Robert Trout say the inaugural address was "rumored to be short, although not on a par with Washington's 135-word second inaugural," then summarize Kennedy's speech to the Massachusetts legislature, reminding viewers that he had said, "Our success or failure will be measured by the answer to four questions: were we men of courage, judgment, integrity, and dedication?" The inaugural address would be "a very serious speech," Trout added, and would challenge Americans to demonstrate similar qualities.

Trout's commentary, like many of the editorials commenting on the address, implied that challenging Americans to acts of courage and sacrifice would be a new departure. In fact, the speech sitting on Kennedy's empty chair at the Capitol would reiterate much of what he had been saying throughout his campaign. It would inspire Americans but not surprise them. Just as a nation exhausted by the Civil War wanted to hear "With malice toward none;

with charity for all," and Britons in 1940 were ready for "we shall neither flag nor fail. . . . We shall go on to the end," Americans in 1961, more prosperous and better educated than ever before yet experiencing a midlife crisis at mid-century, were longing for a New Frontier and aching for "ask not."

Americans had been more fascinated and excited by politics during the 1960 election than at any other time in the century. *Life* had devoted its July 4, 1960, issue to "Politics: A Great Game and a Sight to Behold." The columnist Arthur Krock contributed an essay to it titled "The Year Everybody Cares." On November 6, 63.8 percent of eligible American voters cast ballots, the highest percentage since 1908, and a record remaining unbroken. The parties estimated that four million Americans had been actively involved in the campaign, organizing rallies, stuffing envelopes, and canvassing neighborhoods. People participated because they had been caught up in the televised drama of the debates, and because they believed in the power and benevolence of the federal government—a *Newsweek* poll reported that 70 percent of Americans believed the federal government "would do the right thing most of the time" (a level of trust falling to 29 percent within thirty years)—and that electing the right man to the presidency would make a difference in their lives.

To understand the appeal of Kennedy's pledge "to get this country moving again," one must divide the 1950s into an era of contentment followed by a time of American drift and apparent Soviet triumphs. During this latter period, beginning roughly in 1956, Eisenhower suffered a heart attack, bungled the U-2 spy plane incident, and dispatched federal troops to Little Rock to enforce the court-ordered desegregation of a high school. Also alarming was Castro's assumption of power in Cuba, the Soviet launch of the Sputnik space satellite and testing of hydrogen bombs, and Chairman Nikita Khrushchev's threat to "bury" the United States. Meanwhile, the U.S. economy was falling into recession and unemployment reaching its highest level in two decades. In the *Washington Post* on Inauguration Day, the British economist Barbara Ward warned of "a revolutionary world streaming forward and of America standing still," and a 1960 *New York Times* editorial described "a nation drowning in a sea of luxury and mesmerized by the trivialities of the television screen." Further darkening the mood was a much-publicized letter from John Steinbeck to Adlai Stevenson addressing what Steinbeck called the "vacancy" in America's soul, and concluding, "I am troubled by the cynical immorality of my country. It cannot survive on this basis." On the morning of January 20, Steinbeck was sitting next to John Kenneth Galbraith in the VIP section beneath the presidential stand, awaiting an inaugural address that he, like many Americans, hoped would fill this vacancy in the national soul.

During his campaign, Kennedy had addressed the national unease with materialism, large organizations, and conformity. This unease had already been diagnosed and encouraged by a robust literature of social criticism that included *The Organization Man, The Status Seekers, The Hidden Persuaders, The Lonely Crowd, The Waste Makers,* and *The Man in the Gray Flannel Suit,* books whose very titles had become household words and a shorthand for the alleged failure of postwar prosperity to make Americans fulfilled or happy. The most influential was Sloan Wilson's *The Man in the Gray Flannel Suit,* a novel that contrasted the purpose and sacrifice of the war years with the executive suite conformity and suburban boredom of the 1950s, and whose bleak opening sentence, "By the time they had both lived seven years in the little house on Greenacre Avenue in Westport, Connecticut, they both detested it," perfectly captured the postwar angst.

Rather than merely riding a wave of *Man in the Gray Flannel Suit* dissatisfaction with consumer durables as the final fruit of the Second World War, Kennedy had long been ahead of it. In a May 7, 1945 (V-E Day), story he filed from the United Nations conference in San Francisco during his brief stint as a Hearst reporter, he had written that it was understandable that American servicemen should be concerned with the result of the conference "because any man who has risked his life for his country and seen his friends killed around him must inevitably wonder why this happened to him and most important, what good it will do. . . . It is not surprising that they should question the worth of their sacrifice."

The students who were gathering at this moment in auditoriums and dormitories across the country to watch the inauguration were as dissatisfied, and as eager to be challenged, as some of their parents. By 1960, the so-called Silent Generation had largely disappeared, African-American students were staging sit-ins at lunch counters, and campus political rallies were attracting audiences three times larger than in 1956. A 1960 survey showed 94 percent of young Americans agreeing with the statement that "there is still a good chance for adventure." When offered a choice between a range of accomplishments and possessions, less than 2 percent claimed to want a new car, while the first choice of 62 percent was "attending university and earning a doctorate." An article running in *Look* magazine that same year spoke of an "Explosive Generation" with "a strong desire for goals and causes."

Kennedy had offered this generation the Peace Corps. On the evening of October 13, 1960, he had stepped up to a microphone on the steps of the University of Michigan Student Union and, inspired by an audience of enthusiastic students, shouted, "How many of you who are going to be doctors are willing to spend your days in Ghana? . . . How many of you are willing to work in the Foreign Service and spend your lives traveling around the world? . . . On your willingness to contribute part of your life to this country I think will depend the answer of whether a free society can compete." An aide dashed into the restaurant where the speechwriters Goodwin and Sorensen were eating a late supper to report that Kennedy had just proposed a Peace Corps. "Within two days after Kennedy's extemporaneous advocacy, seven hundred students at the University of Michigan had signed up for service in the nonexistent agency," Goodwin later wrote. "Inadvertently, intuitively, Kennedy had tapped into a still-emerging spirit of the times."

Throughout the 1960 campaign, Kennedy had told eager students and dissatisfied Organization Men that they had become materialistic and soft, and that their nation lacked courage and ideals. Americans had "lost their way, their will, and their sense of historic purpose," he said, and needed to demonstrate "courage, not complacency" (a message that would end the career of any politician foolhardy enough to voice it today). His New Frontier, he said, asked them to choose "between public interest and private comfort." It appealed to their pride, not their pocketbooks, and held out "the promise of more sacrifice instead of more security."

In a nationally televised speech in September, he had warned that history would judge Americans by their willingness to deny themselves material comforts, saying, "If we meet our public and our private responsibilities and obligations, if we recognize that self-government requires qualities of self-denial and restraint, then future historians will be able to say, 'These were the great years of the American Republic.'" He often referred to what he called the "contest between the comfortable and the concerned," declaring, "I do not want it said of Americans what T. S. Eliot wrote in his poem 'The Rock,' 'And the wind shall say: "These were decent people, their only monument the asphalt road and a thousand lost golf balls."'" It was a wickedly clever verse that appealed to the unhappy Organization Men and conjured up the most highly touted accomplishment, the Interstate Highway System, and the favorite pastime, golf, of the elderly president beside whom Kennedy was sitting as they were driven to the Capitol, where he would deliver a speech offering Americans something more glorious than highways and golf balls.

The dignitaries seated in VIP sections on the Capitol steps had been requested to take their places by 11:00 A.M. But when Kennedy walked into the

Capitol rotunda at 11:44 A.M. many had been delayed by the treacherous driving conditions and were still arriving. Before he could be seated, everyone else would have to file out through the bronze doors at the eastern end of the vast domed room. The delay and confusion unsettled Jackie, who complained to her husband's military aide, Major General Chester Clifton, "No one has told me what to do. I just don't know . . . Jack's told me nothing."

Clifton relayed her message, and Kennedy asked him to clear a room where they could be alone. (Much the same thing had happened in Palm Beach on January 15 when, after quarreling with Rose about attending lunch with Lyndon Johnson, Jackie had appeared at breakfast and insisted on seeing Jack alone in their bedroom.) After spending five minutes with her in a room off the rotunda, he emerged and told Clifton, "Let's go! Let's keep it running."

Whatever happened in that room must have worked. Afterward the cameras caught Jackie engaged in an animated conversation with the Johnsons' daughters, Luci and Lynda Johnson. Her posture was regal, her smile cold but unwavering. She was following her own advice, "Just smile, Frank."

Richard Nixon was camera-savvy, too, but trying too hard and talking too much. He stood close to Eisenhower while gesturing expansively at the interior of the dome where a fresco, *The Apotheosis of Washington,* depicted the first president of the United States rising to the heavens in glory.

The CBS commentator Howard K. Smith described Kennedy as "bronze," "very healthy looking," and "already looking rather in command of the situation." While the whole world was waiting for him, Smith boasted, Kennedy was talking with the CBS reporter Nancy Hanschman (later Nancy Dickerson), the first woman to be a television network correspondent. Left unsaid was that Kennedy had dated Hanschman before meeting Jackie.

Hanschman pitched Kennedy an easy question, "When did you first imagine yourself becoming President?"

"Ever since I was a boy," he replied quickly, an answer of dubious honesty that must have surprised Hanschman, since it was widely assumed his political ambitions dated from his brother Joe's death.

If newspapers are "a rough draft of history"—and one could say the same thing about television news—then the rough draft of Kennedy's inauguration would be written, narrated, and managed by journalists like Nancy Hanschman, Arthur Krock, Joe Alsop, Ben Bradlee, and Charlie Bartlett, whose relationships with him were closer and more complicated than most suspected.

Eight years before, Hanschman had pulled strings to get Kennedy extra seats to Eisenhower's inauguration, and four years hence, she and her husband would buy Merrywood, the Virginia estate where Jackie had spent much of her childhood. Such coincidences and relationships were typical of a time when elites were smaller, and the worlds of money, journalism, art, entertainment, literature, politics, and café and social register society more overlapping and homogeneous. By the standards of 1961, it was not really *that* surprising that Jack Kennedy had cuckolded Oleg Cassini with the actress Gene Tierney, or that his father had sabotaged Cassini's engagement to the actress Grace Kelly, or that fourteen years before Cassini designed Jackie's Inauguration Day outfit his brother, the gossip columnist Igor Cassini, had named her Debutante of the Year. Nor that surprising that sitting near Cassini at the Capitol was the author John Hersey, who had broken Kennedy's heart by marrying Frances Ann Cannon, and a year later had written the *New Yorker* article about PT 109 that had established him as a war hero. Also in the audience was Henry Luce, who would hear in the inaugural address echoes of his own American Proposition that "America's mission is to make men free," and sitting next to him was his strong-willed wife, Clare Boothe Luce, who had slept with Joe Kennedy Sr., had given Jack Kennedy the good luck charm he wore around his neck in the South Pacific, and may have seduced him as well, or vice versa. Then there was the *New York Times* columnist Arthur Krock, who had helped Joe Kennedy write *I'm for Roosevelt,* then helped Jack Kennedy polish *Why England Slept,* presented him with the gift of his own valet when he came to Washington as a new congressman, found jobs at the *Washington Times-Herald* for Jack's lover Inga Arvad, his sister Kathleen, and, before she became his wife, for Jackie, too.

Kennedy whistled nervously and rocked on his heels while waiting to proceed from the rotunda to the presidential stand. "When the hell do you think we'll start?" he asked Hanschman. So much for being "in command of the situation."

As he moved out of earshot, Hanschman told the CBS anchorman Walter Cronkite that he had been "obviously anxious to get the proceedings going." She later wrote that he had reminded her of a groom nervously awaiting a tardy bride.

The dignitaries began filing out at noon, the hour when the ceremony was supposed to commence. First went the diplomats in plumed hats and national dress; then the Supreme Court, leaders of Congress, Kennedy cabinet, and Kennedy family; finally the Johnsons, Nixons, Eisenhowers, and Jackie. Oleg Cassini had been waiting for this moment all morning. He was "fantastically nervous," he says, and convinced the next five minutes would determine the new first lady's destiny, and his. When Mamie, Lady Bird, and Pat appeared in heavy furs, his spirits rose, and he noted with pleasure that none of their coats was very new or very chic.

As Jackie descended the Capitol steps, the crowd rose to its feet, cheering and applauding. Cassini sensed victory. Her fawn coat, with its understated sable collar, matching pillbox hat, and small sable muff, communicated youth, simplicity, and elegance. She was the gorgeous petal in a dowdy bouquet of fur. He had promised she would stand out but was still astonished when it happened exactly that way. He sensed he was witnessing a turning point in fashion history—the celebritization of fashion, and the iconization of Jackie Kennedy—and once her husband began speaking, he realized that her outfit perfectly complemented his spare and elegant prose.

PIVOTAL MOMENTS IN THE LIFE OF JOHN F. KENNEDY THAT WERE REFLECTED IN HIS INAUGURAL ADDRESS

An unnamed British officer briefs Kennedy on the situation in Jerusalem in the spring of 1939. Kennedy traveled extensively throughout Europe and the Middle East on the eve of the Second World War. He learned that it is more difficult for a democracy than a totalitarian state to mobilize its citizens for war, and that to overcome this vulnerability, democratic leaders had to inspire their citizens to voluntary acts of sacrifice. These are the philosophical underpinnings of "Ask not . . . " *(John F. Kennedy Library)*

On the morning of September 3, 1939, Kennedy (right) walks to the House of Commons with his brother Joe Jr. and his sister, Kathleen. After Prime Minister Neville Chamberlain announces that Britain is at war with Germany, Winston Churchill will deliver a five-minute speech whose words will echo through Kennedy's inaugural address. *(John F. Kennedy Library)*

Kennedy (far right) and some of the crew of PT 109 one month before a Japanese destroyer rammed and sank their ship. The two sailors who perished were probably on Kennedy's mind when he referred to "the graves of young Americans who answered the call to service . . . " *(John F. Kennedy Library)*

Kennedy delivers a speech at Memorial Day ceremonies in 1946, as a candidate for the House of Representatives in Massachusetts. He often became emotional when speaking to veterans, and his reference to the American war dead would be the turning point of his inaugural address. *(John F. Kennedy Library)*

During the inaugural parade in 1961, Kennedy rose to his feet and cheered his former crew members who stood lining the deck of this PT 109 replica. *(John F. Kennedy Library)*

Right: Kennedy (second from right) and Secretary of the Navy James Forrestal (far left) during a visit to Berlin in July 1945. The pulverized buildings of postwar Berlin and the suffering of its citizens lay behind the plea in his inaugural address for Soviets and Americans to "begin the quest for peace, before the dark powers of destruction engulf all humanity." *(John F. Kennedy Library)*

Left: Kennedy is met by French officials on his arrival at Saigon's Tan Son Hut Airport on October 19, 1951. Robert Kennedy believed that this trip made a "very, very major impression" on his brother. It was reflected in several lines in the inaugural address, including the pledge that "one form of colonial control shall not have passed away merely to be replaced by a far more iron tyranny." *(John F. Kennedy Library)*

Right: Kennedy speaks with miners during the 1960 West Virginia presidential primary. According to a friend who accompanied him to the state, "If you go into a coal miner's town or into his house . . . you can't help but be moved." In his inaugural speech, Kennedy made more references to the "poor" and "poverty" than any other president before him. *(John F. Kennedy Library)*

Above: The Kennedy family on election day in Hyannisport. *(John F. Kennedy Library)*

Right: Kennedy and Sorensen. Sorensen has written that by the time of the 1960 election, "our style and standard had become increasingly one." *(John F. Kennedy Library)*

Left: Kennedy's devoted secretary Evelyn Lincoln *(John F. Kennedy Library)*

Kennedy (right) and his brothers and sisters at their parents' villa in Palm Beach, in the late 1940s. The one-story stucco wing behind them contains the bedroom where Jack and Jackie slept during the week of January 10, 1961, and where he revised his inaugural address that same week. *(John F. Kennedy Library)*

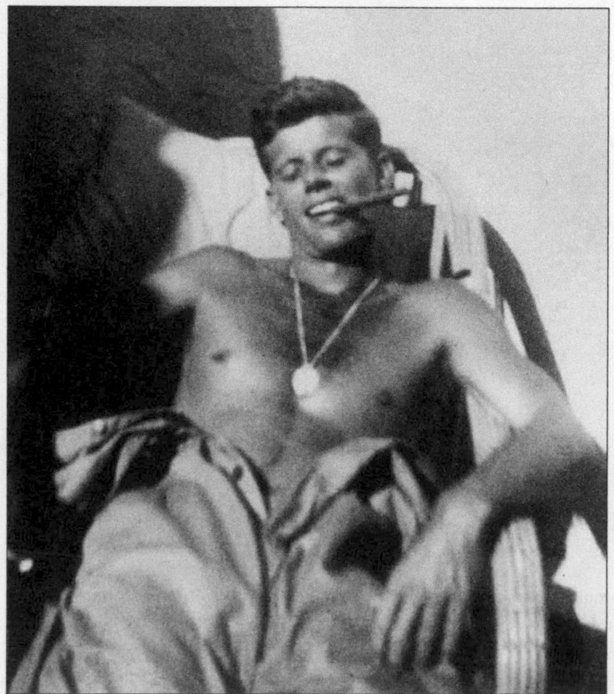

Kennedy deepens his tan in Palm Beach during the winter of 1944. Tanning was a lifelong obsession, and during the ten days preceding the inauguration he worked at maintaining a dark one that would show up on black-and-white television. *(John F. Kennedy Library)*

33

During a flight to Washington three days before the inauguration, Kennedy copied this passage from his inaugural address in his handwriting in order to establish his authorship. It is often mistakenly identified as part of a handwritten "first draft."
(John F. Kennedy Library)

Kennedy stayed at his apartment in New York's Carlyle Hotel on the night of January 17, 1961, and devoted the following day to polishing his physical appearance.
(Robert Knudsen, White House, in the John F. Kennedy Library)

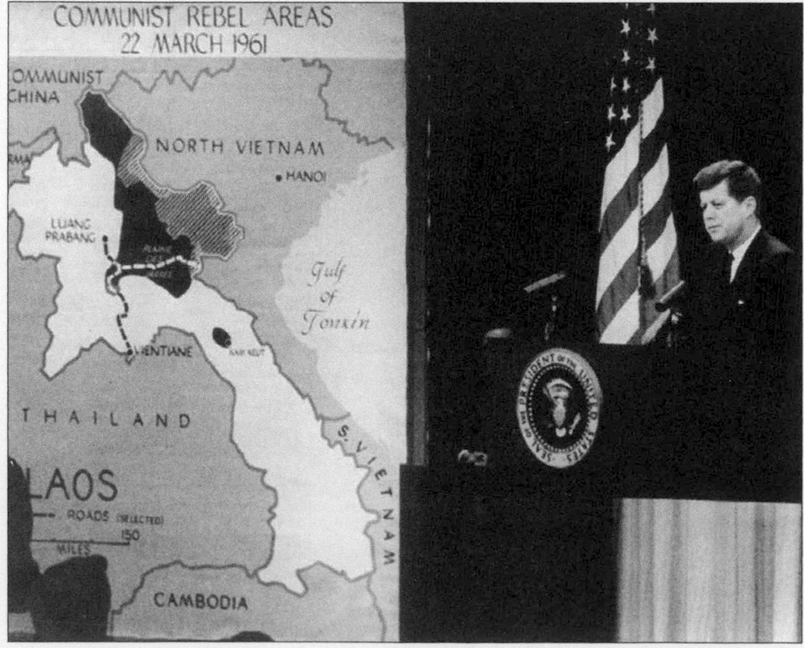

CBS executives Fred Friendly and Blair Clark suggested ways for Kennedy to make his television appearances more visually arresting. He took some of their advice to heart when he delivered his inaugural address. During this March 23, 1961, briefing on the crisis in Laos, Kennedy used a map to illustrate his discussion. *(John F. Kennedy Library)*

The Inaugural Committee
requests the honor of your presence
to attend and participate in the Inauguration of
John Fitzgerald Kennedy
as President of the United States of America
and
Lyndon Baines Johnson
as Vice President of the United States of America
on Friday the twentieth of January
one thousand nine hundred and sixty one
in the City of Washington

Edward H. Foley
Chairman

The Inaugural Committee mailed out 40,000 engraved invitations on the assumption that most of their recipients would consider them souvenirs and not attend. Instead, so many ward heelers and campaign volunteers descended on Washington that two inaugural balls had to be added at the last minute. *(John F. Kennedy Library)*

Diagram of Seating on

President's Platform

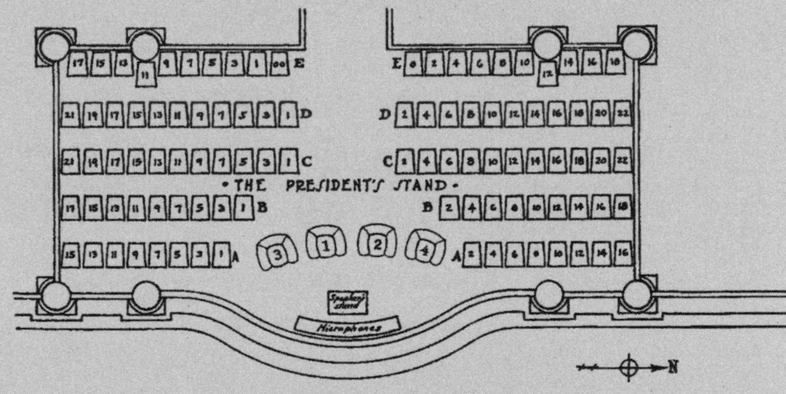

1. President-elect John F. Kennedy
2. Vice President-elect Lyndon B. Johnson
3. President Dwight D. Eisenhower
4. Vice President Richard M. Nixon

A

1. Mrs. John F. Kennedy
2. Honorable John Sparkman
3. Mrs. Lyndon B. Johnson
4. Ex-President Harry S. Truman
5. Mrs. Dwight D. Eisenhower
6. Mrs. Harry S. Truman
7. Mrs. Richard M. Nixon
8. Speaker Sam Rayburn
9. Ex-President Herbert Hoover
10. Miss Lynda Bird Johnson
11. Honorable Joseph P. Kennedy
12. Miss Lucy Baines Johnson
13. Mrs. Joseph P. Kennedy
14. Mrs. Birge Alexander
15. Miss Ann Gargan
16. Mr. Birge Alexander

Diagram of Seating on the President's Platform
(John F. Kennedy Library)

B

1. Chief Justice Earl Warren
2. Honorable Carl Hayden
3. Mrs. Earl Warren
4. Honorable Styles Bridges
5. Mrs. R. Sargent Shriver
6. Honorable John McCormack
7. Mr. R. Sargent Shriver
8. Honorable Charles A. Halleck
9. Mrs. Peter Lawford
10. Honorable Henry A. Wallace
11. Mr. Peter Lawford
12. Mr. A. J. Taylor
13. Mrs. Robert F. Kennedy
14. Mrs. A. J. Taylor
15. Mrs. Stephen Smith
16. Mrs. James D. Moss
17. Mr. Stephen Smith
18. Mr. James D. Moss

C

1. Mrs. John Sparkman
2. Mr. Franklin B. Dryden
3. Mrs. Tazewell Shepard
4. His Eminence Richard Cardinal Cushing
5. Mrs. Alben Barkley
6. Reverend Dr. John Barclay
7. Mrs. Woodrow Wilson
8. His Eminence Archbishop Iakovos
9. Mrs. Franklin D. Roosevelt
10. Miss Marian Anderson
11. Mrs. John McCormack
12. Mr. Robert Frost
13. Mrs. Styles Bridges
14. Rabbi Dr. Nelson Glueck
15. Mrs. Charles A. Halleck
16. Mrs. Oscar P. Bobbitt
17. Mr. Edward M. Kennedy
18. Mr. Oscar P. Bobbitt
19. Mrs. Edward M. Kennedy
20. Mr. Sam Houston Johnson
21. Mr. K. Lemoyne Billings
22. Miss Rebekah Alexander

D

1. Honorable Dean Rusk
2. Honorable James R. Browning
3. Honorable Adlai Stevenson
4. Justice Hugo L. Black
5. Honorable C. Douglas Dillon
6. Justice Felix Frankfurter
7. Honorable Robert S. McNamara
8. Justice William O. Douglas
9. Honorable Robert F. Kennedy
10. Justice Tom C. Clark
11. Honorable J. Edward Day
12. Justice John M. Harlan
13. Honorable Stewart L. Udall
14. Justice William J. Brennan, Jr.
15. Honorable Orville R. Freeman
16. Justice Charles E. Whittaker
17. Honorable Luther H. Hodges
18. Justice Potter Stewart
19. Honorable Arthur J. Goldberg
20. Justice Stanley F. Reed
21. Honorable Abraham Ribicoff
22. Justice Harold H. Burton

E

1. Honorable Zeake W. Johnson, Jr.
2. Honorable Joseph C. Duke
3. Mrs. Edward H. Foley
4. Mrs. Diana Tschursin
5. Mr. Edward H. Foley
6. Miss Susan Taylor
7. Mrs. T. J. Reardon, Jr.
8. Mr. Dale Miller
9. Mr. T. J. Reardon, Jr.
10. Mrs. Dale Miller
11. Mrs. Everett M. Dirksen
12. Honorable Mike Mansfield
13. Honorable Everett M. Dirksen
14. Mrs. Mike Mansfield
15. Mrs. Hugh D. Auchincloss
16. Mrs. W. A. Thomas
17. Mr. Hugh D. Auchincloss
18. Mrs. J. E. Bartley

Chief Justice Earl Warren administers the oath of office. *(John F. Kennedy Library)*

Looking out at the audience, and straight into the cameras and history, Kennedy delivers his inaugural address. *(John F. Kennedy Library)*

Kennedy stands before the nation bareheaded and without the topcoat that he has left folded on his chair. *(John F. Kennedy Library)*

go forth to lead the land we love,
asking His blessing and His help,
but knowing that here on earth God's
work must truly be our own.

John F. Kennedy
January 20th 1961

Kennedy's signature on the last page of the Reading Copy of the inaugural address is bolder and more careful than his usual scrawl. *(John F. Kennedy Library)*

Kennedy and Johnson on the inaugural parade reviewing stand. Joe and Rose Kennedy are seated at Jackie's right. *(John F. Kennedy Library)*

The Kennedys arrive at one of the inaugural balls. *(John F. Kennedy Library)*

The Kennedy inauguration and assassination haunt each other. We see him on January 20, 1961, in the Capitol rotunda, impatiently waiting for the ceremony to begin; we see him again, lying in state in the rotunda on November 24, 1963. *(John F. Kennedy Library)*

10

The Capitol

JANUARY 20

⚜

The apotheosis of John F. Kennedy began at 12:12 P.M., when he left the twilight of the domed room where in 1,038 days he would lie in state, and strode through the great bronze doors of the Capitol into the brilliant noonday sunshine. The light reflecting off the snow and marble was so dazzling that many in the crowd wore sunglasses. Like spectators at a tennis match, they turned their heads toward him in unison. There was a hush, then cheers as his presence transformed this cold and restive crowd into an audience.

He took his seat on a stand that had been used for inaugurations since Franklin Roosevelt's first. It resembled a small Greek temple, with a flat roof perched on eight Corinthian columns. It sat at a ritual distance above the crowd, making it the nearest the American Republic comes to having a pulpit or throne. The dome rising behind it had been repainted, the exteriors of the House and Senate wings cleaned, and the sandstone on the East Front replaced with marble. It was agreed the Capitol had never looked more magnificent.

The CBS commentator Edward R. Murrow said he was impressed "by a sense of solemnity, not so much about the manner and bearing of the President as about the audience here at the Capitol." Kennedy's demeanor during the campaign had contributed to this atmosphere, and the speech he was about to deliver would reinforce it. Unlike some of his successors, he had, if anything, erred on the side of overestimating the literacy and intelligence of the American people. During the campaign he had quoted from Francis Bacon at the Bergen Mall in Paramus, Edmund Burke at Frontier Park in Cheyenne, T. S. Eliot at a Minnesota bean feed, Aristotle in Pittsburgh, *King Lear* in Buffalo, Emerson in Duluth, and, at rallies here and there, from

Victor Hugo, Johann Wolfgang von Goethe, and Oscar Wilde—"Experience is the name that everyone gives to their mistakes." Without sounding pretentious, he had told Massachusetts legislators, "For what Pericles said of the Athenians has long been true of this Commonwealth: 'We do not imitate—for we are a model to others,'" and reminded delegates to the Democratic National Convention of Longfellow's "Humanity with all its fears / with all its hopes of future years / is hanging breathless on thy fate." Perhaps it was naive, or a form of subtle flattery, like inviting noted academics to contribute to his speeches, but consider that during the weekend between his assassination and funeral fifty thousand Americans expressed their grief over his death by writing poems and mailing them to the White House, and that within days of his inauguration high school students had sent him Greek and Latin translations of his inaugural address. If he *had* overestimated the American people, no one was complaining, and if he was the last president to make such assumptions, perhaps it was because 1961 was the last time they were warranted.

Park policemen, ushers, and Secret Service agents also turned their faces toward him as he arrived, and hundreds of spectators took advantage of their inattention to leap walls, crawl under ropes, duck barricades, and sneak into the reserved standing areas. Add to them 23,000 official standees, 18,000 people in reserved seats, 2,000 journalists, and dozens of young men sitting in trees, and you approach the *Washington Post* estimate of 50,000 spectators, more than twice the number who had gathered here in better weather for Eisenhower in 1957. Many had spent the night on sofas, floors, and cots in makeshift shelters, walked through snowdrifts and down ice-covered sidewalks, and stood for hours in the twenty-two-degree cold and twenty-mile-an-hour winds, wrapped in blankets and sleeping bags, stamping feet and blowing on hands. The Kennedy glamour had bewitched some; others expected that a Pulitzer Prize–winning author would deliver a historic address. They saw one of the most handsome men ever to become President standing before them in the bitter cold without a hat, coat, or scarf. They saw a man with a mahogany tan and thick chestnut hair who appeared to be, as the newspapers were reporting, "a picture of health." Jackie's mother, Janet Auchincloss, like others in her generation, perceived "a sort of [Charles] Lindbergh quality" in him. The Boston political operative Billy Sutton thought he resembled Jimmy Stewart, who had played Lindbergh in a recent film. Those more attuned to Hollywood saw an honorary member of Sinatra's Rat Pack, and a few may even have sensed that his combination of show-business cool and flinty New England reserve was an uneasy one.

As Kennedy arrived on the stand, Jackie raised her eyebrows at him and smiled. It was a fleeting gesture, but the expression crossing her face was mischievous and—there is no other way to describe it—sexy. It was a window on their hidden narrative. Before the wink had come her joke about his top hat as they were leaving N Street, then their five minutes together in a room off the rotunda. More would happen before the day ended to contradict one journalist's observation that "nothing seemed to pass between the two during the long public hours together."

Kennedy picked up the binder containing his inaugural address from the second of four leather chairs arranged in a semicircle around the podium, then sat down between Eisenhower and Johnson. Nixon was farther to his left, beyond Johnson in the fourth chair. The ninety-eight other dignitaries on the presidential stand occupied numbered and assigned seats in five rows of folding chairs that flanked a narrow aisle. In row A, alongside the four leather chairs, Jackie Kennedy, Lady Bird Johnson, Mamie Eisenhower, Pat Nixon, Joe and Rose Kennedy, and their niece Ann Gargan sat in odd-numbered seats on the left-hand side of the aisle. In the even-numbered ones across the way were Senator John Sparkman, President and Mrs. Truman, Sam Rayburn, Lynda Bird and Luci Baines Johnson, and their aunt and uncle. Behind them, in rows B through E, sat the Supreme Court, congressional leadership, Kennedy cabinet, members of Jack's and Jackie's families, and several close friends. Protocol had dictated much of the seating, but one detects Kennedy's hand in the row C seat for his prep school pal Lem Billings, and the distant row E seats allotted to Jackie's mother and stepfather, Hugh Auchincloss, a life-long Republican who had thought it amusing to announce that his contribution to the Kennedy campaign would be to refrain from giving any money to Nixon.

An empty seat in row A had been reserved for former president Herbert Hoover, who had been unable to land in the storm the night before. An empty seat in row C was for Eleanor Roosevelt, who had chosen to sit down below with the diplomatic corps. A seat in row B had been assigned to Peter Lawford, who, hungover and still in his bathrobe, preferred watching the ceremony on television in his hotel suite with Frank Sinatra, whose elaborate inaugural costume was hanging in his closet, unworn. For Sinatra and Lawford, the main event had been the previous night's vaudeville show. The inauguration ceremony was a subplot, and freezing your ass off on the presidential stand was for chumps.

Surrounding Kennedy was an elite of poetry and power that had shaped the political, intellectual, and artistic life of the last half century and would determine much of the next. There was Earl Warren, Robert Kennedy, Sam Rayburn, Edward Kennedy, Dean Rusk, Robert McNamara, Henry Luce, Allen Dulles, J. Edgar Hoover, Roy Wilkins, James Michener, Clark Clifford, Walter Reuther, John Kenneth Galbraith, Archibald Cox, Felix Frankfurter, John Steinbeck, Aaron Copland, Robert Lowell, and Reinhold Niebuhr. There were six former and future presidents—Truman, Eisenhower, Kennedy, Johnson, Nixon, and Ford—and eight first ladies, four in row A, Edith Wilson in row C, Betty Ford seated with the congressional wives, and Eleanor Roosevelt with the diplomats. According to a Gallup poll, the Ten Most Admired Women in America in 1960 were, in order, Eleanor Roosevelt, Mamie Eisenhower, Queen Elizabeth II of Great Britain, Helen Keller, Clare Boothe Luce, Pat Nixon, Jacqueline Kennedy, Senator Margaret Chase Smith, Madame Chiang Kai-shek, and Marian Anderson. All but the queen, Madame Chiang Kai-Shek, and Helen Keller were at the inauguration.

Also present were most of the current and future giants of American journalism, men such as Edward R. Murrow, Anthony Lewis, Tom Wicker, Russell Baker, Ben Bradlee, and Walter Cronkite. Some sat on, in, or underneath the press box, a gimcrack rectangular structure towering over the crowd on stilts. Many photographers and reporters occupied bleachers rising from its flat roof; others worked at desks beneath it. The television anchors, already media princes, were inside, watching through picture windows situated at eye level with the presidential stand so that when Kennedy delivered his speech he would be staring straight into the eye of a camera.

Cardinal Cushing was supposed to begin his invocation once Kennedy had been seated. Instead, there was a seven-minute delay as Senate pages dashed back into the rotunda to fetch more folding chairs to accommodate additional VIPs in a reserved section on the Capitol steps. Seats there were supposed to match the number of ticket holders but were unnumbered. Like those breaking police lines and dashing into the reserved standing areas, people with enough pull to be admitted to the rotunda had then wormed their way onto the steps. A Secret Service agent had slipped Congressman Tip O'Neill into this area, placing him next to George Kara, an influential Boston wheeler-dealer who had bagged a prime aisle seat without having a ticket. Kennedy had paused on his way down the stairs to greet O'Neill and Kara, and since he had personally signed off on the VIP seating, he must have been surprised to see them sitting there. As he left, Kara told O'Neill, "Years from now, historians will wonder what was on the young man's mind as he strode to take his oath of office. I bet he's asking himself how George Kara got such a good seat."

The delay presented the dignitaries on the presidential stand with the unexpected, and for many unwelcome, prospect of spending an unscripted seven minutes in one another's company, all the while being scrutinized by reporters with binoculars, photographers fixing them in the crosshairs of telephoto lenses, and a television audience of sixty million.

Walter Cronkite filled the time with typical anchorman banter, describing the stand as a "white pavilion with four columns" (it actually had eight) as if he were still a radio announcer, and noting it had cost a quarter of a million dollars. When he was at a loss for words, he reminded everyone that Kennedy was the youngest man to be elected President, and Jackie the fourth-youngest first lady. He noticed Kennedy glancing down at a loose-leaf notebook in his lap. Cronkite assumed it contained his inaugural address, and that Kennedy was using these final minutes to memorize it. Instead, he was probably deciding on which changes to make as he delivered it, taking to heart Galbraith's advice that "the difference between a brilliant speech and a good one . . . is what happens to it in the last half hour."

During these seven minutes Kennedy also resumed his D-Day conversation with Eisenhower, leading Cronkite to remark that there had been no such friendly banter between Eisenhower and Truman in 1953, and that Eisenhower, whom the camera showed gesturing with one hand and tapping his hat on his knee with the other, appeared to be carrying the conversation. Alistair Cooke reported in the *Manchester Guardian* that Eisenhower had been "voluble" and Kennedy "impassive." On NBC, Chet Huntley said Kennedy's demeanor during the delay proved he had "nerves of cast iron," adding, "It would take a great deal to make him reveal any kind of emotional excitement . . . but this has to be a great moment for any man." A more perceptive reporter for the *Times* of London suspected his impassiveness was a mask, concealing a "repressed nervous energy" that he revealed with a series of "small impatient gestures." Those who knew Kennedy best would have agreed. Here he was at his own inauguration, making small talk with Eisenhower about a book the man had not even read, while suffering through a delay that could only be sapping the attention span of this cold and restless audience.

Meanwhile, Truman kissed Edith Wilson, tapped his feet to the Marine Corps band, and remarked that his overcoat was twenty years old and he hoped no one would steal it. He made such a convincing show of enjoying

Nixon's company that Cooke described him "chatting happily" with a man he would loathe until he drew his last breath. Adlai Stevenson passed the time in glum silence, perhaps because he was seated between Dean Rusk, whom Kennedy had appointed to the job he had wanted, secretary of state, and Douglas Dillon, whom Kennedy had made secretary of the treasury despite his being a Republican who had served in the Eisenhower administration.

Jackie Kennedy, who understood the tyranny of the television camera, maintained her frozen smile. *Newsweek* called it "the subtle smile of a self-restrained pixie," but Myra Mannes, who was covering the inauguration for the *Reporter,* saw "a smile that had nothing public about it, that spoke of things withheld and guarded," and possessed the quality of "serene removal" found in Greek statuary.

Some filled these minutes by fuming over their placement on the stand. Rose Kennedy, who lived by ritual, routine, and etiquette, was the most aggrieved. She and her husband and niece were in the front row, but at the very end, not good enough, she thought, for the first parents in history to attend their son's inauguration. She remained upset for years, complaining in her 1974 memoirs that "since the photographers were focusing on the middle [of the platform] we were left out of everything except the panoramic pictures. . . . I have never seen one in which I am recognizable; in fact, some friends asked later where I had been during the ceremonies." A decade later she remarked ("crossly") to her secretary, Barbara Gibson, "They put the parents at the end of the podium where we couldn't really see what was happening."

Jackie's mother, Janet Auchincloss, had more cause to be peeved. She and her husband had been relegated to seats E15 and E17, at the end of the last row. The presidential stand was meant to be an honor, but it was a curious one since everyone on it except those sitting in the front row behind the podium stared at the speakers' backs. Auchincloss complained that her children had a better view from their seats below, and twelve-year-old Jamie Auchincloss grew up believing Jackie had placed their mother in the back to punish her.

Grudges and politics go together. Still, so many of the VIPs at the Kennedy inauguration had such a long and contentious history of slights and rivalries that had their thoughts been vocalized, the air would have crackled with a Babel of competing voices, like dozens of broadcasts jammed onto a single short-wave radio band.

Nixon had called Johnson an "ignoramus" and said Truman and Stevenson were "traitors of the high principles in which many of the nation's

Democrats believe." Kennedy told the journalist Peter Lisagor in 1957 that he considered Johnson a "man of no very firm principles." By the time of the 1960 convention, he was calling him "that fucking bastard."

Lyndon Johnson looked at Bobby Kennedy and saw "that little shitass" who had tried to muscle him off the ticket hours after his brother offered him the vice presidency. Bobby considered Johnson "mean, bitter, vicious—an animal in many ways." Adlai Stevenson hated Bobby, too ("That young man never says please. He never says thank you, he never asks for things, he demands them"), and Bobby claimed JFK was "disgusted" with Stevenson because of the petulant way he had behaved after being offered the consolation prize post of U.S. ambassador to the United Nations. Tip O'Neill said of Bobby, "To be blunt about it, I never really liked him"; Bobby called O'Neill "that big fat Irish bastard." Jackie Kennedy disliked O'Neill so much she left his line blank on her 1960 absentee ballot.

Joe Kennedy was so contemptuous of Humphrey and the other Democrats that he told Nixon during the primaries, "Dick, if my boy can't make it, I'm for you." After losing West Virginia, Humphrey excoriated "Papa Joe" for buying his son "anything he wanted, even an election," and later wrote, "Underneath the beautiful exterior [of the Kennedy organization] there was an element of ruthlessness and roughness that I had trouble accepting or forgetting."

Chief Justice Earl Warren believed Richard Nixon was "a bad man," and must have been relieved not to be swearing *him* in as the thirty-fifth president of the United States. In the final days of the campaign Pat Nixon had asked an aide, "How can we let the American people know what kind of a man Kennedy is?" Douglas Dillon's wife avoided making eye contact with Nixon during the ceremony because she knew he considered her husband a traitor to the Republican Party for joining the Kennedy administration.

Eisenhower loathed Truman so much that when he stopped at the White House in 1953 to pick him up for the ritual drive to the Capitol, he refused to leave his limousine. A female reporter for the *Times-Herald* noticed strains between Bess Truman and Mamie Eisenhower (who were sitting in the same row today), and wrote that "Mamie's lively laughter could be heard far back in the crowd," while "Mrs. Truman sat solidly with her gaze glued on the blimp overhead through most of the ceremony."

Johnson, Truman, and Bobby and Joe Kennedy were all champion grudge nursers. Joe Kennedy had once told Tip O'Neill, "Bobby's my boy. When Bobby hates you, you stay hated." He thought Jack was too soft: "You can trample all over him and the next day he's there for you with loving arms." The "loving arms" were a father's hyperbole. In truth, Kennedy had a sharp memory and seldom wiped a political slate entirely clean. Any man who could drive down a street in Boston and recall which stores displayed his campaign posters fourteen years earlier, and had said, "Forgive your enemies, but never forget their names," surely recalled Nixon calling him a "barefaced liar" and Humphrey comparing his campaign organization to the Nazi Party, a slur that Theodore White believed had "envenomed and embittered" Kennedy. And how could Kennedy have forgotten that after he had received the last rites in New York Hospital in 1954, Senator Styles Bridges, who was today seated one row behind him, had thrown a celebratory cocktail party in anticipation of the Republicans gaining control of the Senate upon his death?

Eleanor Roosevelt claimed to be sitting with the diplomatic corps because the acoustics were better below the stand, but no one else sitting on it complained of being unable to hear, and that included eighty-eight-year-old Edith Wilson, who was left sitting next to Roosevelt's empty chair. More likely, Roosevelt had changed seats because she could not bear sitting so close to Joe Kennedy.

When Gore Vidal asked Kennedy why he thought Eleanor Roosevelt disliked him, he ascribed the lowest possible motives to her, saying, "She hated my father and she can't stand it that his children turned out much better than hers." But she had some principled reasons for her antipathy, among them his failure to condemn Senator Joseph McCarthy. She alluded to this in December 1958, when she told a national television audience she was hesitant to support the presidential candidacy of "someone who understands what courage is and admires it but has not quite the independence to have it." Then, having skewered him for his moral cowardice, she took a swipe at his father, alleging that he had been "spending oodles of money all over the country" to buy his son the nomination, a statement inaccurate only in its timing, since he had not yet spent "oodles." Kennedy accused Roosevelt of using McCarthyite tactics to smear him. She countered that his father was spending "to make his son the first Catholic President of this country." This chapter in their feud ended with a wicked telegram from Roosevelt: "My dear boy I only say these things for your own good. I have found in lifetime of adversity that when blows are rained on one it is advisable to turn the other profile."

A year later, she was working tirelessly to deny him the nomination. After he won it, he worked just as tirelessly to charm her. She campaigned for him but was disappointed he did not appoint Adlai Stevenson secretary of state. No other Democrat would listen to his inaugural address with a more critical ear. In her January 19 newspaper column she had listed the qualities of a strong president: confidence, optimism, and a flexible mind. And now, seated below Kennedy's stand instead of on it, she was waiting to see if he would display them.

Representative Howard Smith, a conservative Virginia Democrat, was the only person to reveal his feelings by leaving his seat and walking back into the Capitol as Cardinal Cushing began his invocation. He watched the ceremony on a television monitor in the rotunda for a few minutes, but when Marian Anderson began singing the National Anthem he ambled back to his office, apparently unable to stomach an inauguration showcasing a Roman Catholic cardinal and a black American singer, and culminating in an Irish Catholic becoming president.

Smith would probably have preferred that Kennedy deliver a rambling and undistinguished speech. Nixon, Stevenson, and Johnson may not have been praying for a catastrophe, but one doubts they were hoping to hear an address that would immediately be hailed as a classic. Kennedy, with his sharp political instincts, must have sensed this, perhaps making him even more determined to deny the members of what he had once called the "stop-Kennedy coalition" a sweet moment of schadenfreude.

Cardinal Cushing's eight-minute invocation was a dull little sermon delivered in the monotone some clergymen adopt when addressing the Almighty. Few in the audience can have paid much attention to it, or someone would have pointed out that when he urged Americans to focus "not on what we can get out of it [a community], but what we can put into it," he was unwittingly foreshadowing "ask not."

The deceased are present at large family gatherings, and during the invocation the Kennedys had eight minutes of prayerful silence to remember Joe Jr. and Kathleen. It is inconceivable that Joe Kennedy did not think of the dead son he had groomed for this office, or that Jack Kennedy did not imagine his eldest brother here in his stead. After Joe's death, the headmaster of Choate had written his father that he was sure Jack would never forget that "he must live Joe's life as well as his own."

Kennedy admitted his mind wandered during the prayer. "I knew it would be long," he confessed, "but halfway through I was saved by the thought that here is Kennedy, the first Catholic President being inaugurated, and Cardinal Spellman [the archbishop of New York] is having to watch it on television." (Three weeks before the election, Spellman had blessed Nixon's candidacy by meeting him at LaGuardia Airport and joining his motorcade.)

Kennedy had weighed every word in his speech, while Cushing appeared to have weighed none. Jackie knew Cushing's rambling invocation had to be exasperating her husband, and as he droned on, extravagantly wasting words and time, she could not repress an amused smile. Paul Fay, who was seated a few rows behind her on the Capitol steps, recalled how Cushing had bored the congregation at Jack and Jackie's wedding. Kennedy had told Fay afterward, "There is a man I'd hate to follow on the podium."

Secret Service chief U. E. Baughman had positioned himself in the aisle behind Eisenhower and Kennedy. Several minutes into Cushing's invocation, he noticed smoke spiraling from the lectern. The wooden stand was a tinderbox, its only exit up a single narrow aisle. If it burst into flames, two sets of presidents and vice presidents, the cabinet, and the entire leadership of Congress could be incinerated. Baughman considered ordering an evacuation but, fearing the crowd would panic, instead summoned a fireman with a handheld extinguisher.

Cushing believed the smoke came from a smoldering bomb meant for Kennedy. He immediately slowed his delivery even more so that he could absorb the blast and save Kennedy's life. Leonard Reinsch, who had supervised the installation of the wiring, suspected a short circuit in the tangle of wires running to the lighting, sound, and heating systems. He ducked underneath the podium, made a lucky guess, and yanked the wire leading to a mechanism adjusting the height of the podium. The smoke dissipated, and Cushing finished. Eisenhower turned to Kennedy and said, "You must have a hot speech."

By the time Reinsch poked his head out from the podium, Kennedy was impatiently flipping through the pages of his speech. "Is everything set?" he demanded. Reinsch said it was. Kennedy checked his gold Cartier wristwatch, a fourth-anniversary present from Jackie, and said, "Well, let's get going!"

The ceremony gathered momentum. Marian Anderson sang "The Star-Spangled Banner," and Kennedy was observed mouthing its second verse. A Greek Orthodox archbishop prayed for three minutes, then Sam Rayburn administered the vice presidential oath to Lyndon Johnson, who tripped over its words. This was followed by a meandering four-minute prayer delivered by Dr. John Barclay, the minister of Lyndon Johnson's church in Austin, Texas. As Barclay finished, Kennedy instinctively began to cross himself, then, realizing this would be an inappropriate conclusion to a Protestant prayer, raised his hand to his forehead instead and brushed his hair. Senator John Sparkman took the podium to introduce Robert Frost. His announcement that Frost was about to deliver "an original composition" must have surprised Kennedy. Suddenly it seemed as if Frost might, as he had feared, upstage him at his own inauguration.

Frost had not started composing his poem until arriving in Washington on January 18. By the time Stewart Udall arrived at Frost's hotel two days later to drive him to the Capitol, he had written forty lines but considered it unfinished. He told Udall that he wanted to say "a few things" before reading "The Gift Outright"; "Will that be all right?" he asked. Udall was stunned. How long would this introduction take? he asked. Frost returned to his room, shut the door, and read it aloud, timing himself. As they drove to the Capitol, he complained that the ribbon on the hotel typewriter he had used was so old he was having trouble reading the poem.

The wind blew Frost's white hair straight into the air and ruffled the pages of his manuscript. The glare off the snow and marble was intense, and after sitting on the platform for over an hour Frost was thoroughly chilled. Squinting and holding his pages in trembling hands, he looked even older than eighty-three. He was so befuddled that he announced his poem was dedicated "to the President-elect, Mr. John Finley," a classics scholar who was the master of Harvard's Eliot House.

He began, "First, the dedication," then stumbled over the first word. After correcting himself he said in a tremulous voice, "Summoning artists to participate . . ." He paused, corrected himself, then stumbled again. He kneaded the palms of his hands with his fingers in frustration. "No, I'm not having a good light here at all," he muttered. After mangling another line he declared, this time in a louder voice, "I can't see in the sun."

Eisenhower and Kennedy looked pained. Kennedy was probably torn between worrying about the content of Frost's poem, and fearing his great public gesture to the arts was backfiring. Lyndon Johnson stood up and held his top hat over the page, trying to shield it from the sun. Frost grabbed the hat and said, "Here, let me help you." The crowd laughed nervously. As Johnson returned to his chair, Frost said, "This was to be a preface to the poem I can say to you without seeing it." Then, abandoning his new poem, he straightened his shoulders, stared into the television cameras, and in a firm, assured voice gave a stirring recitation of "The Gift Outright."

The land was ours before we were the land's.
She was our land more than a hundred years
Before we were her people. She was ours

In Massachusetts, in Virginia,
But we were England's, still colonials,
Possessing what we still were unpossessed by,
Possessed by what we now no more possessed.
Something we were withholding made us weak
Until we found out that it was ourselves
We were withholding from our land of living,
And forthwith found salvation in surrender.
Such as we were we gave ourselves outright
(The deed of gift was many deeds of war)
To the land vaguely realizing westward,
But still unstoried, artless, unenhanced,
Such as she was, such as she would become.

He included the change Kennedy had requested. After reciting the final line, he said, "Here, for this occasion, let me change that to 'what she *will* become,'" then finished to cheers and applause.

Kennedy shot to his feet to offer congratulations. It had turned out even better than he could have dared imagine. Frost's electrifying recovery from near disaster had delivered him an audience that had become emotionally involved in the ceremony, and provided a moving introduction for a speech by a man who was sometimes criticized for lacking passion and warmth.

Even those who knew Kennedy well have conceded that his passion and idealism were "carefully concealed," and his wit and warmth "private qualities" he seldom communicated in his speeches. His friend the columnist Joe Alsop believed that Kennedy's natural reserve inhibited him from showing the depth of his feelings. "Any public exhibition of emotion gave him gooseflesh," Alsop said. "So foolish people said he was a cold, unfeeling man, although few men in our time have had stronger feelings about those things that mattered to him."

During the campaign, Frost had urged him to "be more Irish than Harvard"—to be more guided by his heart than his intellect. George Kennan believed he possessed "a certain warmth," but one masked by his inherently shy nature. When Harris Wofford congratulated him for launching his bid for the presidency, he closed his letter with "As you know one thing holding back many liberal Democrats and sensitive people of some influence, such as Mrs. Roosevelt, to name one of many, is to see some sign of passionate courage on your part, or, to state these separately, courage and passion."

James MacGregor Burns had faulted his "detached attitude" and "cold insight," concluding that "to him, to be emotionally or ideologically committed is to be captive." Burns would later reconsider this judgment, writing in 2002, "Kennedy came across to me as essentially pragmatic and un-passionate, but in retrospect I see a kind of intellectual passion that showed itself in his most important speeches and decisions."

In fact, when Kennedy spoke about religion, veterans, courage, and sacrifice, he often displayed much more than an intellectual passion. Some men go through their lives without shedding tears. But Kennedy had tears in his eyes when he won the presidency. He wept after the August 1963 death of his newborn son, and the loss of life during the Bay of Pigs invasion brought him to tears, as did the 1961 Vienna summit, because he feared it had made a nuclear war more likely. At a gathering of Gold Star Mothers in the American Legion Hall in Charlestown during his 1946 congressional campaign, his aide Dave Powers had watched in mounting despair as he plodded through a prepared speech larded with banalities about the sacrifices of war. Suddenly, Kennedy surprised everyone by abandoning his text and saying, "Well, I think I know how you ladies feel. My mother, too, lost a son in the war." The women applauded, wept, and rushed the podium to touch him. "From that minute onward," Powers said, "you could see the tide turn his way."

Those close to Kennedy knew that certain events and audiences could unlock his emotions. McGeorge Bundy and Ken O'Donnell would try to dissuade him from addressing the survivors of the Bay of Pigs fiasco at a December 1961 rally in the Orange Bowl because they feared he might become carried away and say something complicating his already difficult relationship with Khrushchev. Sure enough, when the Cuban veterans presented him with a flag they had carried ashore during the invasion, he departed from his cautious text to shout, "This flag will be returned to the brigade in a free Havana." A similar scenario would occur in Berlin on June 26, 1963. Sixteen days earlier, Kennedy had delivered a landmark speech at American University, advocating disarmament and coexistence with the Soviet Union. But faced with the Berlin Wall and a million Berliners chanting his name, he delivered a blistering attack on communism that O'Donnell characterized as "spontaneous and unprepared, put together from a few thoughts that came to him that morning." After delivering his famous line that "today, in the world of freedom, the proudest boast is '*Ich bin ein Berliner,*'" he thundered, "There are some who say Communism is the wave of the future. Let them come to Berlin." Even the fiercely loyal O'Donnell believed Kennedy had been carried away by the audience.

* * *

Kennedy stood at the podium facing Chief Justice Earl Warren. He was bareheaded and had left his overcoat draped over the back of his chair. Jackie moved forward and studied his face intently, as if discovering it for the first time. He raised one hand and placed the other on the Fitzgerald family Bible. A hush fell over the crowd. This was the moment he had promised during his campaign: a Catholic president taking the oath of office and swearing his allegiance to the Constitution. It was also a moment that Nixon, Johnson, Stevenson, and Humphrey had imagined for themselves, although only Humphrey would admit it in his memoirs, writing, "When John Kennedy stood and took the oath of office, I must admit to a moment of envy. . . . I thought, 'There, but for the grace of God, go I.'"

Kennedy could not still his left hand and inadvertently dropped it from the Bible, a misstep leading some Protestant pastors to argue that his oath had been invalid. The presidential oath is too brief to allow time for lengthy interior monologues, but at one of the inaugural balls that evening Kennedy would tell Tip O'Neill that as he was saying, "I do solemnly swear that I will faithfully execute the office of President of the United States, and will to the best of my ability preserve, protect, and defend the Constitution of the United States," he was thinking, "How the hell did Kara get that seat?"

Alistair Cooke noticed Jackie's "smooth throat" twitch for a moment as her husband repeated the oath. When she had covered the 1953 inauguration, she had reported that "Ike planted a kiss on Mamie's cheek right after taking the oath" and that as he walked across the platform he shot his arms into the air, making the "V for Victory" sign. Instead of waving or kissing his wife, Kennedy suffered through an energetic Nixon handshake. Then he took his place behind the mahogany podium and, framed by the shimmering dome of the Capitol and the cobalt-blue sky, opened the Reading Copy of his inaugural address and began:

> Vice President Johnson, Mr. Speaker, Mr. Chief Justice, President Eisenhower, Vice President Nixon, President Truman, reverend clergy, fellow citizens: We observe today not a victory of party, but a celebration of freedom—symbolizing an end, as well as a beginning—signifying renewal as well as change. For I have sworn before you and Almighty God the same solemn oath our forebears prescribed nearly a century and three quarters ago.

When George Washington delivered his first inaugural address, his hands had trembled so badly that one witness said he was "agitated and embarrassed more than he ever was by the leveled cannon or pointed musket." John Adams told his wife after his inauguration that he had been so frightened he could barely speak, and wondered if he should not omit an inaugural address and simply recite the oath of office. When Kennedy declared his candidacy for the presidency, his voice had quivered and he had rushed his words. But he delivered this opening paragraph slowly and deliberately, stressing each word in the phrase "the . . . same . . . solemn . . . oath." His voice was firm, but passionless, his hands were not trembling, but neither were they chopping the air or pounding the lectern.

Kennedy's right hand was his "tell." If he thought a passage was important, he would move his palm up and down like an elevator, slice the air in a wood-chopping motion, point a finger, or make it into a fist he pumped up and down in time to his words. Sometimes he reined in his hand by slipping it into the outside pocket of his jacket. When he began his inaugural, he kept it behind the podium, hidden from the audience. Sorensen believes he started so tentatively because he was concerned with selling himself to those who had opposed his nomination. In this first passage he was reminding Sam Rayburn, John Sparkman, Harry Truman, Styles Bridges, Eleanor Roosevelt, and anyone else still harboring reservations about a Catholic president that he had sworn an oath to uphold the Constitution.

Next came his promise that this Irish Catholic president would promote the "revolutionary beliefs" of Washington, Hamilton, Jefferson, and Adams.

> The world is very different now. For man holds in his mortal hands the power to abolish all forms of human poverty and all forms of human life. And yet the same revolutionary beliefs for which our forebears fought are still at issue around the globe—the belief that the rights of man come not from the generosity of the state, but from the hand of God.

Here, what would become known as the "Speech as Delivered" began diverging from the Reading Copy. The second sentence of this paragraph had read, "For man holds in his mortal hands the power to abolish all form of human poverty and to abolish all forms of human life." Kennedy changed *form* to the plural, *forms,* eliminated the repetitious *to abolish,* and said, "For man holds in his mortal hands the power to abolish all forms of human poverty and all forms of human life."

Few politicians possess the confidence and literary skills to change the most important speech of their lives while delivering it live to an audience of millions. Because Kennedy considered the Reading Copy a historical document, he had not edited its pages in advance. This makes it impossible to know which alternations he settled on while rereading the speech earlier, and which he made as he spoke. We only know that he made thirty-two changes, and all made grammatical or logical sense, or rendered his sentences tighter or smoother. He made them because he was as fussy about his oratory as his appearance and understood that the words he spoke were the ones history would remember.

In his third paragraph he changed "cold and bitter peace" to "hard and bitter peace," and said:

> We dare not forget today that we are the heirs of that first revolution. Let the words go forth from this time and place, to friend and foe alike, that the torch has been passed to a new generation of Americans—born in this century, tempered by war, disciplined by a hard and bitter peace, proud of our ancient heritage—and unwilling to witness or permit the slow undoing of those human rights to which this Nation has always been committed, and to which we are committed today at home and around the world.

He had not just dictated, but had *lived* the words in this passage. They told his story: "born in this century," "tempered by war," and "disciplined by a hard and bitter peace." As he delivered them, he became more emphatic and passionate, turning his right hand into a fist and pumping it up and down as he said, "the torch has been passed." It was here that his nervous energy, heightened by the delays and prayers, began surfacing in his delivery, and he began forging an emotional bond with the audience.

"Let the word go forth" had a classical ring. The passed torch evoked ancient Greece, a society that celebrated physical beauty, athleticism, and the intellect. The audience saw a decorated war hero, standing in a pavilion inspired by ancient Greece, and surrounded by the old men who were letting this torch fall from their grip. He was urging young Americans to merge their heroism with his, dedicate their lives to a noble cause, the preservation "of those human rights to which this Nation has always been committed," and join him in grabbing this torch. Seldom have the words of any speech been echoed so perfectly and movingly by its surroundings.

As Kennedy completed this sentence with "and to which we are committed today at home and around the world," he pounded the lectern for the first time, and for the first time was interrupted by cheers and applause.

After distancing himself, his cabinet, and his generation from Eisenhower, Truman, Rayburn, Sparkman, Stevenson, Bridges, and, although they were only separated by nine years, Lyndon Johnson, he said:

> Let every nation know, whether it wishes us well or ill, that we shall pay any price, bear any burden, meet any hardship, support any friend, oppose any foe, to assure the survival and the success of liberty.

Out of context, this sentence sounds bellicose. What saves it are the last words of the preceding paragraph, in which Kennedy had pledged that the new generation would protect human rights at home and abroad. In this controversial sentence he was simply stating what Americans will do to protect these "human rights" and to "assure the survival and success of liberty."

Kennedy paused between these five pledges to underline their gravity. He stressed *any,* the only word repeated in all five, in the same way Churchill made *fight* the drumbeat of his promises to fight on the beaches, fight on the landing grounds, fight in the fields. Both sets of pledges demanded courage and sacrifice and promised a struggle to the finish. Kennedy made his pledges tighter and more Churchillian by eliminating the unnecessary *or* and *in order* from the text as spoken, so that "or oppose any foe in order to assure the survival and success of liberty" became "oppose any foe to assure the survival and success of liberty."

When the applause for this sentence subsided, he lowered his voice and added, "This much we pledge—and more." At first glance the line seems excessively melodramatic, since if you have already pledged to "pay any price" and "bear any burden," how can you pledge any more? In truth, it was more literary device than policy, a transition to the next six paragraphs, a litany of promises addressed to different audiences that repeated the words *we* and *pledge,* the latter a word that evoked the gallantry and nobility of King Arthur's knights.

> To those old allies whose cultural and spiritual origins we share, we pledge the loyalty of faithful friends. United, there is little we cannot do in a host of cooperative ventures. Divided there is little we can do—for we dare not meet a powerful challenge at odds and split asunder.
>
> To those new States whom we welcome to the ranks of the free, we pledge our word that one form of colonial control shall not have passed away merely to be replaced by a far more iron tyranny. We shall not always

expect to find them supporting our view. But we shall always hope to find them strongly supporting their own freedom—and to remember that, in the past, those who foolishly sought power by riding the back of the tiger ended up inside.

To those peoples in the huts and villages across the globe struggling to break the bonds of mass misery, we pledge our best efforts to help them help themselves, for whatever period is required—not because the communists may be doing it, not because we seek their votes, but because it is right. If a free society cannot help the many who are poor, it cannot save the few who are rich.

To our sister republics south of the border, we offer a special pledge—to convert our good words into good deeds—in a new alliance for progress—to assist free men and free governments in casting off the chains of poverty. But this peaceful revolution of hope cannot become the prey of hostile powers. Let all our neighbors know that we shall join with them to oppose aggression or subversion anywhere in the Americas. And let every other power know that this Hemisphere intends to remain the master of its own house.

To that world assembly of sovereign states, the United Nations, our last best hope in an age where the instruments of war have far outpaced the instruments of peace, we renew our pledge of support—to prevent it from becoming merely a forum for invective—to strengthen its shield of the new and the weak—and to enlarge the area in which its writ may run.

Finally, to those nationals who would make themselves our adversary, we offer not a pledge but a request: that both sides begin anew the quest for peace, before the dark powers of destruction unleashed by science engulf all humanity in planned or accidental self-destruction.

As Kennedy spoke, he eliminated the superfluous *new* from, "United there is little we cannot do in a host of *new* cooperative ventures." He cut *now* from "To those new states whom we *now* welcome to the ranks of the free" and *every* from "We shall not always expect to find them supporting our *every* view." He turned "the tiger's back" into the "back of the tiger," changed the awkward "If *the* free society cannot help the many who are poor" to "If *a* free society cannot help the many who are poor," and "not because the communists *are* doing it" to "not because the communists *may be* doing it," perhaps because the first version gave the communists too much credit.

These pledges are the liberal heart of the Kennedy inaugural. None are preserved at Arlington, and only the tiger metaphor can be found in the quotation anthologies. But his promises to "assist free men and free governments in casting off the chains of poverty," support the United Nations as "our last best hope," and "begin anew the quest for peace" stirred the liberal soul more than any words since the New Deal, and prepared the audience for his master sentence, since how could anyone *not* ask what he could do for such a courageous and high-minded country?

It was not just these liberal words but the passion Kennedy invested in them that was so stirring.

He punctuated "because . . . it . . . is . . . right" by pounding the podium so loudly it was heard over the loudspeakers.

He pounded his fist again in cadence with "this Hemisphere intends to remain the master of its own house."

His right hand flew outside the podium and sliced the air with each word of "If a free society cannot help the many who are poor, it cannot save the few who are rich."

Again and again, he looked down at the page, then up at the audience, slowing his delivery and connecting listeners to the written text, a relationship the teleprompter has severed.

The audience, cued by his hands and his emphasis, applauded his most idealistic pledges: his promise to the people of Africa, Asia, and Latin America "to convert our good words into good deeds" and to break "the bonds of mass misery" imprisoning them.

The color film of the inauguration commissioned by the Democratic National Committee remained tightly focused on Kennedy as he spoke, but there are still distractions. John Sparkman's wife, looking testy and miserable, pulls her mink tight around her neck, then waves her white handkerchief like a flag before blowing her nose as Kennedy says, "But this peaceful revolution of hope cannot become the prey of hostile powers." Lyndon Johnson checks his watch as Kennedy says, "The world is very different now," then whispers to a Secret Service agent crouched behind the podium during "Let both sides seek to invoke." As Kennedy asks, "Will you join in that historic effort?" Johnson reaches down and picks up a piece of paper, takes his reading glasses from his breast pocket, puts them on, studies both sides of the paper, and finally slips it into his pocket. Still, Kennedy's words, gestures, and demeanor are the central focus of this film, and a viewer can concentrate on them.

The sixty million Americans watching television had a different experience. At the 1953 and 1957 inaugurations the cameras had mostly remained on Eisenhower, and viewers saw "a man reading." But when Kennedy spoke, the network cameramen (particularly those working for CBS) shot him from the front, back, and in profile, cut to the crowd, the Capitol facade, and back to the presidential stand for reaction shots of Jackie Kennedy, Eisenhower, and Johnson. Viewers had to divide their attention between what they were seeing and hearing, and at times the speech became a soundtrack. The CBS production staff had apparently decided, perhaps on the basis of the advance release text provided by Salinger, or perhaps because of the conversation between Kennedy and CBS executives Blair Clark and Fred Friendly at the Carlyle two days earlier, that the "ask not" and "the torch has been passed" lines were the poetic heart of the speech, and when Kennedy delivered these, he was shown facing the camera.

But when he said, "The belief that the rights of man . . . ," viewers saw his back.

He said, "To assure the survival and the success of liberty," and on CBS, Eisenhower's face filled the screen.

He said, "For we dare not meet a powerful challenge at odds and split asunder," and Nixon appeared.

When he said, "This Hemisphere intends to remain the master of its own house," he was at the far right of the screen while the camera focused on his empty chair.

When he said, "We dare not tempt them with weakness," CBS cut to the crowd.

He said, "Nor will it be finished in the first 1,000 days, nor in the life of this Administration," and viewers saw Ike and Jackie, shot from the rear.

He said, "In the long history of the world," and Lynda Bird Johnson fidgeted and dropped her program.

And so it went, with CBS cutting from reaction shots to the crowd, then back to Kennedy. The multiple cuts and camera angles were presumably part of the "whole new concept" Friendly and Clark had proposed to Kennedy in December, their solution to the problem of there never having been a successful political speech delivered on television. The "new concept" heightened the drama of the occasion but distracted from the text, since whenever the camera left Kennedy, one paid less attention to his speech. When it returned, it underlined whatever he was saying, leaving us to wonder if some of his sentences became so celebrated because television had put them in boldface.

The last of his promises, Kennedy said, was "not a pledge but a request: that both sides begin anew the quest for peace." This was a bridge to his second litany: seven paragraphs offering proposals for reducing tensions with the Soviet Union. The first two paragraphs provided the transition.

> We dare not tempt them with weakness. For only when our arms are sufficient beyond doubt can we be certain beyond doubt that they will never be employed.
>
> But neither can two great and powerful groups of nations take comfort from our present course—both sides overburdened by the cost of modern weapons, both rightly alarmed by the steady spread of the deadly atom, yet both racing to alter that uncertain balance of terror that stays the hand of mankind's final war.

Then Kennedy offered Khrushchev an outstretched hand.

> So let us begin anew—remembering on both sides that civility is not a sign of weakness, and sincerity is always subject to proof. Let us never negotiate out of fear. But let us never fear to negotiate.
>
> Let both sides explore what problems unite us instead of belaboring those problems which divide us.
>
> Let both sides, for the first time, formulate serious and precise proposals for the inspection and control of arms—and bring the absolute power to destroy other nations under the absolute control of all nations.
>
> Let both sides seek to invoke the wonders of science instead of its terrors. Together let us explore the stars, conquer the deserts, eradicate disease, tap the ocean depths, and encourage the arts and commerce.
>
> Let both sides unite to heed in all corners of the earth the command of Isaiah—to "undo the heavy burdens . . . and to let the oppressed go free."
>
> And if a beachhead of cooperation may push back the jungle of suspicion, let both sides join in creating a new endeavor, not a new balance of power, but a new world of law, where the strong are just and the weak secure and the peace preserved.
>
> All this will not be finished in the first one hundred days. Nor will it be finished in the first one thousand days, nor in the life of this Administration, nor even perhaps in our lifetime on this planet. But let us begin."

Kennedy raised his voice and chopped the air as he delivered the "Let us never negotiate out of fear. But let us never fear to negotiate" line, then dropped it and thumped the podium as he said, "But . . . let . . . us . . . begin."

These seven paragraphs had all been in the Sorensen Draft. Kennedy delivered the first and last with the most feeling and emphasis, and the following day the press would consider this invitation to reduce cold-war tensions to be the most newsworthy portion of the address.

His next sentence was borrowed from Abraham Lincoln's first inaugural. Lincoln had said, "In your hands, my dissatisfied fellow-countrymen, and not in mine, is the momentous issue of civil war." Now Kennedy said,

> In your hands, my fellow citizens, more than in mine, will rest the final success or failure of our course.

Then, under the gaze of Roosevelt's widow, and standing where Roosevelt had when he declared, "This generation has a rendezvous with destiny," he proclaimed in an even louder and more urgent tone of voice:

> Since this country was founded, each generation of Americans has been summoned to give testimony to its national loyalty. The graves of young Americans who answered the call to service surround the globe.

And among those giving testimony to their loyalty, whose graves could be numbered among those answering the call to service, were Harold Marney and Andrew Kirksey of PT 109, and Joseph P. Kennedy Jr.

His next paragraph had the fervor of a hymn and the rhythm of a Psalm.

> Now the trumpet summons us again—not as a call to bear arms, though arms we need—not as a call to battle, though embattled we are—but a call to bear the burden of a long twilight struggle, year in and year out, "rejoicing in hope, patient in tribulation"—a struggle against the common enemies of man: tyranny, poverty, disease and war itself.

He raised his voice still louder, booming out, "the trumpet summons us," then dropping it for, "though arms we need" and "though embattled we are."

The next sentences contained his only rhetorical questions.

> Can we forge against these enemies a grand and global alliance, North and South, East and West, that can assure a more fruitful life for all mankind? Will you join in that historic effort?

At this, hundreds of voices cried out, "Yes! Yes! Yes!"

If the liberal engagement in world affairs has a high-water mark, this was it: a president summoning Americans to a global crusade against tyranny, poverty, disease, and war that would guarantee "a more fruitful life" for all mankind. No president, before or since, has made such an ambitious and idealistic proposal.

With shouts of "Yes!" still ringing through the crowd, Kennedy proclaimed that,

> In the long history of the world, only a few generations have been granted the role of defending freedom in its hour of maximum danger. I do not shrink from this responsibility—I welcome it. I do not believe that any of us would exchange places with any other people or any other generation. The energy, the faith, the devotion which we bring to this endeavor will light our country and all who serve it—and the glow from that fire can truly light the world.

When he said, "I do not shrink from this responsibility," he dropped his voice to a confidential tone, as if speaking directly to Khrushchev, then defiantly spat out, "I welcome it," and heard more applause.

When he said, "I do not believe that any of us would exchange places with any other people or any other generation," the audience cried, "No! No! No!"

He shouted out the words *energy, faith,* and *devotion,* pausing as if each was a sentence in itself, then raising his voice again for, "and the glow from that fire can truly light the world."

His Boston accent thickened when he spoke from his heart, and so *danger* became *dangah, endeavor, endevah,* and *fire, fiyah.*

How much of the passion was genuine? How much a rhetorical act? He was delivering lines that engaged his deepest emotions, yet he retained the presence of mind to change "each generation has been summoned" to "each generation of *Americans* has been summoned" and "the graves of young Americans who answered *that* call" to "the graves of young Americans who answered *the* call to service."

His voice remained firm. He never choked up, hesitated, or stumbled. His instructions to Sorensen to "shorten sentences & words" and learn and apply the "secret" of the Gettysburg Address had produced a speech lending itself to a smooth delivery.

Finally, after delivering sentences inspired by the most traumatic and memorable moments of his life, and speaking with an emotional intensity he seldom revealed, and inspiring the audience at the Capitol to cry out like a congregation at a revival meeting, he delivered his master sentence.

He ran it into the preceding passage to prevent the moment being shattered by applause, and the climax he and the audience were approaching together being delayed any longer.

He began, "And so," crucial words signaling that everything had been leading to this moment.

And so, at a moment he considered as crucial to the survival of Western democracies as 1939, and believing that the survival of human rights might depend on his ability to inspire his fellow countrymen to acts of courage and sacrifice, and training an eye on the High Court of History, he said, "And so, my fellow Americans," and began setting millions of lives on courses many are still following.

"And so, my fellow Americans," he said.

Because you are a courageous and heroic people . . .

Because you are heirs of the American Revolution . . .

Because earlier generations have given their lives to preserve rights secured by that revolution . . .

Because these rights are under assault and you have pledged today to pay any price and bear any burden to preserve them . . .

Because you have also pledged to help the wretched of the earth cast off their chains of poverty, to begin anew the quest for peace, to defend freedom in its hour of maximum danger, and assure a more fruitful life for all mankind . . .

"And so," because of all of this, "my fellow Americans," he said, looking out at the audience and straight into the cameras, and history.

"And so, my fellow Americans," he said, crooking his right index finger, jabbing it at the crowd, and even now editing his speech and turning "ask not what your country *will* do for you" into the stronger "*can* do for you."

And so, Kennedy delivered at last the master sentence that was a distillation of his philosophy and experience, the chrysalis of countless campaign speeches, and the logical and emotional climax of his inaugural address.

He said, "And so, my fellow Americans: ask not what your country can do for you—ask what you can do for your country," and it was at this moment that Americans walked with him through a membrane in time, entering the next decade, and a new era.

The following sentence, "My fellow citizens of the world: ask not what America will do for you, but what together we can do for the freedom of man," was anticlimactic, and Kennedy, perhaps sensing that history would overlook it, did not bother replacing its *will* with *can*.

It is customary for an inaugural address to call upon the Almighty for His blessing and assistance, and Kennedy adhered to this formula in his concluding paragraph.

> Finally, whether you are citizens of America or citizens of the world, ask of us here the same high standards of strength and sacrifice which we ask of you. With a good conscience our only sure reward, with history the final judge of our deeds, let us go forth to lead the land we love, asking His blessing and His help, but knowing that here on earth God's work must truly be our own.

As he finished, Rose Kennedy was reminded of a verse from Luke she had often recited to him: "Of those to whom much has been given, much will be required." Then, paraphrasing a line from Cardinal Newman's prayer, one she had also made part of his upbringing, and that he had woven into the last sentence of his speech, she told herself, "He will do good, he will do God's work." Only in retrospect has it become apparent that, more than any of the analysis and praise soon to be lavished on the address, it is Rose Kennedy's thoughts at this moment that best explain why her son's inaugural address had sent half-frozen tears rolling down so many cheeks.

II

Washington

JANUARY 20, 1961, TO THE PRESENT

⚜

The High Court of History can take decades to deliver its verdict on a speech, an intolerable delay for someone as impatient as John F. Kennedy. Moments after leaving the stand, he began soliciting comments on his address from those whose judgment he trusted, and whose opinions might influence its reception.

Jackie gave the first review. He had turned to her first after concluding his address, and she had flashed him what the *New York Times* called a "you-did-all-right smile." "I was so proud of Jack," she said later. "There was so much I wanted to say! But I could scarcely embrace him in front of all those people." Back inside the rotunda, however, she stroked his cheek and told him he had been "wonderful."

At the traditional postinauguration buffet luncheon in the Capitol, Kennedy was described as "grinning and flushed with pleasure." He signed Truman's menu "with a flourish" and accepted compliments from the House and Senate leadership, although their praise was like that accorded a bride at her wedding, part of the ritual.

During the inaugural parade he left his seat to greet members of the Supreme Court. The elderly and cantankerous Justice Felix Frankfurter said, "Mr. President, I want to congratulate you on your inaugural; I particularly want to congratulate you more on what you didn't say than on what you did say. I congratulate you for making no promises." Frankfurter considered this high praise, but Kennedy was disappointed. Asked later if he thought the inaugural had been "a good speech," Frankfurter replied, "I never think any speech written by somebody else, for somebody else, is any good. I don't want to listen to Ted Sorensen."

Kennedy attended a dinner party that evening at the home of his former prep school classmate George Wheeler. Among the guests were James Michener, Stan Musial, Angie Dickinson, Arthur Schlesinger, and other members of the informal "Kennedy Caravan" that had barnstormed through states he had little chance of winning. Kennedy shared a table with the *New York Times* columnist Arthur Krock. He asked what Krock had thought of his inaugural. Krock replied, "Your inaugural address was the finest political document written in this country since the death of Woodrow Wilson, and in its style, spirit, and thought it reminded me of Wilson more than any other President we've had since."

"Are you going to write that?" Kennedy asked quickly, knowing that Krock's judgment would influence millions.

"Mr. President," he replied, "I already have."

Krock came to believe that the Kennedy inauguration launched "the most glamorous period" in his life and in that of the nation. Others have echoed this sentiment. William Colby, who later headed the CIA, believed the world saw in Kennedy "the embodiment of a good America." Shortly after the inauguration a French diplomat with years of Washington experience told the columnist Drew Pearson, "We have felt so sad in Europe lately. We have always looked to you as the great and powerful country . . . and recently you hadn't been leading. . . . We are so glad that the old America is coming back again."

Kennedy returned to the White House at 9:00 P.M. to collect Jackie and begin making the rounds of the inaugural balls. She had left the parade after an hour and taken to her bed, claiming to be too exhausted even to attend a White House reception for her own family being held one floor below.

Kennedy had settled into a chair and lit a cigar when she appeared in the doorway wearing a white chiffon sheath veiled in a gossamer cape. Thayer, speaking for Jackie, wrote, "The President glanced up, drew a quick breath, and in a reflex gesture stubbed out his cigar. 'Darling, I've never seen you look so lovely,' he said in a low voice. 'Your dress is beautiful.'" The low voice, quick breath, and abandoned cigar hint at sexual arousal and make it easier to imagine him later carrying her over the thresholds of two White House bedrooms.

Kennedy ordered champagne. A steward brought a bottle of Dom Perignon that Jackie had ordered sent over from N Street for this very moment, and the president raised his glass to her and said, "This calls for a celebration." This scene, sometimes recounted as evidence of Kennedy's high spirits and devotion to his wife, has a sad undertone. It is, after all, her dress and beauty that captivate him, but only momentarily. At an inaugural ball at the Statler Hilton, he will leave her alone in their box for thirty minutes while attending a party in Frank Sinatra's suite. At the armory, when an aide tells him he is walking so fast his wife cannot keep up, he will snap, "Well, she'll just have to walk faster."

That evening Kennedy displayed many of the other characteristics (besides his fascination with Hollywood and impatience) that had brought him this far. His dry wit was in evidence when he looked down onto the floor of the Mayflower Hotel ballroom from his box and told those gazing up at him, "I don't know a better way to spend an evening—you looking at us and we looking at you!" He demonstrated his ability to connect with the common man when he spotted Joe Leahy, who had worked in his 1946 campaign, standing in a crowd outside the armory and asked him to sing a few bars of "Danny Boy." It was the proudest moment of his life, Leahy said. Kennedy's restlessness surfaced when crowds at the armory blocked the aisles leading to his box and he vaulted over the railings, shaking hands with the occupants of other boxes as he made his way to his seat. His competitive spirit was there in the attention he paid to compliments on his address, such as Tip O'Neill's remark, "Your inaugural address will go down in the annals of American history as one of the great speeches of all time."

After two inaugural balls Jackie returned to the White House, leaving him to attend the next three alone. At 1:46 A.M. he climbed into his limousine outside the Statler Hilton and, to the surprise of his Secret Service agents, asked to be driven to Joe Alsop's house in Georgetown.

Alsop had spread the word that he would be serving champagne and terrapin soup to all comers. Thirty guests had crowded into his living room when there was a loud knocking on his front door. He opened it to find Kennedy standing outside. A cortege of black Secret Service cars and limousines filled the street, and lights blazed in the windows of surrounding houses. Neighbors stood at open windows in their dressing gowns, cheering and applauding. A few snowflakes had lodged in Kennedy's hair, and he looked to Alsop as if he were still in his thirties. "Exhilaration always rejuvenated him," Alsop wrote later, "and he had been greatly exhilarated by his inauguration."

The guests were a mixture of Hollywood and Washington and included Peter Lawford, the actor Henry Fonda's former wife Afdera, and the future bandleader Peter Duchin, who was Averell Harriman's stepson. Kennedy took a straight-backed chair and accepted a glass of champagne. Everyone arranged themselves around him in chairs or on the floor. Duchin recalls being "spellbound" and cannot remember "a more wonderful moment." For the next ninety minutes Kennedy chatted effortlessly about the day.

He told Alsop's guests he was exhausted and had come to the party to unwind. But Alsop's explanation for his presence is probably closer to the truth. "Everyone told him he had been a success . . . [and] paid him compliments, which he, being a normal man, enjoyed," Alsop recalled. "I soon observed that what he really wanted was one last cup of unadulterated admiration and the people crowding my living room gave him that cup freely, filled to the brim."

Kennedy left at 3:21 A.M. and was back at the White House nine minutes later. Still reluctant to end the evening, he stood in the North Portico talking with a group of reporters who had been following him all day. A chill wind blew, it was nineteen degrees, but he remained hatless and coatless. He apologized for keeping them up, saying he had not planned to stay at the party so long. He said good night, and the last thing the reporters saw was the tip of his cigar, glowing red in the dark as he walked into the White House.

Decades later, Jackie Kennedy was seated next to Walter Cronkite at an informal dinner party in Hyannisport and told him what happened next. "Oh, Walter, Jack was so funny," she said. "He insisted that we go into the Lincoln bedroom first, and despite his bad back he wanted to carry me across the threshold like a bride. We got into the bedroom and he dropped me on the bed . . ." Then her voice trailed away. She continued: "Oh, we laughed so, but then, Walter, we went over to our bedroom and he picked me up and had trouble getting us both through the door. Then he went over to the bed again and he . . ." Again her voice fell to a whisper. Twice Cronkite asked her to repeat the story—"as much as decency would allow," he said—but both times her voice faded away, leaving him, and us, to imagine the rest.

Harry Truman arrived at the White House the next morning for a 10:00 A.M. meeting that would be the first of Kennedy's presidency. At a dinner party the night before he had declared that the inaugural address had been eloquent, forceful, scholarly, and "a magnificent political speech." Now he told reporters gathered in the White House driveway that history would rank it as one of the greatest inaugurals of all time. "It was short, to the point, and in language anyone can understand," he said. "Even I could understand it, and therefore the people can."

As Truman left the Oval Office, Kennedy noticed the Reading Copy of his speech lying on Evelyn Lincoln's desk. He signed it, backdating it January 20,

1961, and told Lincoln, "I read the other day that one of the former presidents was offered $75,000 for his inaugural address." Usually his handwriting was an illegible scrawl. But on this day, signing for history, his signature was elegant and John Hancock–sized. It filled a quarter of the final page of the Reading Copy and is distinguished by graceful loops in the *y* in *Kennedy* and *January.* It has since become his signature of record, often reproduced in books and articles. He handed the speech back to Lincoln with a joke. "Here, keep this $75,000 for me."

A *New York Times* editorial praised the inaugural as "eloquent," "superb," and an inspiring "promise of hope." Its columnist James Reston wrote that "The evangelical and transcendental spirit of America has not been better expressed since Woodrow Wilson and maybe not even since Ralph Waldo Emerson. . . . For, like all true expression of the American ideal, this was a revolutionary document." Other columnists, and editorial writers called it "firm," "crisp," "moral," "Puritanical," "youthful," "idealistic," "vigorous," "classical," "elegant," "stirring," "superb," and "immortal." Kennedy, however, wanted also to hear these words from people he knew and respected. Sometime that morning he placed the first call of his presidency to the Archbishop Philip Hannan, a Jesuit priest with whom he had developed a somewhat clandestine friendship. "Your inaugural address was a masterpiece, the best in a hundred years," Hannan told him, a compliment he recalls making Kennedy "extremely happy." Hannan discussed the address with him on other occasions, too, and remembers him being immensely proud of it, and bitterly resenting the rumors that Sorensen had written it.

Kennedy was annoyed to learn that John Kenneth Galbraith was claiming to have contributed the "Let us never negotiate out of fear. But let us never fear to negotiate" line to the speech. ABC had given Galbraith a car and driver and followed him with a television camera throughout the day. He invited John Steinbeck to accompany him to the Capitol, and after the ceremony had maneuvered him into asking about his contributions to the address. Galbraith, an "unloved dog" of a ghostwriter no longer, quickly and proudly laid claim to his "scrap" on national television.

Kennedy found out about the broadcast and called Galbraith the next day to complain. He pretended to treat the incident as evidence of Galbraith's roguish charm but was obviously nettled. "I've lived in this city almost twenty years and have witnessed every kind of self-advertisement that you can imagine," he said. "But picking out that phrase and then getting Steinbeck to ask about it is beyond anything I've seen."

* * *

Accolades poured into the White House in the days following the inauguration. Perennial Socialist presidential candidate Norman Thomas wrote, "Permit me to add to the thousands of congratulations that are pouring upon you for the appropriate excellence of your inaugural address in style and substance. If you and we can implement it properly, it will go down in history with Lincoln's and Roosevelt's." Columbia University president Grayson Kirk complimented Kennedy for not using "a single tired cliché," adding, "Your inaugural address was superb! The style was exquisite—graceful, simple and forceful." Eleanor Roosevelt sent a handwritten note: "I think 'gratitude' best describes the kind of liberation & lift to the listener which you gave. . . . I have reread your words several times & I have been filled with thankfulness." The letter probably meaning the most to Kennedy came from Hamlin Turner, a Harvard classmate of his late older brother. Turner recounted an all-night college bull session with Joe Kennedy during which the conversation turned to Jack. He wrote, "Joseph said (and I quote as well as my memory serves) 'the kid has always been able to say the right thing when he has to. I never have. I think you'll hear him say the right things some time.'"

Kay Halle asked the Invited Intellectuals to contribute a message and informal photograph for a commemorative scrapbook. Many who responded had been unable to attend the ceremony on such short notice but had watched it on television. Kennedy repeatedly badgered Halle about this book, demanding to know when he could see it. When she finally brought it to the White House that spring, he leaned back, put his feet up on his desk, and read every page. From the novelist Carson McCullers came, "I think that I have never been moved by words more than I was by your inaugural address. . . . It reminded me of the great speeches of FDR and Winston Churchill. Indeed, it is one of the great addresses of our age." Eudora Welty had felt "a surge of hope about life in general." Carl Sandburg saluted him for "wonderfully appropriate appointments & two speeches [his inaugural and State of the Union speech] that are to be American classics." Conrad Aiken praised "an imagination of the noblest sort" and believed that "its effect is already visible in the remarkably increased respect for our country abroad." John Steinbeck called Kennedy's words "nobly conceived and excellently written and delivered," adding that the address had "that magic undertone of truth which cannot be simulated." For the architectural critic Lewis Mumford, it was "a fresh wind from the high slopes of an older America."

Ernest Hemingway had watched the inauguration on television from the

Mayo Clinic in Rochester, Minnesota. Kennedy liked his inscription so much he read it aloud: "Watching on the screen I was sure our President could stand any of the heat to come as he had taken the cold of that day. . . . It is a good thing to have a brave man as our President in times as tough as these for our country and the world."

Many of the intellectuals linked their praise for the address to expressions of gratitude that someone had finally acknowledged their importance, leaving one to wonder if their comments would have been less fulsome had Kennedy not invited them. Carson McCullers added, "It is a great thing that the arts and letters are at last being recognized." Robert Lowell was "happy that at long last the Goths have left the White House." Mark Rothko was "overjoyed that at last literacy and civilization are welcome." Lincoln Kirstein thanked Kennedy "for restoring to the United States the pleasures and powers of the mind." John Steinbeck said, "Personally, of course, I am honored to have been invited, but much more sharply felt is my gratification that through me you have recognized a good many of my profession as existing at all."

The intellectuals' praise for the address undoubtedly influenced its reception in some quarters, but the most important audience that afternoon would prove to have been the members of Kennedy's own future administration. The Peace Corps, Alliance for Progress, space program, Nuclear Test Ban Treaty, and the Vietnam War would all be promoted, negotiated, led, and managed by men who had been at the Capitol and heard Kennedy speak—by Robert McNamara, Sargent Shriver, McGeorge Bundy, and Dean Rusk, and by future treasury secretary Douglas Dillon, who told the speechwriter Mike Feldman afterward, "I've never heard a speech like that," and by Mike Feldman, who was inspired to read every previous inaugural and came to the conclusion that the only one possessing a similar inspirational quality was Abraham Lincoln's second.

Kennedy, too, was stirred by his own words and just hours after delivering them began fulfilling his promise to promote "human rights . . . at home and around the world." After noticing there were no black cadets in the Coast Guard Academy unit marching in his inaugural parade, he summoned Richard Goodwin to his side and said, "Did you see the Coast Guard detachment? There wasn't a black face in the entire group. That's not acceptable. Something ought to be done about it." Goodwin hurried into the White House, called Douglas Dillon, who oversaw the Coast Guard, and relayed what was in effect Kennedy's first presidential directive: an order to integrate the Coast Guard Academy. As Goodwin laid down the receiver he thought, "With this telephone we can change the world!"

Kennedy was not alone in making a connection between his speech and domestic issues such as race and poverty. To many listeners, the inaugural address appeared to concern only foreign affairs. But when some heard "man holds in his mortal hands the power to abolish all forms of human poverty," they thought of Appalachia, and when they heard Kennedy promise to "pay any price to assure the survival and success of liberty," they thought of civil rights in Mississippi. This may be why the Reverend Fred Shuttlesworth, a colleague of Martin Luther King Jr., would tell a meeting at St. James Baptist Church in Birmingham, Alabama, "What a wonderful President we have now!"

Every great speech is supposed to express a great idea. Within hours of the inauguration the editors of America's newspapers had decided that Kennedy's great idea had been his invitation to reduce cold-war tensions. Headlines on January 21 read, "Kennedy Is Sworn In—Asks Grand Alliance for Peace" (*San Francisco Chronicle*), "Kennedy Takes Oath as President, Proclaims a 'New Quest for Peace'" (*Washington Post* and *New York Herald Tribune*), "Kennedy Asks World Peace Quest" (*Philadelphia Inquirer*), and "Kennedy Sworn In, Bids for Peace" (*Washington Evening Star*).

This "rough draft of history" had identified the most newsworthy aspect of the speech but missed its great idea: Kennedy's call to extend the promises and guarantees of the Declaration of Independence to the entire world. There was nothing new about this idea—Woodrow Wilson, Henry Luce, and others had voiced it before him—but it was ideally suited to a time when the United States and the Soviet Union were competing for the allegiance of eighteen new Asian and African nations, and when the United States was offering only a sterile anticommunism, while the Soviets were promising an ideology that appeared to have transformed their once backward nation into a superpower in four decades.

Kennedy had argued for mobilizing the Declaration of Independence and sending it into cold-war battles in his 1957 Senate speech on Algeria: "The strength of our appeal to these key populations—and it is rightfully our appeal, and not that of the communists—lies in our traditional and deeply felt philosophy of freedom and independence for all peoples everywhere." He expressed the concept more forcefully in his remarks at his October 1960 campaign rally in front of the Hotel Theresa: "The world revolution which we see all around us is part of the original American Revolution. When the Indonesians revolted after the end of World War II, they scrawled on the walls, 'Give me liberty or give me death.' Not Russian slogans but American slogans." He had told Hugh Sidey during their flight to Washington on January

17 that he wanted to get across "that the spirit of the revolution was still present in America," and three days later in his inaugural he urged Americans to carry "the same revolutionary beliefs for which our forebears fought" into the world, asking them to "pay any price, bear any burden . . . to assure the survival and success of liberty," and to guarantee "those human rights to which this Nation has always been committed, and to which we are committed today at home and around the world."

In 1961, televisions were rare in the third world, but radios were everywhere, and millions of Asians, Africans, and Latin Americans heard Kennedy's address, either in English or translated into their native languages. His words had the desired effect. Throughout his administration, Americans were more admired and emulated in the third world than ever before or since, and there is an undeniable connection between Kennedy's description of colonialism as an "iron tyranny" and the John F. Kennedy bridges, schools, and boulevards scattered across these former European colonies, between his pledge to help "those peoples in the huts and villages across the globe" and the photographs of him hanging on the walls of those huts.

Kennedy's proclamation that Americans have a responsibility to promote freedom and democracy abroad has proven difficult to rescind. It became a two-edged sword during the Vietnam War: cited by Lyndon Johnson and former members of the Kennedy administration as an argument for preventing the North Vietnamese Communists from taking over South Vietnam, and by opponents of that war as an argument for not supporting a South Vietnamese government demonstrating little respect for human rights and the principles of the Declaration of Independence. It was expressed by Johnson in his 1965 inaugural address when he said that "the American covenant called on us to help show the way for the liberation of man," and by Jimmy Carter, who declared in his 1977 inaugural that "because we are free we can never be indifferent to the fate of freedom elsewhere." It has survived its cold-war raison d'être and been voiced as an argument for taking military action against hostile totalitarian states and as an argument for withdrawing American support from friendly ones. George W. Bush declared in his 2001 inaugural that "the enemies of liberty and our country should make no mistake: America remains engaged in the world by history and by choice, shaping a balance of power that favors freedom. . . . And to all nations we will speak for the values that gave our nation birth." When he announced the end of major combat operations in Iraq in May 2003, he proclaimed that "in this battle we have fought for the cause of liberty," and that "the advance of freedom is the surest strategy to undermine the appeal of terror in the world." What had been, then, in Kennedy's hands, a strategy for combating the spread of communism to third-world nations had become in Bush's hands a justification for the invasion of Iraq and, possibly, for future wars.

One feels that there must be more to explain the passionate response to Kennedy's speech than his call for Americans to become cold-war missionaries for freedom and democracy, more than the prospect of bringing democracy to, say, Pakistan, Mali, or Laos. There must have been, in short, some hidden heartbeat to the speech that resonated powerfully with the American people.

One can detect this heartbeat in Kennedy's October 1960 address at Wittenberg College. The prepared text had been a dry little exercise enumerating the eight principles he would observe in choosing people to serve in his administration. But inspired by an enthusiastic student audience, he delivered instead an extemporaneous speech posing a series of challenges, asking, "How many young students at this college are willing to spend . . . part of their time in this college . . . preparing themselves as doctors or teachers or engineers or scientists, or nurses, or public health officials, or Foreign Service offers, to contribute part of your talents, part of the benefits of your education to society as a whole?" He concluded, "This college was not founded and has not been maintained merely to give this school's graduates an economic advantage in this life struggle. There is a higher purpose."

Kennedy's belief in a higher purpose, and his conviction that every individual could contribute to achieving it by using his talents "to assure a more fruitful life for all mankind," was the hidden heartbeat of his inaugural address. It spoke to the need to live for something grander and more noble than physical comfort and material luxury. It appealed to the deeply religious strain in the American character, since a higher purpose implies the existence of a Higher Power. It affirmed the worth of every life by promising that the energy, faith, and devotion each individual brought to the task of "defending freedom in its hour of maximum danger" could ignite a fire whose glow could "truly light the world." It electrified the restless and unfulfilled Gray Flannel Suited veterans of Kennedy's generation and stirred the souls of their children. The man who had written home from the Pacific that "all war is stupid" and had seen the full dimensions of its stupidity in the ruins of Berlin was offering his generation a sense of purpose like that which they had experienced during the war, but without the bloodshed and with the promise of deterring future wars. (The inaugural: "when our arms are sufficient beyond doubt can we be certain beyond doubt that they will never be employed.")

God and the High Court of History were two sides of the same coin for Kennedy, and he lived in expectation of being judged by both. He had urged the Massachusetts legislators on January 9 to exhibit courage, judgment, integrity, and dedication, not just because it was their responsibility as citizens but because "from whomsoever much is given, of him shall much be required," and "at some future date the High Court of History sits in judgment on each one of us." Eleven days later he had proclaimed in his inaugural address that a good conscience would be our "only sure reward" and history our "final judge," and brought God into the equation by saying, "Let us go forth to lead the land we love, asking His blessing and His help, but knowing that here on earth God's work must truly be our own." This was Kennedy's God, a deity who gives us freedom and judges us on how well we use it, on whether or not we live up to the words of Cardinal Newman in the prayer that Rose Kennedy had drilled into him, "God had not created me for nought. I shall do good."

Just as Kennedy had drawn on earlier speeches for his inaugural, he was soon drawing on his inaugural for later speeches, and his reiteration of its themes and phrases served to root them more deeply in the American soul. He employed another litany of "lets" ten days later in his State of the Union message, proclaiming, "Let every public servant know . . . ," "Let it be clear . . . ," and "Let the public service be a proud and lively career." In that speech, he turned the "hour of maximum danger" into "an hour of national peril," then repeated it in his conclusion, saying, "Each day we draw nearer the hour of maximum danger." He recycled the tiger metaphor on December 23, 1961, when he said, "Khrushchev reminds me of the tiger hunter who has picked a place on the wall to hang the tiger's skin long before he has caught the tiger. The tiger has other ideas." In speeches and impromptu remarks throughout his presidency, he emphasized the responsibility of Americans to defend and spread freedom throughout the world. Had he not been assassinated on November 22, 1963, he would have said at a luncheon at the Dallas Trade Mart that day, "We in this country, in this generation, are—by destiny rather than choice—the watchmen on the walls of world freedom."

The Kennedy assassination and inauguration haunt each other. The inauguration magnifies the tragedy of his death, while his death and funeral lend an added poignancy to the words of his inaugural address. The optimism of one, and the despair of the other, have become so tightly woven that those attending both, or witnessing both on television, can recall them with a dual vision that can be disturbing, and illuminating.

Television footage of Kennedy and Eisenhower traveling by motorcade from the White House to the Capitol on Inauguration Day conjures up the motorcade in Dallas and the horse-drawn caisson carrying Kennedy's corpse to the Capitol, rolling slowly up Pennsylvania Avenue to the beat of muffled drums on another sunny day.

Kennedy stands at the podium on Inauguration Day hatless and coatless, unprotected from the cold, and we see him driving to the Dallas Trade Mart on November 22, also hatless, coatless, and vulnerable.

We see him waiting in the Capitol rotunda, nervously rocking on his heels, made impatient by a twenty-minute delay, then lying in the rotunda, impatient no longer. In the rotunda on Inauguration Day, a bewildered Jackie tells General Clifton she does not know what to do, and 1,038 days later Clifton stands in this same place, blinded by tears as he watches Jackie (who this time knows precisely what to do) kneel and kiss the flag-draped coffin, and watches Caroline slip her hand under the flag to touch the wood.

The next time many of the world leaders who praised Kennedy's inaugural address so extravagantly will search for similar phrases to express their deepest emotions will be in the days following his death. The Israeli statesman Abba Eban will call the assassination "one of the most authentically tragic events in the history of nations," and the Lebanese statesman Charles Malik will say it is difficult to find another instance in history of a man whose death was so universally mourned. Albert Schweitzer will declare that Kennedy "could have been the savior of the world," and a columnist in the *Manchester Guardian* will write, "For the first time in my life I think I know how the disciples must have felt when Jesus was crucified."

The next time many of the people seated in VIP sections on inauguration day will gather in Washington again, and the next occasion many of the men will have to wear their top hats again, will be at Kennedy's funeral. On November 24, 1963, there will be a navy instead of Marine Corps band playing "Hail to the Chief," although at a more mournful tempo, as a military detail carries Kennedy's casket up the same steps he descended to the presidential stand on January 20, 1961. As it passes Ted Sorensen, who will be one of thirty-six aides lined up as a civilian honor guard, will gaze down at his feet and realize he is standing on the same spot where he was sitting when Kennedy delivered his inaugural address.

Chief Justice Earl Warren, who administered the oath to Kennedy on January 20, 1961, will deliver a eulogy before his coffin on November 24, 1963, blaming a climate of hatemongering for his assassination. He will write Jackie that "no American during my long life ever set his sights higher for a better America," and will later head the commission carrying his name that will issue a controversial report. The next time most Americans will see Cardinal Cushing on television again will be at the funeral, where he will electrify mourners in St. Matthew's Cathedral by unexpectedly breaking into English at the conclusion of the Latin High Mass, crying out, "May the angels, dear Jack, lead you into Paradise!" Archbishop Philip Hannan, who told Kennedy the following morning that his speech had been the best in a century, will recite excerpts from it at the funeral, and this will be the first time since the inauguration that Americans will hear, booming from loudspeakers, although this time in Hannan's grieving voice, "We observe today not a victory of a party, but a celebration of freedom," "The torch has been passed to a new generation of Americans," "Now the trumpet summons us again," "And so, my fellow Americans, ask not what your country can do for you."

Jackie Kennedy called her husband's address "beautiful and soaring," and "one of the most moving speeches ever uttered," and predicted history would rank it with Pericles' Funeral Oration and the Gettysburg Address. In the hours following his death, she would translate its eloquent sentences into an eloquent funeral, and so the torch that Kennedy claimed for the new generation became the eternal flame at his grave, and the trumpet summoning Americans to a "long twilight struggle" against tyranny, poverty, disease, and war became the trumpet playing taps during his interment. In fact, the spare and classical language of the Kennedy inaugural was so easily translated into the spare and classical Kennedy funeral that you could almost say that when he dictated it to Evelyn Lincoln on January 10, he was also dictating his funeral.

Soon after Kennedy's death, others began borrowing words and ideas from his inaugural address. Six months after Dallas, Bobby Kennedy delivered a speech he had written himself to students at the Free University in Berlin. He said, referring to his brother, "There were many who felt . . . that the torchbearer for a whole generation was gone," and declared that "the torch still burns, and because it does, there remains for all of us a chance to light up the tomorrows and brighten the future." During a visit to South Africa in 1966 he told an audience of young people, "It is a revolutionary world we live in and this generation, at home and around the world, has had thrust upon it a greater burden of responsibility than any generation that has ever lived."

Many of those echoing the words and ideas of the inaugural have done it in sentences so ham-fisted they leave one longing for Kennedy. In his second inaugural address Richard Nixon translated "ask not" into "In our own lives, let each of us ask—not what the government will do for me, but what can I do for myself? In the challenges we face together, let each of us ask—not just how government can help, but how can I help?"

Kennedy had pledged, "We shall pay any price . . . to assure the survival and the success of liberty." Ronald Reagan said in his first inaugural, "The price for this freedom at times has been high, but we have never been unwilling to pay that price."

One hears Kennedy, too, in both of Bill Clinton's inaugural addresses, in sentences such as "Each generation of Americans must define what it means to be an American"; "We must do what no generation has had to do before"; "I challenge a new generation of Americans to a season of service"; "We have heard the trumpets"; and in "And so, my fellow Americans," which he followed with a flaccid "at the edge of the 21st century, let us begin with energy and hope."

The Republican National Committee used footage of Kennedy delivering his inaugural to introduce George W. Bush at its 2000 convention. Five months later, Bush concluded his own inaugural with a version of "ask not." Kennedy had needed a single comma, colon, dash, and sentence, and twenty-two words to make his point. Bush needed four commas, three semicolons, one colon, three sentences, and fifty-nine words to turn "And so, my fellow Americans: ask not what your country can do for you—ask what you can do for your country" into "What you do is as important as anything government does. I ask you to seek a common good beyond your comfort, to defend needed reforms against easy attacks; to serve your nation, beginning with your neighbor. I ask you to be citizens: citizens, not spectators; citizens, not subjects; responsible citizens, building communities of service and a nation of character."

Those appropriating the words and themes of Kennedy's address have failed to appreciate that the text was only part of its magic. There was also an extraordinary convergence of people, events, and history. There was the snowstorm, Jackie's wardrobe, Frost's recitation, and an audience already longing for his words. There was a man who left nothing to chance—not his tan, his haircut, or teeth, not even the cut of his suit, or the seating of dignitaries on his platform—and who spoke with the urgency of someone who had narrowly escaped death and cared passionately about the judgment of history. There was a speech he had not only composed but lived; one that was a distillation of the spiritual and philosophical principles forming his character and guiding his life, and that he delivered with a passion that reached deeply buried hearts and elicited from the American people, as Gore Vidal had predicted, "a remarkable emotional response."

After everyone has passed away who heard Kennedy speak the words carved onto that sweeping granite wall at Arlington, there will still be tears. Some will be for the man buried under the slab of black slate, some for the faded glamour of Camelot, some for a president who refused to underestimate the literacy and idealism of the American people. But as the Kennedy presidency grows more distant, many will read these sentences and mourn a time when a speech could move a nation and launch an era of idealism, optimism, and joy.

Afterword

POETRY AND POWER

⚜

Kennedy did not read the poem that Robert Frost had composed for his inauguration until the poet visited the White House two days later and gave him a signed and handwritten copy. Its final stanza predicted:

The glory of a next Augustan age
Of a power leading from its strength and pride,
Of young ambition eager to be tried,
Firm in our free beliefs without dismay,
In any game the nations want to play.
A golden age of poetry and power
Of which this noonday's the beginning hour.

"Be more Irish than Harvard," Frost said as he left the Oval Office. "Poetry and power is the formula for another Augustan Age. Don't be afraid of power." At the bottom of a typed thank-you note to Frost, Kennedy wrote, "It's poetry and power all the way!" During the next thousand days, he followed Frost's advice.

There was poetry in his September 1962 address at Rice University, when he told students, "We choose to go to the moon in this decade and do the other things, not because they are easy, but because they are hard," and reminded them that the founder of the Plymouth Bay Colony had warned the Pilgrims that "all great and honorable actions are accompanied with great difficulties" and must be overcome "with answerable courage." There was more poetry during the Cuban Missile Crisis, when he spoke of a worldwide nuclear war "in which even the fruits of victory would be ashes in our mouth," and declared that "our goal is not the victory of might, but the vindication of right."

There was poetry in his June 10, 1963, commencement speech at American University, when he answered the rhetorical question, "What kind of peace of peace do we seek?" with, "Not the peace of the grave or the security of the slave. . . . not merely peace for Americans but peace for all men and women—not merely peace in our time but peace for all time." There was more poetry the next day when he proclaimed, during a nationally televised speech on civil rights, "We are confronted primarily with a moral issue. It is as old as the scriptures and is as clear as the American Constitution."

Frost died in January 1963 and in October Kennedy spoke at the groundbreaking for a library at Amherst College named in Frost's honor. After making extensive changes to his prepared speech during the flight from Washington, he delivered one of the finest orations of his presidency. "It is hardly an accident that Robert Frost coupled poetry and power," he said, "for he saw poetry as the means of saving power from itself. When power leads man toward arrogance, poetry reminds him of his limitations. When power narrows the areas of man's concern, poetry reminds him of the richness and diversity of his existence. When power corrupts, poetry cleanses. For art establishes the basic human truth which must serve as the touchstone of our judgment."

He concluded by predicting "a future in which our country will match its military strength with our moral restraint, its wealth with our wisdom, its power with our purpose," and a nation "which will not be afraid of grace and beauty, which will protect the beauty of our natural environment . . . will reward achievement in the arts as we reward achievement in business or statecraft," and "commands respect throughout the world not only for its strength but for its civilization." He was speaking, of course, of what he hoped to achieve in his second term.

Twenty-seven days later he was dead and Frost's golden age of poetry and power ended. But this age and its spirit cast a shadow over the presidents who followed, and over their inaugural addresses, sometimes placing them in an unflattering light.

In his 1965 inaugural address, Lyndon Johnson promised that his Great Society would not be "the ordered, changeless, and sterile battalion of the ants," and turned JFK's stirring "the torch has been passed to a new generation," into "for every generation, there is a destiny." Richard Nixon proclaimed that "the American dream does not come to those who fall asleep," and that "our destiny offers, not the cup of despair, but the chalice of opportunity." Jimmy Carter described American spirituality and love of liberty as "that unique self-definition which has given us an exceptional appeal." Ronald Reagan's first inaugural address was the best since Kennedy's, but he echoed JFK's pledge to "pay any price . . . to assure the survival and the success of liberty," with a clunky, "the price for this freedom at times has been high, but we have never been unwilling to pay that price." George H. W. Bush told Americans they were living in "a time when the future seems a door you can walk right through into a room called tomorrow." In both of his inaugural addresses, Bill Clinton used JFK's iconic, "And so, my fellow Americans . . ." but followed them with banal exhortations.

Historians have ranked Kennedy's performance in office as high as sixth and as low as eighteenth in polls taken over the last thirty years. The public has been more generous, placing him as high as second and no lower than sixth. When 137 scholars of rhetoric chose the one hundred best American speeches of the twentieth century, they ranked Kennedy's inaugural address second, below only Martin Luther King, Jr.'s "I have a dream" speech. (The only inaugural address delivered after Kennedy's to make the list was Reagan's first, at number thirty.) When the editors of *Time* chose the top ten greatest American speeches, they placed the Kennedy inaugural address at number seven, one place above "I have a dream," and just three below the Gettysburg Address.

Long after everyone who watched the frigid January air turn Kennedy's words into white smoke is gone, it is likely that those words will continue to be counted among his greatest achievements, along with his skillful handling of the Cuban Missile Crisis, the Apollo moon program, and his 1960 election which, by demonstrating that a Catholic could become president, kicked open a door through which members of minority groups, including Barack Obama, have followed.

The similarities between Obama's and Kennedy's political trajectories are striking. Kennedy's *Profiles in Courage* won a Pulitzer Prize. Obama's *Dreams from My Father* spent months on bestseller lists, and both books helped launch their authors' prospective presidential campaigns. Both men came to national attention by delivering eloquent speeches at the Democratic conventions that preceded their nominations. Kennedy concluded his 1956 speech nominating Adlai Stevenson with the stirring, "The time is ripe. The hour has struck. The man is here; and he is ready. Let the word go forth [a phrase he would use again in his inaugural address] that we have fulfilled our responsibility to the nation." In an even more eloquent keynote address at the 2004 convention, Obama said, "There's not a liberal America and a conservative America; there's the United States of America," and defined the politics of hope as, "Hope in the face of difficulty, hope in the face of uncertainty, the audacity of hope."

Kennedy attempted to defuse the issue of his Catholic faith by telling a gathering of Protestant ministers in Houston, "It is apparently necessary for me to state once again—not what kind of church I believe in, for that should be important only to me—but what kind of America I believe in." In 2008, Obama addressed the issue of his race in a speech in Philadelphia, saying, "We may have different stories, but we hold common hopes."

Both men were the only presidential candidates ever to accept their party's nomination in an outdoor stadium. At Denver's Mile High Stadium Obama declared, "We meet at one of those defining moments, a moment when our nation is at war, our economy is in turmoil, and the American promise has been threatened once more." Kennedy also spoke of a defining moment when he accepted his party's nomination at the Los Angeles Coliseum, saying, "We stand today on the edge of a New Frontier—the frontier of the 1960s—a frontier of unknown opportunities and perils, a frontier of unfulfilled hopes and threats." But whereas Obama in Denver was forceful and confident, Kennedy faced a low afternoon sun that forced him to squint, and his delivery was so halting that it convinced Nixon that he could easily beat him in a televised debate. (Six weeks later, a majority of Americans who heard the first Nixon-Kennedy debate on the radio—rather than seeing it on television, where Kennedy looked much better—believed Nixon had won.) Throughout the fall campaign Kennedy, unlike Obama, proved himself to be a mediocre orator, visibly nervous, and sometimes speaking in a hurried monotone. He overcame his shortcomings in his inaugural address, but he traveled with a speech coach during the campaign.

Kennedy and Obama both had an underlying belief in the intelligence of the American people. After reading the transcripts of Nixon's campaign speeches, Kennedy asked journalist Theodore White, "Did you ever read such shit?" Nixon was a "queer man," he added. In their private conversations, Nixon struck Kennedy as smart and forthright, but during the campaign he had made the fatal error of "talking down" to the American people. Instead, Kennedy said, a candidate should always "talk up" to the American people, even if that meant talking over their heads. Obama, too, talked up to the American people during his campaign, and continued doing so during the first year of his presidency, leading former Kennedy speechwriter Ted Sorensen to complain that he sometimes spoke *too* far over their heads, saying, "He [Obama] is clearly well-informed on all matters of public policy, sometimes, frankly, a little too well-informed. And as a result, some of his speeches are too complicated for typical citizens."

Obama's inaugural address was expected to match Kennedy's, inspiring a new generation to a season of sacrifice and ushering in another age of poetry and power. Obama had proven himself to be an even more polished and confident public speaker. The inauguration of the nation's first black president was creating excitement similar to that surrounding the inauguration of the first Catholic, and the huge crowds descending on Washington were as enthusiastic as those that had gathered for Kennedy. Both men were married to women who would be celebrated for their elegance and style. Ted Sorensen, Caroline Kennedy, Ted Kennedy, and Ethel Kennedy had become fervent Obama supporters, further contributing to the comparisons with the Kennedy inauguration. A week before the inauguration, Sorensen appeared to be encouraging Obama to deliver a Kennedy-esque address, telling the *New York Times* that he believed there was a connection between inspirational oratory and inspirational leadership. "The most important quality for a president, as Kennedy and Roosevelt demonstrated, is not how many roll call votes he answered while sitting in the Senate, but his qualities as a leader who can mobilize people, inspire them, galvanize them, arouse them to action," Sorensen said. "The ability to inspire and excite an audience on the campaign trail is one of the reasons I think Obama will be a success as president."

Obama's inauguration day was as moving as Kennedy's. His address was solid, better than any speech since Ronald Reagan's first, but compared to his soaring campaign oratory, and compared to the Kennedy inaugural address it was a disappointment. It contained some good lines, such as, "But our time of standing pat, of protecting narrow interests and putting off unpleasant decisions—that time has surely passed," but no memorable ones. Other great inaugural addresses were echoed, but not equaled. At a similarly perilous time in history, Franklin Roosevelt had declared that "the nation asks for action, and action now" and, like some wrathful Old Testament prophet, had condemned the nation's bankers, saying, "Practices of the unscrupulous money-changers stand indicted in the court of public opinion, rejected by the hearts and minds of men." But after saying, "The state of our economy asks for action and action now," Obama could muster only a tepid, "Our economy is badly weakened, a consequence of greed and irresponsibility on the part of some."

In Obama's hands Kennedy's vivid, "To those people in the huts and villages of half the globe struggling to break the bonds of mass misery, we pledge our best efforts to help them help themselves . . . not because the communists may be doing it, not because we seek their votes, but because it is right," became the more prosaic, "To the people of poor nations, we pledge to work alongside you to make your farms flourish and let clean waters flow."

Instead of a succinct "Ask not," Obama offered a more verbose call to sacrifice: "What is required of us now is a new era of responsibility—a recognition, on the part of every American, that we have duties to ourselves, our nation, and the world, duties that we do not grudgingly accept but rather seize gladly, firm in the knowledge that there is nothing so satisfying to the spirit." Instead of the kind of master sentence that can define a presidency and an age, such as "Ask not," FDR's "We have nothing to fear but fear itself," or Lincoln's "With malice toward none, with charity for all," the most memorable sentence of Obama's inaugural address, the one replayed the most, quoted the most, and even repeated by Obama himself a year later during his State of the Union address, was, "Starting today, we must pick ourselves up, dust ourselves off, and begin again the work of remaking America." It was a paraphrase of lyrics from "Pick Yourself Up," sung by Ginger Rogers and Fred Astaire in the 1936 musical *Swing Time*.

A speech for the ages like Kennedy's inaugural address usually requires the convergence of a dramatic event, a pivotal historical moment, a skillful orator, eloquent words, and an audience hungering to hear them. All five were present for Kennedy. But Obama lacked—or at least imagined that he lacked—an audience hungering for the kind of stirring inaugural address that would launch another age of poetry and power. By the time he delivered his address, the year-long campaign by his opponents to paint his eloquence as a vice rather than a virtue, an effete substitute for action and accomplishment, and to depict Obama as a man of beautiful words but little substance, had taken its toll on Obama and on the American people. His principal adversary in the primaries, Hillary Clinton repeated Mario Cuomo's quotation that, "You campaign in poetry, but you govern in prose," while her supporter Robert F. Kennedy Jr. warned of the danger of too much "poetry or lofty language." In his speech to the 2008 GOP convention, Senator Joseph Lieberman declared that "eloquence is no substitute for a record," and Republican candidate John McCain pledged to "work hard to make sure Americans aren't deceived by an eloquent but empty call for change."

My suspicion that Obama had toned down his rhetoric for the inauguration was confirmed a year later, as he prepared to deliver his first State of the Union address. Asked if Obama would deliver the kind of eloquent speech that had marked his campaign, aide David Axelrod responded that "serious times" like these were ill suited to what he called "for rhetorical flights of fancy." No matter that the Depression had prompted "We have nothing to fear," Pearl Harbor had been answered by Roosevelt's "Day of Infamy" speech, and the threat of a Civil War had summoned forth Lincoln's "Angels of our better nature." Or that two years before Obama himself had responded to Clinton's attacks by saying, "Her dismissive point, and I hear it a lot from her staff, is all I have to offer is words. Just words." He then continued, to applause and cheers, "'We hold these truths to be self-evident that all men are created equal'—just words. Just words. 'We have nothing to fear but fear itself.' Just words. 'Ask not what your country can do for you, ask what you can do for your country.' Just words. 'I have a dream'—just words."

Kennedy's sensitive political antennae had told him that the American people were hungering to be inspired. Obama appears to have reached a different conclusion, and took his foot off the oratorical accelerator just before delivering the two speeches—his inaugural and first State of the Union—that promised to be among the most watched of his presidency. He appears to have read the national mood correctly. No one praised his inaugural as a speech for the ages, but no one accused him of engaging in a rhetorical flight of fancy either. Perhaps sound bite politics, the Internet, and Twitter have dulled the appetite of the American people for "beautiful words" and stirring speeches. If Americans get the government they deserve perhaps they also get the inaugural address they want. But one thing is certain: until they want another golden age of poetry and power, Kennedy's inaugural address will remain unequaled.

Notes

ABBREVIATIONS

JFKL = John F. Kennedy Library
JFKLOH = JFKL Oral History Collection
POF = Presidential Office Files, in JFKL
PP – John F. Kennedy Personal Papers, in JFKL
PPP = John F. Kennedy Prepresidential Papers, in JFKL
USS SUB = The Speeches of Senator John F. Kennedy: Presidential Campaign of 1960—Final Report of the Committee on Commerce, United States Senate, prepared by its Subcommittee of the Subcommittee on Communications

THE INAUGURAL ADDRESS

This version of the speech conforms to *Inaugural Address of President John F. Kennedy—As Actually Delivered,* the text released by the Office of the White House Press Secretary on the afternoon of January 20, 1961 and found in Box 34, POF. It incorporates the changes Kennedy made while delivering the address and conforms to the punctuation and capitalization found in the Reading Copy. The version reproduced in Theodore Sorensen's book, *Kennedy,* and in his compilation of Kennedy's speeches and writings, *"Let the Word Go Forth,"* contains some additional commas, and capitalizes *communists*.

PROLOGUE: ARLINGTON NATIONAL CEMETERY

PAGE

3 The granite at Arlington: Author's interview with the stonemason William "Billy" Cleland, 2002.

4 "oppose any foe, to assure the survival and the success of liberty": The comma after *foe* is absent from the original White House press release, *Inaugural Address of President John F. Kennedy* As Actually Delivered (Box 34, POF), and from the text of the speech that Theodore Sorensen reproduced in his 1965 book, *Kennedy.* It was added to the sentence when it was chiseled into stone at Arlington, and Sorensen included it in the text of the speech found in *"Let the Word Go Forth,"* a 1988 collection of Kennedy's speeches, statements, and writings that Sorensen edited. Sorensen made other small changes in punctuation between the official 1961 version and the 1988 version. Another example: he removed the comma following the word *that* in the phrase "and to remember that, in the past, those who foolishly sought power by riding the back of

the tiger ended up inside" so that it read "and to remember that in the past, those who foolishly sought power by riding the back of the tiger ended up inside." Throughout this book I use the official 1961 White House version.

5 In *The Kennedy Promise,* p. 2, Henry Fairlie also points out that not only are Washington, Lincoln, and FDR buried elsewhere, but not even Churchill and de Gaulle have such a magnificent grave.

6 The physician administering amphetamine injections to JFK was Dr. Max Jacobson. *New York Times,* December 4, 1972.

6 Rose Kennedy was fuming over her row-end seat: Rose Kennedy, p. 386.

6 these seven sentences would remain, carved into stone and woven into lives: United Nations ambassador Richard Holbrooke, United Nations secretary-general Kofi Annan, and Senator Joseph Lieberman are among the dozens of public figures who were college students in 1961 and have credited the inaugural address with inspiring them to pursue careers in politics, diplomacy, or public service.

6 A college student who would join the first class of Peace Corps volunteers: Quotation found in March 2001 exhibit at the Kennedy Library commemorating the fortieth anniversary of the Peace Corps.

6 Donna Shalala comment: Author's interview with Donna Shalala, 2003.

6 "vigorous, classical, sacred eloquence": Pope Paul VI, JFKLOH.

7 James Meredith was inspired: Lord, pp. 96–97. Schlesinger (*Thousand Days*), p. 940.

7 "the energies Kennedy released . . .": Schlesinger (*Thousand Days),* p. 1031.

7 "We find it hard to believe that . . .": *New Yorker,* February 4, 1961.

7 "the cadence of Abraham Lincoln's oratory . . .": *Times* (London), January 21, 1961.

7 Archibald MacLeish: Box 3, Halle papers, JFKL.

7 E. B. White: Schlesinger (*Thousand Days),* pp. 731–32.

7 *Life:* January 27, 1961.

7 Barry Goldwater: David Bell, JFKLOH.

8 Words are mighty things: Emily Dickinson wrote about the power of poetry: "I used to think when I was an ungifted girl that words were cheap and weak. Now I don't know of anything so mighty." Quoted on *Morning Edition* (National Public Radio), November 27, 2001.

8 "It is not merely the thing that is said . . .": Sorensen (*"Let the Word"),* p. 6.

8 Nixon refused to comment on inaugural: *Evening Star* (Washington, D.C.), January 21, 1961. The paper reported that "only former Vice President Nixon, Mr. Kennedy's presidential opponent in the campaign, was noncommittal. His only comment was: 'Today is President Kennedy's day, and I wish him and country well.'"

8 "It's easy for Kennedy to get up . . .": "Richard Nixon's Biggest Crisis," *Redbook,* July 1962, cited in Golden, p. 348.

8 "Theodore Sorensen, not the author . . . ": Wills (*Kennedy Imprisonment*), p. 135.

8 Katharine Graham claimed to be "a real Kennedy enthusiast": Graham, p. 273.

9 "the author of so many of Kennedy's speeches . . .": *Time,* October 24, 1988.

9 "John Kennedy's inaugural address has been praised . . .": The Kennedy inaugural address segment was aired on PBS on January 25, 2002. The statement about Sorensen's authorship is found in "JFK's Trumpet Call," on the PBS Web site.

9 The speech is generally acknowledged to have been the greatest oration of any twentieth-century American politician: A joint survey conducted by the Texas A&M and the University of Wisconsin polled 137 experts in speech making and rhetoric, asking them to rate the top one hundred American speeches of the twentieth century based on social and political impact and rhetorical artistry. The top ten speeches were: (1) Martin Luther King Jr.—"I have a Dream"; (2) John F. Kennedy—inaugural address; (3) Franklin Roosevelt—first inaugural address; (4) Franklin Roosevelt—war message ("A date which will live in infamy"); (5) Barbara Jordan—keynote speech to the 1976 Democratic National Convention; (6) Richard Nixon—"Checkers" speech; (7) Malcolm X—"The Ballot or the Bullet"; (8) Ronald Reagan—address to the nation on

the Challenger disaster; (9) John F. Kennedy—1960 speech to the Greater Houston Ministerial Association; (10) Lyndon Johnson—address to Congress on the Voting Rights Act ("We Shall Overcome"). Four of the top ten speeches were delivered during the 1960s, and only two were delivered in the last thirty-five years of the decade.

10 "History made him [Kennedy] what he was . . .": Box 40, Theodore White papers, JFKL.

10 "[Kennedy] began reeling off a list . . .": White (*In Search*), p. 486.

10 "At some future date . . .": Ibid., p. 57.

10 "overnight raised Lamar . . .": John F. Kennedy (*Profiles*), p. 141.

11 "a sort of slow-motion leukemia . . .": Perret (*Jack*), p. 148.

11 "Ted Sorensen is getting to be . . .": Author's interview with Fay, 2002.

11 Sorensen described his collaboration with JFK: Sorensen (*Kennedy*), p. 240.

11 "the final shape of every text . . .": Sorensen (*Kennedy Legacy*), p. 82.

12 "too rhetorical": Richard Goodwin, p. 114.

12 JFK dictated to Gloria Sitrin: Author's interview with Sitrin, 2002; Gloria Sitrin, JFKLOH.

12 "in the vast majority of cases . . .": Sorensen (*Kennedy*), p. 177

12 "assistant artisans": Ibid., p. 241.

12 "principal architect": Sorensen (*Kennedy*), p. 241.

12 "Now this is very delicate ground . . .": Author's interview with Sorensen, 2002.

13 "all his hopes, dreams . . .": Martin and Plaut, p. 225.

13 The most important of these documents: Box 7, Lincoln papers, JFKL.

13 Kennedy asked Evelyn Lincoln to bring her stenographer's pad: Lincoln (*My Twelve Years*), p.182.

CHAPTER ONE: ON BOARD THE *CAROLINE*, JANUARY 10

17 Kennedy dictated the college honors thesis: Herzstein, p. 154: "Assisted by five stenographers, [Kennedy] rushed to complete his paper by the deadline."

17 Kennedy dictated contributions to *Profiles:* Sitrin, JFKLOH. Sitrin, a secretary in Kennedy's Senate offices who normally worked for Ted Sorensen, flew to Palm Beach to take dictation from Kennedy.

17 Mary Davis on JFK dictation skills: Mary Davis, JFKLOH.

17 JFK speech at Los Angeles convention center: Lincoln (*My Twelve Years*), pp. 131–32.

18 Audiotapes of Kennedy's dictation: Audiovisual archives, November 9, 1954, JFKL.

18 The St. Patrick's Day dinner: Box 40, PP.

18 Memorial Day ceremonies in Brookline: Ibid.

18 He began dictating the announcement of his presidential candidacy: Lincoln (*My Twelve Years*), pp. 105–6.

19 The Neustadt memorandum: Box 31, POF.

19 "to ask the ablest men in the country . . .": Sorensen (*"Let the Word"*), p. 51.

19 James Reston: *New York Times,* January 15, 1961.

19 "the way Mr. Kennedy has conducted himself . . .": *Washington Post,* January 18, 1961.

20 and liking to be teased "about the fact . . .": Bradlee, p. 39.

20 "kiddies day at the circus": Lincoln (*My Twelve Years*), p. 183.

20 letters and telegrams during the transition: Box 1, Holborn papers, JFKL.

20 A former lover wanted him to remember her: Box 1091, PPP.

21 He drove to Cambridge: *New York Times,* January 10, 1961.

21 January 9, 1960, speech to Massachusetts State Legislature: Sorensen (*"Let the Word"*) pp. 56–58.

21 Kennedy worried the speech might have been too good: Sorensen (*Kennedy*), p. 240.

21 Franklin Roosevelt's 1932 tribute to George Norris: John F. Kennedy (*Profiles*), p. 192.

21 "God, but you must be rich . . .": Lawrence, p. 256. Kennedy would not dictate his inaugural until the following evening. His comment that he had "a good inaugural" may have been a reference to his ideas for the speech, or he may have been trying to

convince an influential reporter that his inaugural would be one of the greatest. After composing the address, he told another reporter that it was "a smash."

22 Flight to Washington with Kennan and Kennan's memorandum: George Kennan, JFKLOH.

23 "Dictated several pages of the Inaugural Address . . .": Box 2, Lincoln papers, JFKL.

23 We like to imagine great speeches are born: It has also been said that Lincoln wrote the Gettysburg Address at the White House, or the night before in Gettysburg, or on the very morning of the ceremony. See Donald, p. 461 and footnotes.

23 aviation enthusiasts believe the speed and mobility that it afforded him: An article about the *Caroline* on the Web site of the Smithsonian Air and Space Museum says, "Historians credit this aircraft with providing Kennedy with the narrow margin of victory for it allowed him to campaign more effectively during that very hotly contested race [1960]. The *Caroline,* named after Kennedy's daughter, revolutionized American politics; since 1960 all presidential candidates have used aircraft as their primary means of transportation."

24 Sorensen writes in *Kennedy* about their first inaugural address discussion: Sorensen *(Kennedy),* p. 240.

24 the notes Sorensen took at this meeting: Box 62, Sorensen papers, JFKL. It appears that prior to this meeting Sorensen had written a list of six points that he believed Kennedy should address in the inaugural. It is unknown if he gave this memorandum, titled "Possible Themes for the Inaugural," to Kennedy, but very few of these suggestions made it into the speech. Kennedy certainly ignored the first three: "Tribute to Eisenhower—National Unity—continuity," "The Gold Crisis—meet it with positive policies, not retrenchment," and "The domestic slump—the same." Had Kennedy followed the advice in this memorandum, his inaugural address would have been focused largely on domestic affairs.

25 "leave them wanting more": Author's interview with Hugh Sidey, 2002.

25 "a largely undistinguished lot . . .": Sorensen *(Kennedy),* p. 240.

25 Feldman recalls Sorensen telling him that the inaugurals had provided some useful ideas: Author's interview with Mike Feldman, 2002.

25 Sorensen draft of inaugural address: Box 34, POF.

25 "actual drafting did not get under way . . .": Sorensen *(Kennedy),* p. 240.

25 "pages, paragraphs, and complete drafts . . ." and, these contributors supplied "several phrases, sentences, and themes": Ibid., p. 240.

25 "no Kennedy speech ever underwent so many drafts": Ibid., p. 241. During an interview held in 2002, Sorensen said, "It's almost impossible to say how many drafts the speech went through." He added: "A lot of the writing took place in Washington. Some of it by myself in my home; some of it—and it seems to me I was writing in Mike's [Mike Feldman's] house that morning [January 14 or 15] while waiting for the brunch—some of it may have taken place in the Senate office, judging from that stationery [the Senate memoranda paper he used to compute the length of his draft]."

26 Kennedy was angered by rumors he did not write *Profiles:* Sorensen *(Kennedy),* p. 68.

26 Robert McNamara's first question: O'Donnell and Powers, p. 237; Shapley, p. 84.

26 Kennedy wrote out announcement of McNamara appointment: McNamara, p. 17; O'Donnell and Powers, p. 238. O'Donnell and Powers write, "McNamara was fascinated when he saw Kennedy himself writing in longhand on a yellow legal pad the statement that he would read to the reporters outside on the front steps."

26 "That was a very sensitive subject . . .": Sorensen oral history, among Herbert S. Parmet's interviews in Columbia University Oral History Project.

26 Sorensen wrote first draft at Feldman's house on Thanksgiving: Author's interview with Feldman.

26 Feldman and Sorensen flew together to Palm Beach to meet Kennedy, and Feldman read Sorensen's draft: Author's interview with Feldman, 2002. Feldman's recollection is confirmed by the December 21 entry in Lincoln's appointment book (box 2,

Lincoln papers JFKL): "Spend all day with Dave Bell, Dock Neustadt, Elmer Staats, Mike Feldman, Ted Sorensen."

27 "And if the fruits of . . .": Sorensen *(Kennedy),* p. 242.

27 A slip of U.S. Senate memorandum paper: Box 62, Sorensen papers, JFKL.

27 Sitrin believed she typed the draft: Author's interview with Sitrin, 2002.

28 a repertoire of his favorite lines: These can be found by checking the index of USS SUB.

28 Goodwin supplies JFK with civil rights speech: Richard Goodwin, p. 114.

28 "These were the great years . . .": USS SUB, p. 193.

29 September 15 speech in Harrisburg: Ibid., p. 250.

29 JFK "dictated and dictated . . .": Lincoln (*My Twelve Years),* p. 182.

29 Lincoln's shorthand notes tell a different story: These notes, cited here and on subsequent pages in this chapter, can be found in box 7, Lincoln papers, JFKL.

29 "more than the usual run of prank mail": *Washington Post,* January 19, 1961; Baughman, p. 256.

29 "We are sick of dirty black Catholics . . .": Baughman, p. 255.

30 "moments of grace": Walt Rostow, JFKLOH.

30 The Sorensen draft that Kennedy consulted on January 10: Box 34, POF.

32 speech at Bangor, Maine: USS SUB, p. 82.

32 Kennedy's notebooks have not survived, or at least are not available at the Kennedy Library. However, Ted Kennedy drew on them for *Words Jack Loved,* a privately published book that he gave to friends and family members as a Christmas gift in 1976.

32 "I think this nation will rise to the test . . .": USS SUB, p. 298.

33 "soaring hubris": MacNeil, p. 13.

33 Tom Wicker called the speech "bellicose": Wicker, p. 263.

33 "That business of bearing any burden . . .": Strober, p. 483.

33 "reflected the Cold War atmosphere of the time": Sorensen *("Let the Word"),* p. 5.

33 "extravagant rhetoric": Schlesinger (*Cycles of American History),* p. 412.

33 Schlesinger and other Kennedy aides have explained the bellicosity of "bear any burden": Author's interview with Arthur Schlesinger, 2002. Schlesinger said, "In retrospect I think it was an overreaction to Khrushchev's speech."

33 Kennedy was alarmed by Khrushchev speech: Ibid.; Guthman and Schulman, pp. 310–11. Robert Kennedy recalled in his oral history for the Kennedy Library that "the speech that impressed the President most by Khrushchev was his speech on January 6, 1961, about wars of national liberation. . . . The President made everybody on the National Security Council read the speech. He also made all the military read the speech."

33 Khrushchev speech had no influence on inaugural address: The speech was published in *Kommunist,* no. 1, January 1961 on January 17 and was broadcast in English by the Soviet Home Service at 8:00 A.M. Greenwich mean time on January 19, 1961. The English translation of the speech is contained in the January 19 *Daily Report: Supplement, USSR & East Europe* by the Foreign Broadcast Information Service. The *Daily Report* was presumably the one supplied to Kennedy on the morning of January 19 and can be found in box 126A, POF.

34 Kennedy told Lincoln to insert pages "3, 4, 5" from the Sorensen Draft into his dictation: These three pages from the draft are found in box 34, POF, and correspond to material that was included in the final version of the inaugural address. This is more evidence that this was the draft that Kennedy was consulting while he dictated to Lincoln on January 10, 1961.

34 "This heritage has been passed on to us . . .": Box 102 (chap. 8, p. 19), Sorensen papers JFKL.

35 "I have developed an image of America . . .": Sorensen *("Let the Word"),* p. 90.

36 They also owe something to three quotations: The quotations can be found in Ted Kennedy's *Words Jack Loved,* JFKL.

36 "The way Jack worked . . .": Parmet (*Jack*), p. 328.
36 "He prepared his speeches with the utmost care . . .": John F. Kennedy (*Profiles*), p. 59.
37 Kennedy asked Lincoln to prepare a typescript: Lincoln (*My Twelve Years*), p. 182.
37 "In that dictation, in its original form . . .": Lincoln (*My Twelve Years*), p. 182.
37 "Oh, I see you have it done": Ibid.

CHAPTER TWO: PALM BEACH, JANUARY 11 TO JANUARY 15

38 "It is a long distance . . .": Rose Kennedy, p. 116.
38 "quiet beauty and good taste": Lincoln (*My Twelve Years*), p. 164.
38 Oleg Cassini recalls cracked linoleum: Author's interview with Cassini, 2002.
39 Joseph Kennedy Jr. photograph on piano: Lincoln (*Kennedy and Johnson*), p. 5.
39 Mary Gallagher thought Williams should have been modeling: Gallagher, p. 74.
40 Rose Kennedy at La Guerida: Collier and Horowitz, p. 211; Gibson, p. 8.
40 People stood for Rose Kennedy: Gibson, p. 25.
40 Caroline teetered in high heels: Author's interview with Vogelsinger, 2002.
40 Miss O'Malley "massage-hopped": Gallagher, p. 79.
40 Jackie and Caroline often retreated: Article by Laura Berquist in *Look*, February 28, 1961.
40 People left cash with Secret Service agents: Author's interview with Leo Racine, 2003.
40 Senator Mansfield stumbled into Miss O'Malley's bedroom: Rose Kennedy, p. 380.
40 Surf made the house shudder: Gibson, p. 77.
41 Kennedy had "settled down": *Washington Post*, January 12, 1961.
41 Kennedy is described as working on "several drafts": *New York Times*, January 13, 1961.
41 "except for a swim . . .": Salinger, p. 53.
41 Lincoln's appointment book and diary: Boxes 2, 3, and 4, Lincoln papers, JFKL.
41 Consider January 11: Box 2, in ibid.
41 The Kennedy tanning fetish: Author's interview with Sidey, 2002.
41 Kennedy used sun lamp in 1946 campaign: George Taylor, JFKLOH.
42 "one full day off per week in a pleasant surrounding . . .": Lincoln (*My Twelve Years*), p. 113.
42 Gore Vidal's description of Kennedy: Vidal, p. 355.
42 "pondering drafts . . .": *Washington Post*, January 12, 1961.
42 Sorensen writes of Kennedy working on his "thoughts": Sorensen (*Kennedy*) p. 242.
42 Feldman watched Kennedy reading while speaking on the telephone: Author's interview with Feldman.
43 Description of Kennedy bedroom in Palm Beach: Tour of the house by the author in 2003.
43 Jackie heard JFK reciting inaugural address: Thayer (*White House Years*), p. 75.
43 Jackie gathered up the notes: Leamer (*Kennedy Women*), p. 540.
43 "Underneath a veil . . .": Schlesinger (*Thousand Days*), p. 17.
43 "All my life I have had . . .": Thayer (*Jacqueline Bouvier*), p. 122.
43 "morning after morning . . .": Schlesinger (*Thousand Days*), p. 162.
43 the historian Michael Beschloss also gives him a cigar: Beschloss, p. 47.
44 Letter from Evan Thomas to Emily Danton: Box 84, Sorensen papers, JFKL.
45 the next available draft of the inaugural is a typescript that can be found in box 34, POF.
45 "but I guess it's OK": Sorensen (*Kennedy*), p. 243.
45 Kennedy collected quotations: Sorensen (*Kennedy*), p. 62: "The Senator was the chief source of his own best quotations. Some were in the black notebooks he had kept since college—some were in favorite reference books on his desk, such as Agar's

The Price of Union—most were in his head." Schlesinger, p. 105: "Some quotations he carried verbatim in his own mind. Others he noted down."

45 "sticky mind": Gormley, p. 101.
45 "There's an old saying . . .": Richard Reeves, p. 101.
45 He claimed it was "an old saying": Author's interview with Schlesinger, 2002.
46 He often stopped at roadside markers and "I'm collecting material . . .": Author's interview with the Reverend Philip Hannan, 2002.
46 Rose Kennedy's "Expressions Book" and "Like a schoolgirl . . .": Gibson, 183.
46 Jackie in Palm Beach: Gallagher, pp. 76–81.
46 Jackie's inauguration guest list: Box 16, Lincoln papers, JFKL.
46 Diana Vreeland suggested muff: Vreeland, pp. 170–71.
46 "all the other ladies . . .": Cassini, p. 307; Author interview with Cassini, 2002.
46 Jackie got it immediately: Cassini, p. 306.
47 "I knew Jack Kennedy . . .": Author interview with Cassini, 2002.
47 "a very awkward situation": Lincoln *(Kennedy and Johnson),* p. 12. Lyndon Johnson was apparently oblivious to the trouble he caused the Kennedy household, but his wife was not, and in her oral history for the Kennedy Library she said, "I remember at one point Senator Kennedy invited, and here I'm afraid that he invited just Lyndon alone, but anyhow, Lyndon, who would always say, 'Come and bring your family,' or at least, 'Bring your wife,'—that was his sort of general pattern—and he understood that I was invited."
47 Rose Kennedy complained about chaos in Palm Beach: Rose Kennedy, pp. 380–82.
48 "You might remind her . . .": Gallagher, pp. 75–76.
48 "smoldering irritability": Lincoln *(Kennedy and Johnson),* p. 2.
48 Kennedy visited LBJ ranch: Ibid., pp. 16–21.
48 The telegram from Johnson to Kennedy: Ibid., p. 26.
48 "spavined hunchback": The comment was made by India Edwards, whom Jeff Shesol characterizes as "a Democratic grande dame." The spavined hunchback comment was made to reporters in private, but on July 4, 1960, she announced publicly that Kennedy had Addison's disease, the insufficient operating of the adrenal glands, a charge that was vigorously denied by the Kennedy camp as unfounded, but which turned out to be true. The future Texas governor John Connally joined Edwards in making the charges. For more details see Shesol, p. 35.
49 "Lady Violet had a great habit . . .": John F. Kennedy *(Prelude to Leadership),* p. 12.
49 classic Kennedy signals of discomfort: Lincoln *(Kennedy and Johnson),* p. 6. Lincoln writes, "But while Mr. Johnson talked, Mr. Kennedy's right foot was continually twitching, and his fingers made a rat-ta-tat noise on the arm of his chair."
49 Kennedy kept moving: Ibid., p. 10.
49 The Johnson-Kennedy newspaper incident: Ibid., pp. 8–10.
49 an impatient man who finished your sentences: Vidal, p. 379.
49 Kennedy's nervous tics: Author's interview with Fay, 2002; Fairlie, p. 181.
50 the obsessive Kennedy: Author's interview with Sidey, 2003; Bishop, pp. 10, 40.
50 "The Senator asked me to close the door . . .": Box 3 (diary entry for January 1, 1961), Lincoln papers JFKL.
50 to find a way to fly "Barbara Lansing" from Paris: Box 2, in ibid. These restricted pages from Lincoln's diary were opened at my request in May 2002. I changed the name of the woman in question since it has not been previously released. Further evidence that her relationship with Kennedy was clandestine is supported by the fact that the January 25 letter she wrote to him after the inauguration was addressed to Evelyn Lincoln at her home address (box 3, Lincoln papers JFKL).
51 "I always make it on . . .": George Taylor, JFKLOH.
51 Notes that Kennedy took in 1955 on Lord Melbourne: Box 40, PP.
51 Conversation with Priscilla McMillan: Author's interview with McMillan, 2002.
51 "Oh, it'll be much easier . . .": Author's interview with Marie Ridder, 2002.

52 "positive force for public good": Edward Moore Kennedy, *Words Jack Loved*.
52 "he may be a fine politician . . .": Author's interview with Marie Ridder, 2002.
52 Harris Wofford on being a Kennedy speechwriter: Author's interview with Harris Wofford, 2002.
52 Kennedy edited speech about Lyndon Johnson: O'Donnell and Powers, p. 179.
52 Kennedy changed speech about Nobel Prize winners: Author's interview with Schlesinger, 2002.
53 The "Gridiron team": Clifford, p. 113; box 16, Sorensen papers JFKL.
53 "Would you be so good . . .": Box 16, Sorensen papers JFKL.
53 dictating and redictating material to Lincoln: Lincoln *(My Twelve Years)*, pp. 83–84. Lincoln says that he worked on the speech for weeks, "and he would pace the floor, walk into the bathroom, take a look at himself in the mirror, push his hair to one side, dictating all the time. He said, 'No, strike that, take this down,' so many times my notebook looked like a racing card."
53 "I have just received . . .": Sorensen *("Let the Word")*, p. 89.
53 "a truly excellent speech" and following exchange between Kennedy and his father: Rose Kennedy, p. 388.
54 "I'm not going to listen to the old man . . .": Author's interview with Charlie Bartlett, 2002.
54 "the most vital force . . .": Fay, p. 33; Author's interview with Fay, 2002.
55 JFK was in almost daily communication with his father: Rose Kennedy, p. 362.
55 "It's not the Pope . . .": Miller, p. 187.
55 "That doesn't make any difference . . .": Clifford, p. 336.
55 Clifford flew to New York: Ibid., pp. 336–39.

CHAPTER THREE: PALM BEACH, JANUARY 16

57 On Monday morning, January 16: *Evening Star,* January 16, 1961.
57 Sorensen writes in *Kennedy*: Sorensen *(Kennedy)*, p. 242.
57 Lincoln's appointment book: Box 2, Lincoln papers, JFKL.
57 Lincoln's accounts of events at La Guerida: Box 4, in ibid.
57 Meeting between Berquist and Kennedy: Laura Berquist Knebel, JFKLOH.
58 Sorensen's account of January 16 meeting at La Guerida: Sorensen *(Kennedy)*, p. 242.
58 Sorensen's account of the December meeting: Ibid., p. 239.
58 "sat around and schmoosed . . ." and other exchanges between Kennedy and Berquist: Knebel, JFKLOH.
58 Spaulding believed he was happier: Charles Spaulding, JFKLOH.
58 "was unable to hide his own tremendous sense of exhilaration": Thomas, p. 300.
59 "My God, look at that fat face . . .": Lincoln *(My Twelve Years)*, p. 183.
59 "Aren't you thrilled . . .": Ibid., p. 180.
59 "All these dismal questions!": Knebel, JFKLOH.
60 "We are the great revolutionary people . . .": USS SUB, p. 582.
60 "I would like the people of the world . . .": Ibid., p. 382.
60 JFK's rivalry with Castro: The journalist Marie Ridder (interview with author) also knew both men and believed Kennedy envied Castro's oratorical abilities, saying, "Kennedy wanted to inspire, even to inflame a crowd the way Castro did, to stir great passions, yet he wanted to do it without losing his reserve, his dignity." Ridder also noticed that both men had a similar libido, saying about Castro that "one did have the feeling as one was interviewing him that he would have been extremely interested in the next step."
60 Graham and Smathers arrived for lunch: Box 4, Lincoln papers, JFKL. Lincoln's diary entry shows that Smathers and Graham came at 12:45 and then left with Kennedy to have lunch and play golf at the Seminole Country Club.
61 Quoting Deuteronomy in Oakland: Box 911, PPP.

61 "the Bible said it long ago . . .": USS SUB, p. 649; he used the line several times during the campaign, as in San Diego on November 2, USS SUB, p. 860.
61 "sailing close to flattery": Author's interview with Sorensen, 2002.
61 Billy Graham handed Kennedy a list of suggestions: *Washington Post,* January 17, 1961.
61 JFK had resisted on inviting Graham: Pollock, p. 167.
61 Graham had to get Nixon's approval: Graham wrote in his autobiography that he was "delighted" with the invitation but concerned about what his friend Nixon would think, "depressed as [Nixon] was over losing the election." Graham was originally scheduled to meet Kennedy in late November but arrived in Florida on the same evening that Jackie gave birth to John Kennedy Jr., so their golf game was postponed until January.
61 Graham had done everything short of formally endorsing Nixon: In his autobiography, Graham wrote, "Frankly, I thought Nixon's eight years in the Eisenhower administration qualified him better than Kennedy's terms in the House and Senate" (pp. 390–91).
61 Luce pulled the Graham article from *Life*: Pollock, p. 298.
61 "on the basis of which candidate . . .": *Life,* November 7, 1960.
61 "Do you know why you're here . . .": Graham, pp. 394–95.
61 "When Jack was elected . . .": Ibid., pp. 394–95.
62 The Kennedy-Graham golf game and their discussion about the Second Coming are recounted by Graham in his autobiography, pp. 394–96.
63 "casual about religious rituals . . ." and knelt by his bed in prayer: Rose Kennedy, p. 165.
63 "care a whit for theology": Sorensen *(Kennedy),* p. 19.
63 "because he was born into the faith . . .": Schlesinger *(Thousand Days),* pp. 107–8.
63 "wore his religion, like his patriotism, lightly": Cushing, p. 5.
63 Mark Dalton had been "amazed": O'Donnell and Powers, p. 70; Mark Dalton, JFK-LOH.
63 While recuperating in Palm Beach: Box 40, PP.
63 "I know there is a God . . .": Lincoln *(My Twelve Years),* pp. 229–30. In an August 24, 1998, letter to *Time,* Schlesinger argues that the quotation is highly suspect and that "William Herndon, Lincoln's law partner, and most scholars doubt that Lincoln ever said anything like that." Schlesinger also writes that Kennedy used the quotation to express his determination to resist the spread of communism, and that it should not be construed as a premonition of his death. However, in this instance, after a rocky summit meeting with Khrushchev that left Kennedy fearful that the chances of a nuclear war were greater than ever before, the "storm" is clearly a nuclear war, and the quotation reflects Kennedy's invocation of the Almighty in avoiding it. Richard Reeves writes that at the conclusion of the summit, Kennedy had said to Khrushchev, "Then, Mr. Chairman, there will be war. It will be a cold winter" (p. 171).
64 "Billy, there are about . . .": Graham, p. 396.
64 "newsmen were surprised . . .": *Evening Star,* January 17, 1961.
64 "I think some of you . . .": Box 7 [Salinger], Presidential Papers, White House Files, JFKL.
64 "Mr. Kennedy was using me . . .": Graham, p. 396.
64 "I don't think that Mr. Kennedy being a Catholic . . .": Ibid., p. 396.
64 "I suspect that the religious issue . . .": Sidey, p. 28.
64 "That afternoon, as he was busy . . .": Sorensen *(Kennedy),* p. 242.
64 The two copies of the "Clean Draft" that Sorensen assembled that afternoon: Box 34, POF; box 62, Sorensen papers, JFKL.
65 sheets of yellow paper that Jackie Kennedy had been gathering: Thayer (*White House Years*), p. 75.
65 the torch metaphor: John F. Kennedy (*The Strategy of Peace,*) pp. ix–x.

66 Sorensen used back of a telegram as scratch paper: Box 62, Sorensen papers, JFKL.
66 Sorensen copied Kennedy mannerisms: Tanzer, ed., chap. by Alan L. Otten, p. 8.
66 Dungan's reflections on Sorensen: Ralph Dungan, JFKLOH.
66 "a little boy in so many ways": Martin and Plaut, p. 255.
66 "passionate self-effacement": Knebel, JFKLOH.
67 In a 2002 interview Sorensen said that although he may have first had the idea of using a particular phrase or sentence in the inaugural address, many of them were ones that Kennedy had used in his conversations and previous speeches or had culled from literature.
67 the Sorensen Draft: Box 34, POF.
67 Draft showing changes made by Kennedy and Sorensen in Palm Beach: Ibid.; box 62, Sorensen papers, JFKL.
67 quotations Kennedy saved in notebooks: Edward Moore Kennedy, *Words Jack Loved*.
67 Miami on October 18: USS SUB, p. 649.
67 Philadelphia on October 29: Ibid., p. 809.
67 San Diego on November 2: Ibid., p. 860.
67 New Haven on November 6: Ibid., p. 914.
67 Seattle on September 6: Ibid., p. 135.
67 Fresno on September 9: Ibid., p. 179.
67 New York City on September 14: Ibid., p. 241.
67 Raleigh on September 17: Ibid., p. 273.
67 Salt Lake City on September 23: Ibid., p. 352.
67 Milwaukee on October 23: Ibid., p. 724.
67 "we arm to parley": JFK used the phrase at least a dozen other times during the campaign. One instance came during his speech in Manhattan at a Democratic women's luncheon on September 14, 1960, when he said, "A Democratic administration can never and will never negotiate with the Russians in a position of weakness. Over 11 years ago, Winston Churchill said it succinctly: 'We arm to parley'" (USS SUB, p. 231).
68 Kennedy studied Churchill's wartime memoranda: Sidey (*John F. Kennedy*), p. 55.
68 *Profiles* is a version of *Great Contemporaries:* Richard Reeves, p. 668*n*.
68 Kennedy read Churchill while recuperating: Fay, p. 149; Author's interivew with Fay, 2002.
68 Dutton found Kennedy listening to Churchill's recordings: Fred Dutton, JFKLOH.
68 "mobilized the English language . . .": Sorensen (*"Let the Word"*), p. 319.
68 "We will need in the sixties . . .": Ibid., p. 22.
68 Joe Alsop column: *New York Herald Tribune,* January 18, 1961.
69 Sorensen was supposed to solicit suggestions: Sorensen *(Kennedy),* p. 240.
69 Advice was solicited for JFK acceptance speech: Box 25, Sorensen papers, JFKL.
69 Sorensen sent telegrams on December 23: Box 62, Sorensen papers, JFKL.
70 Nevins draft and covering letter: Ibid.
70 Letter from Dillon: Ibid.
70 "Your wire arrives at most difficult time for me . . .": Ibid.
70 "Due to a myriad of other pressing 'priorities' just now . . .": Johnson, p. 604.
70 Stevenson's draft and suggestions: Ibid., pp. 604–9.
71 "When it comes to oratorical flights . . .": Galbraith *(Letters),* p. 11.
71 Galbraith was flattered; Kennedy was determined to deliver an inaugural ranking among the best: Author's interview with John Kenneth Galbraith, 2002.
71 Galbraith and Kennedy met in Palm Beach on December 23: Box 2, Lincoln papers, JFKL; Galbraith (*Ambassador's Journal*), p. 5.
71 "the tone and tenor of the inaugural address": Galbraith *(Ambassador's Journal),* pp. 5–9.
72 "It looks pretty heavy": Author's interview with Galbraith, 2002.
72 "Over the weekend I will work . . .": Box 29a, POF.
72 Galbraith's second draft of inaugural address: Box 76, in ibid. Galbraith wrote in his draft: "And the work of this new administration will not be over in a hundred days, or

in five hundred days. Its work will continue without surcease all of the next four years." Also, author's interview with Galbraith, 2002.
72 "did not suffer fools gladly": Galbraith *(Letters)*, p. 1.
72 "The conclusions I suppose must evoke God . . .": Box 76, POF.
73 Harris Wofford believes it came from Chester Bowles: Author's interview with Wofford, 2002.
73 "modernize our thinking . . .": Box 84, Sorensen papers, JFKL.
73 "To forge ahead in all fields . . .": Ibid.
73 Lou Harris ideas: Box 30, POF.
73 The best advice came from Gore Vidal: Box 84, Sorensen papers, JFKL.

CHAPTER FOUR: PALM BEACH, JANUARY 17

75 Sorensen and Kennedy met on January 17 to polish draft: Sorensen *(Kennedy)*, p. 243.
75 cricket writer Neville Cardus on the master ball: Moran, p. 142.
75 "a spy sent out . . .": Ibid.
76 "Those were the years . . .": USS SUB, p. 193.
76 JFK acceptance speech: Sorensen *("Let the Word")*, pp. 96–102.
76 "Either we move with new leadership . . .": USS SUB, p. 104.
76 He added "our country": Ibid., p. 113.
76 Archibald Cox's version of Detroit speech: Box 190, PPP.
76 *Detroit News* review of Cox speech: Gormley, p. 130.
76 *New York Times* on the Cox speech: *New York Times,* September 6, 1961.
77 The second, Sorensen-Kennedy, version of the Detroit speech: Box 910, PPP.
77 The Cadillac Square speech as actually delivered by Kennedy: USS SUB, pp. 111–14. The "ask not" sentence is on p. 113.
77 "I do not run for the Presidency to emphasize . . .": Ibid., p. 136.
77 "We do not campaign stressing what our country . . .": Ibid., p. 298.
77 Sorensen Draft version of "ask not": Box 34, POF.
78 "When a line proved successful . . .": Sorensen *(Kennedy)*, p. 177.
78 "This thought had lain in Kennedy's mind . . .": Schlesinger *(Thousand Days)*, p. 4*n*. Kennedy used the Rousseau quotation in a speech in Pennsylvania to young Democrats on August 21, 1946, telling them, "Remember the words of Rousseau: 'As soon as any man says of the affairs of state *What does it matter to me?* the state may be given up as lost'" (Hamilton, p. 784).
78 Warren Harding: *Bartlett's Familiar Quotations* (15th edition), p. 1073.
78 Oliver Wendell Holmes: Ibid., p. 1073.
78 "not what Choate does for you . . .": *Time,* January 28, 1966.
79 "But we shall have to be . . .": John F. Kennedy *(Why England Slept)*, p. 229.
79 "But in public life . . .": John F. Kennedy *(Profiles)*, p. 7.
79 "In short, it is our job . . .": Sorensen *("Let the Word")*, p. 341.
79 "Look Ted, I'm not going to ask you . . .": *Denver Rocky Mountain News,* December 3, 2000.
80 JFK's prewar travels in Europe: Hamilton, pp. 263–72; Perret *(Jack)* pp. 73–77; Leamer *(Kennedy Men)*, pp. 132–35.
81 "Everything that I had worked for . . .": Hamilton, p. 281.
81 Kennedy was electrified by Churchill's speech: According to the JFK biographer Ian Hamilton, "For Jack Kennedy, however, it was Winston Churchill's speech that remained indelibly engraved in his memory" (pp. 281–82).
81 Criticisms of Churchill speech: Jenkins, p. 551.
81 "to prove itself not unworthy . . .": Hamilton, p. 282.
81 Speech to American Legion post in Massachusetts: Box 94, PPP.
81 "Greater love hath no man . . .": Mary McNeely, JFKLOH, cited in Perret *(Jack)*, p. 141.

81 PT 109 incident: Renehan, pp. 253–76; Hamilton, pp. 575–602; Leamer (*Kennedy Men*) pp. 186–90; Perret, pp. 112–16; Robert J. Donovan, pp. 130–94; "A Reporter at Large: Survival," *New Yorker,* June 17, 1943; Gerard Zinser obituary, *New York Times,* August 29, 2001.
82 "It was absolutely involuntary . . .": Adler, p. 53.
82 Joe Kennedy had paid to have the *Reader's Digest* article reprinted: Hamilton, p. 755.
83 "This is a book . . ." and "Grace under pressure . . .": John F. Kennedy *(Profiles),* p. 1.
83 "the tears were streaming . . .": Perret (*Jack*), p. 116. See also Hamilton, who cites a letter JFK sent to his parents after the incident in which he said, "It was a terrible thing, though, losing those two men" (p. 606).
84 Kennedy's diary entries about Berlin in July 1945: John F. Kennedy *(Prelude),* pp. 43–50.
84 Reaction of Leahy and Truman to Berlin: McCullough, p. 415.
85 "very, very major impression": Guthman and Shulman, p. 439.
85 "formative experience": Collier and Horowitz, p. 181.
85 Bobby kept a diary: Box 24, RFK Preadministration Personal Folders, JFKL. RFK also described the trip in his oral history for the Kennedy Library (Guthman and Shulman, pp. 436–39). He stressed the impact that the briefing from Gullian had on JFK.
86 "We've allied ourselves": *Meet the Press,* December 2, 1951.
86 He repeated the same criticism a year later: Ibid., November 9, 1952.
86 "without the support of the native population . . .": Ibid., February 14, 1954.
86 "a failure to appreciate how the forces of nationalism . . .": *Foreign Affairs,* October 1957.
86 JFK speech on Algeria: Sorensen *("Let the Word"),* p. 331–337.
87 Stevenson's criticism of the speech: Parmet *(Jack),* p. 405–6.
87 "capture the imagination of the world," etc.: USS SUB, p. 510.
87 "a systematic attack . . .": Johnson, p. 607.
88 "communicated itself with the emotion . . .": White *(In Search),* p. 460.
88 "If you go into a coal miner's town . . .": Spaulding, JFKLOH.
88 Kennedy often spoke of West Virginia poverty: JFK's opening statement to the first televised debate included this line about West Virginia: "I saw cases in West Virginia, here in the United States, where children took home part of their school lunch in order to feed their families" (Box 914, PPP). In his speech to the Greater Houston Ministerial Association, Kennedy spoke of "the hungry children [he] saw in West Virginia" (Sorensen [*"Let the Word"*], p. 130).

Laura Berquist said JFK was "shocked" by West Virginia poverty (Knebel, JFKLOH), and Jackie was apparently also moved by it. Sarah Bradford points out that she took pains to ensure the contract to make the presidential glassware went to a West Virginian company (p. 126).
89 "he was with them completely": Baughman, p. 256.
89 "people like Muggsy . . .": Author's interview with Deirdre Henderson, 2002.
89 "To think that I . . .": John F. Kennedy *(Prelude),* p. 15.
89 "I was taken into the kitchen . . .": John F. Kennedy, CD, band 3, "A Dictated Letter (Circa 1959) to Jacqueline Kennedy on Weekend in Rhode Island."
90 "When do you think the nice people . . .": Pottker, p. 138.
90 "Now they know their worst fears . . .": Ibid.
90 "Do you know it is impossible for an Irish Catholic . . .": Fay, p. 108. JFK had joined the Spee Club at Harvard. His biographer Ian Hamilton writes that by joining the Spee Club, JFK became "the first Kennedy ever to break into the inner sanctum of Boston's WASP world" (p. 208).
90 Lincoln kept her diary and appointment book in fits and starts: Boxes 2–4, Lincoln papers, JFKL.
90 Lincoln's 1961 *National Diary:* Box, 2, in ibid.
91 "By that time we had been working . . .": Author's interview with Sorensen, 2002.

91 Discussion of antithetical statements in the inaugural address: I am indebted to Kenny, who points out the rhetorical impact of antithetical statements in his article "Another Look at Kennedy's Inaugural Address," in *Today's Speech,* November, 1965, pp. 17–79.
92 "The opening and closing paragraphs . . .": Sorensen oral history among Parmet's interviews in Columbia University Oral History Project.
92 "Lincoln never used . . .": Sorensen *(Kennedy),* p. 240.
92 "Some have claimed, simplistically . . .": Wills *(Lincoln),* p. 174.
92 "Lincoln interlocks his sentences . . .": Ibid., p. 172.
92 "on a few words in different contexts": Ibid., p. 173.

CHAPTER FIVE: ON BOARD THE *CAROLINE*, JANUARY 17

94 Relationship between JFK and Sidey: Author's interview with Sidey, 2002; Peter Lisagor, JFKLOH.
94 "I knew he was after *Time* magazine": Author's interview with Sidey, 2002.
94 "basically a serious man on a serious mission": Ibid.
95 the nine sheets of lined yellow legal paper: Box 34, POF.
95 "an early draft of the inaugural speech": Kenney, pp. 56–58.
95 Conversation between JFK and Sidey on the *Caroline*: Ibid.; Sidey (*John F. Kennedy*), pp. 29–31.
97 "If John Kennedy is characteristic . . .": John F. Kennedy *(Why England Slept),* pp. 13–14 (1961 edition).
97 "I like Luce . . .": Hugh Sidey, JFKLOH. In *A Thousand Days* Schlesinger writes that after having lunch with Luce during the campaign Kennedy had told Schlesinger: "I like Luce. He is like a cricket always chirping away. After all, he made a lot of money through his own individual enterprise. . . . I don't mind people like that. They have earned the right to talk that way. After all, that's the atmosphere in which I grew up. My father is the same way" (p. 63).
97 Luce ran flattering cover stories about Joe Kennedy: Swanberg, pp. 154, 173.
97 Joe Kennedy slept with Luce's wife: Hamilton, p. 310.
97 "good, tough one that both men enjoyed": Hugh Sidey, JFKLOH.
97 Joe Kennedy and Luce watched JFK deliver his acceptance speech: Swanberg, p. 410.
97 Luce's speech at Yale: Ibid., pp. 42–43.
98 "Amprop" and "we and we only among the great powers . . .": Ibid., p. 176.
98 "in the 1960s every American is summoned . . .": *Time,* December 5, 1960.
98 "the means of contributing . . .": Rockefeller Panel, p. xix.
98 "The critical weakness of our society . . .": *Life,* June 20, 1960.
99 "We Must Climb to the Hilltop": Ibid., August 22, 1960.
99 JFK acceptance speech: Sorensen (*"Let the Word"*), pp. 96–102.
99 "I believe we stand for a great national purpose": USS SUB, p. 585.
99 Kennedy wrote five more pages on yellow legal paper: Box 34, POF.
100 Haynes Johnson article: *Evening Star,* January 21, 1961.
101 "Later that day . . .": Sorensen *(Kennedy),* p. 243.
101 "I don't know what this is . . ." and "Let me tell you a little story . . .": Author's interview with Sorensen, 2002. Sorensen said in this interview that writing, polishing, and editing the inaugural address "was certainly a collaborative process," citing their discussions over the telephone earlier in the week, their meetings in Palm Beach, and the revisions they made to the speech during the flight of January 17.
101 "looking at that typed copy" and making the "occasional slight twitch": Ibid.
102 JFK told Clark Clifford he could not allow the Pearson allegation to stand: Clifford, pp. 306–7.
102 Kennedy gave Oakes a letter affirming his authorship: Parmet *(Jack),* p. 331.
102 Kennedy pressed his notes on Senator Richard Neuberger: Ibid., p. 331.

102 Kennedy displayed the notes and PT 109 coconut on his desk: Collier and Horowitz, p. 234.
103 "[Kennedy had received] more help than you or I . . .": James MacGregor Burns, JFKLOH.
103 Parmet analysis of authorship of *Profiles:* Parmet *(Jack),* pp. 324–33.
103 Gloria Sitrin took *Profiles* dictation: Gloria Sitrin, JFKLOH.
103 Sorensen memorandum: Box 27, PP.
103 "The greatest debt is owed . . .": John F. Kennedy *(Profiles),* p. xiv; handwritten notes: Box 27, PP.
103 He had initially written, "Theodore C. Sorensen . . .": Box 27, PP.
104 "The speech was one of those very few . . .": Rosenman, pp. 89–90.
104 "inside the warm living room . . .": Burns *(The Lion and the Fox),* p. 161.
105 "Six days before . . .": Schlesinger *(The Crisis of the Old Order),* p. 7.
105 Raymond Moley's account of how FDR "wrote" his inaugural address: Moley, pp. 96–119.
107 The sheet of paper sold for $39,000: *Newsday,* March 19, 1999.
107 "Kennedy's first attempt to write . . .": CNN interactive Web site, March 18, 1999.
107 Evelyn Lincoln described as a "compulsive collector": *St. Petersburg Times,* November 11, 1999.
108 Lincoln pursued a job in Kennedy's Senate offices: Lincoln *(My Twelve Years),* pp. 7–11. Lincoln wrote, "But most of all, I was impressed by what he had to say in his speeches and his obvious sincerity" (p. 5).
108 "a very close, almost wordless understanding": Najeeb Halaby, JFKLOH.
108 "If I said just now . . .": Sorensen *(Kennedy),* p. 56.
108 The Lincoln-Kennedy relationship had its rocky moments: Lincoln (*My Twelve Years),* pp. 51–52. To his credit, Lincoln's husband refused to fire her for Kennedy and told him, "I don't think that I can do it. I think no one should do it but you" (p. 52).
108 White turned over some of the documents and defended Lincoln's collection: *AP Online,* March 19, 1999; *St. Petersburg Times,* November 11, 1999.
108 in a 1989 letter: On April 5, 1989, Lincoln wrote to White, "Many of these personal items have been saved from extinction by me. . . . many items were given to me by John F. Kennedy. Others were discarded items" (*St. Petersburg Times,* November 11, 1999).
108 "After the Senator left that evening . . .": Lincoln *(My Twelve Years),* p. 143.
109 "an occasional slight twitch . . .": Author's interview with Sorensen, 2002.
109 The draft that Kennedy and Sorensen worked on during the flight: Box 34, POF.
110 The COPY: Box 62, Sorensen papers, JFKL.

CHAPTER SIX: WASHINGTON AND NEW YORK, JANUARY 17

113 Jackie compared White House to Camelot during interview with White: Box 40, White papers, JFKL.
113 "farewell to an America never to be recaptured . . .": White *(In Search),* p. 547.
114 The last "Minorities Dinner," and the "Colored People's Ball": Don Oberdorfer, "Inaugural Hoopla," *New York Times Magazine,* January 17, 1965.
114 Kennedy's inauguration broke down barriers for other ethnic groups: White *(In Search),* pp. 474–75. White writes that Kennedy "was the man who broke up the old patterns of American politics," who ended "an old world of politics and government," and served as a "gatekeeper" who unlatched a door through which "marched not only Catholics, but blacks, and Jews, and ethnics, women, youth, academics" (474).
114 "more Negro participation . . .": *Ebony,* March 1961.
114 Kennedy introduced Martin as a member of his "political family" and danced with African-American women: Branch, p. 384.
114 "a new era in the national life": Bartlett syndicated column, "News Focus," November 27, 1960.

114 Linus Pauling could not get a passport: Serafini, pp. 146–47.
115 National Symphony Orchestra was forbidden to play Copland composition: Parmet *(Eisenhower),* p. 164.
115 "During our forthcoming administration . . .": Lincoln Kirstein, "The New Augustan Age," *Nation,* February 4, 1961.
115 Wilson's inaugural address was unintelligible: *Washington Post,* January 9, 1961.
115 Media coverage of the inauguration: *New York Times,* January 20, 1961.
115 Kennedy mounted a literary campaign for the presidency: Parmet *(Jack),* pp. 479–81.
116 Kennedy became increasingly aware of the influence and requirements of television: Sorensen *(Kennedy),* p. 195.
116 "never forgot that he was an actor . . .": Blair Clark, quoted in Hersh, p. 224.
116 Kennedy's use of television during the West Virginia primary: White *(In Search),* pp. 483–84.
116 Lawford gave Kennedy advice: Spada, p. 231.
116 Reinsch's activities during televised debates: J. Leonard Reinsch, JFKLOH.
116 Kennedy told the newsman Howard K. Smith he had won the election after the first debate: Smith, pp. 263–64.
117 "It has a new star . . .": *New York Times,* January 26, 1961.
117 Kennedy stood in front of maps of Laos: Clifford, p. 344.
117 Sorensen memorandum: Box 60, Sorensen papers, JFKL.
117 "something new and rather imperial . . .": Letter from Miller to author, June 7, 2002.
117 "Camelot-like glorifications . . .": Sorensen *(Watchmen),* p. xv.
117 "our National Capital in the eyes of many . . .": *Washington Post,* January 12, 1961.
118 Inauguration preparations, necessity of adding more balls, etc.: *New York Times, Evening Star, Washington Post,* January 15, 18–19, 1961.
118 Tom Wolfe on inauguration: *Washington Post,* January 20, 1961.
118 Kennedy met with David Bell: Box 2, Lincoln papers, JFKL.
119 The Smith dinner dance: *New York Times,* January 18, 1963.
119 The Eisenhower farewell address was televised live at half past eight and lasted about thirty minutes, explaining why JFK was said to arrive at the Smith party a few minutes after nine o'clock.
119 Some would consider the speech superior to the Kennedy inaugural: An article by Douglas Brinkley in the September 2001 issue of *American Heritage* is a good summary of the liberal infatuation with the Eisenhower farewell speech. Brinkley says that "books and articles by such Left-leaning intellectuals as Noam Chomsky, Eugene McCarthy, and the like turned Eisenhower's warning of an arms industry run amuck into liberal boilerplate."
119 Text of Eisenhower's speech: *New York Times,* January 18, 1961.
119 "Government at all levels has certain obligations . . .": Fairlie, p. 108.
119 "The Eisenhower concern, as I read it . . .": Bliss, p. 366.
120 "a combination of the Lincoln Memorial . . .": *Evening Star,* January 21, 1961.
120 "the glamour of a Hollywood premiere": *Washington Post,* January 18, 1961.
120 Description of scene outside Smith house and arrival of Frank Sinatra: *New York Times, Washington Post, Evening Star,* January 18, 1961; Fay, p. 73; Author's interview with Fay.
120 Sinatra destroyed his own helipad: O'Donnell and Powers, p. 380.
121 Kay Halle's reflections on JFK at parties: Halle, JFKLOH.
121 "but also displaying that slight uneasiness . . .": Fay, p. 73.
121 The Hollywood entertainers felt "slightly out of place" and "I've got to go peeps": Author's interview with Bartlett, 2002.
121 Kennedy asked Fay to perform: Author's interview with Fay, 2002; Fay, pp. 74–77.
121 The Lytton party at the Statler Hilton: *Evening Star,* January 18, 1961.
122 Description of the Carlyle penthouse: *New York Times,* January 4, 1961; Lincoln *(My Twelve Years),* p. 174; Samuel Lewis, JFKLOH; *Washington Post,* January 10, 1961.
122 "an encouraging sign": Roy Wilkins, JFKLOH.

CHAPTER SEVEN: NEW YORK AND WASHINGTON, JANUARY 18

123 Pierre Salinger told reporters: *Washington Post,* January 19, 1961.
123 Kennedy on Daniel Webster: John F. Kennedy *(Profiles),* pp. 59–60.
124 Kennedy chose an official portrait: *Life,* January 20, 1961.
124 Kennedy was photographed by a fashion photographer: Lacy, p. 204. Lacy says that Kennedy visited the studio of the photographer Howell Conant "in the mid-1950s" and that studying the contact prints of the shoot helped him "to develop the dashing, sideways glance into the middle distance which came to symbolize his style."
124 The conundrum of Kennedy's vanity—his youthful appearance: Evidence that this was a concern in the Kennedy camp is confirmed by a memorandum that Sorensen prepared (box 26, Sorensen papers, JFKL), which showed that the average age of the signers of the Declaration of Independence was 44.9 years, and listed twenty-seven "Historical Popular Leaders and Americans Prominent in their Youth," which placed Kennedy in the company of James Monroe, Theodore Roosevelt, John Jay, Patrick Henry, Alexander Hamilton, John Marshall, Christopher Columbus, Alexander the Great, Napoleon, and Julius Caesar.
124 Appointments in New York on January 18: Box 2, Lincoln papers, JFKL.
124 "I'll have my usual breakfast": Ibid.
124 Meeting with Eddie Adams: Author's interview with Eddie Adams, 2003.
124 Bradlee's letter describing meeting with Clark and Friendly: Box 84, Sorensen papers, JFKL.
124 Bradlee cannot recall any details: Author's interview with Ben Bradlee, 2002.
126 Tretick threatened to photograph him combing his hair: Stanley Tretick, JFKLOH.
126 Jackie liked him in a top hat: Manchester, p. 118.
126 Kennedy had "an ideal head" for a hat: *Washington Post,* January 19, 1961.
126 "Certainly, two button . . .": *New York Herald Tribune,* January 19, 1961
126 Kennedy was conscious of his appearance: Jackie Kennedy's personal maid, Providencia Parades, sometimes helped to supervise JFK's clothes when he was traveling. "He liked everything perfect," she recalled, adding that "he was a very quick dresser, and very particular about his clothes" (Thayer [*White House Years*], p. 47).
126 Kennedy scolded Bill Walton for wearing brown shoes: Bradford, p. 116.
126 "Too Ivy League": Fay, p. 176.
127 Kennedy left his coat behind at the Carlyle: *Washington Post,* January 19, 1961.
127 "JFK reads typed transcript . . .": *New York Daily News,* January 19, 1961.
127 The transcript or draft typed by Lincoln on January 17 containing the handwritten changes made by Kennedy: Box 34, POF.
127 The COPY that Sorensen kept with him in Washington: Box 62, Sorensen papers, JFKL.
127 Sorensen had lunch with Lippmann: Walter Lippmann, JFKLOH; Steel, pp. 524–25.
127 "a natural leader, organizer and ruler of men": Steel, p. 522.
127 "Without pretending that everything is perfect . . .": *New York Herald Tribune,* January 19, 1961.
128 Lippmann suggested replacing *enemy*: Steel, p. 525; Lippmann, JFKLOH.
128 Sorensen told himself Kennedy would approve of change: Author's interview with Sorensen, 2002.
128 a "remarkably successful piece of self-expression": *New York Herald Tribune,* January 24, 1961.
128 "A few years later he would deplore the speech . . .": Steel, p, 525.
128 Sorensen spent the afternoon in Kennedy's Senate offices revising the speech and soliciting suggestions: Sorensen *(Kennedy),* p. 23; Author's interview with Sorensen, 2002.
128 Galbraith could not conceal his disappointment: Galbraith *(Ambassador's Journal),* pp. 15–18.
128 Galbraith had written for a nation of readers: Box 96, POF.

129 Galbraith account of January 18 meeting with Sorensen: Galbraith *(Ambassador's Journal)*, pp. 15–16; Author's interview with Galbraith, 2002.
129 "the distinctive note": Schlesinger *(Cycles of American History)*, p. 412.
129 Galbraith made "mostly cosmetic suggestions"; argued against the term *joint ventures* and the tiger metaphor: Author's interview with Galbraith, 2002; Galbraith *(Ambassador's Journal)*, p. 16.
130 The influence of weather on previous inaugurations: "The Weather on Inauguration Day," *Weatherwise*, December 1988.
131 Helen Thomas tried to cover Jackie during transition: Thomas, pp. 56–58.
132 "I seem to be mercilessly exposed . . .": Cassini, p. 310.
132 "You must come and visit us . . .": Author's interview with Cassini, 2002.
132 "I shall be seeing you very soon . . .": John Bartlow Martin, p. 570.
132 "strains seriously threatened the Kennedy marriage . . .": Clifford, p. 361. Others close to the Kennedys have confirmed Clifford's observation. Sorensen: "Their marriage was not always smooth in its early years" (*Kennedy Legacy*, p. 32).
132 Story of Ridder luncheon and "Look, he's got a really good chance . . .": Author's interview with Marie Ridder.
132 "How does a married woman cope . . .": Pottker, p. 145.
132 Jackie worked as Inquiring Camera Girl: Bradford, pp. 53–54; Davis (*Jacqueline Bouvier)*, pp. 160–65.
133 The Reception for Distinguished Ladies: *Washington Post, Evening Star*, January 19, 1961.
133 "The Presidents' Ladies": *Washington Post*, January 15, 1961.
133 Jackie arrived in Washington: *New York Times*, January 19, 1961.
134 Description of conditions at N Street: Thayer (*White House Years)*, p. 45.
134 Jackie secluded herself on "the comparatively peaceful second floor": Ibid.
134 Johnson party at Statler Hilton: *Dallas News, Washington Post*, January 19, 1961.
135 Kennedy and Sorensen met at N Street to compare notes: Author's interview with Sorensen, 2002.
135 "He was a man who wanted to be . . .": Ibid.
135 The Sorensen COPY: Box 62, Sorensen papers, JFKL.
135 Gloria Sitrin believes she typed the Reading Copy: Author's interview with Sitrin, 2002.
135 Text of "Changes in Inaugural Speech . . .": Box 34, POF.
135 Harris Wofford and Louis Martin wrote the memorandum: Wofford, pp. 98–99; Author's interview with Wofford, 2002.
136 "the challenging, revolutionary sixties . . .": Wofford, p. 124.
136 "with the stroke of a presidential pen": USS SUB, p. 961.
136 "To the extent that these tasks . . .": Box 910, PPP.
137 "I intend to be as brave as I dare": Joseph Clark, JFKLOH.
137 Kennedy decided which of the Wofford-Martin suggestions to add to his inaugural address: The fact that "at home and around the world" was added in small capital letters means that Kennedy had to have made his decisions after the Reading Copy was typed late on the evening of January 18. After Kennedy left Bill Walton's house in Georgetown on the afternoon of January 19, he was separated from the Reading Copy for several hours and then began his round of social engagements.
137 George Taylor on Kennedy and the black girls during 1946 campaign: George Taylor, JFKLOH.
138 "a moral issue as old as the scriptures . . .": Sorensen *("Let the Word")*, p. 194.
138 "the future first lady rested . . .": *New York Times*, January 19, 1961.
138 Kennedy attended the Mahoney party: *Washington Post*, January 19, 1961.
139 Kennedy discovered Frost's poetry while in prep school: Knebel, JFKLOH.
139 "If more politicians knew poetry . . .": Sorensen *("Let the Word")*, p. 43.
139 "a pretty lofty book . . .": Meyers, p. 322.
139 "You can't imagine how gifted . . .": Ibid.

139 "The next President of the United States . . .": Thompson and Winnick, p. 266.
139 Kennedy thanked Frost with a graceful letter: Ibid., p. 270. In the letter, Kennedy said, "I don't know how you said that, but thanks just the same" (Meyers, p. 322).
139 Frost wondered if his support had elected Kennedy president: Thompson and Winnick, p. 276.
139 Friendship between Frost and Udall: Thomas G. Smith, "Robert Frost, Stewart Udall, and the 'Last Go-Down,'" *New England Quarterly,* March 1970, pp. 4–5.
139 "You know Robert Frost always steals . . .": Thompson and Winnick, p. 277; Stewart L. Udall, "Robert Frost, Kennedy, and Khrushchev: A Memoir of Poetry and Power," *Shenandoah,* winter 1975, p. 54; Stewart L. Udall, JFKLOH.
140 "Couldn't he read a poem . . .": Thomas G. Smith, "Robert Frost, Stewart Udall," p. 5.
140 Frost's telegram: Thompson and Winnick, p. 278.
140 Frost agreed to change the ending: Thomas G. Smith, "Robert Frost, Stewart Udall," p. 6. After agreeing to change the word, Frost told a reporter for the *Evening Star,* "I'll tell you a secret. I'm going to change that word to 'will' at Mr. Kennedy's suggestion. I think it's a good idea. I'm all for it. Nobody's ever changed a word before, but I'm willing to do it" (*Evening Star,* December 19, 1960).
140 The conversation between Frost, Kennedy, and Truman: *Washington Post,* January 19, 1961.
140 "The courage we desire and prize . . .": Edward Moore Kennedy, p. 8.
140 "I just don't want Joe Kennedy's boy . . .": Rowland Evans, JFKLOH.
140 "could not overcome his visceral dislike . . .": Truman, p. 415.
140 Truman tried to sabotage Kennedy's candidacy: Box 26, Sorensen papers, JFKL. This transcript of the Truman press conference at the Truman Library in Independence, Missouri, corrects the gaffe that Truman made when he delivered his remarks. The videotape of the press conference shows him confusing JFK with his father.
141 "Based on my observation of him . . .": Sorensen (*"Let the Word"*), p. 91.
141 Kennedy and Truman met in August at Truman Library: *New York Times,* August 21, 1961.
141 "You and I are stuck with the necessity . . .": McCullough, p. 974.
141 Truman had not seen Joe Kennedy since the Ritz-Carlton Hotel incident: Miller, p. 187.
141 Ritz-Carlton Hotel incident: Ibid., pp. 186–87.
142 Elliot Roosevelt witnessed explosion of Joe Kennedy Jr.'s plane: Hamilton, p. 661.
142 "One of the most . . .": Miller, p. 342.
142 " as big a crook as . . .": Ibid., p. 187.
142 "I just don't like that boy . . .": Ibid., p. 409.
142 "All they're interested in . . .": Ibid., p. 409.
142 "a gutless wonder": Ibid., p. 415.
142 "I know you will solve . . .": *Washington Post,* January 19, 1961.
142 Kennedy was woken by a motorcycle: *New York Times, Washington Post,* January 20, 1961.

CHAPTER EIGHT: WASHINGTON, JANUARY 19

143 Kennedy was observed brushing his hair: *Washington Post,* January 20, 1961.The *Post* reporter, Carroll Kilpatrick, wrote, "Mr. Kennedy left his Georgetown home at 8:49 a.m. yesterday, and rode without escort to the White House. He sat alone in the back seat of his limousine, brushing at his hair, reading from a looseleaf notebook in his lap, and occasionally chatting with Gerald A. Behn, chief of the President-elect's Secret Service detail."
143 Eisenhower disliked the whole family: Clifford, p. 342.
143 Eisenhower's nicknames for the Kennedys: Richard Reeves, p. 221.
143 "a serious, earnest seeker of information": Ambrose, p. 607.

143 "a non-President": Spaulding, JFKLOH; Clifford, p. 342. In the memorandum that Kennedy dictated to Lincoln after the meeting, he described Eisenhower as "looking very fit, pink cheeked and unharassed."
143 Writing the speech was a "job" for Eisenhower: Ambrose, p. 36.
143 "I read it more for your blue pencils . . .": Ibid., p. 36.
144 "Only the tough problems . . .": Kennedy dictation, box 29a, POF. In a televised conversation with journalists on December 17, 1962, Kennedy said that Eisenhower had told him, "There are no easy matters that will ever come to you as President. If they are easy, they will be settled at a lower level" (Sorensen [*"Let the Word"*], p. 32). The most accurate version of Eisenhower's words can be presumed to be the one Kennedy dictated minutes later.
144 The officer with the satchel, and the Marine Corps helicopter landed on the White House lawn: Eisenhower, p. 617; Ambrose, p. 614. In his dictated memorandum, Kennedy says merely, "We spent the next 45 minutes going through emergency procedures that might be called upon in the case of an immediate attack" (box 29a, POF).
144 "a sober one": Dwight D. Eisenhower, p. 617.
144 Eisenhower shocked the Kennedy team with his emphasis on Laos: box 29a, POF; Clifford, pp. 342–44.
145 "a great tragedy" and "just a question of time": Ibid., p. 343.
145 Laos was "the cork in the bottle": Perret *(Eisenhower)*, p. 600.
145 "If we permit Laos to fall . . .": McNamara memorandum, box 29a, POF.
145 How long would it take for an American combat division . . .": POF, Ibid.
145 "The tone of the old soldier . . .": Clifford, p. 344.
145 The memorandum Kennedy dictated to Lincoln: Box 29a, POF.
145 McNamara took notes: McNamara's notes of the meeting are preserved in ibid.
145 One of eleven pivotal events and decisions leading to Vietnam: McNamara, pp. 33–34, 37.
145 McNamara said there was "no thoughtful analysis," and that the conference made a deep impression on Kennedy and his cabinet: Ibid., p. 37.
146 "There he sat, telling me . . .": O'Donnell and Powers, p. 244.
146 "Eisenhower and Herter both got a certain inner satisfaction . . .": McNamara, p. 36.
146 "In the long run the United States cannot allow the Castro government . . .": Box 29a, POF.
146 "That boy doesn't know what the hell he's doing . . .": Dallek, p. 352.
147 "things were really just as bad . . .": O'Donnell and Powers, pp. 244–45.
147 "a battlefield of beauty . . .": Gallagher, p. 81.
147 Jackie dictated a handbook for new owners of N Street: Gallagher, p. 82.
147 Jackie told Bill Walton that her time at the White House had been happy: Box 2, William Walton papers, JFKL.
148 The two hours Kennedy spent at Walton's house: Thayer (*White House Years*), pp. 55–57.
148 Lyman Lemnitzer came for a meeting: Lyman Lemnitzer, JFKLOH.
148 Ted Sorensen noticed the Reading Copy of the inaugural on a chair: Author's interview with Sorensen, 2002.
148 "a man very much relaxed . . .": Halaby, JFKLOH.
148 Kennedy "appeared the calmest man . . .": *New York Times,* January 20, 1961.
148 PT 109 crew gathered at Touchdown Club: *Evening Star,* January 20, 1961.
149 Lunch on January 19 at Walton's house: Thayer (*White House Years*), p. 55–57.
149 The governors' reception: *Washington Post, Evening Star,* January 20, 1961.
149 The tea at Walter Lippmann's house: *Washington Post,* January 20, 1961; *Nation,* February 4, 1961.
150 Women Democrats gathered to plot Kennedy's 1964 campaign: *New York Times,* January 20, 1961.
150 Nixon's last press conference: *Evening Star,* January 20, 1961.

150 Pat Nixon was in "a funny mood": Julie Nixon Eisenhower, p. 201.
150 "If they had counted the votes right . . .": *Wall Street Journal,* May 10, 1961.
150 Suellen Fulstone arrived in Washington: *Washington Post,* January 20, 1961.
150 Fulstone would spend twenty minutes talking with Jackie: Author's interview with Suellen Fulstone, 2003.
150 Nettie Moulden: *Evening Star,* January 16, 1961; obituary: *Evening Star,* January 24, 1961.
151 Descriptions of the Washington snowstorm: *Washington Post, Evening Star, New York Herald Tribune, New York Times,* January 20, 1961, January 21, 1961.
151 "Southern efficiency and Northern charm": Adler, p. 58.
151 Kennedy and Truman returned to N Street: Thayer (*White House Years*), p. 58; *Evening Star,* January 20, 1961; *Washington Post,* January 20, 1961.
152 "[Kennedy is] a nice, decent young man . . .": Thayer (*White House Years*), p. 58; *Evening Star,* January 20, 1961.
152 Cassini found a heavier lining for Jackie's coat: Author's interview with Cassini, 2002. Cassini said, "I could see it was going to be cold and the lining was too light. I realized that the inauguration would be the first entrance she would make in the world arena, and I didn't want her to freeze to death."
152 Hoover returned to Miami; Morglieth died; Herter was trapped in his limousine: *New York Times,* January 20, 1960.
152 Bernstein and Davis flagged down police car: Anderson, p. 246.
152 Vogelsinger brought copy of speech to Truman: Author's interview with Vogelsinger, 2002.
153 Events during the snowstorm: *Washington Post, Evening Star,* January 20, 1961. Clifford wrote that "women in long dresses struggled through snowdrifts to get to parties; a dreamlike quality suffused the scene" (p. 347). According to Leonard Bernstein, "It was gay—the way a city becomes when a blizzard falls on it and everybody feels helpless anyway and perfect strangers embrace and everybody becomes friends and sings and jumps in the snow" (*A Life,* p. 201).
153 N Street during the snowstorm: Thayer (*White House Years*), pp. 57–58; Gallagher, pp. 82–83.
153 "Aren't you ladies going to the Gala?": Lincoln (*My Twelve Years*), p. 186.
153 Conversation between Kennedy and Sorrentino: Kelley, p. 109.
153 Monroe was in Mexico filing for a divorce: *New York Times,* January 22, 1961.
153 Gallagher sent message from Jackie to Thayer: Box 33, POF.
154 Kennedy asked Gallagher's advice about Jackie's necklace: Gallagher, p. 83.
154 Kennedy called Walton, and Jackie asked his and her husband's opinion about necklaces: Thayer (*White House Years*), p. 3.
154 The Kennedys left N Street and drove to Constitution Hall: Ibid., pp. 3–4, 60.
154 Photographs of Jackie leaving N Street: *New York Times,* January 20, 1961; *United Press International,* January 20, 1961; *New York Herald Tribune,* January 20, 1961.
155 Kennedy traveled to Constitution Hall: *Washington Post,* January 20, 1961.
155 Kennedy asked celebrities to contribute essays: *Evening Star,* January 11, 1961.
155 Description of the concert: Thayer (*White House Years*), pp. 60–61.
156 Review of the concert by Irving Lowens: *Evening Star,* January 20, 1961.
156 Lincoln Kirstein's comments on concert: *Nation,* February 4, 1961.
156 "We made her sit forward . . .": Thayer (*White House Years*), p. 62; Bill Walton interview on "The Presidents," broadcast on PBS *American Experience* series, 1992 (transcript, p. 22).
156 Kennedy compared Jefferson's writings with his own inaugural: Thayer (*White House Years*), p. 62.
157 "It's a smash!": Salinger, p. 108.
157 "elegantly tailored and terribly chic": *Washington Post,* December 31, 1960.
157 Sinatra was angered by the publicity: Ibid., January 7, 1961.

157 "Look, Frank. Just smile . . .": Taraborrelli, pp. 25–26.
157 "a thoughtless act of rudeness": *Washington Post,* January 20, 1961.
157 "not that he would ever read such a thing": Taraborrelli, p. 25.
158 Jackie suspected Sinatra of procuring women for Jack: Bradford, p. 137.
158 Jackie refused to attend rallies with Sinatra: Ibid., pp. 136–37.
158 Preparations for the gala: *Evening Star,* January 6, 1961, January 15, 1961, January 18, 1961; *Washington Post,* January 17, 1961, January 19, 1961.
158 "the finest older talent in the country": *New York Herald Tribune,* January 20, 1961.
159 Descriptions of the gala: Spada, pp. 237–38; Patricia Lawford, pp. 124–27; Thayer pp. 62–63; Bradford, pp. 163–64. *Washington Post, Evening Star, New York Times, New York Herald Tribune,* January 19 and 20, 1961; *Washington Post,* January 21, 1961; *New York Post,* January 22, 1961; visit by author to D.C. Armory, 2002.
159 Sinatra drank and hurled obscenities: Spada, p. 237.
159 Reviews of the gala: *Washington Post, Evening Star, New York Times, New York Herald Tribune,* January 20, 1961. *Washington Post,* January 21, 1961; *New York Post,* January 22, 1961.
159 "I don't get big laughs . . .": *New York Herald Tribune,* January 20, 1961.
159 "The happy relationship between the arts . . .": Lawford, p. 126; Spada, p. 238.
160 "I hope Sinatra will live up to . . .": Fay p. 80; Author's interview with Fay, 2002.
160 Lawford told Sinatra that Kennedy would not be staying with him: O'Donnell and Powers, pp. 379, 380.
160 Joe Kennedy's party: Author's interview with Fay, 2002; Fay, p. 80; Author's interview with Cassini, 2002.
160 The party was Joe Kennedy's last great moment of reflected glory: Author's interview with Cassini, 2002.
160 "I just don't think you should have used . . .": Ted Kennedy interview on "The Presidents," broadcast on PBS *American Experience* series, 1992 (transcript, p. 23).
160 "Have you ever seen so many attractive people . . .": Fay, p. 80.
160 "In a few hours you've got to deliver . . .": Author's interview with Fay, 2002.
161 "I'll give anyone here a thousand-to-one odds . . .": Ibid.
161 "You two are living like Presidents . . .": O'Donnell and Powers, p. 247.
161 Jackie was too excited to sleep: Schlesinger, p. 2. During a 2002 interview with the author Schlesinger said that he believed that Jackie had told him she was too excited.
161 "Just wait until you see the party . . .": *Washington Post,* January 21, 1961.

CHAPTER NINE: WASHINGTON, JANUARY 20

162 Kennedy's morning routine, and Thomas knocked gently on his bedroom door: Bishop, pp. 7–10.
162 Kennedy asked Lincoln for inaugural address and read it in bath: Lincoln *(My Twelve Years),* pp. 186–87.
162 Kennedy was a mediocre public speaker: Richard Goodwin, p. 111; Rose Kennedy, pp. 316, 374; Lincoln *(My Twelve Years),* p. 77.
163 The journalist Cabell Phillips praised his performance: *New York Times,* October 25, 1959.
163 At a news conference following his January 2, 1960, announcement of his candidacy: *New York Times,* January 3, 1960.
163 Nixon believed he could whip him in a debate: White (*Making of the President*), p. 178.
163 Kennedy wrote, "I always swore one thing I'd never do": William Atwood, JFKLOH.
163 Kennedy worked to improve his delivery: White *(Making of the President),* p. 251; *Boston Globe,* August 1, 1976; Silvestri (*Speaking in the Wisconsin and West Virginia Primaries*), pp. 147–53; Robert Healy, JFKLOH; Lincoln writes that "the next Monday the President addressed the United Nations. He was determined that this

speech, laying down the position and policy of the United States in the world situation, be properly delivered. He had made marginal notations: 'slow,' 'deep,' 'quietly,' and 'very quietly and slow.' He had also underlined the words he wanted to emphasize" (*My Twelve Years,* p. 235).

164 The Kennedy breakfast: Bishop, p. 11. Salinger and Sorensen described the same breakfast in their memoirs.

164 Salinger at N Street: Salinger, pp. 108–9.

164 Rose Kennedy's breakfast: Gibson, pp. 80–81.

164 Rose Kennedy attended church: Rose Kennedy, pp. 384–85; Cameron, pp. 176–77.

165 "I realized he was there of his own volition . . .": Rose Kennedy, p. 384.

165 Gibson believed that Kennedy ignored his mother: Gibson and Schwarz, p. 218.

165 Hugh Sidey observed Kennedy at Holy Trinity: Author's interview with Sidey, 2002.

165 "My religion is the religion . . .": Halle, JFKLOH.

166 Kennedy asked Lincoln for the Reading Copy: Lincoln *(My Twelve Years),* p. 187.

166 Salinger briefed press about Kennedy's health: *New York Herald Tribune,* January 21, 1961; *New York Times,* January 20, 1961. After JFK died, Bobby Kennedy said about his health that "at least one half of the days that he spent on this earth were days of intense physical pain" (Salinger and Vanocur, p. 156). But it appears that the inauguration, and the days immediately preceding it, were relatively pain-free days for Kennedy.

166 Bartlett and Bradlee were ignorant of important facts of Kennedy's life: Author's interviews with Bradlee and Bartlett, 2002.

167 Kennedy could not button his collar: Thayer (*White House Years*), pp. 66–67.

167 "Lyndon, you better run . . .": Author's interview with Sorensen, 2002. In 1956, when JFK was lobbying for the vice presidential nomination, Rayburn had told Adlai Stevenson, "If we have to have a Catholic, I hope we don't have to take that little pissant Kennedy" (Mathews, p. 111).

167 Kennedy was impatient to leave: Gallagher, p. 85.

167 Jackie had set his watch ahead: "Just Married," *Providence Sunday Journal,* August 10, 2003. Jackie's stepbrother, Hugh Auchincloss, said during an interview about the 1953 wedding that "Jackie wanted to make sure that Jack was on time. He was always late. On his inauguration day, Jackie was nervous about Jack not being at the White House in time to have coffee with the Eisenhowers. She set his watch 20 minutes ahead so when he got there he discovered he was 10 minutes early, not ten minutes late and had to drive around the White House grounds to get there exactly on time."

167 "You look handsome either way . . .": Gallagher, p. 85.

167 "Come on, Jackie!": Ibid., p. 85.

167 "It's a great day for the Irish!": *Washington Post,* January 21, 1961.

167 "I want you to wear it . . .": Ibid.

167 Rosemary Sorrentino saw him leave N Street: Kelley (*Jackie Oh!*), pp. 110–11.

168 CBS broadcast: Audiovisual archives, JFKL.

168 Pat Nixon ignored Jackie: Thayer (*White House Years*), p. 69.

168 December 9 visit to the White House by Jackie Kennedy: West, pp. 192–93.

168 The drab White House left Jackie in tears: Bradford, p. 143; Thomas, p. 245.

168 Jackie compared White House to Lubyanka: Anderson, p. 243; Kelley *(Jackie Oh!),* p. 100. According to Anderson, Jackie said, "It's the worst place in the world. So cold and dreary. A dungeon like the Lubyanka. It looks like it's been furnished by discount stores."

168 "decorated by a wholesale furniture store . . .": Thomas, p. 4.

169 Mamie complained to West about Jackie occupying the Queen's Room: West, p. 194.

169 "painfully strained": Thayer (*White House Years*), p. 69.

169 "Doesn't Ike look like Paddy . . .": Schlesinger (*Thousand Days*), p. 2; Thayer (*White House Years*), p. 69.

170 Jackie was seven-eighths Irish: Pottker, p. 130

170 "the wedding will be just awful . . .": Ibid., p. 133.

170 Millions of Americans voted against Kennedy because he was Catholic: Bernstein, p. 38. Bernstein writes that "one informed estimate is that 4.5 million Protestant Democrats switched from Stevenson in 1956 to Nixon in 1960."
170 Kennedy and Eisenhower discussed *The Longest Day*; Kennedy told his brother Bobby that Eisenhower appeared not to have read very much at all: Guthman and Shulman, p. 55.
170 "rumored to be short . . .": CBS coverage of inauguration, audiovisual archives, JFKL.
171 The 1950s: Goldman, pp. 341–46; Halberstam, chaps. 35, 39–46; Isserman and Kazin, pp. 7–22.
171 "a nation drowning in a sea of luxury . . .": Isserman and Kazin, p. 9.
171 "I am troubled by the cynical immorality . . .": Halberstam, p. 665.
171 Steinbeck and Galbraith sat together: Author's interview with Galbraith, 2002.
172 "By the time they had both lived . . .": Wilson, p. 7.
172 "because any man who has risked his life . . ." Hamilton, pp. 700–1.
172 Survey of young Americans: *Look*, January 3, 1961.
172 An "Explosive Generation": Ibid.
172 Kennedy proposed the Peace Corps: Richard Goodwin, pp. 102–21; Perret (*Jack*), pp. 268–69.
173 "courage, not complacency": USS SUB, p. 101.
173 "between public interest and private comfort . . .": Ibid., p. 102.
173 JFK used the Eliot poem in five formal campaign speeches and in numerous off-the-cuff remarks: Ibid., pp. 428, 620, 644, 654.
174 "No one has told me what to do . . .": Ralph G. Martin, p. 10.
174 Much the same thing had happened in Palm Beach: Box 3 (diary), Lincoln papers, 2002.
174 "Let's Go! Let's keep it running": Ralph G. Martin, p. 10.
174 Description of events in the Capitol rotunda: Commentary by Smith, Cronkite, Hanschman: CBS inauguration broadcast, audiovisual archives, JFKL.
174 Hanschman had pulled strings to get JFK extra seats to Eisenhower's inauguration: Dickerson, pp. 59–60.
175 Jack Kennedy had cuckolded Oleg Cassini: Tierney, pp. 141–52.
175 Joe Kennedy had sabotaged Cassini's engagement: Cassini pp. 263–65.
175 Igor named Jackie Debutante of the Year: Igor Cassini obituary, *New York Times*, January 9, 2002.
175 Clare Boothe Luce gave charm to JFK: Hamilton, p. 602.
175 Exchange between Hanschman and Kennedy: CBS inauguration broadcast, audiovisual archives, JFKL; Dickerson, p. 60.
175 Cassini was "fantastically nervous": Author's interview with Cassini, 2002.
176 Cassini's reaction to Jackie's appearance: Ibid.

CHAPTER TEN: THE CAPITOL, JANUARY 20

177 Edward R. Murrow comment: CBS inauguration broadcast, audiovisual archives, JFKL.
177 Quotations Kennedy used in campaign speeches: USS SUB, p. 1018 (Bacon), p. 339 (Burke), p. 428 (Eliot), p. 551 (Aristotle), p 397 (*King Lear*), p. 442 (Emerson), p. 1160 (Hugo), p. 1239 (Goethe), p. 421 (Wilde).
178 Pericles quotation: Sorensen (*"Let the Word"*), p. 56.
178 Longfellow quotation: Ibid., p. 96.
178 Americans sent poems to White House: Box 912, White House Central Subject Files, JFKL.
178 Students sent translations of inaugural address: Ibid.
178 Spectators flooded into reserved sections: *Washington Post*, January 21, 1961.

178 "a sort of Lindbergh quality": Janet Auchincloss, JFKLOH.
178 Billy Sutton thought JFK resembled Jimmy Stewart: Billy Sutton, JFKLOH.
179 Jackie raised her eyebrows: *Being with John F. Kennedy,* sixty-minute video produced by Robert Drew and Nancy Dickerson, Direct Cinema Limited, 1992.
179 her joke about the top hat: *Washington Post,* January 21, 1961.
179 "nothing seemed to pass between the two . . .": Mayra Mannes in the *Reporter,* February 26, 1961.
179 Seating arrangement on presidential stand: *New York Times,* January 21, 1961.
179 Hugh Auchincloss's contribution to campaign: Bradlee, p. 200.
179 Eleanor Roosevelt preferred to sit below stand: *New York Times,* January 21, 1961.
179 Peter Lawford skipped ceremony: Spada, p. 238.
180 Kara told O'Neill, "Years from now . . .": O'Neill, p. 102.
181 Cronkite filled the time: Audiovisual archives, JFKL.
181 Cronkite noticed Kennedy glancing at notebook: Author's interview with Walter Cronkite, 2002.
181 Alistair Cooke's report: *Manchester Guardian,* January 21, 1961.
181 NBC broadcast of inauguration: Audiovisual archives, JFKL.
181 Kennedy's "repressed nervous energy": *Times* of London, January 21, 1961.
181 Truman said he hoped no one would steal his overcoat: Thayer (*White House Years*), p. 72.
182 Truman was "chatting happily": *Manchester Guardian,* January 21, 1961.
182 "the subtle smile . . .": *Newsweek,* January 27, 1961.
182 "a smile that had nothing public about it": *Reporter,* February 16, 1961.
182 "since the photographers were focusing . . .": Rose Kennedy, p. 386.
182 "They put the parents at the end . . .": Gibson, p. 158.
182 Auchincloss seating on presidential stand: Pottker, p. 176.
182 "an ignoramus": USS SUB, p. 878.
182 "traitors of the high principles . . .": Miller, p. 178.
183 "a man of no very firm principles": Lisagor, JFKLOH.
183 "that fucking bastard": Ibid.
183 "that little shitass": Schlesinger (*Robert Kennedy*), p. 210.
183 "mean, bitter, vicious . . .": Shesol, p. 3.
183 "That young man never says please . . .": Collier and Horowitz, p. 250.
183 Bobby claimed JFK was "disgusted" with Stevenson: Robert F. Kennedy, p. 6.
183 "To be blunt about it . . . ": O'Neill, p. 83.
183 "that big fat Irish bastard": Farrell, p. 177.
183 Jackie left O'Neill's line blank: Ibid.
183 "Dick, if my boy can't make it . . .": Mathews, p. 133.
183 "anything he wanted . . .": Collier and Horowitz, p. 238.
183 "underneath the beautiful exterior . . .": Humphrey, p. 208.
183 "a bad man": Cray, p. 398.
183 Dillon's wife avoided making eye contact with Nixon: Clarence Douglas Dillon, JFKLOH.
183 Truman and Eisenhower did not exchange a word: *New York Times,* January 21, 1961.
183 "Mamie's lively laughter could be heard . . .": *Times-Herald,* January 21, 1953.
183 "Bobby's my boy . . .": O'Neill, p. 83.
183 "You can trample all over him . . .": Ibid.
184 "Forgive your enemies but never forget their names": Adler and Folsom, p. 194.
184 a "barefaced liar": USS SUB, p. 822.
184 Humphrey had said, "If you want efficiency in politics, you can go to the communists or totalitarians": White (*Making of the President*), p. 90.
184 "envenomed and embittered": Ibid., p. 90 *fn*.
184 Styles Bridges's cocktail party: Author's interview with McMillan, 2002. McMillan said, "I wonder how Kennedy ever dealt with Bridges again."

184 Eleanor Roosevelt sat with the diplomatic corps: *New York Times,* January 21, 1961; *Washington Post,* January 21, 1961.
184 "She hated my father . . .": Gore Vidal, "The Holy Family," *Esquire,* April 1967.
184 December 1958 feud between JFK and Eleanor Roosevelt: Lash, pp. 280–81; box 32, POF.
185 Representative Howard Smith left his seat: *Washington Post,* January 21, 1961.
185 "he must live Joe's life . . .": Collier and Horowitz, p. 146.
185 "I knew it would be long . . .": Ibid., p. 247.
186 Jackie's amused smile: *New York Times,* January 21, 1961.
186 "There's a man I'd hate to follow . . .": Leamer (*Kennedy Women*), p. 457.
186 Baughman summoned a fireman: Baughman, pp. 2–4.
186 Cushing slowed his delivery: Boller, p. 137.
186 Reinsch stopped the fire: Reinsch, JFKLOH.
186 "You must have a hot speech": Ibid.
186 Kennedy was impatient to start: Ibid.
186 Kennedy was observed mouthing words: *Washington Post, New York Times,* January 21, 1961.
187 Exchanges between Frost and Udall about poem and Frost's reading at the inauguration: Thompson and Winnick, p. 279; Udall, "Robert Frost, Kennedy, and Khrushchev"; Thomas G. Smith, "Robert Frost, Stewart Udall"; *Washington Post, New York Times,* January 21, 1961.
188 "carefully concealed": Clark, JFKLOH.
188 Alsop's comments about Kennedy and emotions: Salinger and Vanocur, p. 29.
188 "be more Irish than Harvard": Thomas G. Smith, "Robert Frost, Stewart Udall."
188 Kennan believed he had "a certain warmth": Kennan, pp. 316–17.
188 "As you know one thing holding back . . .": Box 26, Sorensen papers, JFKL.
189 Burns's comments about Kennedy's character: Burns (*John Kennedy*), p. 260.
189 "Kennedy came across to me. . . .": Letter from Burns to author, 2002.
189 Kennedy had tears in his eyes: White (*In Search of History*), p. 509.
189 Kennedy wept over the grave of his infant son: Salinger and Vanocur, p. 11; Leamer (*Kennedy Men*), pp. 697–98.
189 The Bay of Pigs invasion brought him to tears: Rose Kennedy, p. 400.
189 He cried after the 1961 Vienna summit: Author's interview with Sidey, 2002.
189 At a gathering of Gold Star Mothers: O'Donnell and Powers, pp. 53–55.
189 "This flag will be returned . . .": Ibid., p. 277.
189 Kennedy's 1963 speech in Berlin: Ibid., p. 361.
190 Hubert Humphrey admitted to being envious: Humphrey, p. 245.
190 Kennedy dropped his hand from Bible: Kittler, p. 217.
190 "How the hell did Kara . . .": O'Neill, p. 102.
190 Jackie's "smooth throat" twitched: *Manchester Guardian,* January 21, 1961.
190 Ike planted a kiss: Ralph G. Martin, p. 12.
190 George Washington's hands trembled: Boller, p. 77.
191 John Adams was frightened: Ibid.
191 Sorensen believed Kennedy started tentatively: Author's interview with Sorensen, 2002.
191 Reading Copy of inaugural address: Box 34, POF.
195 Color film of the inauguration: Audiovisual archives, JFKL.
196 the "whole new concept": Box 84, Sorensen papers, JFKL.
199 "shorten sentences & words": Box 62, in ibid.
199 The "secret" of the Gettysburg Address: Sorensen (*Kennedy*), p. 240.
201 Rose Kennedy's reaction to speech: Rose Kennedy, p. 388.

CHAPTER ELEVEN: JANUARY 20, 1961, TO THE PRESENT

202 "I was so proud of Jack . . .": Thayer (*White House Years*), p. 75.
202 "grinning and flushed with pleasure": Ibid., p. 77.
202 Exchange between Frankfurter and Kennedy at parade: Felix Frankfurter, JFKLOH.
203 Exchange between Kennedy and Krock at Wheeler dinner: Krock, p. 367; Arthur Krock, JFKLOH.
203 "the most glamorous period" in his life: Arthur Krock, JFKLOH.
203 "the embodiment of a good America": Strober and Strober, p. 495.
203 "We have felt so sad . . .": *Washington Post,* January 25, 1961.
203 "The President glanced up . . .": Thayer *(White House Years),* p. 90.
204 JFK left Jackie alone for thirty minutes: O'Donnell and Powers, p. 248.
204 "Well, she'll just have to walk faster": Ralph G. Martin, p. 14.
204 "I don't know a better way to spend an evening": Thayer *(White House Years),* p. 92.
204 JFK asked Leahy to sing: O'Donnell and Powers, pp. 248–49; box 32, POF.
204 JFK vaulted over railings at the armory: Thayer *(White House Years),* pp. 93–94.
204 "Your inaugural address will go down . . .": O'Neill, p. 102.
204 The Alsop party: Alsop, pp. 434–35; Author's interview with Peter Duchin, 2003; Joseph Alsop, JFKLOH; *Evening Star,* January 21, 1961.
205 "Everyone told him . . .": Alsop, p. 435.
205 Kennedy spoke with reporters outside the White House: Author's interview with Sidey, 2002; Sidey (*Kennedy*), p. 35; *New York Times,* January 22, 1961.
205 Jackie told Cronkite about inauguration night: Cronkite, pp. 219–220.
205 "a magnificent political speech": *Washington Post, New York Times,* January 22, 1961.
205 "It was short, to the point . . .": Thayer *(White House Years),* p. 100.
206 "I read the other day that . . .": Lincoln *(My Twelve Years),* p. 192.
206 *New York Times* editorial: *New York Times,* January 21, 1961.
206 "The evangelical and transcendental . . .": *New York Times,* January 22, 1961.
206 Kennedy-Hannan conversation about inaugural: Author's interview with Hannan, 2002; Manchester, p. 588.
206 Kennedy-Galbraith conversation: Author's interview with Galbraith, 2002.
207 Norman Thomas letter: Box 84a, Sorensen papers, JFKL.
207 Grayson Kirk letter: Ibid.
207 Eleanor Roosevelt letter: Box 32, POF.
207 Hamlin Turner letter: Box 84a, Sorensen papers, JFKL.
207 Kay Halle brought commemorative book to the White House: Halle, JFKLOH.
207 Comments from Invited Intellectuals about inaugural address: Box 32, POF.
208 Hemingway's comment: Schlesinger *(Thousand Days),* p. 732.
208 "I've never heard a speech like that": Author's interview with Feldman, 2002.
208 Feldman read other inaugural addresses: Ibid.
208 "Did you see the Coast Guard . . .": Richard Goodwin, p. 4.
208 "With this telephone . . .": Goodwin's article in *New York Times Magazine,* December 26, 1976.
209 "What a wonderful President we have . . .": Branch, pp. 383–84.
209 "The strength of our appeal to these key populations . . .": Sorensen *("Let the Word"),* p. 337.
209 Hotel Theresa speech: USS SUB, p. 581.
210 "that the spirit of the revolution . . .": Sidey (*Kennedy*), p. 30.
211 Kennedy's address at Wittenberg College: USS SUB, pp. 633–39.
211 "How many young students . . .": Ibid., p. 638.
212 State of the Union message: Sorensen (*"Let the Word"*), p. 59.
212 "Khrushchev reminds me of the tiger hunter . . .": *New York Times,* December 24, 1961.
212 "We in this country . . .": Sorensen *("Let the Word"),* p. 404.
213 Jackie and Caroline at the rotunda: Manchester, p. 542.
213 "one of the most authentically tragic events . . .": Salinger and Vanocur, p. 125.

213 Charles Malik's comment: Ibid., p. 118.
213 "could have been the savior": Ibid., p. 69.
213 "For the first time in my life . . .": Ibid., p. 114.
213 Sorensen was standing on the same spot: Manchester, p. 535.
213 Warren blamed a climate of hatemongering: Cray, pp. 413–14; Manchester, p. 541.
214 "May the angels, dear Jack . . .": Manchester, p. 589.
214 Hannan delivered the eulogy: Hannan interview; Manchester, p. 588.
214 Jackie's comments on the inaugural: Thayer (*White House Years*), p. 75.
214 Bobby Kennedy's speech in South Africa: Salinger et al., p. 2.
216 "a remarkable emotional response": Box 84, Sorensen papers, JFKL.

Bibliography

Adler, Bill, ed. *The Kennedy Wit*. New York: Bantam, 1965.

Adler, Bill, and Tom Folsom, eds. *The Uncommon Wisdom of JFK: A Portrait in His Own Words*. New York: Rugged Land, 2003.

Alsop, Joseph W., with Adam Platt. *"I've Seen the Best of It": Memoirs*. New York: Norton, 1992.

Ambrose, Stephen E. *Eisenhower: The President*. New York, Simon and Schuster, 1984.

Anderson, Christopher. *Jack and Jackie: Portrait of an American Marriage*. New York: William Morrow, 1996.

Baker, Robert Gene. *Wheeling and Dealing: A Capitol Hill Memoir*. New York: Norton, 1980.

Baughman, U. E. *Secret Service Chief*. New York: Harper and Row, 1961.

Bernstein, Irving. *Promises Kept: John F. Kennedy's New Frontier*. New York: Oxford University Press, 1991.

Bernstein, Leonard. *A Life*. New York: Knopf, 1994.

Beschloss, Michael R. *The Crisis Years: Kennedy and Khrushchev, 1960–1963*. New York: HarperCollins, 1991.

Bishop, Jim. *A Day in the Life of President Kennedy*. New York: Bantam Books, 1964.

Bliss, Edward R., ed. *In Search of Light: The Broadcasts of Edward R. Murrow, 1938–1961*. New York: Knopf, 1967.

Boller, Paul F. *Presidential Inaugurations*. New York: Harcourt, 2001.

Bradford, Sarah. *America's Queen: The Life of Jacqueline Kennedy Onassis*. New York: Viking, 2000.

Bradlee, Benjamin C. *Conversations with Kennedy*. New York: Norton, 1975.

Branch, Taylor. *Parting the Waters: America in the King Years, 1954–63*. New York: Simon and Schuster, 1988.

Brauer, Carl. *Presidential Transitions: Eisenhower Through Reagan*. New York: Oxford University Press, 1986.

Burns, James MacGregor. *John Kennedy: A Political Profile*. New York: Harcourt, Brace, 1960.

———. *Roosevelt: The Lion and the Fox*. New York: Harcourt, Brace, 1956.

Burnshaw, Stanley. *Robert Frost Himself*. New York: George Braziller, 1986.

Cameron, Gail. *Rose: A Biography of Rose Fitzgerald Kennedy*. New York: Putnam's, 1971.

Cassini, Oleg. *In My Own Fashion: An Autobiography*. New York: Simon and Schuster, 1987.

Churchill, Sir Winston. *While England Slept: A Survey of World Affairs, 1932–1938.* New York: G. P. Putnam's Sons, 1938.
Clifford, Clark. *Counsel to the President.* New York: Random House, 1991.
Collier, Peter, and David Horowitz. *The Kennedys: An American Drama.* New York: Summit Books, 1984.
Cray, Ed. *Chief Justice: A Biography of Earl Warren.* New York: Simon and Schuster, 1997.
Cronkite, Walter. *A Reporter's Life.* New York, Knopf, 1996.
Cushing, Richard Cardinal. *The Faith of JFK.* New York: E. P. Dutton, 1965.
Dallek, Robert. *An Unfinished Life: John F. Kennedy, 1917–1963.* Boston: Little, Brown, 2003.
Davis, John H. *The Bouviers: From Waterloo to the Kennedys and Beyond.* Washington, D.C.: National Press Books, 1993.
———. *Jacqueline Bouvier: An Intimate Memoir.* New York: John Wiley, 1996.
———. *The Kennedys: Dynasty and Disaster, 1848–1984.* New York: McGraw-Hill, 1984.
Dickerson, Nancy. *Among Those Present: A Reporter's View of 25 Years in Washington.* New York: Random House, 1976.
Donald, David Herbert. *Lincoln.* New York: Simon and Schuster, 1995.
Donovan, Hedley. *Roosevelt to Reagan: A Reporter's Encounter with Nine Presidents.* New York: Harper and Row, 1985.
Donovan, Robert J. *PT 109: John F. Kennedy in World War II.* New York: McGraw-Hill, 1961.
Eisenhower, Dwight D. *The White House Years: Waging Peace, 1956–1961.* Garden City, N.Y.: Doubleday, 1965.
Eisenhower, Julie Nixon. *Pat Nixon: The Untold Story.* New York, Simon and Schuster, 1986.
Fairlie, Henry. *The Kennedy Promise: The Politics of Expectation.* Garden City, N.Y.: Doubleday, 1973.
Farrell, John Aloysius. *Tip O'Neill and the Democratic Century.* Boston: Little Brown, 2001.
Fay, Paul. *The Pleasure of His Company.* New York: Dell, 1967.
Fursenko, Aleksandr, and Timothy Naftali. *One Hell of a Gamble: The Secret History of the Cuban Missile Crisis.* New York: Norton, 1997.
Galbraith, John Kenneth. *Ambassador's Journal.* Boston: Houghton Mifflin, 1969.
———. *Letters to Kennedy.* Cambridge, Mass.: Harvard University Press, 1998.
Gallagher, Mary Barelli. *My Life with Jacqueline Kennedy.* New York: David McKay, 1969.
Gibson, Barbara, with Caroline Latham. *Life with Rose Kennedy.* New York: Warner Books, 1986.
Gibson, Barbara, and Ted Schwarz. *Rose Kennedy and Her Family: The Best and Worst of Their Life and Times.* New York: Birch Lane Press, 1995.
Golden, James L. "John F. Kennedy and the 'Ghosts.'" *Quarterly Journal of Speech,* December 1966, pp. 348–57.
Goldman, Eric F. *The Crucial Decade and After: America, 1945–1960.* New York: Vintage Books, 1960.
Goodwin, Doris Kearns. *The Fitzgeralds and the Kennedys.* New York: Simon and Schuster, 1987.
Goodwin, Richard. *Remembering America: A Voice from the Sixties.* Boston: Little, Brown, 1988.
Gormley, Ken. *Archibald Cox: Conscience of a Nation.* Reading, Mass.: Perseus Books, 1997.
Graham, Billy. *Just as I Am.* San Francisco: HarperSan Francisco/Zondervan, 1997.
Graham, Katharine. *Personal History.* New York: Knopf, 1997.
Guthman, Edwin O., and Jeffrey Shulman, eds. *Robert Kennedy: In His Own Words.* New York: Bantam, 1988.
Halberstam, David. *The Fifties.* New York: Villard Books, 1993.
Hamilton, Ian. *JFK: Reckless Youth.* New York: Random House, 1992.

Hersh, Seymour M. *The Dark Side of Camelot*. Boston: Little, Brown, 1997.

Herzstein, Robert E. *Henry R. Luce: The Political Portrait of the Man Who Created the American Century.* New York: Charles Scribner's Sons, 1994.

Hughes, Patrick. "The Weather on Inauguration Day." Weatherwise, December 1988.

Humphrey, Hubert H. *The Education of a Public Man: My Life in Politics.* Garden City, N.Y.: Doubleday, 1976.

Hunt, Michael H. *Lyndon Johnson's War: America's Cold War Crusade in Vietnam, 1945–1968*. New York: Hill and Wang, 1996.

Isserman, Maurice, and Michael Kazin. *America Divided: The Civil War of the 1960s*. New York: Oxford University Press, 2000.

Jenkins, Roy. *Churchill: A Biography.* New York: Farrar, Straus and Giroux, 2001.

Johnson, Walter, ed. *The Papers of Adlai E. Stevenson*. Vol. 7, *Continuing Education and the Unfinished Business of American Society, 1957–1961*. Boston: Little, Brown, 1977.

Kelley, Kitty. *His Way: The Unauthorized Biography of Frank Sinatra.* New York, Bantam Books, 1986.

——— *Jackie Oh!* Secaucus, New Jersey: Lyle Stuart, 1978.

Kennan, George F. *Memoirs: 1950–1963*. New York: Pantheon, 1983.

Kennedy, Edward Moore, ed. *Words Jack Loved.* Privately published, 1976.

Kennedy, John F. *Prelude to Leadership: The European Diary of John F. Kennedy, Summer 1945*. Washington, D.C.: Regnery Publishing, 1995.

———. *Profiles in Courage*. New York: Harper & Brothers, 1956.

———. *The Strategy of Peace*. New York: Harper & Brothers, 1960.

———. *Why England Slept*. New York: Wilfred Funk, 1940.

Kennedy, Robert F. *Robert Kennedy in His Own Words: The Unpublished Recollections of the Kennedy Years.* New York: Bantam Books, 1988.

Kennedy, Rose Fitzgerald. *Times to Remember.* Garden City, N.Y.: Doubleday, 1974.

Kenney, Charles. *John F. Kennedy—The Presidential Portfolio: History as Told Through the Collection of the John F. Kennedy Library and Museum.* New York: Public Affairs, 2000.

Kenny, Edward B. "Another Look at Kennedy's Inaugural Address." *Today's Speech,* November 1965, pp. 17–19.

Kittler, Glenn D. *Hail to the Chief: The Inauguration Days of Our Presidents.* New York: Chilton Book Co., 1965.

Krock, Arthur. *Memoirs: Sixty Years on the Firing Line.* New York: Funk and Wagnalls, 1968.

Lacy, Robert. *Grace*. New York: Putnam, 1994.

Lash, Joseph P. *Eleanor: The Years Alone*. New York: Norton, 1971.

Lawford, Patricia Seaford. *The Peter Lawford Story: Life with the Kennedys, Monroe and the Rat Pack.* New York: Carroll and Graf, 1988.

Lawrence, Bill. *Six Presidents, Too Many Wars.* New York: Saturday Review Press, 1972.

Leamer, Laurence. *The Kennedy Men: 1901–1963. The Laws of the Father.* New York: William Morrow, 2001.

———. *The Kennedy Women: The Saga of an American Family.* New York: Villard Books, 1994.

Lincoln, Evelyn. *Kennedy and Johnson.* New York: Holt, Rinehart, and Winston, 1968.

———. *My Twelve Years with John F. Kennedy.* New York: Bantam, 1966.

Lord, Walter. *The Past That Would Not Die*. New York: Harper and Row, 1965.

MacNeil, Robert. *The Way We Were: 1963, the Year Kennedy Was Shot*. New York: Carroll and Graf, 1988.

Mahoney, Richard D. *Sons and Brothers: The Days of Jack and Bobby Kennedy.* New York: Arcade, 1999.

Mailer, Norman. *The Presidential Papers*. New York: Putnam's, 1963.

Manchester, William. *The Death of a President: November 1963*. New York: Harper and Row, 1967.

Markmann, Charles Lam, and Mark Sherwin. *John F. Kennedy: A Sense of Purpose*. New York: St. Martin's Press, 1961.

Martin, John Bartlow. *Adlai Stevenson and the World: The Life of Adlai E. Stevenson.* Garden City, N.Y.: Doubleday, 1977.
Martin, Ralph G. *Hero for Our Time: An Intimate Story of the Kennedy Years.* New York: Macmillan, 1983.
Martin, Ralph G., and Ed Plaut. *Front Runner, Dark Horse.* Garden City, N.Y.: Doubleday, 1960.
Mathews, Christopher. *Kennedy and Nixon: The Rivalry That Shaped Postwar America.* New York: Simon and Schuster, 1996.
McCullough, David. *Truman.* New York: Simon and Schuster, 1992.
McNamara, Robert S. *In Retrospect: The Tragedy and Lessons of Vietnam.* New York: Times Books, 1995.
Meyers, Jeffrey. *Robert Frost: A Biography.* Boston: Houghton Mifflin, 1996.
Miller, Merle. *Plain Speaking: An Oral Biography of Harry S. Truman.* New York: Berkley Publishing, 1973.
Moley, Raymond. *The First New Deal.* New York: Harcourt, Brace, 1966.
Moran, Lord. *Churchill at War, 1940–45.* New York: Carroll and Graf, 2002.
Morison, Samuel Eliot. *A Concise History of the American Republic.* New York: Oxford University Press, 1985.
Nevins, Allan, ed. *The Strategy of Peace.* New York: Harper and Brothers, 1960.
O'Donnell, Kenneth P., and David F. Powers. *"Johnny We Hardly Knew Ye": Memories of John Fitzgerald Kennedy.* Boston: Little, Brown, 1970.
O'Neill, Tip. *Man of the House: The Life and Political Memoirs of Speaker Tip O'Neill.* New York: Random House, 1987.
Parmet, Herbert S. *Eisenhower and the American Crusades.* New York: Macmillan, 1972.
———. *JFK: The Presidency of John F. Kennedy.* New York: Dial Press, 1983.
———. *Jack: The Struggles of John F. Kennedy.* New York: Dial Press, 1980.
Perret, Geoffrey. *Eisenhower.* New York: Random House, 1999.
———. *Jack: A Life Like No Other.* New York, Random House, 2001.
Pollock, John. *Billy Graham: Evangelist to the World.* New York: Harper and Row, 1979.
Pottker, Jan. *Janet and Jackie: The Story of a Mother and Her Daughter, Jacqueline Kennedy Onassis.* New York: St. Martin's Press, 2001.
Reeves, Thomas C. *A Question of Character: A Life of John F. Kennedy.* New York: Macmillan, 1991.
Reeves, Richard. *President Kennedy: Profile of Power.* New York: Simon and Schuster, 1993.
Renehan, Edward J. *The Kennedys at War: 1937–1945.* New York: Doubleday, 2002.
Rockefeller Panel. *Prospect for America: The Rockefeller Panel Reports.* Garden City, N.Y.: Doubleday, 1961.
Rosenman, Samuel I. *Working with Roosevelt.* New York: Harper and Brothers, 1952.
Salinger, Pierre. *With Kennedy.* Garden City, N.Y.: Doubleday, 1966.
Salinger, Pierre, and Edwin Guthman, Frank Mankiewicz, and John Seigenthaler, eds. *"An Honorable Profession": A Tribute to Robert F. Kennedy.* New York; Doubleday, 1993.
Salinger, Pierre, and Sander Vanocur, eds. *A Tribute to John F. Kennedy.* Chicago: Encyclopedia Britannica, 1964.
Schlesinger, Arthur M. Jr. *The Crisis of the Old Order: 1919–1933.* Boston: Houghton Mifflin, 1957.
———. *The Cycles of American History.* Boston: Houghton Mifflin, 1986.
———. *Robert Kennedy and His Times.* Boston: Houghton Mifflin, 1978.
———. *A Thousand Days: John F. Kennedy in the White House.* Boston: Houghton Mifflin, 1965.
Serafini, Anthony. *Linus Pauling: A Man and His Science.* New York: Paragon House, 1989.
Shapley, Deborah. *Promise and Power: The Life and Times of Robert McNamara.* Boston: Little, Brown, 1993.
Shesol, Jeff. *Mutual Contempt: Lyndon Johnson, Robert Kennedy, and the Feud that Defined a Decade.* New York: Norton, 1997.

———. *John F. Kennedy, President.* New York: Atheneum, 1964.

Silvestri, Vito Nicholas. *Becoming JFK: A Profile in Communication.* Westport, Conn.: Praeger, 2000.

———. "John F. Kennedy: His Speaking in the Wisconsin and West Virginia Primaries, 1960." Ph.D. thesis, Indiana University, 1966.

Smith, Howard K. *Events Leading up to My Death: The Life of a Twentieth-Century Reporter.* New York: St. Martin's Press, 1996.

Sorensen, Theodore C. *Kennedy.* New York: Harper and Row, 1965.

———. *The Kennedy Legacy.* New York: Macmillan, 1969.

———. ed. *"Let the Word Go Forth": The Speeches, Statements, and Writings of John F. Kennedy, 1947–1963.* New York: Delacorte Press, 1988.

———. *Watchmen in the Night: Presidential Accountability After Watergate.* Cambridge, Mass.: MIT Press, 1975.

Spada, James. *Peter Lawford: The Man Who Kept the Secrets.* New York: Bantam, 1991.

Steel, Ronald. *Walter Lippmann and the American Century.* Boston: Atlantic–Little, Brown, 1980.

Steinbeck, Elaine, and Robert Wallsten, eds. *Steinbeck: A Life in Letters.* New York: Viking Press, 1975.

Strober, Gerald S., and Deborah H. Strober. *Let Us Begin Anew: An Oral History of the Kennedy Presidency.* New York: HarperCollins, 1993.

Swanberg, W. A. *Luce and His Empire.* New York: Charles Scribner's Sons, 1972.

Tanzer, Lester, ed. *The Kennedy Circle.* Washington, D.C.: Luce, 1961.

Taraborrelli, Randy. *Jackie Ethel Joan: Women of Camelot.* New York: Warner Books, 2000.

Thayer, Mary Van Rensselaer. *Jacqueline Bouvier Kennedy.* New York: Doubleday, 1961.

———. *Jacqueline Kennedy: The White House Years.* Boston: Little Brown, 1967.

Thomas, Helen. *Front Row at the White House: My Life and Times.* New York: Scribner, 1999.

Thompson, Lawrence, and R. H. Winnick. *Robert Frost: The Later Years, 1938–1963.* New York: Holt, Rinehart and Winston, 1976.

Tierney, Gene, with Mickey Herskowitz. *Self-Portrait.* New York: Wyden Books, 1979.

Truman, Margaret. *Bess W. Truman.* New York: Macmillan, 1986.

Urofsky, Melvin I., ed. *The American Presidents: Critical Essays.* New York: Garland Publishing, 2000.

U.S. Senate Subcommittee of the Subcommittee on Communications. *The Speeches, Remarks, Press Conferences, and Statements of Senator John F. Kennedy, August 1 Through November 7, 1960.* Washington, D.C.: U.S. Government Printing Office, 1961 [USS SUB].

Vidal, Gore. *Palimpsest: A Memoir.* New York: Random House, 1995.

Vreeland, Diana. *D.V.* New York: Knopf, 1984.

West, J. B. *Upstairs at the White House: My Life with the First Ladies.* New York: Coward, McCann and Geoghegan, 1973.

White, Theodore H. *The Making of the President, 1960.* New York: Atheneum, 1961.

———. *In Search of History: A Personal Adventure.* New York: Harper and Row, 1978.

Wicker, Tom. *One of Us: Richard Nixon and the American Dream.* New York: Random House, 1991.

Wills, Garry. *The Kennedy Imprisonment: A Meditation on Power.* Boston: Atlantic-Little Brown, 1982.

———. *Lincoln at Gettysburg: The Words That Remade America.* New York: Simon and Schuster, 1992.

Wilson, Sloan. *The Man in the Gray Flannel Suit.* New York, Simon and Schuster, 1955.

Wofford, Harris. *Of Kennedys and Kings: Making Sense of the Sixties.* Pittsburgh: University of Pittsburgh Press, 1992.

Acknowledgments

An advantage of concentrating research on a short period of time is that one sometimes stumbles across important documents that have escaped the notice of other writers and researchers. I found much of this new material in the archives of the John F. Kennedy Library in Boston, and I am indebted to its dedicated librarians and staff, chiefly Steve Plotkin, Sharon Kelly, Allan Goodrich, James Hill, and Maryrose Grossman.

Kennedy's friends, aides, and associates have revisited his inauguration in numerous interviews over the years, and I am grateful to those who were willing to do it again for me, particularly to Theodore Sorensen, who was generous with his time and candid in his observations. Mike Feldman's recollection of Thanksgiving Day 1960, when Ted Sorensen wrote a first draft of the inaugural address in Feldman's study, and John Kenneth Galbraith's description of his own contributions to the speech were crucial to my reconstruction of the composition of the inaugural address. My interviews with Harris Wofford, Hugh Sidey, Phillip Hannan, Arthur Schlesinger, Paul Fay, Oleg Cassini, Gloria Sitrin, Priscilla McMillan, Charles Bartlett, Ben Bradlee, Marie Ridder, Suellen Fulstone, Walter Cronkite, and Deirdre Henderson also yielded important details and insights, and I am grateful to them and to others mentioned in the end notes.

I want to thank Betty Schwab for interpreting and transcribing Evelyn Lincoln's shorthand, Tony and Gay Barclay for support and introductions in Washington, Bart and Michel Brownell, Robin and Eileen West, and George Whitney for their friendship and hospitality, Lawrence Leamer and Sheldon Stern for their advice, Leo Racine for giving me a tour of the former Kennedy home in Palm Beach. My wife, Antonia, read this manuscript many times, and her perceptive criticisms are reflected on every page. For more than a decade I have had the good fortune to have Kathy Robbins as an agent. Her encouragement and wise counsel have been, as usual, indispensable. I have worked with twelve editors during a career spanning ten books. George Hodgman is one of the best, and his devotion to *Ask Not* has made it an immeasurably better book.

Index

Acheson, Dean, 141
Adams, Eddie, 124
Adams, John, 32, 156, 191
African Americans, 114, 135–38, 172, 208
Aiken, Conrad, 207
Alexander the Great, 51
Algeria, 33, 86–87, 209
Alliance for Progress, 45, 208
Alsop, Joe, 11, 68, 139, 174, 188, 204–5
"American Proposition" (Luce), 98, 99, 175
Anderson, Marian, 20, 180, 185–86
Aristotle, 177
Arlington National Cemetery grave, 3–5, 35, 65, 216
Arthur, Chester, 151
Arvad, Inga, 175
Asquith, Herbert, 49
Attlee, Clement, 84
Attwood, William, 163
Auchincloss, Hugh, 89, 179, 182
Auchincloss, Jamie, 182
Auchincloss, Janet, 89, 133, 170, 178–79, 182
Auden, W. H., 150
Avedon, Richard, 47, 59
Bacon, Francis, 177
Baker, Russell, 117, 180
Barclay, Dr. John, 186
Bartlett, Charlie, 54, 114, 121, 166, 174
Baruch, Bernard, 155
Batelle, Kenneth, 147, 168
Baughman, U. E., 29, 89, 186
Bay of Pigs, 45, 146, 189
Beale, Betty, 120
Belafonte, Harry, 158
Bell, David, 118
Berle, Milton, 120, 158, 160
Berlin
- trip of 1939, 80
- trip of 1945, 80, 83–84
- trip of 1963, 189

Bernstein, Leonard, 152, 158, 160
Berquist, Laura, 57–60, 66
Beschloss, Michael, 43–44
Bible, 60–61, 63, 67, 79, 96. *See also specific books*
Billings, LeMoyne "Lem," 59, 179
Black, Joe, 20
Bonham-Carter, Lady Violet, 49
Bowles, Chester, 25, 73
Bradlee, Ben, 20, 125, 166, 174, 180
Bridges, Styles, 169, 184, 191, 193

Britt, Mai, 137
Bruce, David, 22
Bundy, McGeorge, 21, 114, 189, 208
Burke, Edmund, 177
Burns, James MacGregor, 103–5, 162, 189
Bush, George, H. W., 219
Bush, George W., 210–11, 215

Callas, Maria, 155
Camelot (musical), 113, 117
Campbell, Judith, 158, 160
Cannon, Frances Ann, 175
Carlyle, Thomas, 140
Carter, Jimmy, 210, 218–19
Cassini, Igor, 175
Cassini, Oleg, 38, 46–48, 132, 147, 152, 154, 169, 175–76
Castro, Fidel, 56, 59–60, 146, 171
Catholic Church, 62–64, 137
CBS News, 125, 168, 170, 174–75, 177, 195–96
Cecil, David, 51
Chamberlain, Neville, 54, 81
Cheshire, Maxine, 120, 157
Chiang Kai-shek, Madam, 180
Churchill, Randolph, 120
Churchill, Winston, 10, 31, 52, 67–69, 75–76, 81, 84, 130, 171, 193, 207
Ciano, Count, 45
Cicero, 78–79
civil rights, 7, 135–38, 171–72, 208–9, 218
Clark, Blair, 47, 116–17, 124–25, 196
Clark, Joe, 137
Clay, Henry, 52
Cleveland, Grover, 24, 151
Clifford, Clark, 23, 26, 53, 55, 102, 132, 145, 146, 180
Clifton, Chester, 174
Clinton, Bill, 6, 215, 219
Clinton, Hillary, 222, 223
Cluster, Alvin, 83
Cohen, Dr. Eugene, 124, 166
Colby, William, 203
cold war, 25, 33, 56, 71, 84, 147, 198, 209
Cole, Nat King, 120, 121, 158, 160
communism, 33, 60, 79, 85–86, 97, 98, 115, 117, 127, 130, 144–47, 189
Conant, James, 98
Cooke, Alistair, 181, 182, 190
Coolidge, Calvin, 27, 115, 151
Cooper, Duff, 49
Copland, Aaron, 115, 180
Corinthians I, 67
Cox, Archibald, 45, 76–77, 180
Crisis of the Old Order, The (Schlesinger), 105
Crisis Years, The (Beschloss), 43
Cronkite, Walter, 175, 180–81, 205
Crosby, Bing, 160
Cuba, 146, 171, 189
Curtis, Tony, 158
Cushing, Cardinal, 63, 180, 185–86, 214

Dalton, Mark, 63
Danton, Emily, 44
Davis, Bette, 152, 158
Davis, John, 125
Davis, Mary, 17, 23
Davis, Sammy, Jr., 137
Declaration of Independence, 32, 137, 209, 210
"Dedication" (Frost), 152
de Gaulle, Charles, 43
de Kooning, William, 155
democracy, 80, 209–12
Democratic National Convention of 1928, 127
  of 1956, 32
  of 1960, 18, 48, 97, 137, 141, 178
Dempsey, Jack, 155
Deuteronomy, 61
Dickerson, Nancy Hanschman, 174–75

Dickinson, Angie, 165, 203
Dillon, Douglas, 23, 69, 70, 144, 146, 182, 183, 208
Disraeli, Benjamin, 165
Donovan, Hedley, 97
Douglas, Kirk, 155
Dreams from My Father (Obama), 219
Duchin, Peter, 204–5
Dulles, Allen, 180
Dungan, Ralph, 66
Durante, Jimmy, 121, 158, 160
Dutton, Fred, 68

Eban, Abba, 213
Ecclesiastes, 63
Einstein, Albert, 36
Eisenhower, Dwight D., 5, 18, 86, 89, 96, 98, 142–47, 151, 168, 170–71, 174–75, 179–81, 183, 186–87, 193, 196, 213
  farewell address, 119
  inaugurals, 24, 25, 27, 114–15, 131, 143–44, 155, 174, 178, 181, 190, 195
Eisenhower, Mamie, 47, 168–70, 175–76, 179–80, 183, 190
Eisenstadt, Alfred, 124
election
  of 1932, 54
  of 1960, 23, 54, 171
Eliot, T. S., 173, 177
Emerson, Ralph Waldo, 177, 206
Evans, Rowland, 149
Everett, Edward, 139

Familiar Quotations (Bartlett), 78, 129
Fay, Paul, 11, 54, 68, 90, 120–21, 126, 160–61, 186
Feldman, Meyer "Mike," 24–27, 42, 208
Fillmore, Millard, 130
Fitzgerald, Ella, 158
Fonda, Afdera, 204
Ford, Betty, 180
Ford, Gerald, 180
Foreign Affairs, 86, 116
Forrestal, James, 83, 84
Frankfurter, Felix, 180, 202
Freeman, Orville, 88
Friendly, Fred, 124–25, 196
Frost, Robert, 20, 139–40, 152, 186–88, 215, 217, 218
Fulstone, Suellen, 150

Gaitskell, Hugh, 123, 126
Galbraith, John Kenneth, 8, 25, 67, 69, 71–73, 114, 128–29, 135, 171–72, 180–81, 206
Gallagher, Mary, 39, 48, 131, 138, 153–54, 167
Garfield, James A., 151
Gargan, Ann, 39, 179
Garside, John, 126
Gates, Thomas, 145, 146
Gettysburg Address. *See* Lincoln, Abraham
Giancana, Sam, 160
Gibson, Barbara, 165, 182
"Gift Outright, The" (Frost), 140, 152, 187–88
Goethe, Johann W. von, 178
Goldberg, Arthur, 69
Goldwater, Barry, 7
Goodwin, Richard N., 24, 28, 73, 173, 208
Graham, Billy, 60–62, 64, 96, 98
Graham, Katharine, 8, 152
Graham, Philip, 152
Grant, Ulysses S., 24, 130, 151
Great American Speeches (TV series), 9
Great Contemporaries (Churchill), 68
Gullion, Edmund, 85

Halaby, Najeeb, 148
Halle, Kay, 120, 207
Hamilton, Alexander, 191

Hand, Judge Learned, 98
Hannan, Archbishop Philip, 206, 214
Hanschman, Nancy (*later* Dickerson), 174–75
Harding, Warren, 27, 78, 115, 151
Harriman, Averell, 22, 120, 126, 204
Harris, Lou, 73
Harris, Samuel, 126
Harrison, Benjamin, 130
Harrison, William Henry, 130
Hartington, Billy, 81
Hayes, Rutherford B., 151
Healy, Robert, 163
Hemingway, Ernest, 83, 207–8
Henderson, Deirdre, 89
Hersey, John, 82, 150, 175
Herter, Christian, 145, 146, 152
Hitler, Adolf, 54, 97, 130
Ho Chi Minh, 85
Hollywood, 119–22, 153, 158, 160–61, 204
Holmes, Oliver Wendell, 78
Hoover, Herbert, 27, 115, 151, 152, 179
Hoover, J. Edgar, 42, 180
Howe, Louis, 106
Hughes, John Emmett, 143
Hugo, Victor, 178
Humphrey, Hubert, 52, 142, 183–84, 190
Hunt, Chet, 181

I'm for Roosevelt (Kennedy), 175
Inaugural Address of January 20, 1961
- antithetical statements, 91–93, 129
- "ask not" master sentence, 36–37, 67, 74–79, 91, 101–2, 107, 119, 128, 171, 196, 199–201
- assassination and, 212–14
- authorship of, 8–13, 80–87
- Bartlett's *Familiar Quotations* and, 129
- "bear any burden" sentence, 33–34, 45, 68, 80, 93, 96, 99, 193
- Biblical quote in, 61
- "Changes in Inaugural Speech—to Be Read and Approved by Senator" (memorandum by Wofford and Martin) and, 135–37
- Churchill and, 68–69, 75–76, 81
- Clean Draft of January 16, 64–67, 69
- COPY shown to Washington circle, 127–30
- delay in writing, to January 10, 19–23
- delivery of, 190–201
- Galbraith and, 71–73
- great idea of, 209
- handwritten first page auctioned, 107, 109
- impact of, 6–7, 9, 214–16
- January 10 dictation, 13, 17–18, 22–23, 25, 27–37, 58, 65–67, 77, 87, 92, 99
- January 10 dictation, copied for January 17 handwritten draft, 95
- January 10 dictation, revised in Palm Beach, 41–46
- January 10 dictation, Sorensen Draft used for, 28, 30–37
- January 16 work on, 57–74
- January 17 COPY changes and, Reading Copy, 135–38
- January 17 COPY typed, 109–10
- January 17 draft, 77–78, 88–89, 94–110
- January 17 handwritten draft, 94–97, 99–102, 104, 107, 109–10
- Jefferson and, 156–57
- JFK draws on, 212
- as JFK's philosophical autobiography, 80–87

Joe Kennedy and, 53–54, 160
"John Fitzgerald Kennedy First Inaugural (Second Version)" (Galbraith) and, 72
magic of, 215–16
major sources and drafts of, 13
memorized, 160
"never negotiate out of fear" sentence, 73, 91, 129, 197, 206
"Possible changes in Preface" (Sorensen note) and, 103
practiced aloud, 6, 143, 162–66
quotations for, 45–46, 61, 67–68, 78–79, 177–78
Reading Copy, 110, 135–38, 148, 190–92
Reading Copy memorandum on changes, 135–38
Reading Copy signed, 205–6
responses to, 7–8, 206–12
rhetorical analysis of, 91–93
seven sentences of, on JFK grave, 3–4, 6
short, desired, 24–25
"Some Miscellaneous Paragraphs" (Stevenson) and, 70
Sorensen compares all inaugurals for, 25
Sorensen discussions on, before January 10, 24–28
Sorensen Draft, 13, 24–27, 36–37, 67, 74, 58, 65–67, 69, 130
Sorensen Draft, first page missing, 30
Sorensen Draft, January 10 dictation and, 23, 30–37, 67
Sorensen Draft, January 17 work and, 42, 45, 57, 58, 64–65, 75, 77–78, 88–92, 94, 99–102, 109–10
Sorensen Draft, JFK's contributions to, 24–28
Sorensen Draft, Speech as Delivered and, 198
Sorensen Draft, Stevenson and Galbraith and, 69–73
Speech as Delivered, 190–92
Stevenson's contribution to, 69–71
suggestions for, solicited, 69–74
television and, 5–6, 20, 115, 125
text of, xiii-xvi
"tiger" metaphor and, 70–71, 110, 129–30, 194, 212
"torch has been passed to a new generation" sentence, 29, 32, 36, 45, 65, 81, 93, 96, 99, 110, 136–38, 192, 196
Truman given copy, 152
"trumpet summons us again" . . . "twilight struggle" sentence, 18, 35, 65, 67–69, 92, 93, 198
typed transcript edited by January 18, 127
weather and, 130–31, 151–53
inaugural balls, 118, 203–4
Inaugural Committee, 118, 120, 131
Inaugural Concert, 115, 153–61
inaugural parade, 202–3
inauguration of 1961, 177–201
imperial presidency and, 117–18
planned, 19–20
Hollywood and, 119–20
television and radio and, 115–17
Inauguration Day, moved, 130–31
Iran, 86
Iraq War, 210–11
Isaiah, 61, 197
Israel, 87

Jackson, Andrew, 134
Jacqueline Kennedy—The White House Years (Thayer), 134
Jefferson, Thomas, 5, 32, 41, 52, 67, 155–57, 160–61, 191
Jenkins, Roy, 81
Job, 63

Johnson, Haynes, 100, 101
Johnson, Lady Bird, 47–48, 133, 150, 157, 168, 175–76, 179
Johnson, Luci Baines, 174, 179
Johnson, Lynda Bird, 174, 179, 196
Johnson, Lyndon B., 5, 23, 47–50, 52, 88, 109, 134–35, 142, 157, 167–68, 175, 179–80, 182–83, 185–87, 190, 193, 195–96, 210, 218

Kara, George, 180–81, 190
Keller, Helen, 180
Kelly, Gene, 120, 158, 175
Kelly, Grace, 124
Kennan, George, 22–23, 34, 188
Kennedy, Caroline (daughter), 39, 40, 41, 47, 107, 108, 213, 221
Kennedy, Edward "Ted" (brother), 121, 143, 180, 221
Kennedy, Ethel (mother), 221
Kennedy, Eunice (sister), 63
Kennedy, Jacqueline Bouvier "Jackie" (wife), 6, 10, 20, 38, 40, 43, 44, 59, 89–90, 94, 116, 121
  assassination and, 213–14
  background of, 175
  Camelot and, 113
  inauguration and, 131–34, 138, 147–48, 150, 153–57, 160–61, 163–64, 167–70, 174–76, 179–80, 182–83, 186, 190, 196, 202–4, 213
  JFK and, 51, 52, 59–60, 203–5
  Rose and, 47–48, 174
  Sorensen and, 66
  wardrobe and, 46–47, 133, 125–26, 152, 176, 215
Kennedy, John Fitzgerald, Jr. "John John" (son), 6, 39–41, 46, 107, 108, 128
Kennedy, John Fitzgerald "Jack". *See also* Inaugural Address of 1961; *Profiles in Courage*
  appearance and wardrobe of, 6, 41–42, 123–27, 166–67, 178–79
  assassination of, 113–14, 178, 212–14
  autobiography of, 80–87
  Berquist interview with, 59–60
  Carlyle Hotel penthouse and, 122
  Churchill's influence on, 67–69
  diary of 1945, 84, 89
  dictation method of composition and, 17–18, 53
  effort of, to establish authorship of inaugural, 28, 100
  egalitarian spirit of, 89
  extemporaneous speaking of, 18, 28
  father and, 54–56
  FDR's influence on, 104–7
  Frost and, 139–40
  grave of, 3–5
  health problems of, 6, 11, 166
  history and, 10–11, 94–95
  Hollywood and, 119–21
  Ike's pre-inaugural briefing of, 143–47
  inaugural delivered by, 188–201
  inauguration and, before speech, 164–65, 167–68, 170, 173–90
  inauguration of, begins new era, 113–17
  LBJ and, 48–50, 134–35
  letters from supporters, 20
  Luce and, 97–99
  marriage strained, 132
  memory of, 45–46, 68
  oratory and, 10–11
  political grudges and, 183–84
  post-inaugural activities of, 202–5
  pre-inaugural concert and Gala and, 114, 153–61
  pre-inaugural socializing and, 138–39, 147–49
  Presidential Office Files of, 65, 109

presidential transition and, 19–22
quotations and, 45–46
religion and, 61–64, 164–65
reserve of, and passion, 188–90
secretary Lincoln and, 107–9
speaking style of, 162–64
speeches of, accepting nomination, 18, 71, 76, 78, 97, 99, 163, 170
speeches of, attention to detail and, 52–53
speeches of, campaign of 1960, 28, 29, 32, 54, 67, 76–78, 98, 139, 172–73, 209
speeches of, congressional, 17, 18, 79, 86–87, 209
speeches of, Massachusetts State Legislature, farewell address, 21, 23, 37, 45, 52, 53, 95–96, 170, 178, 212
speeches of, National Press Club, 68, 79
speeches of, State of the Union, 212
speeches of, to announce candidacy, 18, 35, 43, 163
speeches of, word count and, 24–25, 27
spirit of times caught by, 172–73
television and, 5–6, 8, 115–18, 129
Time and, 95–97
Truman and, 151–52, 205
womanizing of, 20, 50–52, 158, 166, 175
writing on scraps of paper, 66
youth of, 124
Kennedy, Joseph, Jr. (brother), 39, 63, 81, 185, 198, 207
Kennedy, Joseph, Sr. "Joe" (father), 6, 38, 39, 40, 48, 50, 53–56, 61–62, 82–83, 90, 97, 105, 116, 127, 140–42, 152, 160, 161, 164, 175, 179, 183, 184, 185
Kennedy, Kathleen (sister), 39, 175, 185
Kennedy, Robert "Bobby" (brother), 22, 23, 41, 48, 55, 85, 113, 142, 143, 160, 170, 180, 183, 214
Kennedy, Rose (mother), 6, 38–40, 46–48, 50, 54, 90, 133, 152, 164–65, 174, 179, 182, 201, 212
"Expressions Book," 46
Kennedy Legacy, The (Sorensen), 11–12
Kennedy Library, 27, 66, 95, 101–2, 107, 108
Kennedy (Sorensen), 11, 12, 13, 24, 25, 27, 57, 58, 100–101
Khrushchev, Nikita, 22–23, 24, 32, 33, 56, 63, 147, 171, 189, 197, 199, 212
King, Rev. Martin Luther, Jr., 209, 219
King Lear (Shakespeare), 177
Kirk, Grayson, 207
Kirksey, Andrew, 81, 82, 198
Kirstein, Lincoln, 156, 208
Kissinger, Henry, 114
Knebel, Fletcher, 53
Kraft, Joseph, 25, 69
Krick, Dr. Irving, 131
Krock, Arthur, 171, 174–75, 203

Lamar, Lucius, 10
La Montaine, John, 155, 156
"Lansing, Barbara," 50, 57, 122
Laos, 33, 96, 117, 144–47
Lattre, General de, 85
Lawford, Pat Kennedy, 160
Lawford, Peter, 29, 39, 116, 157, 160, 179, 204
Lawrence, Bill, 21
Leahy, Adm. William, 84
Leahy, Joe, 204
Leigh, Janet, 120, 158, 165
Lemnitzer, Gen. Lyman, 148

Letters to Kennedy (Galbraith), 72
Lewis, Anthony, 148, 180
Life, 7, 61, 94, 96, 98, 116, 124, 171
Lincoln, Abraham, 5, 7, 10, 21, 31, 52, 64, 75, 150–51, 170–71, 207, 222, 223
  Gettysburg Address, 8, 23, 24, 42, 92, 139, 199, 214, 219
  inaugurals, 41, 198, 208
Lincoln, Evelyn (secretary), 13, 17–18, 22, 23, 38, 39, 43, 47, 48, 49, 53, 59, 66, 121–22, 138, 145, 146, 148, 153, 162, 166, 206
  appointment book and diary, 41, 42, 50, 57, 71, 90
  Clean Draft and, 64–66
  handwritten draft and, 107–9
  January 10 dictation and, 28, 29–30, 31, 34, 37, 87
  January 17 draft and, 94, 100, 107–8, 45, 110
Lincoln at Gettysburg (Wills), 92
Lindholm, Gudney, 147
Lippmann, Walter, 98, 127–28, 135, 149
Lisagor, Peter, 183
Lodge, Henry Cabot, 160
Longest Day, The (Ryan), 170
Longfellow, 178
Look, 57, 59, 116, 163, 172
Louchheim, Katie, 150
Lowe, Jacques, 154
Lowell, Robert, 180, 208
Lowens, Irving, 156
Luce, Clare Boothe, 98, 175, 180
Luce, Henry, 61, 96–99, 175, 180, 209
Luke, 79, 201
Lytton, Bart, 121, 135

McCain, John, 222
McCarthy, Joseph, 55, 184
McClosky, David, 163
McClosky, Matt, 41
McCullers, Carson, 207, 208
McGovern, George, 33
McKinley, William, 27, 142, 151
MacLaine, Shirley, 158
MacLeish, Archibald, 7, 98
McMahon, Patrick, 82, 148
McMillan, Priscilla, 51
McNamara, Robert, 26, 79, 144–46, 180, 208
MacNeil, Robert, 33
Magnuson, Warren, 90, 94
Mahoney, Florence, 138, 140, 142
Mailer, Norman, 153
Malik, Charles, 213
Manchester Guardian, 181, 213
Man in the Gray Flannel Suit, The (Wilson), 172
Mannes, Myra, 182
Mansfield, Mike, 40
Mantle, Mickey, 155
March, Fredric, 160
Marney, Harold, 81, 82, 198
Martin, Louis, 114, 135–37
Meany, George, 98
Meet the Press (TV show), 86, 163
Melbourne, Lord, 51
Menshikov, Mikhael, 22
Meredith, James, 7, 137–38
Merman, Ethel, 158, 160
Michener, James, 180, 203
Mike Wallace Show, The (TV show), 26
Miller, Arthur, 117, 150, 153
Miller, Merle, 55, 141, 142
Mitchell, Howard, 155–56
Mizner, Addison, 38, 39
Moley, Raymond, 105–7, 109
Monroe, Marilyn, 147, 153
Montgomery, Charles, 165
Montgomery, Helen, 165
Moran, Lord, 75–76
Morglieth, Charlotte, 152
Morrow, Lance, 9
Moulden, Nettie, 150–51

Mumford, Lewis, 207
Muñoz, Luis, 123
Murrow, Edward R., 68, 119, 177, 180
Mussolini, 130
My Twelve Years with John F. Kennedy (Lincoln), 17–18, 29, 108–9

NAACP, 136
Nasser, Gamal Abdel, 87
National Guard Armory Gala, 119, 156–61
Neuberger, Richard, 102
Neustadt, Richard, 19, 22, 34
Nevins, Allan, 65, 69, 70
New Frontier, 76, 77, 140, 171, 173
Newman, Cardinal, 201, 212
Newsweek, 20, 44–45, 95, 102, 171, 182
New York Daily News, 127
New Yorker, 7, 82, 175
New York Herald Tribune, 127
New York Times, 19, 22, 33, 41, 49, 50, 55, 76–77, 117, 134, 138, 166, 171, 175, 202, 206
Niebuhr, Reinhold, 180
Nixon, Julie, 150
Nixon, Pat, 47, 150, 168, 175–76, 179, 180, 183
Nixon, Richard M., 5, 7, 8, 56, 61, 142, 150, 160, 163, 168, 174–75, 180, 182–85, 190, 196, 215, 218, 220
Nixon, Tricia, 150
Nixon-Kennedy debates, 12, 30, 116–17
Norris, George, 21
nuclear war, 80, 144, 208

Oakes, John, 102
Obama, Barack, 219, 220, 221, 222, 223
O'Donnell, Ken, 41, 146–47, 161, 189
O'Leary, Muggsy, 89, 90
Olivier, Sir Laurence, 158, 160
O'Malley, Miss, 39, 40, 42, 153, 166
O'Neill, Tip, 180, 183, 190, 204
"Organizing the Transition" (Neustadt memorandum), 19
Oswald, Lee and Marina, 51

Paine, Thomas, 32
Parades, Providencia, 39, 153
Parmet, Herbert, 26, 92, 102–3
Pauling, Linus, 114
Paul VI, Pope, 6
Peace Corps, 6, 172–73, 208
Peale, Norman Vincent, 60
Pearson, Drew, 26, 102, 203
Pericles' Funeral Oration, 79, 178, 214
Phillips, Cabell, 163
Pitt, William, 8
Poitier, Sidney, 158
poverty, 25, 67, 71, 80, 87–90, 209
Powers, Dave, 89, 90, 161, 189
Profiles in Courage (Kennedy), 10, 11, 15, 17, 21, 26, 36, 43–45, 68, 79, 83, 92, 95, 102–3, 139, 149, 219
Prospect for America (Rockfeller Brothers Fund series), 98
PT 109, 81–83, 148, 175

Quinn, Anthony, 158, 160

Radziwill, Lee, 46, 165
Radziwill, Prince Stanislas, 46
Rayburn, Sam, 167, 179–80, 186, 191, 193
Reader's Digest, 82–83
Reagan, Ronald, 130, 215, 219, 221
Reception for Distinguished Ladies, 133
Reeves, Richard, 68

Reinsch, J. Leonard, 116, 186
Republicans, 7, 78, 215
Reston, James, 19, 206
Reuther, Walter, 180
Reynolds, Billy, 62
Ridder, Marie, 51, 132
Ridder, Walter, 132
Roberts, Chalmers, 42
"Rock, The" (Eliot), 173
Romans, 61
Rommel, Field Marshal, 45
Roosevelt, Eleanor, 6, 22, 54, 105, 142, 152, 179, 180, 184–85, 188, 191, 198, 207
Roosevelt, Elliott, 142
Roosevelt, Franklin D., 5, 10, 20, 21, 29, 41, 54, 58, 69, 75, 76, 113, 140, 151, 207, 221, 222
  inaugurals of, 23, 24, 27, 88, 100, 102, 104–7, 114, 130
  Joe Kennedy and, 141–42
  "nothing to fear but fear itself" and, 106–7, 223
  "rendezvous with destiny" speech, 36, 198
Roosevelt, Theodore, 24, 151
Roosevelt (Burns), 104–5
Rosenbloom, Carroll, 29, 39
Rosenman, Samuel, 104–7
Rostow, Walt, 30, 72, 85, 114
Rothko, Mark, 150, 208
Rousseau, Jean-Jacques, 78
Rubenstein, Helena, 155
Rusk, Dean, 41, 42, 47, 69, 128, 135, 144–46, 180, 182, 208
Ryan, Cornelius, 170

Saint Luke's Gospel, 21
Saint Paul's Epistle to the Romans, 35
Salinger, Pierre, 29, 40, 41, 57, 59, 60, 94, 100, 121, 123, 135, 147, 152, 164, 166, 196
Salisbury, Harrison, 22
Sandburg, Carl, 207
Schlesinger, Arthur, 7, 33, 41, 43–45, 52, 63, 72, 78, 105, 114, 129, 138–39, 169, 203
Schweitzer, Albert, 213
Shalala, Donna, 6
Shriver, Sargent, 128, 135, 208
Shuttlesworth, Rev. Fred, 209
Sidey, Hugh, 41, 50, 54, 94–97, 99–101, 165, 209–10
Sinatra, Frank, 120, 157–60, 178–79, 204
Sitrin, Gloria, 12, 24, 27, 103, 135
Smathers, George, 60, 62
Smith, Al, 127
Smith, Howard (congressman), 185
Smith, Howard K. (journalist), 116, 174
Smith, Jean Kennedy, 118–21
Smith, Keely, 158
Smith, Margaret Chase, 180
Smith, Stephen, 118–21, 163
Sorensen, Theodore "Ted," 23, 41, 47, 53, 61, 63, 80, 116–17, 135, 148, 162, 173, 220, 221. *See also* Inaugural Address of 1961, Sorensen Draft; *Profiles in Courage*
  "ask not" and, 36–37, 77, 79
  assassination and, 213
  assumed to be author of speech, 8–13, 44, 202, 206
  "bear any burden" and, 33
  COPY and, 127–29, 135, 136
  habits of JFK and, 66–68
  inauguration and, 191
  joins JFK staff, 17
  notes of, 24
  Profiles in Courage and, 26
  speeches written by, 36, 77, 91–92
  television and, 125
  White House files of, 65, 110

Sorrentino, Rosemary, 147, 153, 167–68
southern Democrats, 137
Soviet Union, 8, 22–24, 33–34, 83, 119, 127, 130, 140, 171, 197, 209
space program, 73–74, 171, 208
Spalding, Charles, 58, 88
Sparkman, John, 167, 179, 186, 191, 193, 195
Spellman, Cardinal, 185
Sputnik, 171
Stalin, Joseph, 84
Stark, Lloyd, 142
State Department, 114, 149, 150
Steele, Ronald, 128
Steinbeck, John, 149, 171–72, 180, 206–8
Stevenson, Adlai, 22, 25, 32, 67, 69, 87, 98, 132, 142, 152, 171, 182–85, 190, 193, 219
Stewart, Jimmy, 178
Strategy of Peace, The (Kennedy), 65, 116
Sutton, Billy, 178

Taft, Chief Justice, 115
Taft, William Howard, 27, 130, 151
Taylor, George, 51, 137
television, 115–17, 125, 163, 168, 170–71, 174–75, 177, 180–82, 195–96, 206, 212–13
Thayer, Mary Van Rensselaer "Molly," 134, 138, 153–54, 168–69, 203
third world, 6, 33, 70–71, 73, 79–80, 86–87, 98, 110, 129–30, 195, 210
Thomas, Evan, 44, 95
Thomas, George, 39, 162
Thomas, Helen, 58–59, 131–32
Thomas, Norman, 207
Thompson, Randall, 155–56
Thoreau, Henry David, 106
Thousand Days, A (Schlesinger), 7, 43, 78, 169
Tierney, Gene, 175
Time, 9, 41, 48, 54, 94, 96, 97, 101
Times of London, 7, 181
Travell, Dr. Janet, 166
Tretick, Stanley, 126
Trout, Robert, 168, 170
Truman, Bess, 47, 133, 179, 183
Truman, Harry S., 25, 55, 84, 88, 89, 114, 115, 139–42, 151–52, 179–83, 191, 193, 202, 205–6
Truman, Margaret, 140
Tunney, Gene, 132
Tunney, Polly, 132
Turner, Hamlin, 207
Turnure, Pamela, 39, 50, 131
Twain, Mark, 140
Twentieth Amendment, 130–31

Udall, Stewart, 139–40, 187
United Nations, 61, 71, 172, 183, 194–95
U.S. Congress, 130
U.S. House of Representatives, 11
U.S. Senate, 11, 12
Upstairs at the White House (West), 1 68

Vidal, Gore, 42, 73–74, 184, 216
Vietnam
  Eisenhower and, 144–46
  trip of 1951, 80, 85–86
  war, 6, 8, 33, 128, 208, 210
Vietnam War Memorial, 5
Vogelsinger, Sue, 152
Vreeland, Diana, 46

Wall Street Journal, 66
Walton, Bill, 126, 147–49, 154–56

Ward, Barbara, 171
Waring, Fred, 155
Warren, Earl, 180, 183, 190, 213–14
Washington, George, 133, 170, 190–91, 191
Washington, Martha, 133
Washington *Evening Star*, 64, 100, 104, 120, 131, 149, 156, 160
Washington Post, 8, 19, 41, 118, 131, 133, 140, 149, 160, 171, 178
Washington Times-Herald, 132, 175
Webster, Daniel, 36, 52, 67, 123
Welty, Eudora, 207
"We Must Climb to the Hilltop" (Kennedy), 99
West, J. B., 168–69
West Virginia primary, 80, 88, 105, 116, 183
Wheeler, George, 203
While England Slept (Churchill), 68
White, E. B., 7
White, Robert, 107–9
White, Theodore, 10, 47–48, 88, 113, 184, 220
Why England Slept (Kennedy), 17, 68, 79, 80, 97, 175
Wicker, Tom, 33, 180
Wilde, Oscar, 178
Wilkins, Roy, 122, 180
Williams, Bonnie, 39
Wills, Garry, 8, 92
Wilson, Edith, 180, 181, 184
Wilson, Sloan, 172
Wilson, Woodrow, 5, 51, 76, 127, 151, 203, 206, 209
  inaugurals, 24, 27, 31, 41, 115
Winthrop, John, 21
Wisner, Jerome, 21
Wofford, Harris, 52, 73, 128, 135–37, 188
Wolfe, Tom, 118, 151
Working with Roosevelt (Rosenman), 104
World War II, 36, 80–82, 172, 209
Wrightsman, Charles, 138
Wrightsman, Jayne, 138

young people, 172–73, 211